Cybersecurity in the IoT Era

CYBERSECURITY IN THE IOT ERA

Jocelyn O. Padallan

ARCLER PRESS

www.arclerpress.com

Cybersecurity in the IoT Era

Jocelyn O. Padallan

Arcler Press
4164 Lakeshore Road
Burlington, ON L7L 1A4
Canada
www.arclerpress.com
Email: orders@arclereducation.com

ISBN: 978-1-77956-962-2 (Hardcover)

ABOUT THE AUTHOR

Jocelyn O. Padallan is Associate Professor I from Laguna State Polytechnic University, Philippines and she is currently pursuing her Doctor in Information Technology has Master in Information Technology and Master of Arts in Education from the same University. She has passion for teaching been Instruction and College of Computer Studies - Student Council Adviser at Laguna State Polytechnic University.

TABLE OF CONTENTS

LIST OF FIGURES

Figure 10.7. Fifth-generation (5G) networks, for example, offer significant improvements in data transmission speeds and reduced latency, facilitating real-time communication between devices.

Figure 10.8. Real-time monitoring plays a pivotal role as it enables the detection of anomalies that may indicate security breaches or compromised devices.

Figure 10.9. The integration of Federated Learning (FL) offers an innovative solution by allowing distributed data processing without compromising privacy, as it enables the collaborative training of machine learning models while keeping raw data local.

Figure 10.10. Resistance to change or a lack of security training can lead to unintentional breaches or misuse of encryption protocols.

Figure 10.11. By establishing a trustless system, devices can securely authenticate themselves and transact with minimal intervention from centralized authorities.

Figure 10.12. As cyber threats evolve, the vulnerabilities exposed through poorly maintained or outdated authentication mechanisms can lead to severe breaches and data compromises.

Figure 10.13. Quantum technologies have the potential to revolutionize encryption methods, making data transmission across networks more secure against evolving cyber threats.

Figure 10.14. Enhanced public-private partnerships can facilitate the sharing of best practices and resources necessary for building secure IoT environments.

PREFACE

The Internet of Things is no longer something far off; it is a living tapestry of daily existence. Houses raise and lower thermostats on their own, factories broadcast sensor data around the clock, and hospitals link up monitors and pumps to clinical systems in real time. These advantages are built on untold millions of small computers—many low-power, resource-limited, and deployed in the millions. The same attributes that make them revolutionary also expose them: contentious processors which cannot run heavy defenses, longer lifetimes lasting beyond vendor support, and physically exposed systems which will be mounted on a wall, in the field, or inside a vehicle. Security for such systems can't be a legacy IT controls copy-and-paste. It must support bursty short messages, loss networks, periodic power, and heterogeneous devices cobbled together by diverse vendors. Most important, it must be respectful of safety: a faulty security control on an infusion pump or grid sensor is not merely a service outage—it is a killer.

It is not just an issue of securing individual devices but securing the interactions among them. IoT systems combine sensing, actuation, communication, and cloud analytics in extended chains of trust. A compromised link—a default password on a camera, an unpatched gateway protocol, or poorly designed API—is enough to defeat a botnet or a data breach. Attackers have even gotten good at weaponizing scale, taking over dozens of thousands of nodes to spam services or mine sensitive data, but defenders must work within constrained bandwidth and power budgets. Effective IoT security therefore integrates hardware root of trust, performance-aware cryptography, robust identity, carefully bounded network exposure, continuous monitoring, and responsible update techniques. It also requires transparent management—procurement practices, compliance frameworks, and operation runbooks—so that security persists from design and supply chain through deployment and end-of-life.

Cybersecurity in the IoT Era is engineered to meet these realities. The book explains the fundamentals of IoT systems and how attackers might exploit them, and then equips you with real-world defenses that respect device constraints and operational requirements. It finds a middle ground between conceptual simplicity and implementation detail, showing how to design for minimal exposure, select protocols that maintain overhead low, implement cryptography that tolerates limited hardware, and implement detection appropriate to high-volume, low-signal telemetry. Each chapter combines plain-English explanations, structured guidance, and practitioner-experienced methods.

Chapter 1 sets out the basic pieces of IoT and resultant security goals. It defines device classes, gateways, edge computing tasks, and cloud back ends; defines constraints in terms of limited CPU, memory, and power; and maps these facts onto confidentiality, integrity, availability, and safety goals.

Chapter 2 is focused on IoT architecture and the many places an attacker is able to get a foothold. You will see how sensors, actuators, firmware, bootloaders, radios, local networks, gateways, message brokers, APIs, and cloud services create a wide attack surface. The chapter illustrates minimizing exposure using segmented designs, least-privilege connectivity, secure boot chains, and update paths that are rollback and tamper-resistant. Design patterns and anti-patterns are compared to help you make trade-offs early, when they matter most.

Chapter 3 discusses common threats and attacks in IoT, from credential stuffing and device cloning to side-channel abuse, radio jamming, replay, and supply-chain injection. Real-world attack patterns—botnet recruitment, command hijacking, data exfiltration from sensors, and physical tampering—are mapped to kill-chains that identify detection and prevention potential. You will see how careless errors, like leaving dev interfaces open or shipping shared keys, snowball into systemic risk.

Chapter 4 discusses IoT device network and communication protocols and their security implications. It contrasts short-range technologies (BLE, Zigbee, Z-Wave, Thread) with long-range ones (Wi-Fi, cellular IoT, LoRaWAN), and messaging layers such as MQTT, CoAP, AMQP, and HTTP/2. For all of them, the chapter explains authentication modes, session protection, reliability properties, and common misconfigurations. It further discusses segmentation, broker hardening, certificate handling, rate limiting, and gateway policies that preserve function while robustly limiting exposure.

Chapter 5 outlines cryptography for constrained IoT devices with a focus on robustness and feasibility. You will learn when to use symmetric versus asymmetric methods, how to choose curves and ciphers best suited for constrained hardware, and how to manage keys via secure elements, TPM-like hardware, or software vaulting. Secure boot, measured boot, firmware signing, sealed storage, and protocols like DTLS and OSCORE are all covered in this chapter and bring strong protections to constrained stacks. Real-world guidance is given regarding entropy sources, nonce handling, key rotation, and avoiding unsafe shortcuts that make it into embedded code.

Chapter 6 treats privacy and data protection in IoT, where operational and personal data streams flow continuously. It translates principles such as data minimization, purpose limitation, and storage limitation into device and cloud design choices: on-device pre-processing, anonymization at the edge, tokenization, and controlled aggregation. The chapter covers consent models, legal bases for processing, subject data rights, and cross-border transfer implications, translating legal obligations into practices that scale.

Chapter 7 defines access control and identity management with IoT realities. It illustrates how to issue and manage device identities during manufacturing, onboarding, and field replacement; how to bind identities with cryptographic material and attestation evidence; and how to apply authorization models such as RBAC and ABAC to devices, services, and operators. You will find templates for just-in-time provisioning, ephemeral credentials, scoped tokens, and command authorization that resists abuse even if a single node is compromised.

Chapter 8 covers intrusion detection and anomaly detection in systems that are capable of producing sparse, noisy, or high-rate telemetry. It compares signature-based detection, model-based baselining, and physics-informed monitoring, and then shows how to combine them up in resource-aware ways. Topics addressed are selecting signals that warn of device abuse, filtering to reduce false positives, placing sensors on gateways and brokers, and using device attestation and heartbeat checks to spot tampering or cloning. The chapter also addresses how to feed detections into incident response playbooks suitable for fleets of devices across large geographic expanses.

Chapter 9 covers security standards and frameworks that drive procurement, certification, and assurance. It compares large-scale efforts by international organizations and industry consortia, and highlights common controls such as unique identities, secure update, vulnerability disclosure, and baseline cryptography. You will learn how to use these frameworks in your environment, generate compliance evidence during design, and use standardized labels or profiles to encourage vendor responsibility without constraining innovation.

Chapter 10 discusses next-generation IoT security technologies as becoming feasible. Topics include edge confidential computing, post-quantum cryptography preparation for long-lived devices, verifiable supply-chain artifacts (SBOMs with signing and provenance), zero-trust patterns applied to constrained endpoints, and hardware-backed attestation with policy enforcement in the cloud. Chapter 10 rounds out with guidance on evaluating new tools: how to pilot, estimate overhead, and decide when the security benefit is worth the cost and complexity of adoption.

Cybersecurity in the Age of IoT is targeted at professionals tasked with designing, developing, deploying, or assessing connected devices and the systems beneath them. Security practitioners will utilize it to bring enterprise practices to resource-constrained environments. Embedded and firmware developers will benefit from insightful cryptography, secure boot, and update guidance that they can implement on real hardware. Network and cloud architects will inherit the patterns for gateways, brokers, and APIs that govern exposure but not performance. Compliance and risk teams will benefit from the clear linkage to standards and the direction on obtaining credible evidence without slowing down projects. Product owners, technical leaders, and students will get a formalized view that maps device realities to business risk so that they can make informed decisions through the product life cycle.

CHAPTER 1

INTRODUCTION TO IOT AND CYBERSECURITY

Contents

INTRODUCTION

The Internet of Things (IoT) is a great technological innovation, connecting ordinary objects to the internet and bestowing upon them the capacity to share and communicate information. The networked device has transformed various sectors, from smart homes and medicine to industrial applications. By enabling real-time sharing and control of data, IoT provides an opportunity for increased operational effectiveness and decision-making. In doing so, companies can leverage the use of IoT to make predictions for maintenance, make better resource allocations, and respond to consumers effectively. Next, firms can capitalize on new prospects, develop new products and services, and stay ahead in the market. However, the emergence of interconnected devices also presents advanced issues, particularly in the aspect of cybersecurity since exposure associated with these devices can lead to major threats if effectively not addressed. IoT's architecture largely relies on sensors, cloud computing, and analytics. Sensors gather vast amounts of information from the physical world, which get processed in cloud platforms that support storage as well as analysis. This infrastructure not only makes data more accessible but also invites growing smart algorithms to compute the resultant data. It is against this background that cybersecurity becomes imperative, as each component of the IoT system presents itself as a point of vulnerability for rogue actors. It is central to maintaining data integrity, confidentiality, and privacy in guaranteeing users' trust and ensuring the seamless functioning of these interlinked systems. With increased usage of IoT, it is important that businesses implement strict security measures capable of fighting threats and responding accordingly against shifting attacks. With IoT products making their way into daily life, the risk for cybersecurity presents increasingly solemn concerns. Cyber attackers exploit vulnerabilities of IoT networks to make unauthorized attacks, leading to data exposure and compromised personal information. It is compounded by the number of devices that are potential targets for cyber-attacks. In such an environment, a proactive security solution is not only required but must incorporate not only technology but also end-user education and awareness. Organizations must develop comprehensive security strategies that encompass ongoing monitoring, threat detection, and incident response playbooks. Additionally, establishing coordination among stakeholders—spanning from manufacturers to consumers—will be essential in creating a strong IoT ecosystem. With the debate on the future of IoT and its position within society evolving still, the balance between innovation and security will be the decisive factor in the making or breaking of its success and longevity.

Definition and Overview of IoT

The IoT is a paradigm of revolution that entails the connection of common things to the internet and thereby enable them to send, receive, and process information. The ecosystem includes devices such as sensors, wearables, and smart appliances, each with unique identifiers and the capacity to transfer data automatically. With the development of IoT devices accelerating, their applications have expanded to multiple industries including healthcare, agriculture, transport, and smart cities, enhancing operation efficiency and supporting decision-making based on data. The potential of IoT technologies is enormous in economic terms, expected to contribute trillions of dollars to the global economy in the coming several years. But this lightning growth of connectivity raises underlying questions about security controls, personal information, and ethical factors, which make IoT both a cybersecurity challenge for professionals and an innovation potential. The very connectivity of IoT devices itself presents anomalous cybersecurity issues that must be thoroughly examined. With billions of devices likely to be online soon, cyber threats from hackers become increasingly complex and pervasive. The threat profile consists of various vulnerabilities from insecure communication protocols to weaker device authentication mechanisms that can lead to unauthorized access and exploitation of sensitive information.

Figure 1.1. The internet of things (IoT) represents a transformative paradigm characterized by the interconnectivity of everyday objects to the internet, allowing them to send, receive, and process data.

Source: https://www.rtsrl.eu/site/assets/files/11048/what_is_the_internet_of_things.png.

In such situations, cybersecurity needs to keep up with IoT technology to secure data integrity and protect privacy. Devices need robust encryption, real-time monitoring, and robust risk control mechanisms to avoid potential breaches. Further, since numerous IoT devices collect personal information and undertake sophisticated data analysis, that is an issue of privacy that needs to be addressed by legal means to counteract risks of data manipulation and exploitation, as highlighted in the increasing importance of data-breach legislation (Anglano et al., 2018) and the relationship between vulnerabilities in data and online manipulation (Kilovaty et al., 2019). Growing complexity of IoT systems renders it necessary to install effective cybersecurity solutions as well as establish public confidence in such technologies. Having effective cybersecurity solutions in place is at the heart of not only protecting people's privacy but also ensuring the integrity of market systems and social functions that are increasingly reliant on IoT devices. The stakeholders like manufacturers, service providers, and policymakers should get together to define standards that address the risk of IoT deployment and focus on security by design principles that offer value to flexibility and resilience. Education and awareness for users in relation to the risks involved and precautions necessary are also crucial components of a comprehensive cybersecurity strategy. As IoT continues to evolve, bridging the chasm between innovation and security will become imperative, allowing users with a safeguarding against the threats that come with increased connectivity (Figure 1.1).

Historical Development of IoT

The history of the IoT began back in the early 1980s, when it was all theoretical. The term IoT itself was first employed in 1999 by Kevin Ashton to refer to a configuration where physical objects were made internet-enabled and could communicate with each other. This early vision was accelerated further by the appearance of enabling technologies, such as embedded systems and wireless communications. The introduction of IPv6 in the late 1990s also permitted an enormous volume of devices to be linked to the internet, a critical juncture for IoTs future development. As companies increasingly saw these capabilities, IoT began to disrupt traditional business models by making them more operationally efficient and creating new streams of data for analysis and decision-making, ultimately reshaping organizational designs. The significance of this foundational stage cannot be overestimated because it laid the ground for IoTs revolutionizing capabilities across industries. By the early 2000s, the convergence of a number of technological innovations propelled the development of IoT applications into a wide range of sectors. The spread of wireless communication and smartphones provided the basis for increased consumer engagement with networked products. Applications such as smart security systems in homes and web-enabled thermostats began to gain traction, demonstrating the utility potential of IoT for mass consumers. Aside from that, industries like healthcare and transport started using IoT solutions to monitor equipment and operate to enable improved delivery of services and risk reduction. With organizations identifying the economic value of IoT, research on security solutions became a priority. Valuation of vulnerabilities inherent in such networked systems came into focus in protecting the integrity and confidentiality of data exchanges, ultimately leading to the broader debate on IoT and cybersecurity. The ongoing development of IoT technology has created an ever-evolving environment, setting the stage for the emphasis on cybersecurity as a fundamental aspect of IoT development. As more devices proliferate, risks associated with their deployment have received great attention. Cybersecurity measures today also emphasize the importance of embedded security measures and protocols to combat threats from potentially insecure devices. The majority of IoT devices are usually not provided with strong security safeguards, thus making the data more vulnerable to breaches and cyber-attacks, which requires strong means of safeguarding sensitive information. Hence, with the IoT ecosystem expanding, there is an urgent need for developers, regulators, and other stakeholders to sit together and develop security standards that ensure the secure and effective deployment of such technology. The intersection of IoT and cybersecurity thus becomes a critical area of study in securing the future of connected systems and building societal trust in these technologies (Figure 1.2).

Figure 1.2. Cybersecurity frameworks now emphasize the importance of embedded security measures and protocols that can mitigate threats posed by potentially unsecured devices.

Source: https://media.licdn.com/dms/image/v2/D5612AQFKFwgCMH3ZKQ/article-cover_image-shrink_720_1280/B56ZdqBclAHEAQ-/0/1749830461750?e=2147483647&v=beta&t=SSnpWc5RIF5v00mpL8QSHGH0pEqlXasBMOgD0dFhlTc.

Key Components of IoT Systems

The backbone of IoT systems lies in some fundamental constituents that ensure interconnectivity, processing, and security. The underlying architecture of an IoT system is comprised of devices or sensors that detect data from the environment, which is transferred over a network to a central platform for action and analysis.

They range from as simple as a temperature sensor to as complex as a machine system. These are supplemented with gateways that facilitate communication, ensuring data is correctly routed and processed. It is this layering that is at the heart of IoT system functionality, as it facilitates scalable and efficient data management, consistent with the need for robust cybersecurity interventions to protect this sophisticated infrastructure from ever-evolving threats (Daniel et al., 2024). The interaction of these components builds the base for safe, responsive IoT environments. Data analysis is another crucial component in IoT systems, transforming raw data into decision-making information that is helpful for subsequent actions.

Figure 1.3. Data analytics is another critical component within IoT systems, transforming raw data into meaningful insights that drive decision-making.

Source: https://onlinedegrees.sandiego.edu/wp-content/uploads/2022/11/what-is-data-analytics-mads.jpg.

The collected data can be fed through numerous processes of analysis, including real-time analysis, which allows responses in real-time to events as they occur. Cloud computing is often a key player in this context, providing the necessary computational power and storage needs to process the large volumes of data generated by IoT devices. This is a serious concern as far as data privacy as well as security are concerned since the sensitive information is often being handled. Effective models of cybersecurity therefore need to be integrated into the process of analytics so that it can respond to vulnerabilities in a preventative manner, while data integrity and also user trust is maintained during IoT applications (Daniel et al., 2024). As companies increasingly rely on analytics to inform their operations, the integrity of analytics-based insights matters. Finally, the interface and user experience are integral components that dictate how end-users interact with IoT systems. This aspect encompasses designing applications and dashboards to facilitate intuitive data visualization and management by users. Among the considerations that are most important in this design is cybersecurity, which must be woven into the user experience without an obstacle. The users need to feel safe accessing their devices and data; therefore, robust authentication methods, data encryption, and transparency in terms of policy on privacy are essential. Furthermore, as IoT technology moves forward towards linked platforms, such as those in the metaverse, the demand for stable and effective security in a variety of applications increases in significance. Success of IoT systems, however, also hinges on maintaining not only technical functionality but also consumer trust in its security, should it really propagate and develop in this new field (Figure 1.3).

1.1. IMPORTANCE OF IOT IN MODERN SOCIETY

The Internet of Things (IoT) has been a cornerstone of modern society, contributing tremendous innovation to sectors across the board in manufacturing, transport, and healthcare. The interconnectivity of intelligent devices has transformed businesses through increased efficiency in operations and services provided. For instance, real-time monitoring and data gathering have enabled doctors to make effective decisions, leading to improved patient outcomes. Besides, the innovation of IoT-based smart cities has optimized urban infrastructure with less energy consumption and improved traffic management. All these innovations highlight the requirement for a robust system that can securely process the vast amounts of data generated, as it addresses possible vulnerabilities across the IoT chain. Therefore, the uses of IoT are not just for convenience and demand an appreciation of its place in contemporary society infrastructure, particularly in cybersecurity. With IoT devices increasing in prevalence globally, the security risks inherent in them have gained wide interest. The high degree of interconnectivity does not only add more function but also generates millions of entry points for cyber vulnerabilities.

It is necessary to learn these risks because inadequate protection can lead to data breaches, privacy invasion, and domination of critical services. For example, smart domestic appliances, at first considered to improve the standard of living, can become the target of malicious access, with the risk of invading the safety of their owners. Because of these concerns, the development of a culture of cybersecurity awareness and proactive action is vital. Companies can leverage the advantages of IoTs while adopting high-level cybersecurity practices to safeguard sensitive information and secure user confidence. The interaction between IoTs and security practices heralds an insight into the importance of an holistic approach toward embracing challenges from high growth rates among connected devices in society. Beyond technical advancements, the social implications of IoT extend to the boundaries of ethics pertaining to privacy and data security. With the metaverse and other virtual worlds increasingly interconnected with IoT technologies, it is important to be aware of the socio-economic effects. People contribute vast amounts of personal data unconsciously while using IoT devices, exposing them to abuse and clandestine surveillance. To address these challenges, a broad understanding of user trust and the social consequences of large-scale data collection is needed. Researchers and practitioners are then faced with the task of surmounting these challenges, proposing frameworks for ethical data management and governance. The debate on the importance of IoT in society today must then be accompanied by debates on equitable access to technology, so that the benefit of IoT is made accessible to all, thereby making the digital space more inclusive. By acknowledging both the possible benefits and the non-negotiable problems, society will be able to use IoTs transformative power without jeopardizing personal freedoms (Figure 1.4).

Figure 1.4. Enterprises can leverage IoTs advantages while implementing stringent cybersecurity protocols to safeguard sensitive information and uphold user trust.

Source: https://atmecs.global/wp-content/uploads/2024/12/iStock-1450723537-scaled.jpg.

1.1.1. Applications in Smart Homes

Smart homes are currently the most promising application of the IoT in contemporary society, revolutionizing the manner in which individuals live and relate with their homes. A smart home is an integrated system of devices, including smart thermostats and security cameras, that communicate with one another to enhance convenience and efficiency in life. The use of IoT technology allows residents to remotely monitor and manage various systems, thereby increasing energy usage efficiency and security. The connectivity, however, comes with tremendous susceptibilities since each device offers an avenue of vulnerability through which cyber-attacks may happen. Robust security frameworks and efficient risk management are required to safeguard the smart home ecosystem from breaches that may compromise privacy and safety, underlining the superior nexus of IoT deployment and cybersecurity. Cybersecurity is core to safeguarding smart homes against an ever-evolving set of threats. With the pervasiveness of devices that include IoT capabilities, traditional security controls might no longer be sufficient due to the scale and intricacy of the systems at hand. Deployment of a Cognitive Digital Twin (CDT) approach presents a viable solution by providing dynamic threat detection as well as ongoing monitoring. Using artificial intelligence and machine learning techniques, CDTs have the ability to model actual systems under simulation in a virtual world to investigate complex behavior and identify potential security threats even before they materialize.

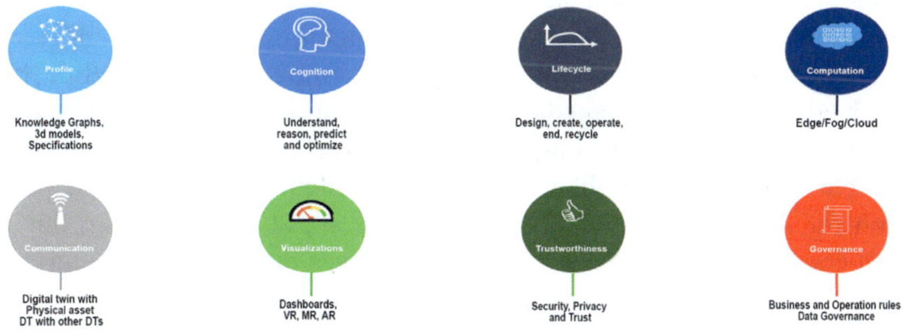

Figure 1.5. The implementation of a cognitive digital twin (CDT) architecture presents a promising solution by facilitating continuous monitoring and dynamic threat detection.

Source: https://www.mdpi.com/applsci/applsci-11-04103/article_deploy/html/images/applsci-11-04103-g001.png.

The preventive approach has the effect of enabling homeowners to redesign security provisions and implement more effective prevention models, thus enhancing the cyberattack resilience of smart homes, as portrayed by Sandeep Pirbhulal et al. (Abie et al., 2023). Furthermore, smart home development is related to the concept of Cyber-Physical Social Machines that characterize the interaction between humans and IoT devices. Besides facilitating automation and efficiency, socio-technical systems also introduce complexity pertaining to security and privacy. By exploiting users' reliance on networked devices, permanent sensing and automation capabilities reshuffle traditional human-machine relationships, which are difficult to express in terms of their socio-cognitive dimensions. The integration of IoT into domestic environments requires a universal platform that addresses these new dangers. Between innovation and security, there must be a balancing act that ensures the comfort introduced by smart home devices without compromising the safety of users and data integrity. This two-way strategy is critical to establishing a trustworthy and accountable smart home environment, as defined within the context of IoT application-related cybersecurity challenges (Creese et al., 2018) (Figure 1.5).

1.1.2. Impact on Healthcare

The addition of the IoT to healthcare systems has facilitated significant innovations in medical practice and patient care. The use of IoT-based devices, such as wearables and remote monitoring solutions, has revolutionized the way healthcare providers interact with patients. These technologies encourage real-time monitoring of vital signs, thereby enabling early interventions and improved patient outcomes, particularly for chronic ailments. While being emphasized as the new telemedicine environment, having access to real-time information through Cloud Computing boosts the accessibility and interaction of patients and healthcare alike, which makes telemedicine a game-changing solution for the healthcare sector (Samsidar et al., 2025). However, this new wave of connected devices also raises urgent issues regarding data security and patient privacy, calling for an integrated approach to cybersecurity practices to ensure patient data integrity. Healthcare cybersecurity threats have expanded in tandem with healthcare's adoption of IoT technology. The highly interdependent and interconnected nature of healthcare systems—covering everything from electronic health records (EHRs) to telehealth platforms and IoT devices—demand very robust security measures to prevent compromises and data theft. Episodes such as the WannaCry ransomware attack have underlined the risks of compromise of proper cybersecurity, which will compromise patient safety and operational integrity (Aldosari, 2025). This is augmented by regulatory compliance and digital health literacy concerns that vary between healthcare workers and patients. Enhancing cybersecurity in health care, thus, is not just a matter of updating technology defenses but also a matter of influencing culture based on awareness and preparedness within health care organizations so that everyone stands in a place to respond to emerging threats. Effective IoT integration in healthcare ultimately relies on innovation against ethical alignment with regard to patient data protection. Healthcare organizations leverage innovative technologies to advance service delivery while inheriting the moral responsibility of safeguarding sensitive information against breaches.

Implementing best practices in cybersecurity such as data encryption, risk management, and employee education is essential to averting threats while guaranteeing regulatory compliance (Aldosari, 2025). Additionally, building trust among patients through open communication regarding data usage and security processes can greatly impact the uptake of IoT healthcare solutions. As institutions aim towards a sustainable model of healthcare focused on accessibility and effectiveness, cybersecurity will continue to be a critical priority to safeguard patient rights and maintain the overall integrity of healthcare services in the future (Figure 1.6).

Figure 1.6. The implementation of IoT-enabled devices, such as wearables and remote monitoring systems, has revolutionized how healthcare providers interact with patients.

Source: https://www.kserve.co.in/wp-content/uploads/2021/06/iot-in-healthcare.jpg.

1.1.3. Role in Industrial Automation

As the world of industrial automation continues to advance, the convergence of the IoT becomes a pivot element reshaping production workflows. Industry 4.0 brings a new age where intelligent factories prevail, with interconnected systems facilitating unprecedented levels of efficiency and flexibility. This transformation is particularly pronounced in industries like the food and beverages industry, where IoT technology makes it possible to personalize the production process according to the requirements of the consumers. The implications of such a transformation are vast, with organizations looking to improve efficiency and reduce wastage through better utilization of resources. Through IoT capabilities, companies can optimize their supply chain and drive forward their manufacturing processes, all in the pursuit of greater Industry 4.0

goals defined in Córdoba-Roldán et al. (2017). In addition to general operating effectiveness, the effects of industrial automatization extend to security issues as well. With increasingly networked devices and systems, industrial environments have heightened vulnerability to cyber-attacks. As described in cybersecurity framework discussions, it is crucial for organizations to set in place strong defense mechanisms in order to protect their operational technology (OT) networks. Securing these interlinked devices is essential not just for service continuity but also for protecting sensitive data that can affect the integrity of the production process. As literature suggests, an integrated strategy for the infrastructure and controls to be used in cyber defense is essential in industrial automation risk mitigation of the IoT threats, as shown in Anglano et al. (2018). Finally, and most importantly, education and awareness play a critical role in maintaining cybersecurity in industrial automation. Training programs encompassing technical and operational aspects of cybersecurity are an essential part of establishing a culture of security awareness among employees. Companies must invest in ongoing learning programs to train employees to be able to identify inherent vulnerabilities and respond appropriately to threats. Such a pro-active approach not only enhances collective resilience but also promotes innovation within the workforce, facilitating a more agile response to the changing threats of Industry 4.0. As industries strive to integrate IoT solutions in responsible and secure ways, ongoing education becomes an enabling enabler offering the twin objectives of operational excellence and cybersecurity resilience (Figure 1.7).

Figure 1.7. The advent of industry 4.0 heralds an era characterized by smart factories, where interconnected systems facilitate unprecedented levels of efficiency and flexibility.

Source: https://www.innovapptive.com/hubfs/Industry5.0-49.webp.

1.2. OVERVIEW OF CYBERSECURITY

The cyber world becomes increasingly important as technology advancements continue to become part of everyday life. With the rapid diffusion of digital environments, dangers arise that necessitate comprehensive protection and resilience mechanisms. Cybersecurity incorporates multiplicity of measures directed towards safeguarding networks, machines, and data from cyber-attacks, such as unauthorized entry and information exposures. As noted in the current debate among the experts, cyber defense continues to evolve, requiring a proper comprehension of infrastructures and controls required by organizations in order to forestall possible threats (Anglano et al., 2018). The growing technicality of cyber threats also requires sophisticated cybersecurity strategies, both technological strategies as well as policies and practices for handling risk. In the IoT context, cybersecurity presents unique challenges and opportunities. As IoT devices proliferate, enabling seamless interaction between the physical and digital worlds, the security of these networked devices takes on a critical significance. The increasing reliance on IoT technology to monitor and control processes creates valuable efficiencies, but in so doing, it also creates vulnerabilities to cyber-attack. Addressing cybersecurity in IoT environments involves a multi-faceted solution that entails innovative technologies and innovative approaches to maintaining confidential information and securing user privacy (Abdolee et al., 2019).

Figure 1.8. As IoT devices proliferate, facilitating seamless interaction between the digital and physical worlds, the security of these interconnected devices becomes paramount.

Source: https://dataconomy.com/wp-content/uploads/2023/08/Future-of-IoT_7.jpg.

The marriage of various technological disciplines like artificial intelligence and blockchain can offer ways to increase IoT systems security to facilitate the secure development of these technologies into everyday applications. Understanding the nuances of cybersecurity within the IoT era also involves an understanding of the roles of awareness, training, and risk management. The success of effective cybersecurity implementation necessitates ongoing education and training for the stakeholders at all levels, i.e., individuals, corporates, and governments. With the increasing sophistication of cyber threats, there becomes an urgent need to build a culture of security awareness. Risk management efforts will continue to allow organizations to identify potential vulnerabilities and take measures to mitigate such risks. Collective action, then, as described in recent literature, in terms of establishing standardized practices and training programs is necessary in order to boost the cybersecurity resilience of an IoT-dependent world (Anglano et al., 2018). These proactive steps not only secure data but also allow users and organizations to thrive in the increasingly digitalized era (Figure 1.8).

1.2.1. Definition and Scope of Cybersecurity

Cybersecurity, the vital discipline in our increasingly digital life, means the protection of computer networks, systems, and information from theft, harm, or unauthorized use. With the IoT continuing to grow, the term cybersecurity also expands to encompass the particular weaknesses presented by networked devices. This expansion is coupled with new challenges as IoT devices come with varying levels of security measures and are generally mounted in places where traditional security measures are not adequate. As far as this is concerned, cybersecurity must also account for several attack points and dynamic threats, which can have significant effects on organizations and individuals alike. By acknowledging the multi-dimensional nature of cybersecurity, stakeholders are adequately poised to make well-informed decisions about reducing risk and resource allocation, ultimately enhancing their overall security position within the vast digital universe of interactions. The agenda of cybersecurity is not merely technical protection; it encompasses legal, ethical, and social elements that are increasingly becoming necessary in a globalized world. As business entities cross borders of regulations and compliance regimes, they must also build a culture of cybersecurity awareness among employees as well as consumers. This is achieved through constant training and education to equip personnel with the capability to detect threats and act accordingly. Cybersecurity also addresses complex issues of data privacy, intellectual property rights, and ethical dimensions around surveillance and monitoring. These issues underscore the necessity for collaboration between various industries, including government, business, and academia, to develop strong cybersecurity policies that counter present and looming threats. As the IoT comes to shape more and more of our digital landscape, it is more and more essential that cybersecurity policies are comprehensive and inclusive in their scope. Because of the dynamics of technological advancement, the definition and scope of cybersecurity must be constantly updated to accommodate new threats. Programs like Industry 4.0 and the soon-to-arrive Industry 5.0 underscore the intertwined nature of technical innovations and security, affirming that cybersecurity is not an after-the-fact response but a foresighted initiative. As the world's economy becomes ever more dependent on digital infrastructures, the consequences of insufficient cybersecurity are multifaceted, and the impact spills beyond companies into sectors and communities. Furthermore, the interconnectivity of the IoT provides a fertile soil for sophisticated cyber-attacks, adding to the saturation of the security landscape. As researches, policymakers, and business leaders come together to navigate these complexities, their combined efforts will go a long way in formulating a resilient cybersecurity policy that can safeguard our virtual future, enabling new technologies like the metaverse to flourish while avoiding threats and vulnerabilities that come with them (Dwivedi et al., 2022; Xu et al., 2021) (Figure 1.9).

Figure 1.9. With the world's economy increasingly reliant on digital infrastructures, the implications of inadequate cybersecurity are far-reaching, affecting not just businesses but entire industries and communities.

Source: https://blogs.worldbank.org/content/dam/sites/blogs/img/detail/mgr/de-risking_digital_development_investments.jpg.

1.2.2. Historical Context of Cybersecurity Threats

The progression of cybersecurity threats can be followed back to the early days of computing, where the weaknesses were mainly a result of technology's infancy. When computer networks improved, so too did the methods employ by the bad guys. Early threats were in the form of simple malware and basic hacking techniques, primarily against home computers. The proliferation of the internet in the 1990s, however, significantly increased the threat picture. With increasingly large numbers of devices getting connected and data exchange growing, opportunistic cybercriminals mounted sophisticated attacks on governments and businesses, using security weaknesses to wreak havoc. This historical trend indicates the evolution of cybersecurity threats to their sophistication from isolated incidents to orchestrated attacks that have a potentially catastrophic impact on national security and economic stability. As technology changed over time, cyber threats became more sophisticated along with the growth of the IoT. In the late 1990s and early 2000s, connectivity among devices grew, leading to concerns about intrusions into networks and data exfiltration.

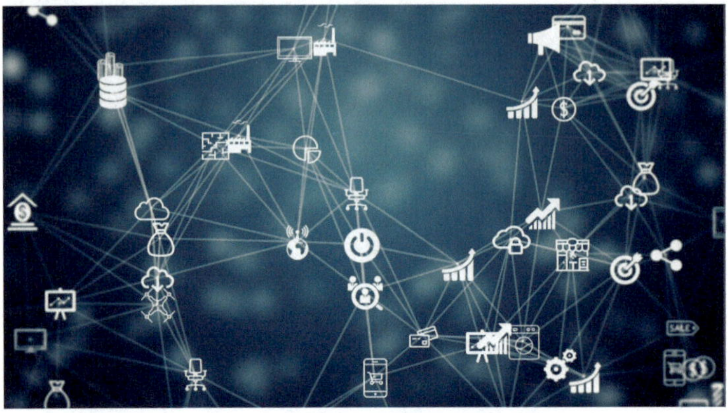

Figure 1.10. Each advancement in IoT technology brought not only greater efficiency but also heightened risks, as these devices often lacked adequate security measures.

Source: https://informationage-production.s3.amazonaws.com/uploads/2022/10/AdobeStock_133171498-scaled.jpeg.

This involved a shift from attacks on individual systems to targeting networks connecting various devices, creating new vulnerabilities. The introduction of digital twins, computer simulations of physical systems, also complicated this environment with the new additional data streams and attack vectors (Botín-Sanabria et al., 2022). Each phase in the development of IoT technology was not only introducing greater efficiency but greater risk as well since the devices never had appropriate security programs installed. Hence, awareness of past threats is the stepping stone to designing effective cybersecurity solutions particularly for contemporary challenges in the IoT environment. Besides that, the existence of the metaverse illustrates the expanded range of cybersecurity threats in an increasingly digitalizing society. As interactive technologies build shared virtual experiences, concerns with trust, privacy, and security have intensified (Dwivedi et al., 2022). The vulnerability to exploitation in metaverse spaces is symptomatic of a larger trend in which distinctions between the physical and digital worlds continue only to blur further. Cyber threats nowadays include not just data breaches but also identity theft, misinformation, and manipulation of the psyche. With these spaces an increasingly integral part of daily life, their vulnerabilities are a tempting target for malicious actors. Understanding such a historical context of evolving threats, particularly with regards to developments like the metaverse, is critical to address future cybersecurity concerns in an interconnected world, thereby ensuring the security and resiliency of users in digital operations (Figure 1.10).

1.2.3. Key Principles of Cybersecurity

With the IoT, it is crucial to know the fundamental principles of cybersecurity in an effort to steer clear of threats through connected devices. One of the basic principles is maintaining confidentiality of information in a way that only the authorized entities have access to it. This principle is particularly critical with IoT-based systems where large amounts of data are pooled and moved from devices like smart home devices and medical trackers. Confidentiality is ensured through the application of robust encryption techniques and access restrictions. On top of that, organizations should remain vigilant for attempted access and potential breaches because unauthorized access may lead to harmful effects. Thus, the design of processes that facilitate confidentiality is a vital aspect in guaranteeing IoT devices and information are safeguarded, leading to wiser and safer deployment within the digital world. Integrity is also an essential building block that is critical to the security of IoT systems and maintaining data integrity from the time of its creation until its end of life. Data integrity is a difficult aspect in a network with a high device-to-device connection because vulnerabilities create opportunities for malicious entities to tamper with device function or corrupt data. In order to counteract these threats, organizations must employ tools such as digital signatures and cryptographic hashing, which enable authentication of the data source and verification of information accuracy. Routine auditing of data transactions and the employment of anomaly detection software can further assist in detecting instances of tampering. By making integrity their primary cybersecurity planning, organizations are able to build trust in their IoT applications such that the users and stakeholders have confidence in the quality and correctness of the data being processed and transferred. Lastly, the availability principle encompasses the need for IoT systems to be operational and usable by users at the time of need.

This rule is important, particularly in sectors such as healthcare and critical infrastructure, where system downtime would result in calamitous impact on individuals and society in general. To enhance availability, organizations must implement redundancy controls such as failover mechanisms to dampen the impact of would-be attacks or hardware failure. Moreover, regular monitoring and a dynamic incident response approach can further enhance availability by facilitating immediate mitigation and minimizing threats or downtime. In recognizing the value of availability in addition to confidentiality and integrity, organizations can establish an end-to-end cybersecurity stance that protects their IoT systems so they can function properly in various environments and uses (Aldoseri et al., 2023; Dwivedi et al., 2022) (Figure 1.8).

Figure 1.11. Integrity is another key principle essential to the cybersecurity of IoT systems, ensuring that data remains accurate and unaltered throughout its lifecycle.

Source: https://kigen.com/wp-content/uploads/2025/01/GettyImages-1469723133-scaled.jpg.

1.3. Cybersecurity Challenges in IoT

The rapid development of the IoT has created opportunities as much as challenges, particularly when it comes to cybersecurity. As IoT devices proliferate in consumer and industrial environments both, their interconnected nature opens them up to cyber-attacks. Each device represents a potential point of entry for cyber-attacks and hence it is important that organizations develop solid security measures. The majority of IoT devices have bad design with minimal processing and outdated firmware. Therefore, these defects hinder applying advanced security features. Contributing to this issue, the majority of users do not keep regular software updates, contributing to the susceptibility of devices. Not only is it hard to find these bugs, but also to integrate effective cybersecurity products as part of the design and functionality of the IoT system. Effective IoT cybersecurity is marred by a number of issues, including the need for advanced intrusion detection systems (IDS) with real-time functionality for identifying malicious behavior. Conventional IDS methodologies are not effective in handling the inherent challenges of IoT environments. The nature of heterogeneity in IoT devices as well as the diversity of potential cyber-attacks makes conventional IDS challenging to maintain its precision and effectiveness. However, emerging technologies such as Deep Learning have proved high potential for enhancing security controls for IoT installations. By improving the ability of intrusion detection, which is such advanced methodologies, organizations can guarantee the integrity of their networks. Aldhaheri et al. (2023) highlights the construction of Deep Learning techniques that support cyber threat mitigation and detection, which is an excellent prospect for research and application in enhancing IoT security. Moreover, the application of Artificial Intelligence (AI) in cybersecurity mechanisms has its chances and dangers. AI-backed systems are able to offer predictive analysis that foresees anticipated threats before they arise, thereby speeding up overall responsiveness. Implementation of AI, however, brings with it an aspect of complexity as the technology itself may be vulnerable to intelligent cybercriminals. The possibility of AI-provided false positives also leads to unnecessary panic or misuse of resources. As more organizations are turning to AI to improve their cybersecurity, there is a necessity to keep pace with innovation while exercising caution. Lloyd et al. (2024) emphasizes the importance of understanding the limitations of AI in cybersecurity and advancing research and development as a way of preventing risks tied to AI while harnessing the potential that AI offers to IoT security systems (Figure 1.12).

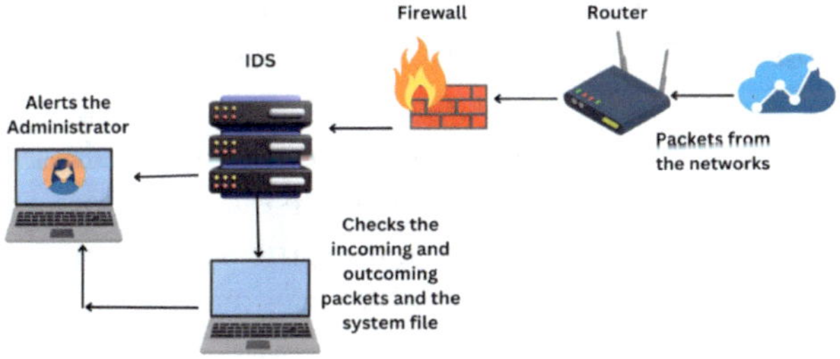

Figure 1.12. Effective cybersecurity measures in IoT face numerous hurdles, including the need for advanced intrusion detection systems (IDS) capable of identifying suspicious activities in real-time.

Source: https://pub.mdpi-res.com/computers/computers-14-00087/article_deploy/html/images/computers-14-00087-g001.png?1741005090.

1.3.1. Vulnerabilities in IoT Devices

With the rise of the IoT, vulnerabilities in IoT devices have become increasingly topical within the field of cybersecurity. Such vulnerabilities are a direct result of various factors, including weak security practices, weak passwords, and weak patch management. With the majority of IoT devices being designed with the convenience of their users as a priority, the security measures they possess end up being weak, making them susceptible to abuse. For instance, although intelligent home appliances offer greater functionality, they can also facilitate easy hacking into personal networks by cybercrooks. The implications of the vulnerabilities are deep, since compromised devices can be used for illicit purposes, such as data breaches and unauthorized surveillance. It needs to be addressed because they rank among the largest of threats to the current cybersecurity landscape, citing the need for a more comprehensive framework in protecting user data and privacy. Interconnected IoT devices make exponents of the risks associated with vulnerabilities, thus turning them into potential multipliers of cyber threats. When one device is breached, the hackers are able to breach more related services and have a cascading effect of breaches. This is further supported by the fact that there are no shared security practices among the extensive IoT ecosystem of devices.

The majority of the manufacturers emphasize rapid development and market entry over security, and the devices that result might be susceptible to infirm manipulation. Second, personal and nonpersonal data collected by such devices are increasingly used for targeted manipulation, not only targeting individual consumers but the entire society as well. Regulators have yet to realize fully the consequences of these flaws against the backdrop of data-breach legislation. Enhanced understanding of data abuse can inform policy innovations that address the dynamic nature of threats derived from IoT vulnerabilities, expanding the discussion on the convergence of technology, privacy, and law (Kilovaty et al., 2019). As security experts strive to vanquish these vulnerabilities, public awareness and user education can never be overstated. End-users must be made aware of the potential dangers and mitigating measures that ensure protection for their IoT devices. Promoting healthy password management, regular software updates, and implementation of network segmentation are crucial steps that can strengthen security. Also, ongoing research on cyber defense strategies focused on IoT ecosystems is the priority of the hour. A joint effort by makers, policymakers, and consumers can lead to stronger security postures, thereby reducing the threats of these gadgets. The strategy should include the creation of industry-wide security standards, and policies holding companies accountable for protecting consumer data. The evolving IoT cybersecurity environment calls for a holistic response where technology developments are complemented with education and awareness, thus ensuring a secure digital environment for all (Anglano et al., 2018) (Figure 1.13).

Figure 1.13. Many IoT devices are designed with user convenience in mind, often resulting in minimal security features that leave them open to exploitation.

Source: https://switchhotelsolutions.com.au/wp-content/uploads/2025/05/image_98cf94f9e73bcad3f13a8c263215b769.jpeg.

1.3.2. Data Privacy Concerns

As the IoT continues to expand, data privacy issues concerning the vast number of interconnected devices have become increasingly imperative. Integrating a multitude of intelligent devices into daily life initiates an advanced ecosystem where individual information is gathered, forwarded, and archived constantly. This data often holds sensitive information about users' locations, health and fitness information, and habits, raising very serious questions about ownership and permission. On top of this, the vulnerabilities in much of the IoT open up possibilities for unauthorized access, and hence potentially very serious breaches of personal privacy. Such concerns require ongoing dialogue between technology developers, policymakers, and consumers in establishing distinct protocols and policies that secure individual information and yet encourage development and utility in the IoT space (Li et al., 2020). The convergence of IoT privacy and cybersecurity concerns is most apparent in wearable technology, whose popularity has increased exponentially due to convenience and their addition of features such as medical monitoring and exercise tracking. These advantages serve to underscore critical concerns regarding data security. Wearable technology does not usually have robust security capabilities, and thus they are an attractive target for cyberattacks. These attacks have the potential to exploit vulnerabilities and facilitate easy access to individual data or change device behavior. Such intrusions not only breach personal privacy but also data gathered integrity and confidentiality. Hence, manufacturers must exercise good security practices and maintain openness into data collection operations (Abad et al., 2023). Resolution of the issues of data privacy in the IoT space also involves creating consumer-focused solutions that enable users to be in control of their personal data.

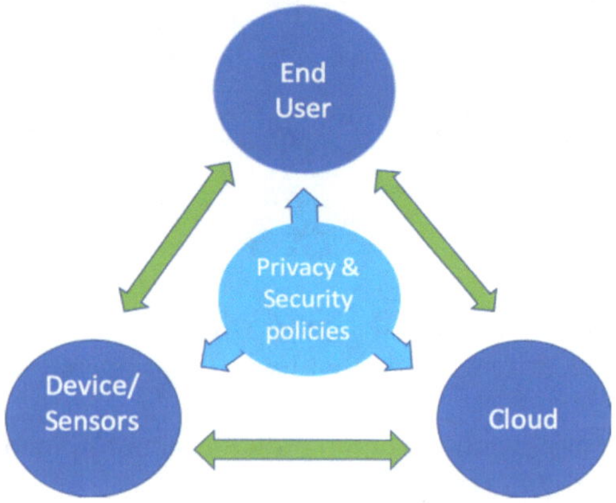

Figure 1.14. Mitigating data privacy concerns in the IoT ecosystem also necessitates the development of consumer-focused solutions that empower users to take control of their personal information.

Source: https://pub.mdpi-res.com/applsci/applsci-10-04102/article_deploy/html/images/applsci-10-04102-g001.png?1592206172.

One of these is having user-controlled data collection mechanisms that enable users to determine what they wish to share and with whom they want to share it. Other actions, such as the deployment of Virtual Trip Line (VTL) and virtual wall technologies, are able to create boundaries that further secure user data. Besides, public awareness by offering comprehensive user guides and security alerts can also encourage greater sensitivity to the dangers posed by IoT devices among consumers. Encryption technology can further play a critical role in safeguarding users' privacy by ensuring that data is sent and stored out of reach from the public (Abad et al., 2023). Collectively, these strategies can help to enable both confidence in IoT technologies and public confidence as a whole in addressing the data privacy complexities of an increasingly interconnected world (Figure 1.14).

1.3.3. Threats From Cyber Attacks

The IoT explosion has transformed the cybersecurity landscape, ushering in newer scales of threat from cyber-attacks. With more devices becoming connected, the attackers' surface area multiplies many times, opening up new opportunities for exploitation. Cyber-attacks on IoT devices range from data theft and identity theft to more dangerous possibilities such as the compromise of critical infrastructure. Such vulnerabilities are traditionally compounded by poor security controls, making devices susceptible to attacks that not only pose risk to user data but also potentially endanger public safety. The peculiar nature of IoT devices, with compromised processing capacity and mixed operating systems, complicate traditional cybersecurity, necessitating a reevaluation of established defense mechanisms against evolving threats. Moreover, the lack of shared security standards within the IoT community is one of the reasons for the growing threat environment. The majority of IoT devices are made with security being an afterthought, and hence there is wide-scale deployment of systems that are fair game for criminals.

For instance, connection of smart home devices and industrial systems is a domino effect; one compromised device serves as an entry point for subsequent attacks across the network. Interconnectedness does not only raise the stakes for mass breaches but also complicates how to react and recover from breaches. With the aforementioned challenges, businesses must prioritize making the creation of far-reaching cybersecurity programs targeted at the unique demands of IoT environments a top priority, as proposed in current research into cyber risk assessment approaches (Ani et al., 2020). Moreover, enhancing organizations' cybersecurity position against future IoT threats also involves proactive threat management and education. As noted in recent publications, a robust self-assessment and readiness procedure is key to enabling organizations to prepare, prevent, and respond adequately to cyberattacks on IoT devices. Developing methodologies that allow organizations to assess their IoT cyber risk posture is critical for preventing vulnerabilities and preparing for prospective attacks. Bridging the existing loopholes in cybersecurity standards and training can empower stakeholders to develop a culture of security awareness and resilience. The inclusion of risk assessment models, for instance, the goal-oriented dependency model, can provide valuable insights into the existing and desired status of the risk of an organization, thereby strengthening a better defense against the sophisticated nature of cyber-attacks in IoT systems (Anglano et al., 2018) (Figure 1.15).

Figure 1.15. Many IoT devices are produced with little consideration for security, resulting in widespread deployment of systems that are easy targets for malicious actors.

Source: https://relevant.software/wp-content/uploads/Untitled-design-2023-11-06T113703197.png.

1.4. REGULATORY AND ETHICAL CONSIDERATIONS

The integration of IoT technologies across various industries, including construction and critical infrastructure, has raised significant regulatory and ethical challenges that need to be addressed to achieve safe and secure environments. Regulation is the key in guiding the deployment of IoT systems since it provides standards and protocols regarding data privacy, security, and operating integrity. For instance, the construction industry is assisted by regulations that govern the use of AI technologies to manage projects and perform predictive maintenance, which prioritize the need to comply with safety and quality standards. Therefore, businesses need to navigate a complex regulatory environment that could differ sharply between jurisdictions, impacting their capacity to adopt innovative solutions without compromising legal and ethical compliance in the dynamic technological landscape (Rane et al., 2024). Aside from regulatory contexts, ethical considerations of IoT deployment are critical in influencing public trust and the success of IoT technology. The consequences of data breaches and unauthorized surveillance raise very profound issues regarding the privacy rights of people and the moral management of personal information. Both organizations and developers who have a stake in IoT applications must promote transparency, responsibility, and consent in handling personal information. To that effect, the guidelines of equity and justice also come into play, particularly since how the IoT technology can affect vulnerable populations or widen digital divides comes under consideration. These ethical dimensions call for productive communication among stakeholders in order to make sure that technological innovation and implications thereof are critically assessed and aligned with societal values, thereby promoting responsible innovation (Adegbite et al., 2023). The overlap of regulatory and ethical aspects under the scenario of IoT and cybersecurity accounts for the need for visionary strategies to favor both compliance and ethical demands. Governments, the private sector, and civil society must cooperate to design end-to-end policies addressing the multifaceted issues that IoT technologies present. By building an environment that prioritizes safe data use, cybersecurity education, and stakeholder engagement, it is feasible to constrain threats while maximizing opportunities for IoT innovations. Technological development cannot occur in isolation but through a policy environment that values human rights, the well-being of communities, and environmental sustainability. By so doing through such interagency collaborations, stakeholders are able to create a trusted and secure environment that enables the future of IoT, thus unlocking its full potential for making positive contributions to society (Rane et al., 2024).

1.4.1. Overview of IoT Regulations

The rapid boom of IoT devices needs a robust structure of regulations to ensure cybersecurity and user privacy. Governments and organizations across the world are now understanding the necessity to create these regulations, addressing the challenges and prospects arising from IoT technologies. An effective regulation policy includes principles that govern data protection, interoperability, and security requirements among devices. This is crucial in the safeguarding of sensitive information, especially in sectors highly impacted by IoT, such as health and infrastructure. The Italian Nations research society recognizes a systematic approach to cyber security, with the need for explicit measures facilitating stronger organizational practices in cybersecurity as discussed in the observations provided in Anglano et al. (2018). These regulations can go a long way in facilitating a safer environment for consumers and industries embracing the IoT revolution. Moreover, IoT regulations must keep pace with the constant growth of technology and the changing landscape of cyber-attacks. The dynamic nature of IoT device roll-out and new uses of artificial intelligence is presenting opportunities for mischievous use. Regulators are between a rock and a hard place when trying to create legislation that both defends consumers and spurs innovation simultaneously. For instance, advanced data analytics techniques can influence personal information in a way that controls consumer behavior, as mentioned in Kilovaty et al. (2019). This attests to the need for laws that do not only address obvious cybersecurity threats but also opportunities for data abuse behind IoT device-collected information. It is crucial, thus, to devise a comprehensive legal framework that facilitates the practice of responsible data handling measures in an effort to minimize risks from IoT devices. Apart from reducing the risk of cybersecurity, IoT legislations must give priority to user education and awareness about data security and privacy. Since people are increasingly relying on connected devices, they do not know the way their data is processed and transferred. Promoting transparency in the IoT infrastructure, in the way of open guidelines and education initiatives, can empower users to make intelligent decisions regarding their device usage. Producers and regulators share the responsibility of making information related to data collection, sharing, and storage readily accessible. Furthermore, training and awareness efforts, as noted in Anglano et al. (2018), should be incorporated into regulations to foster a culture of cybersecurity. This kind of well-educated user base will not only enhance the overall effectiveness of existing regulations but also play a role in the development of a safer IoT world (Figure 1.16).

Figure 1.16. Governments and institutions worldwide are beginning to recognize the importance of establishing these regulations, addressing both the challenges and opportunities posed by IoT technologies.

Source: https://carnegie-production-assets.s3.amazonaws.com/static/media/images/iStock-1394401648.jpg.

1.4.2. Ethical Implications of Data Collection

The advent of the IoT has radically transformed data collection, exchange, and processing, with tremendous ethical implications. The more devices that are connected, they accumulate vast volumes of personal information with or without the expressed permission of the user. This is a critical problem as much as privacy, ownership, and misuse of data are involved. Ethical concerns arise when organizations utilize this data for profitability, usually against personal privacy. The principle of informed consent is most commonly broken in an environment where users may not be aware of the extent of data gathering or the risks of sharing private information. Further, clarity around the utilization of data exacerbates this moral concern, instilling consumers with distrust toward technology providers. In addition to privacy concerns, data harvesting and utilization in IoT systems compromise traditional security principles. By gathering data that reflects a person's everyday activities and hobbies, IoT devices are able to automatically create profiles that can put people at risk of innumerable threats. Nefarious persons may exploit this data to serve malicious purposes, with possible outcomes being identity theft or unauthorized entry into sensitive information.

Figure 1.17. Cybercriminals could leverage this information for malicious purposes, leading to identity theft or unauthorized access to sensitive data.

Source: https://www.idagent.com/wp-content/uploads/2024/02/A-hacker-or-cracker-tries-to-hack-a-security-system-to-steal-or-destroy-critical-information.-Or-a-ransom-of-important-information-of-the-company_-copy.jpg.

The ethical implications also apply to the responsibilities of organizations that develop such technologies; they must ensure the safety of data gathered and the repercussions of possible misuse. For Posadas et al. (2017), the need for a comprehensive legal framework for IoT identifies not only the protection of information but also enhancing consumer protection to ensure ethical use and gathering of data. Finally, the development of IoT technologies must embrace ethical values through practices such as privacy-by-design, which supports the integration of privacy protection in the technology's architectural design at the start. This offers a proactive approach, with a focus on companies designing systems with the privacy of users as a main objective alongside innovation. As Anglano et al. (2018) advocates, awareness promotion, training, and risk management empower developers and users to handle the complexities of data ethics responsibly. Integrating ethical practice into every stage of development enables stakeholders to build public trust in IoT technologies eventually leading to societal benefits while avoiding harm. This balance is most critical in matching the ethical aspects of information collection and ensuring that technological progress does not move into areas of individual rights or societal values (Figure 1.17).

1.4.3. The Role of Organizations in Ensuring Security

Organizations play an imperative role in offering security in the realms of IoT and cybersecurity. They are experienced through strong frameworks and protocols tailored to secure sensitive data and maintain user confidence. These frameworks must evolve with the dynamic technology landscape, adhering to industry norms while resisting emerging threats. As emphasized in studies of developing information technology curriculum guidelines, educational frameworks and career pathways into such programs are critical in building competence in cybersecurity, which supports organizational resilience against cyber problems (Alrumaih et al., 2015). Investing in employee training and cultivating security awareness culture can help organizations develop an informed staff that can identify and respond to potential threats. Furthermore, the integration of security practices into organizational practices demands the adoption of new technologies and methods, particularly as society moves toward "Smart Cities." Organizations' activities must extend beyond compliance with regulations; they need to drive the projects that utilize the strengths of big data, shared micromobility, and other innovative solutions while safeguarding community interests (Cohen et al., 2019). By implementing pilot projects and using metrics to determine the effectiveness of cybersecurity approaches, organizations are able to refine their methodologies and implement successful models across industries. Not only does this enhance security, but it also generates public confidence in the technologies behind existing urban infrastructures. Organizations also have to collaborate with stakeholders like government agencies, technology providers, and community associations to establish balanced security plans. This cooperation enables enhanced sharing of knowledge and provides organizations with a multi-dimensional understanding of likely vulnerabilities in IoT systems. These alliances lead to the development of best practices and common assets that allow organizations to meet cybersecurity threats head-on. Organizations embracing collaboration are better positioned to weather the multi-faceted aspect of cybersecurity since they can draw on varied pools of talent to create robust defenses. Therefore, the organizational contribution towards securing IoT ecosystems is not reactive but must be proactive and strategic, encompassing multifaceted voices and disciplines to ultimately contribute to a safer digital world.

1.5. CONCLUSION

In short, the intersection of the IoT and cybersecurity is an urgent area of concern of debate in modern technology. With the number of IoT devices on the rise, so is the risk of vulnerabilities being exploited by malicious actors. The strange nature of the devices, with minimal processing power and weak security features, calls for innovative solutions in cybersecurity to forestall the wave of threats. The challenge increasingly mounts as the IoT integration in various industries from smart homes to mission-critical infrastructure creates multiple lines of attack. Thus, having a thorough comprehension of the security implications that tend to accompany IoT deployment is instrumental in defining resilience against likely cyber-attacks. Moreover, the ongoing evolution of high-tech technology, such as artificial intelligence, offers viable opportunities for enhancing cybersecurity procedures in the IoT environment. AI can be employed to monitor networks continuously, analyze patterns to identify anomalies, and enable proactive identification of threats. As discussed in the context of AI-based modeling, these technologies play a central role in defining smart systems in various applications, such as cybersecurity. However, this reliance on AI is accompanied by newer complexities, particularly in the context of ethical matters, privacy, and the need for robust regulatory infrastructure to avoid misuse and ensure secure and equitable use. The subtle consequences of these technological developments hold considerable weight on building secure IoT environments. Eventually, addressing the twin challenges presented by IoT and cybersecurity requires an interdisciplinary approach, including interdisciplinarity between actors such as policymakers, industry, and researchers. As the discussion regarding new technologies like the metaverse demonstrates, there exists a critical need for interdisciplinarity incorporating multiple perspectives. By engaging the best brains across different fields, we can better understand the social implications of these advances and address burning issues such as trust, privacy, and data protection. As identified in current studies, a future research agenda on these issues that could be submitted as proposed research can serve as a valuable asset to decision-makers because it could lead to a safer and more secure digital world as IoT continues to expand (Dwivedi et al., 2022; Sarker, 2022).

1.5.1. Summary of Key Points

The rapid development of the IoT significantly influences the cyber security environment, both positively and negatively. IoT devices, characterized by their connectivity and data sharing capabilities, have invaded every aspect of life in various fields, including healthcare, smart cities, and industries. The proliferation of the devices results in a wider attack surface for malicious cyber threats because every device can be a weak link. As noted in recent studies, these weaknesses necessitate a sound approach to cybersecurity that can handle the inherent character of IoT, i.e., scalability and heterogeneity. The need for austerity in cybersecurity solutions becomes clear as one considers the rampant multiplication of devices that need to be secured and the subsequent threats that organizations must navigate in this frenzied environment (Anglano et al., 2018). Moreover, firms must adopt proactive cybersecurity in the IoT arena through good risk management practices. This would not only entail being aware of the possible threats but also developing a list of horizontal measures that entails training and awareness programs for stakeholders and users. The education emphasis underscores the importance of mitigating human error, often exploited by cyber threats as a means of compromising security defenses. By cultivating a culture of security-awareness, organizations can better equip employees to detect and successfully resist cyber threats, embedding a strong cybersecurity posture necessary in today's interconnected world (Atmaca et al., 2020). In addition to organizational activity, the coming together of newer technologies such as machine learning and autonomous systems into the Internet of Things paradigm creates a new frontier and danger. As the Internet of Space Things (IoST) work illustrates, reliance upon advanced communication networks enhances the risk for cyberattacks, leading to an increased threat landscape sophistication. The advent of new technologies creates a continuous necessity for the security architectures to be continuously evaluated to find and minimize emerging threats. Thus, the establishment of reference architectures for modeling applications in these emerging systems is required to anticipate and safeguard against upcoming threats. The convergence of IoT, cybersecurity, and emerging technology paradigms therefore requires a multi-dimensional approach that embraces innovation while upholding strict cybersecurity measures (Anglano et al., 2018; Atmaca et al., 2020).

1.5.2. Future Trends in IoT and Cybersecurity

With the expansion of the IoT, integration of emerging technologies and cyber security techniques will shape future trends. There are more devices connected to the IoT network, which makes the process of cyber threat handling more complex and requires high-level techniques of cyber security. One of the major concerns is the expanding list of IoT devices that lack proper security features, with them being ideal targets for cyber hackers. This anticipated increase in cyber-attacks underscores the importance of organizations evaluating their IoT cybersecurity position on a regular basis. Notably, research brings into focus the development of self-assessment tools to help organizations quantify their vulnerabilities. The addition of a goal-dependent model of dependency, as suggested in recent research, provides a structured process by which organizations can approach and decrease cyber threats associated with IoT devices to lead them into a safer future through increased risk perception and regulation (Ani et al., 2020). Along with the surge in devices, attention to cybersecurity regulations and guidelines will likely rise. Governments and regulators are increasingly conscious of the risks involved in connected devices and are likely to enact stricter requirements on IoT security. Simply regulatory pressure will not only compel manufacturers to put more emphasis on incorporating cybersecurity capabilities into products but create a culture of responsibility within organizations. Stricter regulatory systems will allow for greater alignment of cybersecurity practice with business objectives and drive large-scale training and awareness programs. Furthermore, standard norms will enable organizations to optimally benchmark their cybersecurity position. As it has been pointed out in cybersecurity infrastructure debates, such regulations are paramount in delineating required controls and steps for adequate cyber protection (Anglano et al., 2018).

Figure 1.18. A central concern is the rising number of IoT devices that lack adequate built-in security protocols, making them attractive targets for cybercriminals.

Source: https://img-cdn.publive.online/fit-in/640x430/filters:format(webp)/dq/media/media_files/iot-devices-and-zombie-mushrooms.jpg.

On the horizon, integrating AI and ML into IoT cybersecurity is monumental. These technologies can provide organizations predictive capabilities to identify the possibility of threats before its occurrence, and it enables preemptive strikes against cyber threats. AI and ML enable the processing of high amounts of data generated by IoT devices, thereby facilitating the identification of network irregularities and probable intrusions. This heightened level of threat intelligence not only improves response rates for threats but also informs future security solutioning based on the evolving dynamic of cyber threats. Furthermore, with organizations adopting automated vulnerability scanning and threat detection platforms, the overall IoT ecosystems' resilience will be improved. The interactive dynamics of AI/ML with traditional cybersecurity frameworks will definitely shape the future of IoT security, providing end-to-end protection against increasingly sophisticated cyber-attacks (Ani et al., 2020) (Figure 1.8).

1.5.3. The Importance of Ongoing Research and Development

The technology environment, particularly in the environments of the IoT and cybersecurity, is ever-changing. The evolution of threats follows the evolution of technology, making continuous research and development (R&D) the top priority. This is true because devices that are increasingly interconnected not only become more convenient but are also causally susceptible to huge vulnerabilities. Without consistent R&D, organizations stand the chance of being left behind in the identification of emerging threats and development of proper defense measures. In accordance with a recent study, the Italian scientific environment places particular importance on the need for a structured process of cyber defense, highlighting the necessity of innovative interventions and technologies to be designed for the aim of protecting effectively (Anglano et al., 2018). New types of cyber-attacks make it imperative to have an adaptive approach, which research specifically remains to focus on, building resilience in digital infrastructures. In addition, ongoing R&D is required for developing education frameworks that keep up with technological advancement. Given the ever-changing nature of the information technology industry, developing curricula that properly gets graduates geared up for future requirements is crucial. The blend of knowledge of existing trends and hands-on training ensures that students possess the skills necessary to remain competitive with the evolving cybersecurity and IoT environment. Industry members' overview emphasizes the fact that institutions must analyze these trends in a bid to create effective educational policies (Alrumaih et al., 2015).

This alignment benefits not only the interests of student achievement but also the job market, with graduates contributing to an increasingly reliant workforce on secure and innovative technology. Lastly, the worth of ongoing R&D also applies to cooperative activity among researchers, educators, and industry leaders. These cooperative efforts are necessary to bridge the gap between theoretical knowledge and practical application in real-world settings. With the advancements in the sophistication of cybersecurity threats, cross-disciplinary research has the potential to stimulate innovative solutions that counter such threats holistically. By synthesizing multidisciplinary knowledge from researchers and practitioners, innovative frameworks and technologies can be developed for overall security features. This joint response, as highlighted in current research, allows organizations to actively fend off vulnerabilities and strengthen defense systems against cyber threats (Anglano et al., 2018). Lastly, creating a culture of continuous R&D constructs a stronger technological ecosystem, essential to the future of IoT and cybersecurity.

REFERENCES

1. Abad, H. (2023). Privacy concerns and proposed solutions with IoT in wearable technology. https://core.ac.uk/download/595866282.pdf (accessed on 17th October 2025).
2. Abdolee, R., Maroufi, M., & Tazekand, B. M. (2019). On the convergence of blockchain and Internet of Things (IoT) technologies. http://arxiv.org/abs/1904.01936 (accessed on 17th October 2025).
3. Abie, H., Katt, B., Pirbhulal, S., Shukla, S., et al. (2023). A cognitive digital twin architecture for cybersecurity in IoT-based smart homes. https://core.ac.uk/download/646177235.pdf (accessed on 17th October 2025).
4. Addanki, U. K., Devareddi, R. B., Kamarajugadda, K. K., Movva, P., & Gera, P. (2025). Machine learning-powered intrusion detection system for Agriculture 4.0: Securing the next generation of farming. *International Journal of Innovative Research and Scientific Studies.* https://www.semanticscholar.org/paper/59f71ac0b17b3abe4f315452750c5668cf927269 (accessed on 17th October 2025).
5. Adegbite, A. O., Akinwolemiwa, D. I., Uwaoma, P. U., Kaggwa, S., Akindote, O. J., & Dawodu, S. O. (2023). Review of cybersecurity strategies in protecting national infrastructure: Perspectives from the USA. *Computer Science & IT Research Journal, 4*, 200–219. https://doi.org/10.51594/csitrj.v4i3.658 (accessed on 17th October 2025).
6. Aldhaheri, A., Alwahedi, F., Ferrag, M. A., & Battah, A. (2023). Deep learning for cyber threat detection in IoT networks: A review. *Internet of Things and Cyber-Physical Systems, 4*, 110–128. https://doi.org/10.1016/j.iotcps.2023.09.003 (accessed on 17th October 2025).
7. Aldosari, B. (2025). Cybersecurity in healthcare: New threat to patient safety. *Cureus, 17*. https://www.semanticscholar.org/paper/11da4efb289cba124192186a9280beac0a471df6 (accessed on 17th October 2025).
8. Aldoseri, A., Al-Khalifa, K. N., & Hamouda, A. M. S. (2023). Re-thinking data strategy and integration for artificial intelligence: Concepts, opportunities, and challenges. *Applied Sciences, 13*, 7082–7082. https://doi.org/10.3390/app13127082 (accessed on 17th October 2025).
9. Allioui, H., & Mourdi, Y. (2023). Exploring the full potentials of IoT for better financial growth and stability: A comprehensive survey. *Sensors, 23*, 8015–8015. https://doi.org/10.3390/s23198015 (accessed on 17th October 2025).
10. Almalawi, A., Baecher, B., Boldea, B., Bouchti, B., Brand, B., Byres, E., et al. (2017). Assessing and augmenting SCADA cyber security: A survey

of techniques. https://core.ac.uk/download/293885085.pdf (accessed on 17th October 2025).

11. Alrumaih, H., Byers, B., Gudoniene, D., Hamilton, D., et al. (2015). Multinational perspectives on information technology from academia and industry. https://core.ac.uk/download/86427274.pdf (accessed on 17th October 2025).
12. Amoo, O. O., Osasona, F., Atadoga, A., Ayinla, B. S., Farayola, O. A., & Abrahams, T. O. (2024). Cybersecurity threats in the age of IoT: A review of protective measures. *International Journal of Science and Research Archive.* https://www.semanticscholar.org/paper/6295b61e4b2bdf81489f893a5705304654d96568 (accessed on 17th October 2025).
13. Anglano, C., Aniello, L., Antinori, A., Armando, A., et al. (2018). The future of cybersecurity in Italy: Strategic focus area. https://core.ac.uk/download/188830442.pdf (accessed on 17th October 2025).
14. Ani, U., Anthi, E., Burnap, P., De Roure, D., et al. (2020). Dynamic real-time risk analytics of uncontrollable states in complex Internet of Things systems, cyber risk at the edge. https://core.ac.uk/download/491119431.pdf (accessed on 17th October 2025).
15. Atmaca, U. I., Bradbury, M. S., Cannizzaro, S., Maple, C., et al. (2020). Identifying attack surfaces in the evolving space industry using reference architectures. https://core.ac.uk/download/287605688.pdf (accessed on 17th October 2025).
16. Botín-Sanabria, D. M., Mihăiţă, A. S., Peimbert-García, R. E., Ramírez-Moreno, M. A., Ramírez-Mendoza, R. A., & de Lozoya-Santos, J. J. (2022). Digital twin technology challenges and applications: A comprehensive review. *Remote Sensing, 14*, 1335–1335. https://doi.org/10.3390/rs14061335 (accessed on 17th October 2025).
17. Chilongo, L., & Abubakkar, S. K. M. (2024). Impact of artificial intelligence on cybersecurity: A case of Internet of Things. *I-Manager's Journal on Digital Forensics & Cyber Security, 2*, 1–1. https://doi.org/10.26634/jdf.2.1.21030 (accessed on 17th October 2025).
18. Cohen, A., Davis, R., Dowd, M. K., Shaheen, S., et al. (2019). A framework for integrating transportation into smart cities. https://core.ac.uk/download/289097213.pdf (accessed on 17th October 2025).
19. Córdoba-Roldán, A., de las Heras García de Vinuesa, A., Luque Sendra, A., Peralta-Álvarez, C., et al. (2017). State of the Industry 4.0 in the Andalusian food sector. https://core.ac.uk/download/185608711.pdf (accessed on 17th October 2025).
20. Creese, S., De Roure, D., Hall, W., Madaan, A., et al. (2018). A storm in an

IoT cup: The emergence of cyber-physical social machines. http://arxiv.org/abs/1809.05904 (accessed on 17th October 2025).

21. Daniel, S. A., & Victor, S. S. (2024). Emerging trends in cybersecurity for critical infrastructure protection: A comprehensive review. *Computer Science & IT Research Journal, 5*, 576–593. https://doi.org/10.51594/csitrj.v5i3.872 (accessed on 17th October 2025).
22. Dwivedi, Y. K., Hughes, L., Baabdullah, A. M., Ribeiro-Navarrete, S., Giannakis, M., Al-Debei, M. M., Dennehy, D., et al. (2022). Metaverse beyond the hype: Multidisciplinary perspectives on emerging challenges, opportunities, and agenda for research, practice and policy. *International Journal of Information Management, 66*, 102542–102542. https://doi.org/10.1016/j.ijinfomgt.2022.102542 (accessed on 17th October 2025).
23. Jaime, F., Muñoz, A., Rodríguez-Gómez, F., & Jeréz-Calero, A. (2023). Strengthening privacy and data security in biomedical microelectromechanical systems by IoT communication security and protection in smart healthcare. *Sensors, 23*, 8944–8944. https://doi.org/10.3390/s23218944 (accessed on 17th October 2025).
24. Joy, Z. H., Islam, S., Rahaman, M. A., & Haque, M. N. (2024). Advanced cybersecurity protocols for securing data management systems in industrial and healthcare environments. *Global Mainstream Journal.* https://www.semanticscholar.org/paper/1364a55e699fb463f21ae2e9280872706fa9e6b3 (accessed on 17th October 2025).
25. Kilovaty, I. (2019). Freedom to hack. https://core.ac.uk/download/223239898.pdf (accessed on 17th October 2025).
26. Li, S., Qi, L., Xu, L. D., Zhao, K., et al. (2020). Computational intelligence-enabled cybersecurity for the Internet of Things. https://core.ac.uk/download/326707061.pdf (accessed on 17th October 2025).
27. Mishra, P., & Singh, G. (2023). Energy management systems in sustainable smart cities based on the Internet of Energy: A technical review. *Energies, 16*, 6903–6903. https://doi.org/10.3390/en16196903 (accessed on 17th October 2025).
28. Mourtzis, D., Angelopoulos, J., & Panopoulos, N. (2022). A literature review of the challenges and opportunities of the transition from Industry 4.0 to Society 5.0. *Energies, 15*, 6276–6276. https://doi.org/10.3390/en15176276 (accessed on 17th October 2025).
29. Mughal, A. A. (2019). Cybersecurity hygiene in the era of Internet of Things (IoT): Best practices and challenges. https://core.ac.uk/download/568392999.pdf (accessed on 17th October 2025).
30. Posadas, D. V. (2017). After the gold rush: The boom of the Internet of

Things, and the busts of data-security and privacy. https://core.ac.uk/download/216957487.pdf (accessed on 17th October 2025).

31. Rane, N. L., Desai, P., & Rane, J. (2024). Acceptance and integration of artificial intelligence and machine learning in the construction industry: Factors, current trends, and challenges. https://doi.org/10.70593/978-81-981367-4-9_4 (accessed on 17th October 2025).

32. Samsidar, M. A. (2025). Transforming telemedicine: Optimizing cloud computing and IoT for security, digital trust, and the influence of E-WOM in modern healthcare services. *International Journal of Science Technology and Health.* https://www.semanticscholar.org/paper/b52e58e5521f5ecc40b862897afd36c043825729 (accessed on 17th October 2025).

33. Sarker, I. H. (2022). AI-based modeling: Techniques, applications and research issues towards automation, intelligent and smart systems. *SN Computer Science, 3.* https://doi.org/10.1007/s42979-022-01043-x (accessed on 17th October 2025).

34. Sun, N., Ding, M., Jiang, J., Xu, W., Mo, X., Tai, Y., & Zhang, J. (2023). Cyber threat intelligence mining for proactive cybersecurity defense: A survey and new perspectives. *IEEE Communications Surveys & Tutorials, 25*, 1748–1774. https://doi.org/10.1109/comst.2023.3273282 (accessed on 17th October 2025).

35. Vanhee, J., & Verleysen, C. (2017). Cyber safety: A theoretical insight. https://core.ac.uk/download/156960827.pdf (accessed on 17th October 2025).

36. Xu, X., Lu, Y., Vogel-Heuser, B., & Wang, L. (2021). Industry 4.0 and Industry 5.0—Inception, conception and perception. *Journal of Manufacturing Systems, 61*, 530–535. https://doi.org/10.1016/j.jmsy.2021.10.006 (accessed on 17th October 2025).

37. Yang, E., Jeong, S., & Seo, C. (2025). Harnessing feature pruning with optimal deep learning based DDoS cyberattack detection on IoT environment. *Scientific Reports, 15.* https://www.semanticscholar.org/paper/3437e7c8821258987bd2a31adb79fe747986422e (accessed on 17th October 2025).

CHAPTER 2

IOT ARCHITECTURE AND ATTACK SURFACES

Contents

INTRODUCTION

The Internet of Things (IoT) world is evolving at a very rapid pace, where a huge number of devices are connected together to form a complex ecosystem. It not only makes augmentation and data collection easier but also results in enormous security and privacy concerns. As the number of devices grows, the IoT system's architecture must be examined to identify the various attack surfaces by which the attackers can exploit. The core framework of IoT consists of hardware, software, and network protocol layers, each having their own vulnerabilities. For example, the surging number of smart devices in domestic, business, and industrial environments has opened a huge arena that, although rich in potential capabilities, is replete with the threat of security incidents and data harvesting. An effective analysis of IoT architecture begins by finding out these attack surfaces in order to minimize the associated risks and enhance overall security controls. An overview of the fragile interdependency between IoT architecture and its attack surfaces merits an inquiry into the security implications inherent in emerging technologies. The integration of emerging technologies such as artificial intelligence, machine learning, and blockchain with the IoT platform can not only improve performance but also increase security vulnerabilities. As devices within the IoT interact in diverse contexts, interoperability and scalability become issues of utmost concern. While these technologies hold immense benefits, they also introduce new levels of complexity that can be targeted by hackers. With the rapid-changing rate of technology, companies are driven to counter the threats posed by rogue attackers seeking to exploit such vulnerabilities. Thus, an urgent critical analysis of security and countermeasures that can be implemented for IoT systems becomes a priority in order to secure confidential data and maintain user trust. Another significant area of addressing IoT architecture and attack surfaces is through ongoing assessment of security policies and procedures. As the IoT environment expands, the organisations must craft their security frameworks to take into account the evolving threat landscape. This is technical in nature but also comprehensive in that it encompasses user education and regulatory compliance. Regular evaluation of the effectiveness of the security measures and adopting best practices are critical to creating an IoT ecosystem that is resilient. Moreover, as the complexity of such systems increases, so does the governing institutions that manage their deployment. It is critical to engage various stakeholders, like technologists, policymakers, and users, in crafting strategies that can effectively counter the threats mounted by cyber-attacks in the IoT space. Resolve to advocating an aggressive security approach is paramount to unlocking the full potential of IoT technologies while lowering levels of associated risk.

Importance of IoT Architecture

The IoT architecture is ultimately vital in giving IoT systems smooth integration and functionality across various industries. With the increasing adoption of IoT technologies by businesses, the need for a robust architecture becomes stronger. The architecture serves as the backbone for data management, communication between devices, and security mechanisms necessary for the effective functioning of IoT ecosystems. An efficiently designed IoT architecture not only facilitates operating efficiencies but also maximizes decision-making, enabling firms to respond in a timely manner to market demands. The model of architecture must therefore be extremely scalable to the rapidly changing technologies and fluctuating data volumes as emphasized in recent research asking for a necessity of firms to invest in adaptable IoT solutions. Hence, it is important that any entity that wishes to leverage the highest potential of IoT technologies effectively comprehend the intricacies of IoT architecture since it is the foundation for future innovation and development (Allioui et al., 2023). In a discussion of specific applications of IoT architecture, a notable example is in precision agriculture.

Figure 2.1. A well-designed IoT architecture not only facilitates operational efficiencies but also enhances decision-making processes, allowing businesses to respond adeptly to market demands.

Source: https://smartdev.com/wp-content/uploads/2023/10/isometric-illustration-smart-home-with-people-using-various-devices-control-scaled.jpg.

The area uses IoT technologies towards enhancing agricultural production in a way that reduces the environmental footprint. With the help of advanced sensors and data analytics, farmers can monitor real-time crop health and develop resource optimization enhancements. This kind of application has to be designed carefully in order to handle high amounts of data and provide secure communication between numerous devices. Precision agriculture IoT architecture not only enhances productivity and efficiency but also sets the stage for environmentally friendly farming practices in response to pressures for nourishing the world's increasing population. As described in literature, IoT architectural advancements impact the profitability of operations of such innovative agriculture practices, depicting the architectures intrinsic role in achieving economic as well as environmental objectives within the agricultural sector (Karunathilake et al., 2023). Moreover, the implications of IoT architecture do not stop at operational sustainability and efficiency; they extend far into the realm of security. A proper grasp of the IoT architecture is critical, particularly where its attack surfaces are involved. The more IoT devices, the higher the number of vulnerabilities that hackers can exploit against them. The architecture must incorporate robust security measures to fend off the increasing threat of cyberattacks. Having security as the priority when developing IoT architecture will assist organizations in avoiding future threats and keeping sensitive data. This proactive approach not only enhances users' confidence but also enables regulatory compliance, which is becoming ever more vital across various industries. Thus, the development of secure IoT architecture is not just an IT matter but a fundamental organizational strategy enabling long-term existence in a perpetually evolving digital era (Allioui et al., 2023) (Figure 2.1).

Overview of Attack Surfaces

In the IoT architecture, an attack surface is defined as all the potential means by which an unauthorized user may attempt to take advantage of a system. They include but are not limited to device interfaces, communication, and software applications that interact with various IoT devices. Understanding attack surfaces is critical in formulating effective security protocols. With the rise of more devices and a progressively complex network, there is an increased chance of exploitation; therefore, hackers find it easy to exploit security vulnerabilities on such surfaces. Networks such as zero touch networks (ZTNs), as good and autonomous as they are, can also end up maximizing the attack surface unintentionally through the utilization of public channels of data transfer, which are typically in short supply of adequate security provisions (Kumar et al., 2022). In framing the IoT architecture, distinguishing between various types of attack surfaces is important, including physical, logical, and network vulnerabilities. Physical attack surfaces imply physical devices that can be stolen or physically manipulated, while logical surfaces imply software vulnerabilities in the form of coding faults or exposed APIs that can be remotely attacked. Network vulnerabilities imply the channels through which data exchange with one another, encompassing wireless as well as hard-wired communication. Each component has a specific function in the overall security posture of an IoT network, necessitating targeted countermeasures to mitigate threats. An in-depth analysis of such surfaces also allows one to comprehend the weakness of existing guard mechanisms, demonstrating the significance of emerging methods, such as deep-learning technology and blockchain, in strengthening protection in ZTNs (Kumar et al., 2022). Secondly, the evolving characteristic of the metaverse also brings in other challenges regarding attack surfaces. As immersive technologies blur physical and virtual boundaries, security issues become more complicated. Virtual users introduce trust, privacy, and data integrity issues, which are critical components of any robust IoT infrastructure. The socio-economic impacts of such growth determine the need for interdisciplinary research in understanding the potential vulnerabilities in such platforms. The research needs to be centered on ethical standards and legal principles that can protect users in such platforms, along with designing adaptive security models to address new issues surrounding the integration of IoT technologies into the metaverse (Figure 2.2).

Figure 2.2. Systems such as zero touch networks (ZTNs), while promising in their automation and efficiency, can inadvertently expand the attack surface due to their reliance on public channels for data transmission, which often lack adequate security measures.

Source: https://www.mothersontechnology.com/wp-content/uploads/2025/05/network-security-seprator-01-1024x483.jpg.

2.1. COMPONENTS OF IOT ARCHITECTURE

The structure of the IoT is a sophisticated framework with several fundamental components, each performing a different role in facilitating smooth interconnection among devices. The grounding layer includes sensing things or devices that gather, process, and transmit data. They vary from simple sensors that monitor environmental factors to sophisticated equipment that conducts sophisticated data analysis. The heterogeneous nature of this device contributes more complexity to data interoperability and security, particularly since they usually operate in different protocols and standards. Hence, the need to comprehend and address the potential attack surface in this layer because insecurely set up devices can serve as gateways for cyber-attacks, not only posing danger to individual devices but also the integrity of IoT networks as a whole (Wang et al., 2022). Enhancing the IoT architecture involves robust connectivity and communication protocols that allow such devices to interact with each other and with the core systems. Devices use wireless communications such as Wi-Fi, Bluetooth, Zigbee, and cellular networks for data reception and transmission. Utilization of these transmission channels raises significant security threats.

Figure 2.3. Wireless protocols such as Wi-Fi, Bluetooth, Zigbee, and cellular networks enable devices to transmit and receive data.

Source: https://hackster.imgix.net/uploads/attachments/980620/0_b-MnkRcJ9k-1MIJ73.jpeg?auto=compress%2Cformat&w=1200.

For instance, unauthorized data eavesdropping will lead to information leakage or signal jamming, which hinders the operation of the connected devices normally. Furthermore, new communication standards like 5G present opportunities together with threats that encompass potential higher attacks due to the increased attack surface. Thus, an effective understanding of the potential vulnerabilities in these protocols is crucial in delivering secure transmissions and system integrity (Ning et al., 2021). The final but most important element of IoT architecture is the data processing and management layer, which gathers and analyzes the data collected from devices. This involves cloud computing and edge computing features that provide scalable resources for processing and handling data. Strategic data management allows improved decision-making processes, empowering organizations to derive actionable insights from raw data. Yet, this layer is exposed by nature to any form of attacks, such as data leaks and unauthorized access to analytics algorithms. As data tend to be handled in virtualized environments, security solutions must encompass both the micro and macro levels of networked infrastructures. Including robust security mechanisms, like data encryption and access management, is essential to protect this layer from vulnerabilities and render the overall IoT design robust (Wang et al., 2022) (Figure 2.3).

2.1.1. Sensors and Actuators

Actuators and sensors in IoT infrastructure provide the link between physical and digital. Sensors are responsible for collecting real-time information from surroundings in the form of temperature, humidity, and motion, which constitute the critical inputs for data processing systems. The inputs enable intelligent decisions in several applications from industrial automation to residential homes. With evolving technologies, the capabilities of sensors have grown, usually including premium features such as connectivity and processing power for enhanced functionality. But with the growing dispersal of sensors comes a host of security threats that render them a favorite target for cyber-attacks. The availability of IoT devices and sensory systems in critical infrastructure poses concern with regard to data integrity as well as the potential for severe disruption in service, hence the necessity for security measures installed to protect them from exploitation. The complementarity of actuators to sensors is another performance improvement for IoT systems as it opens up the possibility of physical actions from sensor data. Actuators are controlled by control systems and perform actions in the world, for instance, opening a valve or moving a machine position.

In Industry 4.0, the integration of sensors and actuators introduces automated processes that significantly increase operational efficiency and responsiveness across industries. However, this integration also expands the attack surface for attackers. As emphasized, IoT and WSN make possible the operation of systems that are increasingly vulnerable to hacking and other cyber threats. It is therefore crucial to understand and take into account the actuator security implications as companies become increasingly reliant on and automated using these systems so that performance enhancements are not achieved at the cost of security and privacy. In a consideration of the broader context of IoT architecture and attack surfaces, it is apparent that sensor and actuator deployment and design must take account of the evolving threat landscape. The fourth industrial revolution (IR 4.0) and automation on which it is centered is highly dependent upon the security and dependability of sensor-actuator networks. Recent studies must focus on identifying likely loopholes in the security of such frameworks because any loss of sensors or actuators can lead to lethal outcomes. On top of that, with the advancement in IoT and WSN technology, the potential for more sophisticated attacks is higher. Novel approaches to enhancing security protocols that can change as per these advancements must be investigated. Addressing these kinds of challenges not only makes use of the resilience of IoT systems but also the trust of the users in embracing the transformative energy of these technologies, finally guaranteeing a smoother shift to a complete interconnected digital world (Figure 2.4).

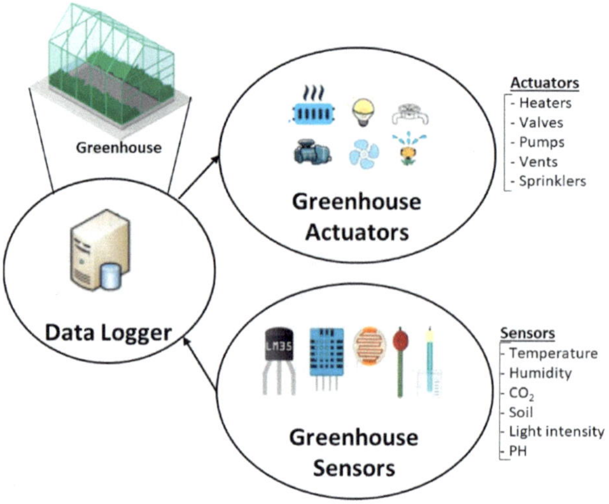

Figure 2.4. Sensors are responsible for collecting real-time data from their surroundings, including temperature, humidity, and motion, which provide crucial inputs for data processing systems.

Source: https://www.mdpi.com/sensors/sensors-24-02647/article_deploy/html/images/sensors-24-02647-g001.png.

2.1.2. Communication Protocols

In IoT architecture, communication protocols are the bricks that confer the degree of interoperability among a range of devices and systems. The protocols are essential to data exchange to enable devices to talk to one another and to cloud services. The device heterogeneity in IoT, ranging from consumer-grade sensors to industrial devices, requires a robust and adaptable communication infrastructure. For example, MQTT and CoAP protocols are the ones that seek to reduce the utilization of low-bandwidth, high-latency networks typical of IoT examples and consequently enhance the efficiency of transmitting data. However, the rising complexities of the communications networks create many attack surfaces available, and hence the security ramifications of these protocols and configurations need to be evaluated. Security flaws increase as

IoT devices further become reliant on both local and cloud-based channels of communication. Such a reliance brings into sharp perspective questions of abuse of such channels, especially where local connectivity would often get ignored in security assessments. According to recommendations established by ENISA and NIST, secure local connections become vital so that the operational reliability of IoT systems is assured, particularly when cloud access is irregular or is disconnected. Failure to provide end-to-end local communication can lead to severe attacks such as replay attacks that make devices prone to unauthorized control and access. This state emphasizes the need for mechanisms capable of identifying and remedying such vulnerabilities in order to offer end-to-end security to all communication surfaces and hence adhering to best practices in IoT reliability and security infrastructure (Lazzaro et al., 2024). New security architectures will need to be designed to counter the multifaceted attack surfaces that come with IoT communication protocols. Research has already shown that existing protection networks tend to lack in securing heterogenous environments, exposing them to intelligent cyber-attacks. By adopting a three-tier security framework, as recommended in recent research, organizations can utilize technologies such as blockchain authentication and adaptive encryption to build a stronger IoT ecosystem. The performance metrics reveal significant improvements in safeguarding against unauthorized access and threat detection. Such advancement highlights the necessity for dynamic solutions addressing not only existing weaknesses but also future-proof emerging threats. Bridging such gaps will become imperative in advancing the cybersecurity condition of IoT structure, ultimately resulting in enhanced and reliable communication protocols more suited to evolving demands from networked devices (Kumar et al., 2024) (Figure 2.5).

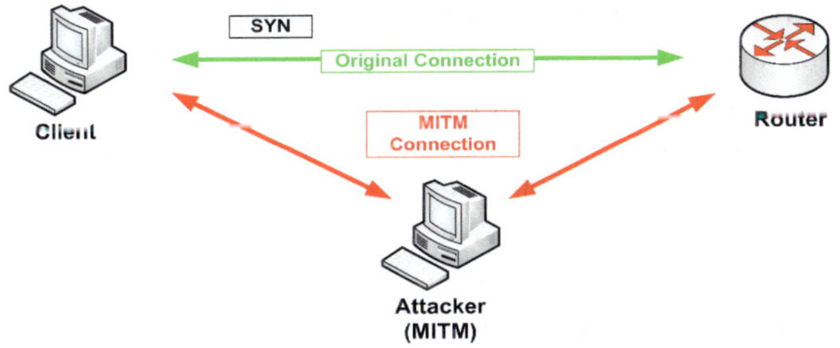

Figure 2.5. Failure to secure local communication can lead to significant threats such as replay attacks, rendering devices susceptible to unauthorized access and manipulation.

Source: https://www.howtonetwork.com/wp-content/uploads/2022/02/1-10-2.png.

2.1.3. Data Processing Units

Integration of Data Processing Units (DPUs) into IoT infrastructure is gaining prominence due to the sophisticated character of cyber-physical systems. DPUs enhance the processing capability of IoT devices to handle vast volumes of data generated by interacting sensors, enabling the devices to process information more insightfully and efficiently. With increasingly increasing IoT networks spreading across, the volume and complexity of data require advanced-level processing capabilities to enable decision-making within time. The incorporation of DPU technology within the IoT framework allows data processing to become decentralized, thereby reducing latency as well as the response time of the network as a whole. In addition to enhancing performance, this decentralized approach also offers security against possible cyber threats because data can be processed closer to its source, thereby limiting data transmission over potentially insecure lines. However, the advent of DPUs births new attack surfaces in IoT systems. As explained in the literature, the inter-connectedness of devices in IoT systems inherently exposes them to a broad spectrum of cyber-attacks. Empirical evidence indicates that the integration of advanced processing units must be accompanied by a firm security framework designed to safeguard the integrity and confidentiality of the data. Most importantly, through DPUs, predictive analytics for threat detection is enhanced, yet it can be compromised if proper safeguards do not exist. This ambivalence emphasizes the importance of an anticipation-based security approach, which is complemented by enormous innovation in processing and storage to fortify IoT platforms. As attack vectors become more complex, the concurrent development of DPUs-specific security protocols is also crucial to ensure robust defenses against emerging threats encompassed by the academic literature. In addition, the relationship between DPUs and IoT security is underscored by the need for a deep learning approach to identify and seal possible security loopholes. The most recent study encourages the use of intelligence in IoT systems that leverages DPUs to scan data patterns dynamically. With continuous monitoring of network behavior, the method aims to identify anomalies and predict future attacks early. As explained by the research, leveraging deep learning models allows systems to label network traffic as benign or malicious accurately. Such predictive capabilities not only maximize response to incidents but also establish an environment in which IoT devices can perform with less risk, exhibiting robustness under the bombardment of an increasingly adversary cyber space. The simultaneous focus on enhancing processing capability while enhancing security measures is the secret to determining the future of IoT architecture, minimizing risks created by its very character of complexities and sustaining growth (Figure 2.6).

Figure 2.6. As IoT networks proliferate, the volume and complexity of the data necessitate advanced processing capabilities to ensure timely decision-making.

Source: https://iotbusinessnews.com/WordPress/wp-content/uploads/2025/04/data-analytics.jpg.

2.2. LAYERS OF IOT ARCHITECTURE

The IoT architecture is a multi-layered framework that provides seamless interaction between devices, networks, and users. Essentially, the architecture is generally divided into four broad layers: perception, network, edge, and application. Physical devices and sensors are the perception layer, which captures live environmental data. This bottom-layer is most critical to provide when it comes to determining the quality and accuracy of input data into the system. In the absence of strict sensing mechanisms, decision-making data subsequently utilized at higher layers is compromised and hence has an impact on overall system performance. As IoT continues to evolve, security and efficiency concerns regarding this bottom-layer need to take precedence to avoid vulnerabilities that could be exploited by malicious actors. Proceeding to the network layer, it is the gateway to facilitate the communication between the IoT devices in the context of the architecture. It accommodates various communication protocols such as Wi-Fi, Bluetooth, Zigbee, and cellular networks. As the IoT devices spread and there is a chance of huge data being circulated, this layer's security is of the most prominent importance. Network-layer vulnerabilities may have enormous attack surfaces that facilitate unauthorized access to sensitive information. As seen in the recent metaverse debates, with new technologies enmeshed in conventional IoT uses, encryption and secure transmission protocols have to be given great attention (Wang et al., 2022). Besides protecting user information, these processes help promote confidence in IoT systems in the face of growing public concern over privacy and security matters. Finally, the application layer is where end-user interaction occurs predominantly, with emphasis on data analysis and decision-making. This layer integrates information processed up to this point, enabling users to gain actionable insights through dashboards and user interfaces. The potential for cyber-attacks still exists here. Applications can unintentionally expose vulnerabilities that might be exploited, leading to data breaches or service downtime, reflecting the intrinsic problematics of the broader digital environment, including the metaverse (Dwivedi et al., 2022). As IoT architecture changes in response to shifting society needs and technology advancements, an integrated understanding of each layer is crucial. It not only assists in fortifying attack surfaces but also provides insight into minimizing risks that accompany increasingly interconnected systems (Figure 2.7).

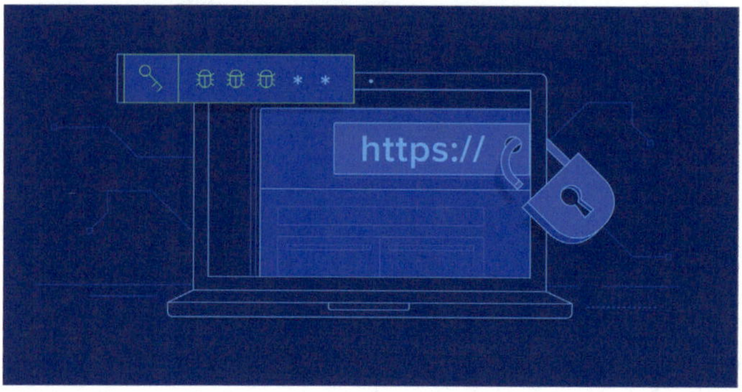

Figure 2.7. Vulnerabilities at the network layer can present significant attack surfaces, allowing unauthorized access to sensitive information.

Source: https://bs-uploads.toptal.io/blackfish-uploads/components/open_graph_image/8960623/og_image/optimized/cover-Redesign-WebSecurityVulnerabilities-Luke_Newsletter-91ee4d294318c967b26187f4d67a8351.png.

2.2.1. Perception Layer

The Perception Layer is one of the basic components of the IoT structure, which is also the first layer of interaction between the physical and digital world information systems. The Perception Layer is primarily responsible for acquiring data through sensors and actuators that monitor environmental parameters such as temperature, humidity, and movement. It is crucial to understand the role of the Perception Layer, for it not only gathers raw data but also influences the timeliness and accuracy of the same, with implications that can directly pertain to decision-making mechanisms in numerous applications. As the volume of data being generated continues to grow exponentially, the necessity for proper and effective data handling processes at the Perception Layer is more apparent. Organizations must account for where these sensors are being deployed, managed, and safeguarded in order to constrain vulnerabilities and ensure that the architecture is resilient against potential attack surfaces due to poor data protection controls. Perception Layer within IoT is not merely about data collection but also about optimizing operational efficiency and overall productivity. By adopting the use of technology, businesses can use the data collected to make better decisions, optimize processes, and improve service delivery. Rapid innovation of IoT technologies, including the development of smart devices, increases the demand for an in-depth understanding of how the Perception Layer communicates with the other layers of the IoT architecture. For instance, with the evolution of communication technologies such as 5G, companies can expect faster data transmission, resulting in instant decision-making. However, this also introduces new problems that might cause the attack surfaces to be bigger since the increasing connectivity might reveal vulnerabilities that an attacker would exploit.

Figure 2.8. Malfunctions or manipulations of sensors can lead to incorrect conclusions and hinder effective operational responses.

Source: https://carnegieendowment.org/static/media/images/data-us-technology-china-iStock-1530973530.jpg.

Hence, the creation of a secure Perception Layer is crucial to maintaining information integrity and winning over user and stakeholder confidence across industries. Moreover, dependence on the Perception Layer for accurate data capture has far-reaching ramifications on system security and reliability. With organizations planning to roll out sophisticated IoT systems, it is imperative for them to consider the threats arising from compromised sensor data. Sensor failure or tampering with sensors can lead to drawing incorrect conclusions and inverting sound operational responses. The strength of the Perception Layer then comes into play; it needs to possess fail-safes and redundancy capabilities as a defense mechanism. Organizations are recommended to put in place holistic security frameworks that incorporate the Perception Layer, not just as an interface but as an essential element that needs to be under tight control and inspected.

While our dependency on IoT systems grows, the ongoing development of the Perception Layer—along with stringent security analysis—will become the key to protection against new threats in an environment characterized by accelerating technological progress and increased vulnerabilities in IoT structures (Allioui et al., 2023; Cheng-Wang et al., 2023) (Figure 2.8).

2.2.2. Network Layer

In IoT architecture, the network layer is a critical component that facilitates inter-device and internet-scale communication. The layer has the responsibility of routing, addressing, and forwarding data packets such that information can be conveyed seamlessly across different inter-connected networks. This layer-based design must accommodate the diversity of devices found within an IoT setup, from simple sensors to complex actuators, each with unique communication needs. As the number continues to grow, the network layer is faced with scalability as well as heterogeneous connectivity options, which are important to provide maximum performance in a heterogeneous ecosystem of device types and various network protocols. Effective control of all these aspects is crucial in order to ensure the integrity and credibility of data transmission across the IoT environment, highlighting the significance of the network layer in providing credible IoT solutions. Network-layer security is vital, particularly in light of the insecurities inherent in IoT devices and infrastructure. IoT networks are susceptible to many attack surfaces, such as data interception, replay attack, and denial of service, thus leading to serious disruption of services or unauthorized access to sensitive data. The fact that they use devices with low processing capability makes it difficult to apply advanced security protocols, thus exposing them to attacks that can exploit basic vulnerabilities, such as weak encryption techniques or factory-set passwords. As specified in Arshi et al. (2023), protecting information and devices at the network layer is crucial to counter possible threats of such security vulnerabilities. Hence, it is necessary to incorporate secure communication protocols and rigorous authentication mechanisms at this layer to preserve data integrity as well as confidentiality in the context of growing security concerns in the IoT environment. Furthermore, the real-time interconnectedness of IoT devices adds additional challenges in the network layer because they need to interact with each other at the same time while continuously adapting to network condition changes. Emergent challenges, for example, scalability and interoperability, become more evident as the environment expands, impacting the efficiency of data routing and resource management. The significance of innovative solutions for addressing these issues is underscored by the dynamic nature of IoT applications in various sectors, as articulated in Wang et al. (2022). As there is an ever-growing set of devices and services that rely on effective network-layer exchange, researchers and practitioners must concentrate on developing responsive frameworks with the ability to service the complexity of this interdependent ecosystem. Having a complete approach with security solutions that incorporate network layer security along with technological innovations will be crucial in the development of a secure and resilient IoT ecosystem to counteract evolving threats (Figure 2.9).

Figure 2.9. Effective management of these factors is essential for preserving the integrity and reliability of data transmission across the IoT landscape, highlighting the critical role of the network layer in achieving robust IoT solutions.

Source: https://www.telit.com/wp-content/uploads/2023/01/iot-security.jpg.

2.2.3. Application Layer

The application layer is a very important part of the IoT framework as it is an interface that enables users and devices to exchange information with one another. It consists of various protocols and standards that govern how applications interact with one another, hence influencing the efficiency and security of the interactions. Applications written on this layer could range from simple device control systems to very complex data analysis systems, making it possible for users to control multiple IoT devices with great ease. This adds to the significance of layering is also amplified by the tremendous volumes of data generated from IoT devices, with efficient data management processes having to be put in place so that information is both accessible and actionable. In the absence of robust application-layer protocols, the intrinsic potential of IoT devices will not be achieved to their maximum capability, which serves to underscore the imperative for continued development and enhancement of these underlying frameworks, particularly that of IoT security vulnerabilities (Arshi et al., 2023). Application-layer security is a problem of particular concern, particularly with IoT devices pervading industries such as medicine and smart cities. With such networks getting increasingly complex, it often leads to an increased attack surface, and therefore they are desirable targets for cybercrime. Application-layer weaknesses may be a result of old software, insecure encryption methodologies, and poor authentication practices. For instance, many IoT devices are shipped with default passwords that would easily be exploited. These security vulnerabilities can lead to intrusion into sensitive data, which has a severe implication on user privacy and faith. As has been indicated in recent discussions about the security of IoT, remediation of these vulnerabilities is critical to the protection of connected devices and getting them to operate in safe environments (A-Amefon et al., 2023). Furthermore, a clear understanding of the function of the application layer is critical in implementing solid governance and protection mechanisms most apt for IoT deployments. As IoTHDs expand and are put to use in critical sectors like healthcare, there must be more focus on the protocols that govern their interactions and data exchange. The architecture must be forward-thinking, with security by design implications that predict forthcoming exploits and eliminate their risks efficiently. Anticipatory design is the way to maintain consumer confidence and operational integrity in IoT systems. As the environment continues to evolve, stakeholders must remain vigilant in their observations and responses to potential threats that target vulnerabilities in the application layer (Arshi et al., 2023).

2.3. IOT DEVICE SECURITY

The growing use of IoT devices in everyday life comes with numerous benefits but also more security risks. As IoT technology pervades across the board to many sectors such as healthcare, agriculture, and transportation, the interconnectedness of the devices creates vast attack surfaces that are open to attackers. Devices typically employ basic processors and ancient operating systems and are hence susceptible to attacks based on security vulnerabilities inherent in their design. For instance, the overwhelming majority of IoT devices contain weaknesses in physical security, encryption practices, and authentication policies. These vulnerabilities threaten not just the short-term operability of the devices but the security of networks that they connect to, underscoring the necessity for efficient security controls and comprehensive threat assessment within today's IoT ecosystem (Arshi et al., 2023). The consequences of the absence of effective security controls in IoT devices can be particularly disastrous in the healthcare industry, such that the inclusion of IoTHDs can generate severe risks to patient data and system integrity altogether. With healthcare organizations adopting these technologies to enhance patient observation as well as care delivery, potential vulnerabilities can reveal sensitive health data, resulting in diminished trust in health systems. The architecture of IoTHDs is often vulnerable to multiple vectors of attack, ranging from unauthorized access to information to interference with critical care processes. Addressing these threats requires a multi-faceted approach that not only evaluates technology in isolation but considers social processes that underpin their deployment. Understanding this holistic context is critical to developing more effective strategies for addressing security threats around IoTHDs (A-Amefon et al., 2023). On top of that, enhancing IoT device security demands an active strategy of finding and blocking vulnerabilities prior to their potential use in attacking the system. Along with the shift in the technological landscape, technologies such as advanced encryption protocols, secure authentication mechanisms, and adaptive controls will take center stage in fortifying IoT systems against potential intrusion. Firms must invest not only in technology but also in security governance frameworks that will ensure compliance with best practice and regulation. By means of security awareness and stakeholder engagement cultures, the sector is in a position to address effectively the complexities of protecting IoT devices. This collaborative effort will be essential not only for safeguarding critical information and systems but also for the maintenance of public trust in the growing interdependence of services provided by IoT technology (Arshi et al., 2023) (Figure 2.10).

Figure 2.10. Devices often operate with basic processors and outdated operating systems, making them susceptible to attacks that leverage security vulnerabilities inherent within their design.

Source: https://assets.gcore.pro/site-media/uploads/how_ai_enhances_waf_waap_fi_7f61ffc2e6.png.

2.3.1. Authentication Mechanisms

In the case of IoT architecture, the role played by authentication mechanisms is pivotal in defending device interaction. As an ever-increasing number of devices become connected at a very fast rate, the problems in making sure that such devices are communicating safely are compounded many times over. Authentication mechanisms are the first line of defense against unwanted intrusion and potential attack, playing the role of a gatekeeper to sensitive data and critical operational capabilities. Effective authentication practices should not only authenticate devices, but they must also provide the proper users access to necessary services without compromising security. Implementing robust practices such as multifactor authentication, public key infrastructure, or blockchain implementations, IoT networks can minimize exposure of multiple attack surfaces that undermine the security of the network and the devices within it. Furthermore, the large range of devices found in an IoT world demands custom authentication techniques catering to specific vulnerabilities inherent in different classes of devices. Lightweight protocols are often used on resource-constrained devices, sacrificing security for efficiency. Greater attention to interoperability is required, since IoT devices of diverse vendors must communicate seamlessly while imposing strict security measures.

Figure 2.11. Effective authentication methods must not only verify the identity of devices but also ensure that legitimate users can access necessary services without compromising security.

Source: https://www.loginradius.com/assets/blog/identity/device-authentication-methods/device-authentication-methods.webp.

This interoperability often adds additional attack surfaces, particularly when combined with legacy devices and modern devices. In order to effectively tackle these issues, knowledge of the built-in issues raised by varying capabilities of devices and connectivity types is needed in order to deploy appropriate authentication that not only enhances existing frameworks but also expands to accommodate the shifting tide of the IoT. By incorporating advanced authentication mechanisms, IoT structures can significantly be fortified against potential attacks. As advancements in new technologies bring the physical and virtual worlds closer, their implications on authentication in the metaverse and other such domains gain importance. The metaverse is centered on achieving smooth interactions within virtual domains, and it will definitely require advanced models of authentication to protect user identity and data. Poor implementation of rigid authentication can create mass privacy intrusions that undermine user trust and the general sustainability of the technology. Therefore, addressing the intrinsic security challenges in IoT frameworks and learning from the hard-won experience of industries embracing the metaverse can inform the development of resilient authentication models that not only safeguard current infrastructures but future-proof against expected attacks (Dwivedi et al., 2022; Wang et al., 2022) (Figure 2.11).

2.3.2. Data Encryption Techniques

In the backdrop of the IoT, encrypting data with robust encryption techniques is vital in protecting sensitive information from potential cyber-attacks. Encryption as a first defense line is employed by encrypting plaintext into coded form and rendering it unintelligible to unauthorized entities. Among widely known techniques, symmetric and asymmetric encryption stand out. Symmetric encryption employs a single key to encrypt and decrypt, though efficient, and this creates secure distribution of keys issues. Asymmetric encryption employs the use of a pair of keys—public and private—to secure communication by avoiding the dangers of exchanging keys. Determination of the method of encryption depends on the application scenario in IoT systems, where both performance and security are critical factors to consider. With the evolving IoT ecosystem, so too does potential attack surface complexity within. Emerging technologies such as machine learning and the Internet of Space Things (IoST) make increasingly necessary advanced encryption techniques that can withstand sophisticated cyberattacks. Cyber attackers are constantly searching for new vulnerabilities to exploit, a factor magnified by increasing levels of attack vectors as quoted in Atmaca et al. (2020). All these developments require an proactive security policy, where encryption is a forethought, rather than an afterthought, and is made part of the IoT architecture. Constantly reviewing and modifying encryption protocols in preparation for future threats significantly reduces susceptibility to attack and maximizes the overall resilience of the IoT system. Also, the integration of advanced encryption technologies into IoT platforms must consider the natural limitations of mobile networks, particularly those transitioning towards 5G. Some security vulnerabilities have been identified in existing mobile network generations capable of violating user information and network integrity, as outlined in Dabrowski et al. (2018). By understanding the origin of these vulnerabilities, researchers and developers can design improved encryption solutions for future IoT applications. Further, fixing problems connected with unsecured pre-authentication traffic and downgraded data transmissions is important to achieving strong security measures. Through a widespread approach that incorporates encryption as a central feature, IoT systems can be protected from all types of cyber-attacks and thus ensure secure and reliable operation in the networked world of today (Figure 2.12).

Figure 2.12. Encryption serves as a primary line of defense by converting plaintext into a coded format, making it incomprehensible to unauthorized users.

Source: https://learn.g2.com/hubfs/G2CM_FI025_Learn_Article_Images-%5BEncryption%5D_V1a.png.

2.3.3. Firmware Updates and Patching

In the context of IoT architecture, successful firmware patching and updates are imperative to securing devices as well as their functioning. With IoT devices becoming an integral aspect of daily life, ongoing software development remains imperative. The need brings with it vulnerabilities that can be exploited by attackers, leading to substantial financial as well as reputational loss for users and manufacturers alike. According to Mishra et al. (2021), the exponential increase in IoT devices presents various challenges, predominantly concerned with security management, which normally come in a secondary position due to issues like size and cost. It is thus crucial to have robust firmware update measures to mitigate such attacks and uphold user confidence in IoT technologies. Firmware updates for IoT devices are usually done using over-the-air (OTA) mechanisms, which come with advantages and disadvantages. Although OTA updates ensure that patch delivery is seamless, they add risk to devices in the guise of centralized update system risk. In such a system, the manufacturers server is a point of failure, potentially hindering the application of critical patches. As observed in Witanto et al. (2020), the conventional centralized architecture is susceptible to latency, which delays essential updates, thereby leaving devices open to ongoing attacks.

This means that a shift towards decentralized methods of firmware updates, such as peer-to-peer protocols, would enhance the reliability and robustness of patching activities, ultimately making IoT architecture more resistant to upcoming cyber-attacks. Recent advances in firmware update protocols, particularly with blockchain technology, offer solution opportunities to the issues of security and integrity for IoT patch management. Utilizing a blockchain-based system, makers can ensure open and tamper-evident recording of firmware updates, which minimize security breach issues during the updating procedure. An execution of protocols that combine both direct and peer-to-peer update methods—proposed in recent studies—enables devices to update more efficiently while sharing the workload among a network of connected devices. This dual approach, as researched in Witanto et al. (2020), not only improves firmware deployment speed but also minimizes risks from central architecture, thereby establishing a safer IoT environment that can withstand the complexities of the modern cyber world (Figure 2.13).

Figure 2.13. As Internet of Things (IoT) devices become increasingly integrated into everyday life, the necessity for ongoing software development remains imperative.

Source: https://www.salvosoftware.com/wp-content/uploads/2022/10/ultimate-guide-to-iot-Salvo-software-scaled.jpg.

2.4. COMMON ATTACK VECTORS IN IOT

The IoT has revolutionized businesses by enabling devices to talk to other devices in real-time and perform automated functions. Widespread adoption of IoT technologies, however, comes with an enormous amount of security vulnerabilities that are vulnerable to be exploited by attackers. The most prevalent attack mode is unauthorized access, facilitated through weak authentication mechanisms. They have either default passwords or no robust encryption protocols that enable an attacker to easily gain access to sensitive data or control operations remotely. Because the majority of IoT devices are part of larger networks on a routine basis, compromising one IoT device can serve as an entry point to subsequent attacks, raising the threat level within networked systems. Therefore, tackling unauthorized access through enhanced authentication mechanisms and encryption algorithms is essential in strengthening IoT architecture against possible threats. Another vital attack area arises from the intrinsic difficulties related to device management and firmware updates. IoT devices tend to run with out-of-date software, which could have unpatched vulnerabilities that can be exploited by attackers.

Most users ignore routine firmware updates either because they are not aware or because they feel it will be inconvenient, hence the devices remain vulnerable to attacks. Also, the heterogeneity of IoT devices makes standardization of update processes difficult, causing differences in security postures among different models and manufacturers. As highlighted in recent studies, the integration of Federated Learning (FL) towards real-time monitoring can serve as an answer by enabling improved attack detection without compromising user privacy. With the implementation of such adaptive security measures, IoT networks can also resist firmware vulnerability threats, achieving a higher degree of security for users. Lastly, distributed denial-of-service (DDoS) attacks are a significant threat to IoT ecosystems. Attackers can conduct DDoS attacks by using compromised IoT devices, causing extensive service disruption through traffic overload of targeted systems. This method has become popular due to the sheer number of devices within the IoT network that can be used as available resources for attackers to utilize. The clustering of important services in smart cities, transport, and healthcare makes them ideal targets for such an attack, which can prove disastrous. It is necessary to counter such attacks by adopting advanced security technologies like anomaly detection systems that monitor traffic flow. Besides, FL can enhance the security infrastructure by facilitating collaborative training on devices without leaking sensitive information, as emphasized in literature on the dynamic nature of IoT security threats (Nguyen et al., 2021) (Figure 2.14).

Figure 2.14. Attackers can orchestrate DDoS attacks by leveraging compromised IoT devices, causing widespread disruption to services by overwhelming targeted systems with traffic.

Source: https://www.corero.com/wp-content/uploads/2024/11/2024_11_BA_The-Most-Famous-DDoS-Attacks_Preview_Graphic.png.

2.4.1. Physical Attacks

Physical attacks are a dire risk to the integrity and security of IoT systems since they involve attacking the physical device and infrastructure components directly. Unlike remote cyber-attacks that may exploit software vulnerabilities, physical attacks involve hardware manipulation or destruction, typically leading to a complete system compromise. Physical attacks like device tampering to alter their purposes and intercepting communications to appropriate sensitive data are prevalent. With the growth of IoT devices in various domains, including health and smart transport, physical access to the devices becomes a greater risk factor, particularly in insecure locations. This calls for the implementation of robust physical security controls because failure to address these vulnerabilities translates to disastrous breaches that compromise user privacy and system integrity in general. IoT system design presents heterogeneous attack surfaces by design, exposing them to several physical attack frameworks. Factors like massive deployment of low-cost and less-secured devices raise the likelihood of successful physical compromises. The majority of IoT devices are designed with little physical security, typically without adequate enclosures or tamper-proof design. This raises a contradiction where the very same benefit of connectivity and data exchange can, in practice, make the systems more vulnerable to such attacks. Moreover, as shown by recent studies, threats due to incorrect installation or antiquated physical defenses can bring about catastrophic ramifications, further complicating the predicament of organizations driven by IoT solutions.

The implications of these security breaches underscore the necessity of full threat assessment protocols that are tailored to the unique characteristics of IoT infrastructures, as posited by Arshi et al. (2023). To address the threat of physical attacks on IoT systems, stakeholders must adopt proactive measures that incorporate physical security upgrades and rigorous operational practices. This means applying safeguarding solutions like secure enclosures, unified access controls, and regular security audits to identify probable vulnerabilities. Furthermore, the implementation of front-runner technologies, e.g., Artificial Intelligence and machine learning algorithms, holds the potential to enhance the ability to notice and respond to physical threats in real-time, as per Yavuz et al. (2022). Technological measures alone will not be sufficient; organizations need to cultivate security awareness culture among staff and stakeholders such that everyone is vigilant against physical vulnerabilities. By adopting a holistic strategy that includes physical and cybersecurity defenses, organizations can create a resilient IoT ecosystem that can resist the diverse challenges presented by the physical attack surfaces (Figure 2.15).

Figure 2.15. To mitigate the risks associated with physical attacks on IoT systems, stakeholders must adopt proactive strategies that encompass physical security enhancements and robust operational practices.

Source: https://www.ituonline.com/wp-content/uploads/2024/01/IoT_devices_and_security.jpg.

2.4.2. Network Attacks

The IoT revolution has changed various industries by ushering in a level of connectivity never seen before. This revolution has, however, brought with it extra vulnerability to network attacks that exploit the intricate interdependence between different IoT devices and corresponding architectures. One such prominent category of these attacks is launched over Wireless Local Area Networks (WLANs), which are primary means of communication among devices. The IoT architecture provides opportunities for attackers to take advantage of WLAN protocols and configurations vulnerabilities, particularly those in Radio Access Control interfaces. Literature indicates that Advanced Persistent Threats (APTs) have been targeting these interfaces persistently in order to hack WLANs, making the whole network vulnerable to critical security threats like unauthorized entry and information breaches (Alamleh et al., 2025). With the increasing connectivity, these exposures need to be mitigated for IoT ecosystem security. Apart from WLAN exposures, the heterogeneity and diversity of IoT devices further complicate network security. The majority of the devices are based on limited resources, so they typically possess weak authentication protocols and inadequate security controls. For instance, the absence of device-specific defenses may expose systems to brute force attacks as well as exploitation of legacy firmware. Additionally, with the evolving nature of attacks, the attackers are employing more advanced methods, such as botnets or side-channel attacks, to penetrate IoT networks. The literature indicates that a robust knowledge base of such attack vectors is a prerequisite for the formulation of effective countermeasures against network attacks (Madu, 2025). This includes advancing information on developing adaptive security models that are incorporated within various forms of IoT architectures, allowing for real-time monitoring and anomaly detection capabilities to avoid unauthorized intrusions. To effectively counter the network attack landscape, there must be a multi-pronged approach to IoT security enhancement. Incorporating robust security layers within IoT architectures can mitigate the attack surface by a significant amount. Advanced strategies incorporating the use of light encryption, elastic security, and robust authentication are essential in countering current attack vectors. Also, experts point out incorporating AI-based systems that can dynamically analyze traffic patterns and detect anomalies in order for instantaneous responses to be triggered to upcoming attacks. These systems not only protect individual devices but also enhance network resilience overall (Alamleh et al., 2025). By adopting an integrated approach to network vulnerabilities and using holistic security approaches, stakeholders can create a more secure IoT platform, resilient enough against the smart attacks prevalent in the current online space (Madu, 2025).

2.4.3. Application Layer Attacks

The complexity of IoT architectures renders them all the more vulnerable to application layer attacks. These attacks exploit weaknesses in the protocols and APIs by which IoT devices talk to applications. Unlike the typical network attacks that primarily target infrastructure, application layer attacks are specifically aimed at controlling the software running on devices, exploiting whatever weaknesses exist. As IoT devices are integrated into the systems with different levels of security, this diversity becomes a critical attack surface for cyber attackers. Thus, robust defenses must be constructed in an effort to learn these vulnerabilities, for example, data breaches, denial-of-service, and unauthorized access. With the increasing reliance on such networked systems across various industries, the need to enhance application layer security within IoT applications is greater than ever before to avert crippling effects that will be experienced in case of successful attacks. Some classes of application layer attacks also validate the intricacies and complexities of IoT security. For instance, command injection, a widespread attack, occurs when malicious input is sent to a susceptible application by attackers, thereby allowing them to execute arbitrary commands.

This type of threat can potentially severely compromise the functionality of IoT devices, such as smart home devices or in critical infrastructure. Consequently, buffer overflow attacks exploit the software vulnerabilities via data overloading in a buffer, causing system crashes or backdoors to be installed for future exploitation. These vulnerabilities can also be exploited by the attackers to gain access to unauthorized areas, resulting in privacy invasions or modification of sensitive information. As highlighted by recent research, it is crucial to understand the layers of IoT architecture when developing potent countermeasures to such attacks, which can lead to insecure systems that are potentially devastating in their effects to users and organizations (Hanine et al., 2024; Zahra et al., 2024). Mitigating application layer attacks requires a multi-layered approach that incorporates integration of robust security frameworks with best practices. IoT developers must implement stringent encryption methodologies, secure development practices, and regular software updates to make devices resilient to attacks. Moreover, the implementation of lightweight security solutions is required to ensure that defense does not impact the performance or operation of limited-resources IoT devices. Lastly, the application of advanced detection models, such as machine learning models, can enhance the rate of detecting anomalies typical of an application layer attack. By merging real-time monitoring functions and connectivity among stakeholders such as users, manufacturers, and developers, the IoT sector can build a comprehensive security system. Lastly, since IoT devices are continuously growing in size, application-layer security has to be prioritized not only for the integrity and dependability of these technologies but also for the safety of our connected digital environment (Hanine et al., 2024; Zahra et al., 2024) (Figure 2.16).

Figure 2.16. As IoT systems integrate devices with differing levels of security, this inconsistency becomes a critical attack surface for cyber adversaries.

Source: https://cdn-dynmedia-1.microsoft.com/is/image/microsoftcorp/MSFT_Security_01-Growing-IoT-and-the-risk-to-OT_375x23 4@2x?resMode=sharp2&op_usm=1.5,0.65,15,0&wid=752&hei=580&qlt=100&fmt=png-alpha&fit=constrain.

2.5. CASE STUDIES OF IOT ATTACKS

The proliferation of IoT devices has significantly expanded attack surfaces and exposed them to various cyber threats. Case studies attest to the critical role of vulnerabilities. For instance, the majority of IoT components, particularly wireless sensor networks, are significantly vulnerable to energy-drain attacks such as denial of sleep attacks. These attacks target devices relying on limited battery resources, jeopardizing their performance and lifespan. A fascinating study examined how security processes like authentication inadvertently increase energy consumption in such sensors, even as it highlights the need for enforcing strict protection protocols. Thus, while heightened security processes might burden device capabilities, threat generation by the exclusion of such processes is detrimental to operational efficiency and IoT device longevity (Udoh et al., 2019). Coupled with the security dilemma are the speed and enthusiasm of manufacturers to enter the IoT market. As the intelligent devices market expanded, the majority of the manufacturers ran in ahead of themselves in launching products with minimal security. As a number of case studies have shown, this has resulted in thousands of unpatched devices that remain vulnerable, in most instances being unable to be upgraded after they were made. These cases illustrate the grave scenario where security considerations are not implemented during the design stage, resulting in networks being full of exploitable vulnerabilities. The implications of such overlook can be dire, with affected devices remotely being controlled and used for ill ends. For example, recent work illustrates how the use of sophisticated filtering methods, including Berkeley Packet Filters, can safeguard such devices from ubiquitous threats with reduced effects on network performance (Cruz et al., 2019). Growing interconnectivity among IoT devices has given rise to advanced attack surfaces that attackers can utilize in different forms. A strong example is one where massive-scale Distributed Denial of Service (DDoS) attacks were launched utilizing compromised IoT devices such as cameras and appliances that were not well protected. The attacks, which collapsed large-scale online services, are a clear demonstration of the vast potential for harm when IoT infrastructure is breached. In addition, the two-way interaction between unsecured devices and the large-scale scalability of IoT solutions provides an overwhelming challenge to cybersecurity professionals. The incidents of such attacks not only underscore the need for strong security measures but also require in-depth analysis of potential attack surfaces in IoT architecture. Accordingly, enhancing security aspects and ensuring constant surveillance of IoT networks is imperative for discouraging such newly evolved threats.

2.5.1. Mirai Botnet Incident

The Mirai Botnet Attack is a stark reminder of the security risk inherent in the IoT architecture. The built-in network interconnectivity of IoT devices that aids innovation and productivity makes them susceptible to severe security risk. The Mirai botnet, which emerged in 2016, took advantage of thousands of vulnerable IoT devices—e.g., security cameras and routers—by employing factory default passwords and poor security practices. This episode demonstrates the law of attack surfaces in IoT networks, where weak security controls provide the attacking party with a means of carrying out mass attacks. The large-scale DDoS attacks conducted by the Mirai botnet disrupted high-level services such as Dyn, emphasizing the criticality of addressing security loopholes in the IoT ecosystem and necessitating a redesign of security paradigms in IoT architecture, as well advanced in a number of studies evaluating attack vectors and countermeasures (Madu, 2025). Besides, the Mirai attack also uncovered the complexity involved in the multi-layered nature of IoT systems, as theorized in the layered security model developed in recent research. The attack showed how vulnerability existed at every level of the IoT architecture—not only on device hardware but also at network and app levels. With the botnet using tens of thousands of compromised devices to generate choking traffic, it was evident that conventional security measures would not be able to protect IoT deployments from smart threats. Security must now go beyond strong authentication; it must become holistic in approach with the incorporation of lightweight encryption, secure communications, and ongoing vulnerability scanning. The significance of these multi-layered security controls is further emphasized by their capacity to potentially preclude future events similar to Mirai, thereby reinforcing the broader IoT ecosystem and precluding ensuing risks (Aggarwal et al., 2025).

Figure 2.17. The Mirai botnet, which emerged in 2016, harnessed thousands of unsecured IoT devices—such as security cameras and routers—by exploiting factory default passwords and lackluster security protocols.

Source: https://smartdev.com/wp-content/uploads/2023/08/representation-user-experience-interface-design-scaled.jpg.

In light of the Mirai Botnet Incident, the necessity for using robust cybersecurity controls in IoT environments has become all the more apparent. This situation has triggered innovation of new-generation technologies meant to enhance the security of IoT devices through more advanced intrusion detection systems and AI-powered anomaly detection. These technologies play an essential role in establishing a secure IoT architecture that can withstand increasingly sophisticated cyber threats. Further, the Mirai incident lessons have also resulted in a call for the establishment of security standards that govern device manufacturing and deployment, with a need for security practices to be standardized across the industry. As firms attempt to assure their IoT environments, adopting a holistic strategy for addressing cross-domain policy enforcement will be needed to develop effective and adaptive security solutions against adaptive attack surfaces in the context of IoT, toward a brighter digital future (Madu, 2025) (Figure 2.17).

2.5.2. Smart Home Device Breaches

The rise of smart home products has increased concerns over security compromise, as these technologies, while making life more convenient and efficient, bring with them remarkable vulnerabilities. The interconnected nature of IoT devices leaves many possible avenues open for cybercriminals to exploit flaws in protocols and architectures that are created to facilitate ease of use at the expense of security. These systems are also often targeted by attackers in order to obtain unauthorized access to sensitive personal data, which results in privacy and network integrity-compromising breaches. One of the most disturbing features of these breaches is that numerous users are not even aware of the inherent dangers of their devices, since manufacturers tend to focus on function at the expense of having good security controls in place. This absence of regulation paves the way for a set of cyberattacks likely to happen in various forms, including data breaches and unauthorized device manipulation, underlining the need for an effective security architecture in smart home systems. To mitigate the dangers posed by the breaching of smart home devices, scholars and experts are promoting innovative security solutions that will enhance the resilience of IoT frameworks. A promising remedy involves the application of more advanced access control systems that are tailored to smart home environments. For instance, the dynamic attribute-based access control (ABAC) system offers an avenue for implementing strong security functionalities while still maintaining user convenience. In hybrid blockchain architecture, such systems are able to monitor access with ease and real-time adaptation, enhancing unauthorized access incidents significantly. Moreover, integrating such models within systems also enables the continuous re-evaluation of device privileges based on behavior patterns, which can greatly increase adaptive capability in smart home systems. Lastly, integrating such sophisticated security systems into IoT frameworks not only protects user data but also improves overall trustworthiness in smart home systems, potentially revamping consumer perception of IoT technology. In addition, the increasing interconnectivity of smart devices gives more emphasis on secure methods of encryption to safeguard data transfer. Traditional communication protocols have the potential to expose IoT devices to eavesdropping and misuse, with the need to deploy safer alternatives. For example, innovations in Bluetooth technology provide a compelling solution through single-connection enforcement mechanisms, which reduce the possibility of unauthorized connections.

By halting simultaneous connection and adhering to standards such as AES encryption for data security, such practices provide a solid security against common vulnerabilities. With smart homes founded on diverse networks and protocols, the guarantee that secure structures are in place becomes essential in the prevention of breaches. A detailed examination of hardware as well as software aspects in the context of smart household appliances will firm their structure, thereby establishing a situation that gives emphasis to user security and data integrity despite evolving threats, as highlighted in Ankita et al. (2025) and Waheed et al. (2025).

2.5.3. Industrial IoT Attacks

Industrial IoT (IIoT) devices are becoming increasingly common in modern manufacturing and infrastructure, which leads to worry about how exposed their security is. Because these networked devices are employed to gather and transmit sensitive data, they are a tempting target for malicious actors. The attack surface of IIoT devices can be immense, extending to the devices themselves, network communications, and the underlying infrastructure. For instance, a compromised IoT device can be used as a portal through which intruders can acquire access to broader industrial networks. The consequences of these intrusions can be catastrophic and lead to not only financial loss but even violent disruption in critical services. Hence, a thorough understanding of the attack surfaces is imperative in developing effective defense technologies that will be capable of addressing risks involved in Industrial IoT attacks. The new architecture of IoT networks is normally a combination of various technologies, including wireless sensor networks (WSNs), which are commonly utilized in Industry 4.0. This transition to automation has made it a paradigm where traditional security measures are no longer sufficient to neutralize the sophisticated techniques employed by cyber attackers. Network attacks in IIoT can be in various forms, ranging from data eavesdropping to denial-of-service (DoS) attacks. Moreover, the faster pace of technological advancement has led to security being overlooked, and this has added to the risk environment as a whole. Effective security controls against making IIoT systems vulnerable are based on understanding various kinds of network intruders and their methods, as per recent studies (Majid et al., 2022). To enhance the security of IIoT ecosystems, there needs to be complete frameworks instituted that take into account the specific challenges posed by these networks. The convergence of diverse devices and technologies results in an ecosystem where security controls need to be responsive and dynamic. Furthermore, solving fundamental issues related to scalability and interoperability can render IIoT architectures stronger. Thus, specialized research must be undertaken to identify major loopholes in existing security protocols and propose innovative solutions tailored to the intricacies of Industrial IoT (Wang et al., 2022). By prioritizing the upgrade of advanced security solutions, industries protect not only their assets but ensure the integrity and reliability of their critical services in the more automated world of the present day (Figure 2.18).

Figure 2.18. Industrial IoT (IIoT) systems are increasingly integral to modern manufacturing and infrastructure, leading to concerns regarding their security vulnerabilities.

Source: https://dadb.com/in/wp-content/uploads/sites/5/2025/05/image-20.jpeg.

2.6. FUTURE TRENDS IN IOT SECURITY

As the IoT ecosystem continues to evolve, future trends in IoT security will disproportionately affect the attack surfaces and architecture of Internet of Things devices. With the increasing interconnectedness of devices, the shift toward a more holistic approach to security will involve both hardware and software methods of protection. More advanced anomaly detection and machine learning techniques are being designed to identify potential hazards in real-time so systems can respond proactively to emerging vulnerabilities. As IoT devices expand to such areas as healthcare, agriculture, and urban infrastructure, the demand for robust security procedures becomes increasingly important. An active response, where there is a focus on detection and prevention of potential attack vectors, will result in a more secure and resilient IoT space because user trust remains critically reliant on security effectiveness. In addition, the interlinkage of IoT with other nascent technologies such as blockchain and artificial intelligence both presents opportunities and threats to IoT security. Blockchain technology has the potential to provide decentralized verification and record-keeping, making transactions between IoT devices more secure (Wang et al., 2022). On top of that, artificial intelligence can make the defense autonomous, so the response will be smarter and faster. For instance, traditional security models that require only perimeter defenses are obsolete nowadays; instead, a diversified response that includes identity-based access control and data encryption is required. Metaverse development also serves as an example of the need for a robust security infrastructure, given that virtual digital interfaces will largely rely on the interactions among different connected devices, each of which would be a potential attack surface (Dwivedi et al., 2022). Implementing such sophisticated technologies is thus needed to establish a secure IoT environment. Lastly, future IoT security trends will also include an increasing focus on regulatory compliance and ethics that impact device makers and developers. As governments and regulatory bodies realize the significance of IoT security, there will be demand for standardized security frameworks and protocols with minimum security requirements among devices (Dwivedi et al., 2022). This governing force will facilitate easier progress of secure software development practices, thereby adding to the overall integrity of IoT networks. Ethical concerns over data privacy and surveillance will also demand a top-down model of governance that is based on user consent and openness. These concerns will be addressed not just to diminish security threats but also to foster user trust, ultimately leading to broader acceptance and user interaction with IoT technologies. As these trends continue to evolve, the dynamics between technological innovation, regulatory environment, and ethical concerns will continue to be most influential in determining the future context of IoT security.

2.6.1. AI and Machine Learning in Security

As IoT continues to evolve, the crossroads of machine learning and AI have serious implications for security architecture in these systems. AI will play a pivotal role in supplementing security functions through the application of sophisticated algorithms that can handle enormous volumes of data generated by devices that are connected. Deep learning-based machine learning algorithms have been effective in intrusion detection system construction as well as the identification of anomalous patterns typical of cyber-attacks. Examples are multilayer perceptron and convolutional neural networks, which are commonly utilized for real-time malware analysis and botnet traffic detection, eventually being used for the development of robust IoT environments that can withstand sophisticated cyber-attacks (Ghillani, 2022). This evolution highlights the necessity of continuous innovation within both AI methodology and IoT infrastructure to contain nascent weaknesses associated with advanced attack surfaces. An integral component of integrating AI and machine learning into security solutions is the flexibility and predictive capabilities embedded in these technologies. Since they can learn from past occurrences, AI-based security systems can identify patterns that typically result in security breaches and hence can take preventive action against future intrusions. This preventive action involves the calibration of the AI models through methods like Stochastic Gradient Descent and Adaptive Moment Estimation, in order to make the networks function efficiently and effectively to analyze sophisticated threat environments (Ghillani, 2022). Moreover, with the accelerating increase in IoT devices, the role of security assurance becomes more complex; thus, organizations must also spend money on strong AI frameworks that can keep up with new technology to make security measures dynamic so that they can resist constantly changing outside threats. Although there has been significant promise made through AI and machine learning of enhancing security in IoT systems, there are significant challenges that must be addressed. One of the fundamental challenges lies in the vulnerability of the AI systems themselves, which could be hacked by malicious hackers interested in finding faults within the learning frameworks. Bypassing security in AI systems could lead to unauthorized access and manipulation of information, with devastating consequences at an organizational level. Moreover, the heterogeneity of the IoT ecosystem presents complexity issues on interoperability and scalability, wherein a uniform security solution will be difficult to implement. Overcoming the above complexities effectively calls for ongoing research focused on securing AI models and developing standardized frameworks that are suitable for the unique requirements of IoT environments. To this end, overcoming the above mentioned challenges will be central in laying the groundwork for a secure and robust IoT architecture (Figure 2.19).

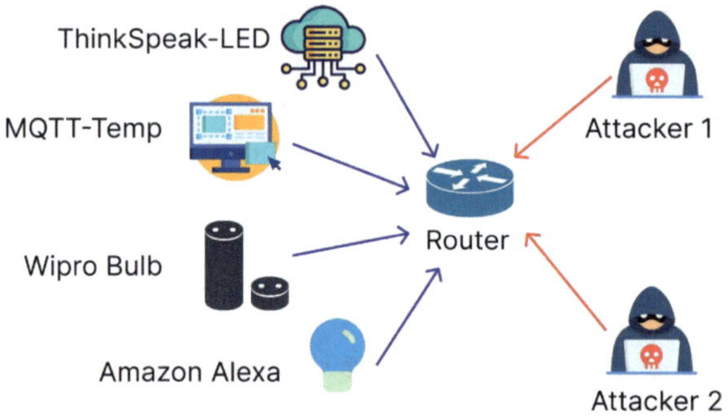

Figure 2.19. Machine learning models, particularly those based on deep learning frameworks, have demonstrated effectiveness in developing intrusion detection systems and identifying anomalies indicative of cyber threats.

Source: https://scx2.b-cdn.net/gfx/news/hires/2025/ai-powered-intrusion-d-1.jpg.

2.6.2. Blockchain for IoT Security

The application of blockchain technology in IoT security is a landmark step toward overcoming the problems of weakness in traditional systems. IoT devices, which are typically known for their weak processing power and memory capacity, are largely vulnerable to a number of cyber-attacks like unauthorized use and data tampering. Blockchain provides a decentralized platform that enables secure and untampered transactions between networked devices. Its immutable ledger capability ensures that all transactions are maintained in a transparent manner and can never be altered retrospectively, thereby ensuring data authenticity and integrity. Since IoT is decentralized, the integration of blockchain will be able to offset the risks posed by single points of failure, as every device contains a replica of the blockchain, meaning more resistance to attacks. Other than that, interoperability challenges of various IoT devices also necessitate the inclusion of blockchain in security frameworks.

Figure 2.20. The diverse nature of IoT architectures often results in fragmented ecosystems where devices from different manufacturers may not communicate seamlessly.

Source: https://www.lonti.com/hubfs/Five%20Challenges%20in%20Mobile%20App%20Data%20Integration.png.

The heterogeneity of IoT architecture is apt to create heterogeneous ecosystems where devices from various sets of diverse vendors may not be able to interact in a seamless way. With blockchain, a uniform and universal transactional framework can emerge so as to facilitate cross-device interaction. In this manner, information exchanged among devices is not only secure but also trustworthy, reducing the attack area significantly. With the evolution of 5G and strategies towards 6G networks, reliance on interdependent IoT systems will only augment, necessitating strong security solutions that blockchain can offer well, supporting the relevance of blockchain in the future of IoT security (Cheng-Wang et al., 2023). In addition, with the virtual environment increasingly developing with the advent of the metaverse, so are the demands of IoT security exacerbated. The immersive world offered by the metaverse demands secure safeguarding of personal data and users' privacy, which can be severely challenged by potential vulnerabilities and privacy invasions. The blockchains distributed nature not just ensures data integrity but also serves to safeguard user privacy through allowing secure, anonymous transactions. This is of especial importance in a metaverse of extended reality and AI, where abusive users can exploit vulnerabilities built into the underlying system. Implementing blockchain in IoT architectures would help alleviate scalability as well as interoperability problems, making security measures as efficient as the virtual landscapes they are meant to protect (Wang et al., 2022). Thus, the convergence of blockchain technology and IoT security is an all-encompassing solution addressing both current as well as future cybersecurity challenges (Figure 2.20).

2.6.3. Regulatory Frameworks and Compliance

The growth of the IoT calls for rigorous regulatory actions that address the unique challenges native to its design and security threats. With IoT devices pervading sectors from healthcare to manufacturing, governments and regulatory bodies need to create guidelines that dictate data protection, user privacy, and cybersecurity in general. For instance, laws such as the General Data Protection Regulation (GDPR) and California Consumer Privacy Act (CCPA) also impose significant burdens on the storage, collection, and processing of personal information. These frameworks are intended to not only safeguard consumer information but also instill a sense of responsibility among organizations dealing with IoT infrastructures. Because non-compliance with these regulations can result in severe penalties and loss of credibility, businesses operating within this technology environment that constantly changes have no choice but to comply. Additionally, the rapidly changing nature of IoT architecture makes it such that regulation policies must continue to be adaptive and visionary in countering changing threats and vulnerabilities. Notably, as companies transition towards multi-cloud and edge computing infrastructures, they encounter increased challenges in data security and compliance. The intersection of machine learning (ML) and artificial intelligence (AI) in cybersecurity policy is the key to enhancing compliance efforts. By applying real-time threat detection and policy response capabilities, organizations are better equipped to navigate regulatory landscapes and steer clear of risk. Frameworks, therefore, must be developed that balance innovation and regulatory compliance in a manner that ensures that technological innovation does not outpace legal and ethical thought.

With time, these adaptational measures will not only keep organizations in line with present standards but also prepare them for future changes in regulatory demands. Interconnectedness of IoT devices contributes to the complexity of compliance since security vulnerabilities in frameworks are being increasingly used by threats like botnets, data breaches, and ransomware. Guidelines for regulations must evolve to encompass these vulnerabilities, recommending organizations implement strong security features like encryption, access control, and intrusion detection. The recognition of future threats such as AI-based attacks and quantum attacks demonstrates the need for an integrated security and compliance strategy across IoT ecosystems. Merging current attack trends and defense tactics, organizations can develop a more secure position against potential attacks while guaranteeing stakeholders' compliance with regulations. As such, the effectiveness of regulatory models does not lie solely in having the authority to dictate compliance but also in being able to instill a culture of security and accountability at all levels of the IoT architecture with the ultimate objective of protecting the user and data integrity within the complex ecosystem (Figure 2.21).

Figure 2.21. The integration of artificial intelligence (AI) and machine learning (ML) within cybersecurity strategies presents a promising avenue for enhancing compliance measures.

Source: https://i0.wp.com/spd.tech/wp-content/uploads/2024/05/AI-and-Machine-Learning-in-Manufacturing.webp?fit=4000%2C2040&ssl=1.

2.7. CONCLUSION

In short, the rapidly evolving IoT landscape demands a good understanding of the natural attack surfaces inherent in its multi-faceted architectures. With the unification of IoT devices increasingly becoming the norm across all sectors, the resulting cybersecurity threats have tremendously risen. The complexity of IoT environments exacerbates these threats, making it increasingly challenging to identify and thwart cyber threats prior to their emergence. This highlights the need to employ cutting-edge methodologies, such as machine learning and AI-based methodologies, in developing anticipatory security mechanisms. These not only have the ability to enhance the resilience of IoT systems but also significantly reduce the magnitude of the damage suffered as a result of cyberattacks, enabling IoT architectures to function securely in increasingly hostile digital environments (Alshammari, 2025). Attack surface analysis is a crucial consideration in ascertaining the security posture of IoT architecture. By using scientific study of the exposure points in such networks, scientists are able to develop targeted interventions to improve the overall resilience of the network. The new methodology outlined in this paper illustrates how tracking some cyberattacks to specific layers in an IoT architecture can provide insight into potential vulnerabilities. By including metrics to measure the attack surface area, stakeholders will be able to effectively prioritize their security controls. Secondly, the use of these metrics allows for a quantifiable means of assessing the risk environment, ultimately resulting in the fortification of IoT environments against threats that are increasingly emerging (Alshammari, 2025). Lastly, the findings emphasize the necessity of developing an enhanced IoT intrusion detection system, as attested through the implementation of the BoT-IoT dataset. This study demonstrated that employing advanced machine learning models, such as an optimally tuned Convolutional Neural Network (CNN), can remarkably improve the detection of novel attacks. A whopping accuracy of 98.23% attests to the effectiveness of the use of such advanced algorithms in security mechanisms specifically designed for IoT setups. With the advancement of sophistication in cyber-attacks, the employment of advanced detection systems will prove to be priceless in maintaining the reliability and integrity of IoT infrastructures. Through the study of the architectural problems and evolution of detection techniques, this paper illustrates an integrated approach to security on the integrated platform of IoT.

2.7.1. Summary of Key Points

IoT structure is central in the operation and effectiveness of networked devices in the healthcare, transportation, and smart cities sectors. Essentially, IoT structure is a set of layers which facilitates communication, processing, and management of the devices. Most frequently, the layers contain perception, network, and application levels with functions of differing natures among the community of devices. The perception layer handles sensor and actuator data gathering, whereas the network layer enables data transport between protocols. The application layer provides user interfaces and data analytics capabilities through which end-users can make informed decisions from raw data. Understanding these layers and their interactions is crucial in establishing potential attack surfaces that are susceptible to threat actors in a more interconnected world, as attested to by the need for efficient security frameworks that can protect different IoT applications. With IoT continuing to evolve, its implications on security in terms of architecture are many. Attack surfaces—every point in a system that an unauthorized user can see or touch the system—are growing as more equipment becomes connected. Each level of IoT architecture thus has unique vulnerabilities that require unique treatment. For instance, the perception layer may be compromised by unauthorized access to information or device manipulation, but the network layer may be threatened by interception as well as by replay attacks. The application layer, being susceptible to web-based attacks, must be protected against application-based attacks and data breaches. Therefore, the security of IoT systems requires a multi-faceted approach consisting of threat modeling, monitoring in real-time, and imposition of best practices in security architecture to address threats, reasserting the necessity of proactive security in the protection of sensitive IoT infrastructure. Future advances in both IoT and related technologies like 5G and the metaverse will extend even further to making the security landscape more complicated. Increased connectivity and innovative applications—characterized by attributes like low latency and high reliability—provide opportunities for efficiency while also providing new routes of attack. With the commercialization of 5G, for instance, industries can leverage ultra-reliable low-latency communications to enhance operational efficiency; with this change, however, there are new sources of cyberattacks and exposure. Also, with the metaverse poised to create virtual experiences that are immersive by nature, there are significant privacy and security considerations with a focus on the requirement of broad frameworks to respond to such evolving threats. As highlighted by recent studies, e.g., those in studies addressing the vision of 6G, it is paramount to take a technology insight and security preparedness lead to protect against imminent threats in an interconnected digital economy (Cheng-Wang et al., 2023; Wang et al., 2022).

2.7.2. Importance of Continuous Improvement

The function of continuous improvement in the case of IoT architecture cannot be overemphasized since the threats of cyberattacks advance to be sophisticated. Continuous improvement provides an environment where organizations are not only reactive but proactive against vulnerabilities in their systems. With the increase in IoT devices, the potential surfaces of attack change, and this necessitates constant assessments and optimizations of security controls. Networked devices, such as CCTV cameras, embody this requirement; studies discovered that devices such as the TP-Link Tapo C200 featured numerous vulnerabilities in the factory settings, ultimately revealing the necessity for incremental increases in security measures. Continuous improvement better equips organizations to adapt their security practices, implement effective updates, and neutralize risks that come with discovered vulnerabilities, thus maintaining a robust defensive position in an ever-changing cyber landscape (Liu et al., 2025). Incorporating feedback mechanisms into the development cycle of the IoT system is crucial in achieving continuous improvement. Through structured analysis of security events and near misses, organizations can learn valuable lessons that inform the future design and risk analysis. This holistic process not only improves security provisions but also infuses a learning and responsive culture within teams that work on creating and sustaining IoT solutions. The integration of advanced frameworks with AI and ML highlights the necessity for such a structured process. These models provide organizations with the capability to monitor threats in real-time and update security policies automatically according to emerging threats, placing the value of continuous improvement in a position of fulfilling requirements to comply with data protection laws and risk minimization for cloud and edge computing systems (Le et al., 2025). Continuous improvement practice also encourages innovation and competition within the IoT ecosystem. As organizations mature their architectures and neutralize potential surfaces of attack, they differentiate themselves as market leaders in an increasingly security-focused market. Prioritizing continuous improvement to IoT solutions enables businesses to improve user expectations around security and privacy more effectively, thereby enhancing consumer loyalty and trust. Lastly, adopting a culture of perpetual improvement allows an organization to not just advance its security position but also enhance strategic partnerships and collaborations that make the overall IoT ecosystem more reliable. In a world where technology evolves so quickly, perpetual improvement is one of the foundation stones upon which sustainable development and resilience can be built and against the ever-increasing numerous cyber-attacks that continue to surface (Le et al., 2025; Liu et al., 2025).

2.7.3. Future Research Directions

The evolution of IoT architecture calls for repeated reassessment of the potential attack surfaces of such technologies. Emerging research must focus on integrating high-level security into IoT system architecture to counter threats from the beginning. Emphasizing proactive security principles, research must examine how varied architectural models can influence security stances in diverse applications. This involves exploring multi-layer security architectures that contain intrusion detection systems (IDS) tailored to be utilized in IoT environments. Such studies will not only improve resistance against intrusions, but it will also become simpler to know how design choices influence scalability and performance in the case of threats. By concentrating on these factors, researchers will be able to make significant contributions to the improvement of security systems that will inevitably be protecting the increasing number of connected devices within a spreading IoT environment (Diana et al., 2025). Another promising line for subsequent research is the use of Explainable Artificial Intelligence (XAI) in the IoT environment, with specific focus on cybersecurity interventions. As ML models occupy the central position of anomaly detection and cyber threat defense, their rationale or decision-making needs to be comprehended. The future work would be how XAI can transform traditional IDS models into interpretable ones so that they win security professionals' trust by making use of AI-based recommendations. Interpretability becomes essential while operating in the domain of IoT networks, where decision-makers are interested in knowing the reasoning behind alerts generated by anomaly-based IDS. Through the analysis of how XAI can be effectively implemented in such systems, researchers can uncover novel methods of enhancing cybersecurity defenses, and eventually the more effective strategies for managing and analyzing the extensive attack surfaces of the IoT environments (Moustafa et al., 2023). Besides, the integration of future technologies like blockchain with the security of IoT is a rich field for future investigation. Blockchains decentralization and inherent security features have the potential to outshine most of the vulnerabilities associated with IoT device management and integrity. The research must focus on how blockchain technology can facilitate IoT device verification processes in enhancing the formation of tamper-proof networks that are secure from varied types of cyberattacks. Future work can more extensively investigate the use of smart contracts to automate security measures and responses in IoT systems. Through developing frameworks combining blockchain with the conventional IoT security measures, researchers can lay the foundation for novel solutions that minimize attack surfaces while improving overall security and reliability of connected systems in mission-critical uses (Diana et al., 2025).

2.7.4. Final Thoughts on IoT Security

As the IoT continues to expand, having solid security controls is becoming essential to protect IoT devices from a host of threats. As cyber-attacks become more complex, a continuous need exists to formulate new security strategies to address emerging vulnerabilities inherent in IoT design. The presence of devices of varying capabilities and functionality complicates the security landscape since traditional cybersecurity models are not good enough at addressing the unique needs of constrained environments. A focused strategy on IoT security will not only include short-term safeguarding measures but also a comprehensive approach that includes developing existing systems and incorporating new technologies. This futuristic mindset is required in building a secure infrastructure that will be quantum-resistant and can accommodate further development in the IoT sector. Among the primary components in improving IoT security is incorporating quantum-resistant cryptography. According to existing research, widespread encryption methods such as RSA and ECC are susceptible to severe vulnerabilities after the advancement of quantum computing. Adoption of lattice-based and hash-based cryptographic techniques is a promising approach towards enhancing device security without burdening their limited resources. Furthermore, this transition necessitates a strategic deployment framework that not only addresses existing quantum threats but also facilitates long-term security goals. Through the integration of such higher-level cryptographic controls into IoT infrastructures, organizations can enhance their security against potential breaches, hence ensuring data confidentiality and integrity within their networks. The urgency of this evolution highlights the need for proactive engagement with security innovations as the IoT environment matures and expands. In addition to these technical solutions, an important component of effective IoT security is to create a culture of awareness and responsibility among stakeholders and users. Appropriate education regarding potential threats and secure behavior can significantly mitigate risks with regard to device vulnerabilities. Furthermore, having governance frameworks and compliance requirements will be a very important element in guiding organizations through the implementation of security standards. The obstacles presented by broken protocols and diverse device ecosystems also highlight the urgent need for common interoperability standards that will harmonize security initiatives on the different platforms. By employing a multi-dimensional approach that combines technical innovation and user education, businesses can establish a robust security ecosystem that is proof against ever-changing cyber-attacks, ensuring the long-term success of IoT ecosystems in the increasingly integrating world.

REFERENCES

1. Abimbola, O., & Idris, O. O. (2025). A critical cybersecurity analysis and future research directions for the Internet of Things: A comprehensive review. https://core.ac.uk/download/657008516.pdf (accessed on 17th October 2025).
2. Acarali, D., Komninos, N., Rajarajan, M., Zarpelao, B. B., et al. (2019). Modelling the spread of botnet malware in IoT-based wireless sensor networks. https://core.ac.uk/download/185244502.pdf (accessed on 17th October 2025).
3. Affia, A. A. O., Finch, H., Jung, W., Samori, I. A., Potter, L., & Palmer, X. L. (2023). IoT health devices: Exploring security risks in the connected landscape. *IoT, 4*, 150–182. https://doi.org/10.3390/iot4020009 (accessed on 17th October 2025).
4. Aggarwal, D., Saxena, A. B., & Sharma, D. (2025). Mitigating cybersecurity risks in IoT: A layered approach to threat detection and prevention. *2025 4th International Conference on Sentiment Analysis and Deep Learning (ICSADL).* https://www.semanticscholar.org/paper/9e7d7d824e00209d8de6b8e53d351653c52b73bc (accessed on 17th October 2025).
5. Alamleh, H., Estremera, L., Arnob, S. S., & AlQahtani, A. A. (2025). Advanced persistent threats and wireless local area network security: An in-depth exploration of attack surfaces and mitigation techniques. *Journal of Cybersecurity and Privacy.* https://www.semanticscholar.org/paper/5875e494525a536731ba35754f51a1bdfbb69d13 (accessed on 17th October 2025).
6. Allioui, H., & Mourdi, Y. (2023). Exploring the full potentials of IoT for better financial growth and stability: A comprehensive survey. *Sensors, 23*, 8015–8015. https://doi.org/10.3390/s23198015 (accessed on 17th October 2025).
7. Alshammari, B. M. (2025). A machine learning-based framework for measuring attack surfaces of IoT systems. *IEEE Access, 13*, 134297–134311. https://www.semanticscholar.org/paper/4943e1bd428f968592bcebd2bff86e6fc12a63ef (accessed on 17th October 2025).
8. Arshi, O., & Chaudhary, A. (2023). Fortifying the Internet of Things: A comprehensive security review. *EAI Endorsed Transactions on Internet of Things, 9*, e1–e1. https://doi.org/10.4108/eetiot.v9i4.3618 (accessed on 17th October 2025).
9. Asokan, N., Frassetto, T., Hafeez, I., Marchal, S., et al. (2016). IoT Sentinel: Automated device-type identification for security enforcement in IoT. http://arxiv.org/abs/1611.04880 (accessed on 17th October 2025).

10. Atmaca, U. I., Bradbury, M. S., Cannizzaro, S., Maple, C., et al. (2020). Identifying attack surfaces in the evolving space industry using reference architectures. https://core.ac.uk/download/287605688.pdf (accessed on 17th October 2025).
11. Awasthi, A. (2025). Quantum-resistant security for IoT systems: Challenges and implementation strategies. *International Journal of Scientific Research in Computer Science, Engineering and Information Technology.* https://www.semanticscholar.org/paper/1793a771fdde668348fcc1930bd1994518806a64 (accessed on 17th October 2025).
12. Baumann, F. W., & Roller, D. (2017). Survey on additive manufacturing, cloud 3D printing and services. http://arxiv.org/abs/1708.04875 (accessed on 17th October 2025).
13. Bulajoul, W., James, A., Li, Y., Obande, T., et al. (2018). Security challenges and solutions for e-business. https://core.ac.uk/download/161525090.pdf (accessed on 17th October 2025).
14. Chen, C. Y., Hasan, M., & Mohan, S. (2018). Securing real-time Internet-of-Things. http://arxiv.org/abs/1705.08489 (accessed on 17th October 2025).
15. Cruz, B., Gómez-Meire, S., Janicke, H., Méndez, J. A., et al. (2019). A practical approach to protect IoT devices against attacks and compile security incident datasets. https://core.ac.uk/download/228199767.pdf (accessed on 17th October 2025).
16. Dabrowski, A., Holz, T., Pöpper, C., Rupprecht, D., et al. (2018). On security research towards future mobile network generations. http://arxiv.org/abs/1710.08932 (accessed on 17th October 2025).
17. Diana, L., Dini, P., & Paolini, D. (2025). Overview on intrusion detection systems for computers networking security. *Computers, 14*, 87–87. https://doi.org/10.3390/computers14030087 (accessed on 17th October 2025).
18. Dwivedi, Y. K., Hughes, L., Baabdullah, A. M., Ribeiro-Navarrete, S., Giannakis, M., Al-Debei, M. M., Dennehy, D., et al. (2022). Metaverse beyond the hype: Multidisciplinary perspectives on emerging challenges, opportunities, and agenda for research, practice and policy. *International Journal of Information Management, 66*, 102542–102542. https://doi.org/10.1016/j.ijinfomgt.2022.102542 (accessed on 17th October 2025).
19. El Hanine, M., El-Yahyaoui, A., & Es-Sadaoui, R. (2024). Three-layer IoT architecture: Attacks and security mechanisms. *2024 11th International Conference on Future Internet of Things and Cloud (FiCloud).* https://www.semanticscholar.org/paper/6b7ae70e7d9d0c4b1a49b956f4cab40bc973c4e3 (accessed on 17th October 2025).

20. Ghillani, D. (2022). Deep learning and artificial intelligence framework to improve the cyber security. *Authorea (Authorea).* https://doi.org/10.22541/au.166379475.54266021/v1 (accessed on 17th October 2025).
21. Jaime, F., Muñoz, A., Rodríguez-Gómez, F., & Jeréz-Calero, A. (2023). Strengthening privacy and data security in biomedical microelectromechanical systems by IoT communication security and protection in smart healthcare. *Sensors, 23*, 8944–8944. https://doi.org/10.3390/s23218944 (accessed on 17th October 2025).
22. Kammara, T. T. (2018). Management and security of IoT systems using microservices. https://core.ac.uk/download/215414662.pdf (accessed on 17th October 2025).
23. Karunathilake, E. M. B. M., Le, A. T., Heo, S., Chung, Y. S., & Mansoor, S. (2023). The path to smart farming: Innovations and opportunities in precision agriculture. *Agriculture, 13*, 1593–1593. https://doi.org/10.3390/agriculture13081593 (accessed on 17th October 2025).
24. Kokate, A., Labade, P., Khedkar, V., & Date, A. R. (2025). Development of secure communication protocol for IoT device. *International Journal of Scientific Research in Science, Engineering and Technology.* https://www.semanticscholar.org/paper/f9d53b993cf6852303087413ee601be70167255e (accessed on 17th October 2025).
25. Kumar, M., Dhingra, M., Bhati, M., & Joshi, S. (2024). Enhancing network security in cloud-integrated IoT devices. *2024 2nd International Conference on Advances in Computation, Communication and Information Technology (ICAICCIT), 1*, 949–954. https://www.semanticscholar.org/paper/10cd84d2fe80b8695754e91b50bbbcffa8b45d43 (accessed on 17th October 2025).
26. Kumar, R., Kumar, P., Aloqaily, M., & Aljuhani, A. (2022). Deep-learning-based blockchain for secure zero touch networks. *IEEE Communications Magazine, 61*, 96–102. https://doi.org/10.1109/mcom.001.2200294 (accessed on 17th October 2025).
27. Latifi, S., Pirouz, M., Raste, N., Tayeb, R., et al. (2018). A cognitive framework to secure smart cities. https://core.ac.uk/download/215451692.pdf (accessed on 17th October 2025).
28. Lazzaro, S., De Angelis, V., Mandalari, A., & Buccafurri, F. (2024). Is your kettle smarter than a hacker? A scalable tool for assessing replay attack vulnerabilities on consumer IoT devices. *2024 IEEE International Conference on Pervasive Computing and Communications (PerCom).*

https://www.semanticscholar.org/paper/65559ce272e7d072995a1ab1600 30aab4d2b7a86 (accessed on 17th October 2025).

29. Le, M. H. (2025). Adaptive cybersecurity frameworks for multi-cloud and edge computing: Addressing threats, regulatory challenges, and autonomous intelligence. https://core.ac.uk/download/664702816.pdf (accessed on 17th October 2025).

30. Liu, X. (2025). Analysis and protection of security vulnerabilities in smart home cameras. https://core.ac.uk/download/657113261.pdf (accessed on 17th October 2025).

31. Madu, V. K. (2025). Security challenges in IoT: A systematic literature review. *Engineering and Technology Journal.* https://www.semanticscholar.org/paper/4a6afa3d5a3d1eb0a24c806445ce486cc95e7dc3 (accessed on 17th October 2025).

32. Majid, M., Habib, S., Javed, A. R., Rizwan, M., Srivastava, G., Gadekallu, T. R., & Lin, J. C. W. (2022). Applications of wireless sensor networks and Internet of Things frameworks in the Industry Revolution 4.0: A systematic literature review. *Sensors, 22*, 2087–2087. https://doi.org/10.3390/s22062087 (accessed on 17th October 2025).

33. Mendez, D. M., Papapanagiotou, I., & Yang, B. (2017). Internet of Things: Survey on security and privacy. http://arxiv.org/abs/1707.01879 (accessed on 17th October 2025).

34. Mishra, N. C., & Pandya, S. (2021). Internet of Things applications, security challenges, attacks, intrusion detection, and future visions: A systematic review. *IEEE Access, 9*, 59353–59377. https://doi.org/10.1109/access.2021.3073408 (accessed on 17th October 2025).

35. Moustafa, N., Koroniotis, N., Keshk, M., Zomaya, A. Y., & Tari, Z. (2023). Explainable intrusion detection for cyber defenses in the Internet of Things: Opportunities and solutions. *IEEE Communications Surveys & Tutorials, 25*, 1775–1807. https://doi.org/10.1109/comst.2023.3280465 (accessed on 17th October 2025).

36. Nguyen, D. C., Ding, M., Pathirana, P. N., Seneviratne, A., Li, J., & Poor, H. V. (2021). Federated learning for Internet of Things: A comprehensive survey. *IEEE Communications Surveys & Tutorials, 23*, 1622–1658. https://doi.org/10.1109/comst.2021.3075439 (accessed on 17th October 2025).

37. Ning, Z., Wang, C., Chen, Y., Zhang, F., & Cao, J. (2021). Revisiting ARM debugging features: Nailgun and its defense. *IEEE Transactions on Dependable and Secure Computing, 20*, 574–589. https://doi.org/10.1109/tdsc.2021.3139840 (accessed on 17th October 2025).

38. Oladimeji, D., Gupta, K., Kose, N. A., Gundogan, K., Ge, L., & Liang, F. (2023). Smart transportation: An overview of technologies and applications. *Sensors, 23*, 3880–3880. https://doi.org/10.3390/s23083880 (accessed on 17th October 2025).
39. Papalkar, R. R., & Alvi, A. S. (2024). Hybrid CNN approach for unknown attack detection in edge-based IoT networks. *ICST Transactions on Scalable Information Systems.* https://www.semanticscholar.org/paper/2129d1dbb80ae9132f7d9e7d1a0d8047eb0375f5 (accessed on 17th October 2025).
40. Rekeraho, A., Cotfas, D. T., Balan, T., Cotfas, P., Acheampong, R., & Tuyishime, E. (2025). Cybersecurity threat modeling for IoT-integrated smart solar energy systems: Strengthening resilience for global energy sustainability. *Sustainability.* https://www.semanticscholar.org/paper/9d4bd6fda03bc804f1d90bd2dee90c57226b9ee1 (accessed on 17th October 2025).
41. Udoh, E., & Udoh, E. (2019). An energy aware and secure MAC protocol for tackling denial of sleep attacks in wireless sensor networks. https://core.ac.uk/download/305119264.pdf (accessed on 17th October 2025).
42. Waheed, U., Khan, S. A., Masud, M. I., Jamshed, H., Jumani, T., & Malik, N. U. R. (2025). Blockchain-based, dynamic attribute-based access control for smart home energy systems. *Energies.* https://www.semanticscholar.org/paper/374aa5b5e63eeff6b7eb0dda7da5c37a0c42674b (accessed on 17th October 2025).
43. Wang, C. X., You, X., Gao, X., Zhu, X., Li, Z., Zhang, C., Wang, H., et al. (2023). On the road to 6G: Visions, requirements, key technologies, and testbeds. *IEEE Communications Surveys & Tutorials, 25*, 905–974. https://doi.org/10.1109/comst.2023.3249835 (accessed on 17th October 2025).
44 Wang, Y., Su, Z., Zhang, N., Xing, R., Liu, D., Luan, T. H., & Shen, X. (2022). A survey on Metaverse: Fundamentals, security, and privacy. *IEEE Communications Surveys & Tutorials, 25*, 319–352. https://doi.org/10.1109/comst.2022.3202047 (accessed on 17th October 2025).
45. Wang, Z. (2025). Applications of embedded IoT systems in smart agriculture: Innovations and challenges. *Applied and Computational Engineering.* https://www.semanticscholar.org/paper/f4b5d1d5701f469a144f5f833671673a4cb42049 (accessed on 17th October 2025).
46. Witanto, E. N., Oktian, Y. E., Lee, S. G., & Lee, J. H. (2020). A blockchain-based OCF firmware update for IoT devices. *Applied Sciences, 10*, 6744–

6744. https://doi.org/10.3390/app10196744 (accessed on 17th October 2025).

47. Yavuz, A. A., Nouma, S. E., Hoang, T., Earl, D., & Packard, S. (2022). Distributed cyber-infrastructures and artificial intelligence in hybrid post-quantum era. https://doi.org/10.1109/tps-isa56441.2022.00014 (accessed on 17th October 2025).
48. Zahra, F. T., Bostanci, Y. S., & Soytürk, M. (2024). LSTM-based jamming detection and forecasting model using transport and application layer parameters in Wi-Fi based IoT systems. *IEEE Access, 12*, 32944–32958. https://www.semanticscholar.org/paper/dcb5b7b245a53110cc553c125c453c859794691f (accessed on 17th October 2025).

CHAPTER 3

COMMON THREATS AND ATTACKS IN IOT

Contents

INTRODUCTION

The booming IoT environment is both unprecedented in opportunity and monumental in challenge, particularly in the realm of cybersecurity. Connected devices facilitate communication and automation and enhance the quality of life. That connectivity can, however, leave people vulnerable to potential threats and attacks on weaknesses of the technology. For instance, the misuse of IoT devices in domains such as IPV has risen to prominence as an urgent issue.

The risks of technology abuse within the context of IoT, according to Slupska and Tanczer, demonstrate the interplay between technological advancement and social issues, calling for wholesome strategies that are both human-centered and cybersecurity-centered (Slupska et al., 2021). The ability of these devices to monitor and control individual environments increases the vulnerability of users, necessitating a deeper analysis of the dynamics of threats. Emerging technologies within the IoT system, such as smart locks, thermostats, and cameras, complicate privacy, and security concepts. IoT devices are designed with the aim of keeping things convenient, but they do not have robust security, and therefore, they become targets for exploiters and abusers. The susceptibility of these devices to be utilized for illegal means is a pointer to systemic design flaws where the lack of proper safeguards disproportionately hurt vulnerable groups. Studies have indicated that IPV perpetrators exploit their detailed knowledge of the victims to leverage security loopholes to attain coercive control through smart technologies (Lim et al., 2020). These despicable dynamic serves to emphasize the need for the practice paradigm of cybersecurity to change towards one that includes socio-technical knowledge in transferring priorities to user security as the primary concern in designing and rolling out IoT devices. Considering the plethora of risks associated with IoT, increased emphasis on threat modeling is paramount in examining and mitigating peril. Threat modeling involves analysis of possible weaknesses, determination of adversarial parties, and developing methods to thwart risks identified, particularly where IPV is involved. By focusing on the efficacy of device use and design, technology creators can shift their focus from classic cyber-attacks to user-centric problems that speak to the dynamics of tech exploitation. As Slupska and Tanczer elucidate, the intricacies of IoT-enabled tech exploitation necessitate collaboration, drawing on technology, sociology, and criminology viewpoints to conceive of frameworks to safeguard individuals against exploitation (Slupska et al., 2021). Lastly, IoT device security is not a technical issue; it is a matter of an interdisciplinarity involvement of understanding the implications of the technological advancement on people's safety and well-being.

Overview of Security Challenges in IoT

The burst in Internet of Things (IoT) devices has brought about unprecedented advances in virtually all industries but also paved the way for a list of security threats. Their intrinsic flaws are the devices' often compromised computational abilities that restrict their ability to implement strong security mechanisms. Most IoT devices lack adequate hardware-based security, which leaves them open to basic cyberattacks such as denial-of-service attacks, brute-force attacks, and unauthorized access. This lack of security infrastructure is further exacerbated by the heterogeneity of IoT networks, which makes it harder to detect and respond to security incidents (Nguyen et al., 2022). There are so many devices and types of devices that traditional security measures are inadequate, and new tactics must be developed to safeguard the integrity and availability of IoT systems (Nguyen et al., 2022). Also, in the light of the IoT era, we notice a critical issue regarding the secure exchange of data. As IoT devices are intended to collect and transfer sensitive information, they are targets of hackers intending to exploit weaknesses in the data transfer.

Figure 3.1. Many IoT devices lack adequate hardware protection, rendering them susceptible to common cyberattacks such as denial-of-service attacks, brute-force attacks, and unauthorized access.

Source: https://www.ibm.com/content/dam/connectedassets-adobe-cms/world-wide-content/stock-assets/getty/image/others/4d/82/4d82aec4-0343-443a-91ff 63cb9814e817.jpg/_jcr_content/renditions/cq5dam.web.1280.1280.jpeg.

The universal issues stem from the distributed nature of IoT networks, where devices have a tendency to operate independently while exchanging data with several platforms and services. This can lead to potential data leaks if there is not appropriate encryption and secure communication protocols. The occurrence of more sophisticated attack vectors necessitates having comprehensive security frameworks that address the entire IoT ecosystem such that end devices and the networks on which they operate are safeguarded from external threats (Bouzidi et al., 2022). The ever-changing IoT landscape further makes security measures even more challenging. New technologies and devices pop up daily, each with its own set of potential vulnerabilities that hackers can take advantage of. As noted in many research studies, these continuous development cycles require a flexible and responsive framework for securing the IoT. Existing detection mechanisms must evolve and recognize a wide variety of attacks on IoT devices, ranging from the design of effective collaborative intrusion detection systems. For instance, proposals such as the MidSiot system aim to categorize IoT devices and recognize malicious traffic patterns with high accuracy, encompassing both present and emerging threats within this constantly growing sector. Such projects are landmark contributions towards the development of an integrated security framework that strengthens the resilience of IoT infrastructures in the face of holistic cyber-attacks (Nguyen et al., 2022) (Figure 3.1).

3.1. TYPES OF IOT DEVICES

The Internet of Things (IoT) is a broad array of devices that are each designed to serve specific purposes and facilitate connectivity in various contexts. Among the most prominent categories of IoT devices are those which are intelligent home appliances, such as thermostats, door locks, and security cameras. These devices are designed to enhance convenience, security, and energy efficiency in homes. However, their mass installation raises grave issues concerning cybersecurity. As highlighted by recent studies, the large numbers of intelligent home devices present a lucrative target among cybercrimes, whereby such criminals can exploit loopholes to achieve unauthorized access to people's private information or initiate massive-scale attacks on the network they occupy, thereby creating the necessity for stringent security protocols (Benlloch-Caballero et al., 2022). In addition to smart household appliances, industrial IoT (IIoT) devices are also important components in manufacturing and resource management process modernization. They include sensors, actuators, and networked equipment that provide real-time data analysis and automate production lines. Despite their capacity to improve efficiency and lower cost, IIoT devices remain equally susceptible to cyber-attack, such as Distributed Denial of Service (DDoS) and malware attacks. Increased complexity and interconnectivity of industrial networks have necessitated advanced security protocols to combat breaches that can cause disruptions in production or loss of valuable confidential information (Benlloch-Caballero et al., 2022). Therefore, as industries use IIoT for competitive purposes, they are constantly at risk of facing potential threats that begin to target their networked infrastructure. Wearable IoT devices form another category, the epitome of the latest advances in health tracking and body fitness. These wearables, from fitness trackers to smartwatches, gather, process, and transfer user data to support individual body health care. With the data sensitivities they possess, such as biometric information and personal health metrics, there is more at risk in case of data breaches. As hackers increasingly target health-related IoT devices with malicious intent, there is the need for strong cybersecurity controls. As seen in current research, technologies such as Self Evolving Host-based Intrusion Detection Systems (SEHIDS) can be game-changers in the provision of device-specific protection through evolution to match the particular threats each type of wearable technology is vulnerable to and constantly updating to meet vulnerabilities (Baz, 2022). This security dynamism is essential for the security of the huge amount of data produced by wearables, justifying the inclusion of strong cybersecurity controls in every kind of IoT devices.

3.1.1. Consumer IoT Devices

The onset of Consumer IoT devices has changed how humans engage with technology in their daily lives. Devices as diverse as smart thermostats and wearable fitness trackers are engineered to make life more convenient and efficient. But this unprecedented level of connectedness opens a wide range of security vulnerabilities, making devices numbering in the millions vulnerable to malicious attacks. Because, as noted, all the devices connected form a potential threat to hacking and the risk of misuse has extremely grave consequences on user privacy and data security, measures to neutralize such weaknesses are called for, as the consequences of a breach can be extensive, resulting in not just financial loss, but also the leakage of sensitive personal information, which ends up damaging consumer trust in such technologies (Dragoni et al., 2017). Despite the obvious risks of consumer IoT products, the overall growth of this market continues unabated. Industry experts have an optimistic outlook on IoT's future, citing its ability to connect devices and permit sharing of resources as primary drivers for growth. Increasingly, businesses and consumers alike recognize the value that IoT devices have to offer, not just convenience but also productivity gains and new opportunity (Anderson et al., 2017). This optimistic viewpoint inspires even more scrutiny, however, regarding how security is being enforced in these devices. As the market increases, the absence of effective security practices will further escalate current threats, placing emphasis on the priority of secure design and consumer education as a fundamental product development approach to manufacturers. Consumer awareness and education of IoT device security is an essential factor in mitigating threats associated with such technology. A vast majority of end-consumers are oblivious to the innate weaknesses that accompany their devices and thus are not properly trained to enforce necessary protective mechanisms. To counter this lack, manufacturers and service providers must emphasize more on education aimed at making consumers sensitive to best practices in securing their IoT environments.

By providing users with knowledge, the rate of successful attacks can be significantly reduced since informed consumers can identify and eliminate threats more effectively. Along the way, a safer and stronger IoT ecosystem can be developed, hopefully mitigating the harm caused by increased connectivity and opening up the world of the internet (Dragoni et al., 2017) (Figure 3.2).

Figure 3.2. The emergence of consumer internet of things (IoT) devices has revolutionized the way individuals interact with technology in their everyday lives.

Source: https://cdn.britannica.com/51/237151-050-BBAD66F8/Scanning-QR-code-self-checkout-NFC-technology-smartphone.jpg.

3.1.2. Industrial IoT Devices

The proliferation of Industrial IoT (IIoT) devices has transformed production and supply chain procedures through increased connectivity and automations. Through an integration of sensors, actuators, and communication technologies, IIoT devices make it possible to monitor and analyze real-time data, resulting in huge efficiency gains. The same connectivity, however, brings a slew of security risks. Because these devices typically operate in exposed environments, they are most likely to attract cybercriminals. The effects of IIoT system breaches can be extensive, ranging from the disruption of operations to data exposure, making effective security controls imperative. The evolving threat landscape necessitates that industries give top priority to security within their digital transformation strategies to counter these new vulnerabilities and ensure uninterrupted operations. One threat linked to IIoT devices is that they may be susceptible to various forms of cyberattacks. Common weaknesses are DoS attacks, which can render devices unusable by overloading them with excessive traffic, and man-in-the-middle attacks, where intruders can intercept and tamper with messages between devices. The network topology of IIoT devices in many cases does not have sufficient built-in security features, exposing them to simple exploitation. In addition, variations in manufacturers and standards lead to disparate security practices, adding to vulnerabilities in a more interconnected industrial environment. As highlighted in recent research, it is essential that there are comprehensive risk assessment frameworks to respond to and mitigate risk against such threats in industrial settings (Anglano et al., 2018). Given that IIoT systems are central to enabling infrastructure, industries must take proactive steps and implement layered security for cybersecurity. This entails implementing best practices such as regular updates of software, device authentication, and encryption of data in transit. Organizations also need to conduct routine risk assessments to identify vulnerabilities particular to their IIoT deployments and create a culture of cybersecurity-aware staff. As the IIoT market continues to mature, collaboration between device manufacturers and cybersecurity experts is necessary in developing hardened systems. By giving priority to security and resilience in IIoT deployment and design, industries can limit the possible effects of cyberattacks, thereby building trust in the technology that is increasingly driving contemporary industrial processes (Romano et al., 2019) (Figure 3.3).

Figure 3.3. By integrating sensors, actuators, and communication technologies, IIoT devices facilitate real-time data collection and analysis, resulting in significant efficiency gains.

Source: https://7834705.fs1.hubspotusercontent-na1.net/hubfs/7834705/Predictive%20Maintenance.jpg.

3.1.3. Smart City IoT Applications

Smart cities leverage the IoT to maximize city living through networked systems and devices that streamline processes, maximize resource utilization, and improve life for people. Applications of IoT span various sectors like energy, transportation, healthcare, and public safety, and hence it is a transformational enabler. For instance, intelligent traffic management systems make use of real-time data from networked sensors to optimize traffic, reduce congestion, and lower emissions. Additionally, smart grids leverage the use of IoT technology for efficient distribution and utilization of energy so that cities can incorporate alternate sources of renewable energy and improve overall sustainability. However, the convergence of these complex systems poses serious cyber security challenges since networked devices become vulnerable to attacks that can trigger disruptions in vital urban services and endanger residents' safety (Johnson et al., 2016). The intricate device network applied in smart city solutions is particularly vulnerable to many threats, such as unauthorized access and data breaches. As more IoT devices are installed, the lack of standardized security measures exacerbates these vulnerabilities, leaving urban infrastructures open to cyber-attacks. For example, intelligent surveillance systems that collect and process information to enhance public safety can be hijacked by attackers who want to manipulate feeds or bring down services. The implications of such actions range from economic losses to large-scale disruption of urban services. Furthermore, standard security controls are prone to failure, as smart city infrastructure usually employs a wide array of devices and protocols through which strong security procedures are challenging to enforce. Remediation of threats is essential, especially with regards to the human impacts likely due to the failure of large-scale IoT usage (Ali et al., 2019). In an effort to mitigate smart city IoT applications' cybersecurity threats, there are multiple strategies that must be put in place taking into consideration both proactive and response measures. Device access and authentication come top as the primary features where only authorized personnel will have access to critical data and systems. In addition to this, policymakers and city planners must collaborate with cybersecurity professionals to design comprehensive security measures like regular software patches, incident response plans, and public awareness campaigns. Stakeholder coordination among government agencies, private businesses, and technology suppliers can be employed to enhance standardized security measures favorable to the resilience of smart cities against cybercrime. Lastly, the effective deployment of IoT applications in smart cities is not only reliant on technological advancements but also on mitigating the underlying security threats that may undermine public trust and safety (Ali et al., 2019; Johnson et al., 2016) (Figure 3.4).

Figure 3.4. Smart cities harness the Internet of Things (IoT) to enhance urban living through interconnected devices and systems that streamline operations, improve resource management, and elevate the quality of life for residents.

Source: https://appinventiv.com/wp-content/uploads/2024/03/smart-city.webp.

3.2. COMMON SECURITY VULNERABILITIES

As the IoT continues to expand, widespread security vulnerabilities inherent in this network of interconnected devices become more common. One of the primary faults is the absence of proper security being utilized in the majority of IoT devices. Businesses prioritize cost and efficiency over security, resulting in devices that have few security functions such as encryption and authentication. This inattention opens enormous opportunities for cybercrime to exploit these lacunae, making the sensitive data vulnerable to unauthorized access and control over the gadgets themselves. The ad-hoc nature of IoT systems also makes it harder to secure as devices belonging to various manufacturers with varying levels of security protocols are meant to communicate seamlessly. Therefore, the coming together of heterogeneous devices with non-uniformed security protocols is able to very organically create enormous gaps through which intruders are able to make their entry into the system, undermining user privacy and safety and destroying the overall confidence in IoT technologies (Mendez et al., 2017). Another significant vulnerability within the context of IoT arises from the difficulty in managing data, more so when it comes to the confidentiality and integrity of the data conveyed via networks. IoT devices tend to produce huge volumes of data, which although valuable, is extremely risky if it is not properly secured. Attackers can make use of unencrypted streams of data, intercepting sensitive data sent from these devices. Further, the plurality of access points implicit in IoT systems presents possible points of compromise. Without adequate controls, like stringent anonymization of data and limiting access, organizations expose themselves to potentially sensitive information. These vulnerabilities are compounded by the related absence of user understanding and education about how to mitigate such threats. As outlined in recent studies, focus on enhancing technical defenses must be paired with an overall educational approach, which galvanizes manufacturers as much as consumers (Dragoni et al., 2017). In the end, the runaway proliferation of IoT devices has evolved at a rate that dwarfs the development of effective cybersecurity measures, which has resulted in a breach-terrain-contaminated environment. A majority of IoT products have outdated software and firmware that are not patched with modern security fixes, as they do not benefit from ongoing support from their vendors. The devices are, therefore, exposed to all publicly available exploits and malware. Default passwords and poor user controls also contribute a lot to the security problem in these devices. When end-users do not change factory-default passwords, they inadvertently grant hacker's simple access. Mitigating such vulnerabilities is not a technology issue only; it needs an adjustment in user behavior and practices as well. To enhance overall security in IoT environments, more emphasis needs to be placed on user education and proactive device management to mitigate risks effectively (Dragoni et al., 2017; Mendez et al., 2017).

3.2.1. Weak Authentication Mechanisms

With the evolving era of the IoT, insecure authentication mechanisms pose a real threat to system integrity and protection of user data. Such mechanisms rely on basic password structures or default usernames and passwords which are likely to be hacked by attackers. With devices continuing to proliferate, the majority of vendors prioritize speedy deployment over stringent security examination, making most connected devices at the mercy of illegitimate users. This condition is particularly pertinent with the broad range of applications that the IoT caters to, from personalized health monitoring systems to industrial control. The implications of such vulnerabilities can lead to mass data breaches and unauthorized entry into sensitive infrastructure, thereby placing greater emphasis on the urgent need for secure authentication protocols that are able to effectively stave off such threats. Moreover, the implementation of new technologies like Federated Learning (FL) in IoT networks provides opportunities as well as challenges for authentication mechanisms. FL enables distributed data processing and enhances privacy by not requiring raw data to be sent outside end devices, but it demands the devices authenticate themselves securely within a collaborative environment. The inherent complexity involved in managing authentication among heterogeneous devices makes the vulnerability that already exists even more challenging. Poor authentication mechanisms can be very dangerous where devices operate in collaboration because a weakness in one device can compromise the whole system. The end result is that it should be a top agenda to upgrade authentication processes in order to develop a secure environment able to support smart IoT applications with maintaining user privacy and data integrity. Since authentication is crucial in the preservation of IoT security, some methods have to be researched to strengthen the weak mechanisms. Techniques such as two-factor authentication (2FA), biometric authentication, and adaptive security deployment can provide protection layers against unauthorized users. As communications networks advance, the necessity for lightweight cryptographic solutions tailored to the limitations of IoT devices becomes more significant. Creating safe devices that can withstand common attacks is a shared responsibility on the developer, producer, and user sides. By having a security-conscious culture and adopting best practices in device verification, it is likely that the weaknesses associated with poor authentication processes will be suppressed significantly, hence enhancing the general security of IoT environments against threats and attacks (Figure 3.5).

Figure 3.5. Techniques such as two-factor authentication (2FA), biometric verification, and the implementation of adaptive security measures can provide layers of protection against unauthorized access.

Source: https://www.f-secure.com/i/964x472/a179b8b311/2fa-hero.webp.

3.2.2. Insecure Communication Protocols

Insecure communication protocols form the biggest flaw in the IoT ecosystem, typically allowing space for unauthorized access and data leakage. IoT devices typically employ basic protocols that neither encrypt data nor confirm connections adequately. This lack of efficiency provides space for intercepted communications where cybercriminals gain access to sensitive data like personal identification details and financial data. Also, as more devices are interconnected, the channels of these attacks increase, increasing the ability to cause harm to individuals and organizations. The efficacy of such attacks is enhanced when less focus is put on maintaining and updating security processes in place over the lifespan of the device, so it is important that users and developers implement cybersecurity standards. The consequences of insecure communication protocols extend beyond individual user issues; they are significant threats to organizational integrity and consumer trust. The attached device when compromised does not just threaten the data associated with that device but can be employed as a gateway to the larger network infrastructures. Many organizations are directly impacted by these vulnerabilities, leading to economic loss, regulatory penalties, and reputational damage. The connectivity that the IoT promotes in theory ought to promote efficiency and innovation, but in the absence of strong security protocols, it results in anarchy that manifests in system crashes and lost revenue. As companies continue to integrate IoT devices into their operational models, discovery and remediation of vulnerabilities that are inherent in communication protocols become forefront as a way of averting sensitive information compromise and guaranteeing functional efficiency. Emerging technology, in that it promises further capability for the IoT, introduces new security threats in protecting communication protocols. As noted by metaverse conversation, the evolving era of networked devices necessitates reconsideration of existing security paradigms. Insecure communication risks are intrinsically magnified through complexity introduced by sophisticated technologies such as artificial intelligence and blockchain. These technologies, being potentially revolutionary in nature, also introduce novel vulnerabilities that can be exploited by attackers. A qualitative understanding of these threats is essential in the development of effective countermeasures that will be able to effectively render risks from insecure communication protocols ineffective. Future research should not only examine the intricacies of such technologies but also develop new measures that enhance cybersecurity in the IoT ecosystem to build trust and maintain privacy in a highly digital world, as evidenced in the findings by researchers in the metaverse paradigm (Dwivedi et al., 2022; Wang et al., 2022).

3.2.3. Lack of Regular Software Updates

Under the IoT, not updating the software periodically creates a major risk, which compromises the security and functionality of connected devices. Software updates not only add fresh features but also plug significant security flaws that are exploited by malicious entities. Without updates, devices will remain susceptible to attacks, presenting an easy point of entry for attackers. For instance, unsecured endpoints may be hijacked and utilized to launch botnet attacks, where they are accessed remotely to perform concerted efforts to impact larger systems, with significant disruptions to the operations. Proactive measures in performing regular updates are, therefore, essential in mitigating these threats and maintaining the integrity of IoT environments. Furthermore, failure to implement systematic software updates can lead to the cascading failure of integrated systems. In IoT networks, devices will communicate and share data with each other, creating a web of interdependency. One device's security flaw can cascade to others, creating a chain reaction that increases the risk of no updates.

Figure 3.6. Software updates often serve not only to enhance features but also to address significant security vulnerabilities that can be exploited by malicious actors.

Source: https://www.quickheal.co.in/knowledge-centre/wp-content/uploads/2025/04/Regular-Software-Updates-991x564.jpg.

This interdependence underlines the importance of a centralized process of IoT device management, whereby the manufacturers and users provide regular maintenance and updates. By fostering a culture of responsibility and vigilance in connection with software updates, stakeholders can collectively improve the overall security posture of IoT systems, reducing exposure to threats and attacks that can have deleterious long-term effects. Further, the issue of maintaining devices at current levels is also compounded by the sheer multitude of IoT devices and manufacturers. Each device will have differing update processes, timing, and levels of support and hence result in inconsistencies in the management of security. This kind of fragmentation will not enable organizations to roll out a standard update policy, increasing their exposure to threats. For these issues to be addressed, policymakers and industry stakeholders must collaborate to establish standards for security updates for devices in the IoT space. These standards can potentially define frequency, priority, and openness of updates so that even lower-supported devices can receive critical patches. By emphasizing the role of software update in IoT, stakeholders can potentially promote a safer digital world where threats are actively being addressed and mitigated to protect users and organizations (Dwivedi et al., 2022; Rasheed et al., 2020) (Figure3.6).

3.3. TYPES OF ATTACKS ON IOT DEVICES

One of the popular types of attacks on IoT devices is the DDoS attack. In this attack, numerous infected devices, typically from a botnet, are employed to flood a victim device or service with an enormous amount of requests. The amount of traffic generated is typically so huge that it results in a service slowdown or total unavailability, rendering systems inaccessible. The unique nature of IoT networks, which operate with limited resources, compels it to be more challenging to tackle such attacks. Traditional anomaly detection tools are unable to distinguish between malicious and benign traffic since there are similarities that could lead to increased rates of false positives, ultimately failing to counter attacks. Ongoing research works towards enhancing DDoS mitigation technologies, combining machine learning algorithms with statistical models to boost the detection rate and offer a more effective defense against this pervasive threat in IoT systems (Alzahrani et al., 2023). Vulnerability exploitation in IoT devices is another critical kind of attack that typically takes place as a result of inadequate security provisions in design and deployment. Such devices usually employ default passwords, which can be guessed, or do not possess robust authentication systems, thus susceptible to unauthorized control. The vulnerabilities may be exploited by threat actors such that they can control and manipulate devices for nefarious purposes, such as surveillance or data exfiltration. Moreover, with the rapid spread of the Internet of Medical Things (IoMT) in recent times, the effect of such an attack can be particularly lethal, with the potential to reveal precious health data and patient confidentiality. The new dynamics of IoMT bring with them unique challenges, the primary need being effective models of risk assessment tailored to challenge the diversified and heterogeneous nature of such devices and vulnerabilities (Pritika et al., 2023). Finally, firmware attacks represent a significant challenge to securing IoT devices. Firmware attacks exploit flaws in the devices' software, oftentimes with the aim of corrupting the firmware or replacing it with an infected firmware. Such vulnerabilities may lead to backdoors being opened, enabling unapproved use and operation of the device. This weakness is compounded by the generally poor update mechanisms in most IoT devices, where manufacturers may forget to release timely patches for found weaknesses. Because these devices are typically deployed in high-risk sectors, such as healthcare and infrastructure, the effects of compromised firmware can be disastrous. Thus, it is important to increase security controls around firmware updates and ensure that devices have robust validation processes in order to prevent the dangers associated with this type of attack (Alzahrani et al., 2023).

3.3.1. Distributed Denial of Service (DDoS) Attacks

The expansion of the IoT has brought new levels of technological and connectivity advancement but, in doing so, also opened new avenues through which malicious attacks can be done, most notably DDoS attacks. These attacks are risky because they have the capability to make services unusable by flooding targets with excessive traffic. IoT devices, typically having very limited security features, are particularly vulnerable to takeover, hence the most suitable candidates to be converted into a botnet. As soon as malicious actors acquire additional devices, they are able to make more substantial DDoS attacks, basically disabling networks and internet services. As noted in recent studies, the open nature of most IoT networks allows such security vulnerabilities, with adequate measures required to defend against such potential invasions (Al-Mohtaseb et al., 2024). One of the major manifestations of DDoS attacks in the context of the IoT is the utilization of IoT devices infected with malware to initiate massive botnets. These botnets are established by infecting a number of devices in a network, and then they are commanded to flood the target IP address with traffic. This strategy not only produces the reduced service but also compromises the integrity of business processes and critical infrastructures. The infamous Mirai botnet is a prime example here, where it has been demonstrated that easily hackable IoT devices can be utilized to launch huge DDoS attacks. It is important to know the way these malwares operate to be able to design effective countermeasures against these advanced threats (Kulbacki et al., 2024). To prevent the ill effects of DDoS attacks, there must be a general and proactive approach to protect the IoT. The initial step is for manufacturers to prioritize robust security features in their devices, making sure default passwords are changed and security updates are routinely delivered. In addition, the network administrators need to install advanced traffic analysis applications and intrusion detection systems with the capability to identify and neutralize suspicious activity in real-time. In addition, there is a necessity to promote an environment of cybersecurity awareness among users, emphasizing the importance of judicious practices in device management. With the continued advancement of IoT technologies, there will be a need for more collaboration between the stakeholders like the policymakers, technology vendors, and users to come up with measures sufficient to combat the threat posed by DDoS attacks (Al-Mohtaseb et al., 2024; Kulbacki et al., 2024).

3.3.2. Man-in-the-Middle (MitM) Attacks

The explosive proliferation of IoT devices has greatly increased connectivity and convenience across industries. However, this increase in connectedness is also accompanied by enormous security threats, particularly through the risk of Man-in-the-Middle (MitM) attacks. In an MitM attack, the attacker intercepts and even has the ability to alter the communication between two parties without their knowledge. Such an attack can breach sensitive information and threaten the integrity of data exchanges. As demonstrated in recent experiments, e.g., experimentation with industrial IoT protocols, MitM attacks expose tremendous vulnerabilities, and the necessity for secure security practices in IoT systems is thereby proven. Such protocols must include protection from the potential for interception and guarantee confidentiality and authenticity of communications, safeguarding users and devices from substantial threats to their reliability of operation and security (Sengar, 2024). The implications of effective MitM attacks on IoT are far-reaching and can result in serious repercussions, such as data theft, unauthorized control of systems, and disruption of operations. For example, researchers have proven that using protocols with inadequate authentication procedures will open up the door for MitM attacks, which enable attackers to perform a wide range of malicious activities. In laboratory tests of IoT device communications, MitM attacks have been shown to hijack data streams and inject malicious commands, potentially leading to disastrous outcomes for users and service providers. For this reason, there is a pressing need to develop improved security protocols that can effectively counter these threats. This pressing need has stimulated research into various cryptographic techniques, such as elliptic curve cryptography, which can enhance device authentication without imposing excessive resource burdens on constrained IoT devices (Ferrag et al., 2022). As well, the growing emphasis on sophisticated machine learning techniques and comprehensive datasets is hand in hand with the removal of MitM vulnerabilities. For example, data sets such as Edge-IIoTset are crafted for studying various cyber-attacks such as MitM attacks. Such data sets facilitate the development of machine learning-based intrusion detection systems that can operate in federated as well as centralized modes for efficient traffic monitoring and anomalous behavior detection. By leveraging attributes based on network communication and device interaction, these systems can effectively facilitate the detection of possible MitM situations before they mature into full-scale breaches. By this token, strengthening defenses against MitM attacks in IoT platforms not only enhances security but also ignites user confidence and trust in the continuous building of smart technology (Sengar, 2024) (Figure3.7).

Figure 3.7. In an MitM attack, an adversary intercepts and potentially alters the communication between two parties without their knowledge.

Source: https://sosafe-awareness.com/sosafe-files/uploads/2024/01/231204_Glossary_MitM_Header.jpg.

3.3.3. Malware and Ransomware Targeting IoT

The IoT device explosion has changed connectivity and automation universally, but it has also increased the stakes for cyber threat, primarily malware and ransomware. The aforementioned malware exploits the typically poor security configurations of IoT devices, which are usually deployed with minimal oversight. IoT malware can serve as a gateway for cyber attackers, through which they can access secret data without authorization or take control of devices to launch extensive cyber-attacks, such as DDoS. Inherent vulnerabilities in these devices present fertile ground for malware to spread rapidly, necessitating the existence of a robust security framework that safeguards IoT ecosystems against possible vulnerability. It is crucial that cyber security best practices be adopted by users and organizations to check such attacks, so as not to destroy desired functionality through the interference of mischief. One of the most insidious forms of malware, ransomware, is a severe threat within the IoT community because it encrypts vital information on compromised devices and demands ransoms for them. This type of attack can be devastating in its consequences, especially in sectors that heavily rely on IoT for business operations, such as healthcare or manufacturing. Attackers tend to utilize social engineering methods in conjunction with technical vulnerabilities to trick users into executing ransomware, thereby compromising the integrity of the IoT infrastructure. Further, the distinct character of IoT devices—i.e., they possess limited processing power and memory—can render the enforcement of good security controls challenging, exposing them to greater susceptibility to ransomware attacks. With the IoT ecosystem expanding, it is important that organizations comprehend and treat the ransomware implications with a view to safeguarding their assets and promoting public trust in connected technologies. The marriage of future technologies, such as the metaverse, and IoT brings additional security issues, particularly in terms of malware and ransomware. Because these systems inherit weaknesses from current technologies, they add to the vulnerabilities that come with cyber-attacks. For instance, the interactive nature of the metaverse heavily employs IoT devices as input devices for the users, thus becoming prime targets for hackers who want to disrupt services or manipulate data. It is important to study the privacy and security implications of such unions, because it not only addresses the current situation but also prospects for potential threats. On studying the intrinsic properties unique to both metaverse and IoT, researchers can identify necessary challenges and recommend effective countermeasures to enhance security protocols. An appreciation of such concerns is paramount, given that the world today is increasingly dealing with an even more complex digital landscape with reduced separation between the digital and physical worlds (Dwivedi et al., 2022; Wang et al., 2022).

3.4. IMPACT OF IOT ATTACKS

The explosion of IoT devices has transformed the technology landscape in a revolutionary manner, yet in doing so revealed inherent vulnerabilities to this interconnected platform. Some of the most pressing threats include Denial of Service (DoS) attacks, which have the ability to take entire networks down by overwhelming them with malicious traffic. Not only do the attacks disrupt the functioning of individual devices but also the entire IoT ecosystem, disturbing essential services in sectors like healthcare, energy, and transport. Based on observation of the impact of such attacks, researchers have been able to identify how they attack the Resource Protocol for Low-Power and Lossy Networks (RPL), leading to extreme data loss and operational freeze in IoT networks. With rising IoT devices, plugging these security gaps becomes of vital significance in determining the resilience and dependability of connected systems, in which more studies and rigorous detection tools are imperative in a bid to ward off potential threats (Sinha et al., 2021). The impact of IoT attacks is not only bringing about disruption; it also has grave sociotechnical impacts, particularly within the framework of intimate partner violence (IPV). Abuse of IoT technology for coercive control is but one illustration of how technological progress can be utilized to produce evil rather than good. Devices meant to be a boon, such as smart locks and speakers, can become tools of surveillance and control, putting the victims under continuous observation and harassment. This convergence of technology and personal safety presents new challenges to victims and the support sector, which must adapt to the advanced security needs of IPV victims.

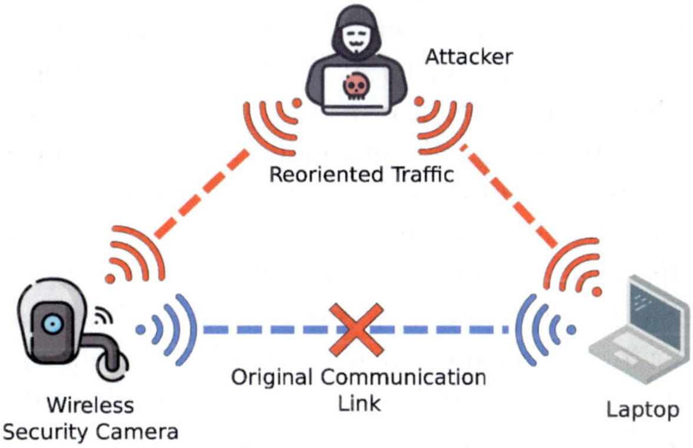

Figure 3.8. The ramifications of IoT attacks extend beyond mere disruption; they also encompass significant sociotechnical implications, particularly in the context of intimate partner violence (IPV).

Source: https://pub.mdpi-res.com/applsci/applsci-11-07228/article_deploy/html/images/applsci-11-07228-g004.png?1628409528.

Addressing these vulnerabilities calls for a comprehensive understanding of user experiences with IoT devices, accompanied by an urgent need for design improvements aimed at user security and safety (Slupska et al., 2021). Compounding the complexity is that the majority of IoT attacks exploit inherent design vulnerabilities rather than sophisticated hacking techniques. Cyber security practitioners need to shift their focus away from conventional outsider threats in order to include the unique challenges of authorized users who misuse their privilege for nefarious purposes. Such an approach emphasizes the imperative for a more sophisticated threat model that takes into consideration the intentions and capability of likely perpetrators, especially where IPV is the context. By combining the knowledge in both IPV and cybersecurity research, actors are able to develop better mitigation techniques that take into account the diverse risks posed by networked devices. Such an interdisciplinary approach not only enhances the security of the IoT systems but also teaches the users about the knowledge and tools needed to protect themselves from the most recent trends in digital abuse (Sinha et al., 2021) (Figure 3.8).

3.4.1. Economic Consequences for Businesses

The monetary implications for businesses trading in the IoT space are gargantuan, particularly when taking into consideration the pervasive security breaches and cyberattacks that penetrate their systems. Once a business organization is victimized by a data breach or a cyberattack, the initial monetary expenses are staggering, ranging from direct monetary loss to recovery costs, lawyer fees, and regulatory fines. Along with these short-term fiscal impacts, companies often encounter long-term damages in the form of reputational damage and loss of customer confidence, reducing market share and profitability. Also, the higher frequency of attacks necessitates increased expenditure on security measures, diverting resources from possibly being invested in innovation or expansion initiatives. Therefore, although IoT technologies promise increased efficiency and connectivity, built-in security threats can translate to enormous economic burdens for organizations that are unable to adequately fend them off. Additional to the economic tangible expenses, organizations also face intricate challenges from the regulatory landscape surrounding IoT security. With governments and institutions still recognizing the need for robust cybersecurity protocols, compliance with evolving regulations can have additional costs to organizations. For example, being out of compliance with data protection laws following a breach can cost them significant fines, lawsuits, and increased scrutiny from regulators. Companies have to invest money in the necessary tools to meet the compliance requirements, which translates to investing in training, policy development, and updating technology. It places a financial strain on the bottom line, particularly for small and medium-sized companies with less to cover the investment. Stress to comply can suppress innovation, for corporations prefer deference to adopting new technologies or methodologies that assist them in capitalizing on market space. The confluence, therefore, of economic necessity and regulatory needs highlights the slippery slope that corporations have to tread when dealing with IoT. The convergence of IoT platforms has the potential to transform operational efficiency; but the economic implications pose a balancing act. Companies need to position themselves strategically against the risk of financial loss by putting into place effective cybersecurity practices and ensuring a culture of security awareness among their employees. Spending money on extensive training programs may help preempt the types of human error that are most likely entry points for cyberattacks. Creating incident response plans can also drastically lower the loss and duration of any breach that does happen. With the metaverse and other such revolutionary technologies evolving, learning about their economic impacts will be ever more relevant to businesses. The nexus of innovation and security mechanisms must direct corporate strategies such that while companies leverage IoT for competitive positioning, they are also directed towards asset protection, customer data, and brand reputation as a whole, thus opening up the opportunities for long-term expansion in an uncertain digital economy (Dwivedi et al., 2022 Wang et al., 2022).

3.4.2. Privacy Concerns for Individuals

In today's rapidly evolving IoT world, the integration of intelligent devices into daily life poses severe privacy concerns for individuals. Because they collect vast amounts of information on individuals, including location, health metrics, and behavioral patterns, avenues for exploitation are daunting. Unauthorized access to this sensitive data can produce a wide range of problems, from identity theft to targeted advertising that takes advantage of individual vulnerabilities. Unlike in traditional computing environments, IoT devices tend to include weak or no security measures, so they are an easy target for cybercriminals. As a result, people are faced with the difficult challenge of benefiting from the convenience of smart technology while at the same time protecting against potential intrusions into their privacy. Moreover, the complexity of IoT ecosystems complicates the privacy landscape further since data easily moves between platforms and devices. Interconnectedness offers several avenues of entry for bad people who intend to exploit vulnerabilities. Alongside advancements in architecture in IoT, so does the level of sophistication in privacy attacks. Individuals may be unaware of the processing and storage of their information, which would lead to exposure that is not intended. Not only are users exposed to outside threats, but they are also facing ambiguous privacy practices and policies by service providers. The integration of IoT into daily life can thus conceal users' awareness of their privacy rights, with greater awareness and alertness being required to mitigate data handling and sharing-related threats. While the advancements in IoT hold great promise for enhancing user experiences, they need to be supported by a serious examination of privacy models. As foreseen in metaverse debates, the synergy between immersive technologies and IoT calls for a revision of how privacy is maintained in such virtual worlds. Research indicates that key industries will be impacted by the evolving character of such technologies, like advertising and health, where the intermingling of physical and virtual worlds poses extremely particular challenges to individual privacy. There is therefore a need for good rules and guidelines available to ensure that individuals can have control over their personal information. Countering these issues will not only protect users but also foster trust between IoT systems, making the digital world a safer place for all involved stakeholders (Dwivedi et al., 2022; Wang et al., 2022) (Figure 3.9).

Figure 3.9. Unauthorized access to this sensitive information can lead to a plethora of issues, ranging from identity theft to targeted advertising that exploits personal vulnerabilities.

Source: https://content.nordlayer.com/uploads/Blog_images_7_ransomware_attacks_in_2023_So_Me_2_1d6b2e7237.webp.

3.4.3. Potential Risks to Public Safety

The possible threat to public safety from IoT devices embedded in critical infrastructure is numerous. With the increasing embedding of smart technologies in cities, the reliance on networked systems to manage utilities, transportation, and emergency services heightens vulnerability to cyber-attacks. One of the significant threats includes the possibility of attackers gaining control of these systems to deliver disruptions to basic services. For instance, autonomous vehicles (AVs), which are dependent on complex algorithms and sensor technologies, are a possible threat to cyberattacks. If compromised, AVs can cause accidents or traffic congestion, exposing passengers' and pedestrians' lives. To neutralize such threats, developing robust threat modeling frameworks is essential to identify and counter new threats to AV applications to provide the continuous safety and reliability of urban transport networks (Ghosh et al., 2023). Besides, the emergent metaverse, a more interconnected digital realm, brings new public safety risks associated with its reliance on various IoT technologies. While offering revolutionary social and economic capabilities, its complexity also brings along privacy invasions and security compromises potentially emanating from underlying technology. These threats can lead to extensive personal harm, including identity theft or unauthorized monitoring, shattering the psychological sense of security in virtual and augmented realities. Accordingly, it is imperative that metaverse platform-developing organizations and companies prioritize installing proactive security measures to secure user data against possible compromise. Integrating the greatest metaverse scalability and interoperability challenges will enhance the efficacy of security measures and solve for the inherent public safety matters in such virtual space (Wang et al., 2022). In addition to looking at individual IoT devices and platforms, cities must also work on the system-level threats of the pervasive interconnectivity of the technologies. With increased reliance on diversified uses of IoT, including intelligent traffic systems or emergency warning systems, the failure of one will have a domino-like effect and lead to far and distant consequences. Furthermore, the potential threat of simultaneous coordinated attacks on multiple IoT devices could overwhelm city infrastructure, exposing vulnerability in municipal response. A model of risk assessment spanning across different IoT systems is needed in order to create a resilient city infrastructure that is capable of withstanding cyber as well as physical assaults. By encouraging collaborations among technology vendors, policymakers, and security experts, cities are better positioned to create a network that significantly minimizes public safety threats inherent in the IoT ecosystem.

3.5. MITIGATION STRATEGIES

Mitigation controls in the IoT context are essential to counteract the sheer volume of threats and attacks that define this fast-evolving industry. One effective strategy is the implementation of overarching cybersecurity policies that comprise risk discovery, threat assessment, and incident response procedures. By the focus on an overarching method of cybersecurity, firms are able to procedurally deal with possible vulnerabilities that are present in IoT systems. This entails robust practices such as regular patching of software, implementation of encryption techniques, and installation of firewalls that can prevent unauthorized entry. As contended in recent literature, the creation of a unique list of infrastructure and controls is key to administering effective cyber protection, which translates to the requirement for safeguarding data as well as system integrity in light of more threats from the IoT (Anglano et al., 2018). Apart from that, promoting training and awareness among stakeholders is a must for enhancing the resilience of IoT ecosystems. This involves developing education programs to enhance users' understanding of potential threats associated with IoT devices and how they operate. As long as users are educated on recognizing malicious behavior and maintaining best practices concerning device security, they make a significant input into the overall defense of the IoT system. Periodic seminars and workshops can be significant platforms for disseminating this information, rendering the entire organizational culture susceptible to cybersecurity. The importance of such horizontal initiatives towards training and awareness cannot be overstated, as they form a significant first line of defense against social engineering attacks and other technical vulnerabilities (Anglano et al., 2018). As pivotal as such strategies are, no less crucial is the embrace of technology innovations to enhance IoT security protocols. The implementation of multidisciplinary approaches is a forward-thinking initiative, as explained through an Integrated Technological System Framework (ITSF) lens. This strategy leverages the synergy of various aspects of technology, including Artificial Intelligence (AI) and machine learning, to enable real-time threat detection and response capabilities tailored to the unique challenges of IoT networks. By using genetic algorithms and other advanced analytical techniques, organizations can not only strengthen their defense mechanisms but also foster a proactive strategy to IoT security management. Such convergence, as witnessed in the literature, indicates an incredible stride in the security management discipline, illustrating the pivotal significance of a multidisciplinary paradigm in addressing challenges unique to IoT.

3.5.1. Implementing Strong Authentication Protocols

The IoT has transformed the way technology is involved in everyday life, but like any revolution, this one too has its challenges. The most pressing challenge that is currently facing IoT is the threat posed by bad security, and specifically poor authentication protocols. These protocols play a vital role in verifying users and devices and keeping the gates closed against unauthorized access of sensitive information. Strong authentication techniques such as multi-factor authentication (MFA) and public key infrastructure (PKI) are crucial in diminishing the threats that compromised accounts and devices pose. By using strong authentication, IoT networks can create a multi-layered security environment that considerably minimizes susceptibility to attack and thereby enhances overall system integrity and user trust. Additionally, the resource-limited environment of IoT devices presents additional complications in applying strong authentication mechanisms. There are many devices in IoT systems that must utilize lightweight solutions because there are limitations on processing power and battery lives. Traditional cryptographic methods, although effective, may not be sufficient in terms of efficiency for these devices, thus prompting investigations into alternative methodologies. That is where technologies such as ML and DL come into play. These emerging technologies provide methods for designing complicated yet efficient authentication methods that are modified to accommodate the constraints of IoT devices. With ML and DL, devices can improve themselves and learn automatically to trends in authentication, significantly enhancing their security against misuse and attacks, which are increasingly prevalent in a networked world (Hussain et al., 2020). In addition to securing authentication procedures, using strong protocols can lead to greater compliance with data protection and privacy regulations. As industries adopt IoT technologies, they must navigate a thicket of legal and ethical concerns. The General Data Protection Regulation (GDPR), for example, demands strict protocols for data protection, so strong authentication is not only the best practice but also obligatory. By adopting holistic authentication methods, organizations not only become prepared to counter breaches but are also better able to attain compliance requirements. Developing a culture of security for authentication can help organizations strengthen their defense against conventional attacks in IoT. Finally, by prioritizing the use of strong authentication procedures, organizations are able to handle the complicated IoT dynamics securely and guard their users as well as their private information (Dwivedi et al., 2022) (Figure 3.10).

Figure 3.10. Strong authentication mechanisms, such as multi-factor authentication (MFA) and public key infrastructure (PKI), are critical in mitigating the risks associated with compromised accounts and devices.

Source: https://emudhra.com/hs-fs/hubfs/MFA-authentication-1.jpg?width=1200&height=600&name=MFA-authentication-1.jpg.

3.5.2. Regular Software Updates and Patch Management

In this dynamic age of the IoT, how essential it is to maintain periodic software updates and smooth patch management cannot be overstated. Software vulnerabilities are most often the doorways to cyberattacks, and it is essential that IoT devices are regularly updated so as to repel newly budding threats. Each software update not only introduces bug fixes but also security patches that prevent unauthorized access and data breaches. Without these updates, devices remain open to attacks by malicious entities, who continually work on developing new complex techniques to circumvent out-of-date security protocols. Therefore, creating a regular update schedule and having aggressive patch management practices in place is imperative in strengthening the security of IoT environments against a background of ongoing cyber threats. In addition, the challenges of patch management in IoT networks are particularly underscored depending on the diversity and quantity of devices being deployed. Many IoT devices are being deployed in environments where updates cannot be realistically performed manually, and this leads to a high percentage of devices being left unpatched for extended durations. This prolonged exposure period to known vulnerabilities can have cascading effects by which an exploited device can offer a jumping board for adversaries to breach larger network infrastructures. Furthermore, the far-reaching diversity of IoT devices, from consumer devices to industrial machines, makes it harder to implement updates. Mechanisms must be established such that in a home setting or an industrial one, devices can be quickly updated without disrupting their fundamental operations and hence enhancing overall security without compromising on operational effectiveness. Finally, organizations with a whole organization approach to patch management and software updates significantly minimize the threats with IoT vulnerabilities. Such an approach should incorporate automated methods of tracking, deploying, and verifying patches across all devices in the network. With cloud computing capabilities, organizations are able to manage numerous numbers of updates with ease, thus ensuring that all connected devices are running on the safest versions of their software. Furthermore, there is a need to notify users of the importance of these enhancements since human problems tend to complicate security programs. By having a robust strategy in place for regular patches and updates, organizations are not only able to minimize their exposure to common IoT-based threats but also promote a cybersecurity-conscious organizational culture, thus enhancing the overall resilience of their digital infrastructure against the increasingly hostile cyber environment (Ahmad et al., 2021; Dwivedi et al., 2022).

3.5.3. Network Segmentation and Monitoring

With the ever-evolving IoT landscape, network segmentation has emerged as a fundamental security tactic. Segmentation of a big network into smaller, independent segments enables organizations to restrict access, in effect minimizing the attack surface available to be leveraged by nefarious actors.

Segmenting the network not only stops lateral movement but also provides improved visibility and control of network traffic. It also permits the implementation of personalized security protocols within diversified segments, enabling critical data to be effectively secured while less significant aspects can operate with more flexibility. In general, robust segmentation is a foundation that supports against widespread threats and incursions, enabling organizations to react well to changing vulnerabilities within the IoT ecosystem. Monitoring is also a critical component of safeguarding segmented networks. Real-time monitoring of network traffic allows organizations to detect atypical behavior and possible compromise in real time.

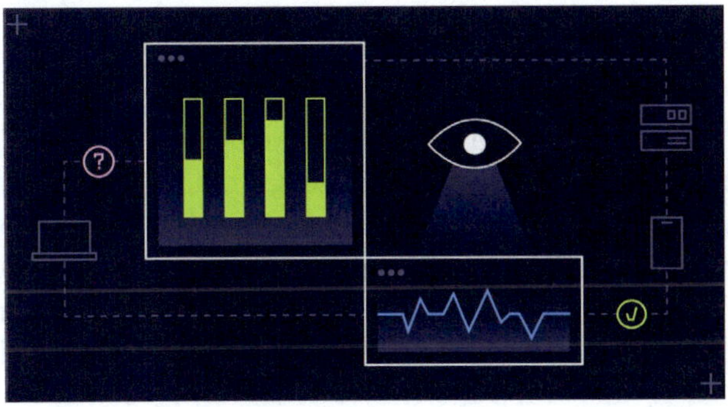

Figure 3.11. Continuous surveillance of network traffic allows organizations to detect suspicious activities and potential breaches in real-time.

Source: https://content.nordlayer.com/uploads/Cybersecurity_monitoring_Cover_52794 2393f.webp.

Contemporary monitoring software has the tendency to utilize anomaly detection technologies, which are able to identify deviations from the standard, depicting possible security problems. For instance, utilization of models such as FusionNet has shown great potential in enhancing anomaly detection performance for IoT networks, where high accuracy can be achieved in detecting abnormal traffic patterns and behaviors (Alsalman, 2024). By the implementation of machine learning-driven algorithms, organizations can automate monitoring and more easily and quickly respond to potential threats. The integration of robust monitoring tools not only enhances security but also provides executives and administrators with valuable insights that can inform future segmentation strategy and operational adjustments. Furthermore, monitoring systems that are incorporated directly into network segmentation can significantly enhance an organization's defenses against attacks targeted at IoT. For example, the development of high-tech real-time monitoring systems for disaster scenarios brings into focus the capacity of the technology to detect anomalies pertaining to environmental risks. Deep neural networks are employed in these systems to analyze data from sensors of multiple types for quick detection of problems like flood risk, which is an issue of the present climate-affected world (Lee et al., 2024). By integrating various inputs of information, organizations can build a common image of their network, enhance situational awareness, and enable proactive response against potential interruptions. This integrated strategy emphasizes the use of both network segmentation and monitoring in minimizing threats, ultimately guarding IoT infrastructure from various mundane attacks experienced currently (Figure 3.11).

3.6. CONCLUSION

Lastly, this shared threat and attack analysis in the IoT emphasizes the need to enforce proper security controls particular to this evolving technological landscape. The diverse range of vulnerabilities, from weak device authentication to data privacy threats, necessitates a convergent approach to cybersecurity. As more and more devices are brought online, the magnitude of potential effect upon successful attacks increases, threatening not just individual consumers but even large networks and infrastructure as well. Thus, proactive steps such as threat modeling and constant traffic monitoring can provide increased resilience against typical threats and secure the IoT ecosystem. Moreover, the incorporation of future technologies can potentially reduce these vulnerabilities in IoT. Techniques such as Federated Learning (FL), which allow devices to train machine learning models in collaboration without revealing raw data, can potentially minimize privacy concerns significantly without affecting functionality (Lim et al., 2020). Additionally, the Digital Twins concept has the potential to offer possibilities for enhanced operational efficiency and predictive maintenance, particularly in manufacturing and healthcare sectors. With the imitation of real-life situations in virtual environments, companies can identify potential security vulnerabilities and design effective as well as situational countermeasures (Fuller et al., 2020). Finally, the future of IoT security is dependent upon collaboration between industry stakeholders, researchers, and regulatory bodies. There is a need to develop total standards and best practices for designing a common security architecture evolving with the dynamically changing nature of threats. Investment in research that explores and counteracts the prevailing issues of communication expenses and resource splitting during the deployment of FLs is vital to the successful implementation and optimization of the technologies for varied applications in the IoT. It is through a coordinated, cross-disciplinary approach that we can hope to secure the future of the IoT from the array of challenges facing it.

3.6.1. Summary of Key Points

The application of IoT devices has transformed numerous industries in a critical manner, enhancing efficiency and connectivity and also introducing with them a range of security challenges. With IoT devices more embedded in essential infrastructures such as power grids and industrial automation systems, the importance of resolving potential weaknesses cannot be overstated. The new arrival of real-time Internet of Things (RT-IoT) systems places a focus on enhancing robust security capabilities that are capable of withstanding sophisticated cyber-attacks. From observations, this extensive connectivity, which enhances the user experience, has an attractive target for cyber attackers in trying to find vulnerabilities in the connected systems (Chen et al., 2018). One of the pressing issues in IoT security is the security of Secure Device Pairing (SDP) protocols, designed to enable secure communication among intelligent devices. One problem of comparing and analyzing different SDP schemes is that they have different assumptions regarding out-of-band channels and adversary models. In the absence of a common analysis framework, it becomes hard to decide on the advantages and limitations of different SDP approaches. The need for a conceptual model facilitating comparative consistency between different SDP schemes is critical because it can discover systemic security weaknesses that must be addressed to enhance the global resilience of IoT ecosystems (Fomichev et al., 2017). Solving the security vulnerabilities inherent within IoT systems means solving this by adopting a multi-disciplinary method in which technological solutions are complemented, if not supplemented, by systemic analyses. Practice professionals and researchers need to emphasize the identification and remediation of generic weaknesses in current security systems. This involves developing techniques that encompass privacy concerns and refining current SDP schemes to thwart identified weaknesses more efficiently. With IoT, creating a culture of forward-looking security measures and continuous change will be essential to safeguard consumers and critical infrastructures from the pervasive threat environment that characterizes the IoT ecosystem (Chen et al., 2018).

3.6.2. The Importance of Proactive Security Measures

The recent explosion of IoT devices has brought into focus the imperative need for proactive security measures. With these devices being an indispensable part of everyday life, weaknesses of these devices are significant threats, not only to individual users but also to wider networks. Unlike conventional computing devices, most IoT devices are designed with very few security controls, and therefore they become the first target for cyberattacks. This deficiency is then worsened by manufacturers prioritizing functionality over security in designs often rolled out into the market with pre-embedded vulnerabilities. The requirement to implement proactive security measures cannot be emphasized enough; aside from securing personal data, these measures also protect the integrity of linked systems from looming attacks, keeping the confidence of customers intact while ensuring maximum overall security within the cyber world. Preemptive security mechanisms, such as the implementation of authentication mechanisms and data encryption, play an important role in mitigating the threats of IoT devices. The methods carry the prospect of providing significant immunity to usual attacks, such as those that target the energy efficiency of the devices. A case in point, denial of sleep attacks, has the capacity to drain the energy reserves of IoT sensors, reducing the operational lifespan while increasing their vulnerability. Enhancing security for these devices demands double priority for protecting sensitive information as well as maximizing the use of resources. The inclusion of robust security features might bring with it higher energy demands, yet potential benefits in terms of improved performance and device longevity assume precedence. Ultimately, achieving security equilibrium will enable IoT systems to function efficiently without subjecting them to unbalanced breach risks (Udoh et al., 2019). Also, addressing the security loopholes of IoT products requires manufacturers to ensure that cybersecurity remains their priority on their list of things to do at the design and deployment phases. The rise of IoT created a lot of demand for connected devices, but most manufacturers have not provided the necessary security fixes after deployment. As the high percentage of unpatched devices makes clear, this complacency creates a high-risk environment where vulnerabilities are readily exploitable. Applying proactive measures such as regular firmware updates, easy security settings, and implementation of advanced filtering technologies can make a big difference in device security. As an example, the development of Berkeley Packet Filters (BPFs) has shown a promising way for IoT device security at minimal performance overhead. Proactive measures for security, stakeholders can pool together to implement actions that mitigate risks and enhance the integrity of the IoT environment (Cruz et al., 2019).

3.6.3. Future Outlook for IoT Security Challenges

The future IoT security challenges are going to transform rapidly to the shifting technology and pervasiveness of connectivity. As fifth generation (5G) networks become widespread, the prospect for improved communication from IoT devices offers opportunities and threats. With more connectivity, there is more room for malicious users to attack the system, and it becomes important for sectors to rethink security measures. As chronicled, research into sixth-generation (6G) systems is already hinting at a list of technical requirements and use cases that try to mitigate these challenges. However, the literature indicates that several open questions remain, highlighting the need for continued innovation in security models to protect against evolving threats. Thus, understanding these dynamics will be critical to anticipating and effectively countering the continuing evolution of IoT security. The convergence of artificial intelligence (AI) with IoT technology further complicates the security landscape. AI systems are increasingly employed to analyze massive datasets generated by IoT devices, enabling real-time threat detection and response mechanisms. However, as highlighted, the application of AI in security measures must also address potential vulnerabilities, as malicious actors may exploit these technologies for their gain. The development of machine learning-driven algorithms to improve IoT security has raised some philosophical issues regarding the ethical limitation and robustness of such systems. As the intersection between AI and IoT continues to change, the development of secure communication channels and the implementation of accountability programs will be instrumental in securing user data without losing trust in the improvement of technology. Future prediction is that there must be a balanced approach, incorporating AI along with augmented security controls, to tackle the various IoT challenges. In the future, collaboration among stakeholders like manufacturers, governments, and academia will determine the future of IoT security. The ecosystem must evolve with increasing threats and ensure security is embedded in the IoT device design from inception. With ecosystems of technology more deeply integrated, regulatory domains must evolve in tandem, addressing issues such as data privacy, device interoperability, and security certification. Discussion of the ethical frameworks governing AI and IoT is heating up, emphasizing the importance of responsible tech development. Besides, next-generation innovations in 6G, as described in Cheng-Wang et al. (2023), and the future implications of next-generation AI systems, as discussed in Gill et al. (2023), will be crucial to developing security paradigms. Therefore, collaborative research and policy action are a must in order to effectively tackle the future IoT security challenges.

REFERENCES

1. Abioye, S., Oyedele, L. O., Akanbi, L., Ajayi, A., Dávila Delgado, J. M., Bilal, M., Akinadé, O. O., et al. (2021). Artificial intelligence in the construction industry: A review of present status, opportunities and future challenges. *Journal of Building Engineering, 44*, 103299–103299. https://doi.org/10.1016/j.jobe.2021.103299 (accessed on 17th October 2025).

2. Ahmad, W., Rasool, A., Javed, A. R., Baker, T., & Jalil, Z. (2021). Cyber security in IoT-based cloud computing: A comprehensive survey. *Electronics, 11*, 16–16. https://doi.org/10.3390/electronics11010016 (accessed on 17th October 2025).

3. Ali, I., Sabir, S., & Ullah, Z. (2019). Internet of Things security, device authentication and access control: A review. http://arxiv.org/abs/1901.07309 (accessed on 17th October 2025).

4. Al-Mohtaseb, A., Hanoon, A. Q., Samara, G., Daoud, E. A., Alidmat, O., Batyha, R., Aljaidi, M., et al. (2024). A comprehensive review of VANET attacks: Predictive models, vulnerability management, and defense selection. *2024 25th International Arab Conference on Information Technology (ACIT).* https://www.semanticscholar.org/paper/34b7b38ef92d5c77c13337b711b07269db340cf9 (accessed on 17th October 2025).

5. Alsalman, D. (2024). A comparative study of anomaly detection techniques for IoT security using adaptive machine learning for IoT threats. *IEEE Access, 12*, 14719–14730. https://www.semanticscholar.org/paper/53eec06b3b814bd3e62cd2064a987960ac4592b2 (accessed on 17th October 2025).

6. Alzahrani, R. J., & Alzahrani, A. (2023). A novel multi algorithm approach to identify network anomalies in the IoT using fog computing and a model to distinguish between IoT and non-IoT devices. *Journal of Sensor and Actuator Networks, 12*, 19–19. https://doi.org/10.3390/jsan12020019 (accessed on 17th October 2025).

7. Anderson, J., & Rainie, L. (2017). The Internet of Things connectivity binge: What are the implications? https://core.ac.uk/download/89472988.pdf (accessed on 17th October 2025).

8. Anglano, C., Aniello, L., Antinori, A., Armando, A., et al. (2018). The future of cybersecurity in Italy: Strategic focus area. https://core.ac.uk/download/188830442.pdf (accessed on 17th October 2025).

9. Baz, M. (2022). SEHIDS: Self evolving host-based intrusion detection system for IoT networks. *Sensors, 22*, 6505–6505. https://doi.org/10.3390/s22176505 (accessed on 17th October 2025).

10. Benlloch-Caballero, P., Wang, Q., & Alcaraz Calero, J. M. (2022). Distributed dual-layer autonomous closed loops for self-protection of 5G/6G IoT networks from distributed denial of service attacks. *Computer Networks, 222*, 109526–109526. https://doi.org/10.1016/j.comnet.2022.109526 (accessed on 17th October 2025).
11. Bouzidi, M., Gupta, N., Cheikh, F. A., Shalaginov, A., & Derawi, M. (2022). A novel architectural framework on IoT ecosystem, security aspects and mechanisms: A comprehensive survey. *IEEE Access, 10*, 101362–101384. https://doi.org/10.1109/access.2022.3207472 (accessed on 17th October 2025).
12. Chen, C. Y., Hasan, M., & Mohan, S. (2018). Securing real-time Internet-of-Things. http://arxiv.org/abs/1705.08489 (accessed on 17th October 2025).
13. Cruz, B., Gómez-Meire, S., Janicke, H., Méndez, J. A., et al. (2019). A practical approach to protect IoT devices against attacks and compile security incident datasets. https://core.ac.uk/download/228199767.pdf (accessed on 17th October 2025).
14. Davis, B. D., Liu, Y., & Anwar, M. (2024). Repository of metadata-related threats and mitigation strategies to enhance security in smart homes. *2024 Conference on AI, Science, Engineering, and Technology (AIxSET).* https://www.semanticscholar.org/paper/27455535cad5c51f5b13dcc5f7b4294ae5e4dedd (accessed on 17th October 2025).
15. Dragoni, N., Giaretta, A., & Mazzara, M. (2017). The Internet of Hackable Things. https://core.ac.uk/download/132703657.pdf (accessed on 17th October 2025).
16. Dwivedi, Y. K., Hughes, L., Baabdullah, A. M., Ribeiro-Navarrete, S., Giannakis, M., Al-Debei, M. M., Dennehy, D., et al. (2022). Metaverse beyond the hype: Multidisciplinary perspectives on emerging challenges, opportunities, and agenda for research, practice and policy. *International Journal of Information Management, 66*, 102542–102542. https://doi.org/10.1016/j.ijinfomgt.2022.102542 (accessed on 17th October 2025).
17. Ferrag, M. A., Friha, O., Hamouda, D., Maglaras, L., & Janicke, H. (2022). Edge-IIoTset: A new comprehensive realistic cyber security dataset of IoT and IIoT applications for centralized and federated learning. *IEEE Access, 10*, 40281–40306. https://doi.org/10.1109/access.2022.3165809 (accessed on 17th October 2025).
18. Fomichev, M., Gardner-Stephen, P., Hollick, M., Steinmetzer, J., et al. (2017). Survey and systematization of secure device pairing. http://arxiv.org/abs/1709.02690 (accessed on 17th October 2025).

19. Fuller, A., Fan, Z., Day, C., & Barlow, C. (2020). Digital twin: Enabling technologies, challenges and open research. *IEEE Access, 8*, 108952–108971. https://doi.org/10.1109/access.2020.2998358 (accessed on 17th October 2025).
20. Garzia, F., & Lombardi, M. (2018). Safety and security management through an integrated multidisciplinary model and related integrated technological framework. https://core.ac.uk/download/159635814.pdf (accessed on 17th October 2025).
21. Ghosh, S., Zaboli, A., Hong, J., & Kwon, J. (2023). An integrated approach of threat analysis for autonomous vehicles perception system. *IEEE Access, 11*, 14752–14777. https://doi.org/10.1109/access.2023.3243906 (accessed on 17th October 2025).
22. Gill, S. S., & Kaur, R. (2023). ChatGPT: Vision and challenges. *Internet of Things and Cyber-Physical Systems, 3*, 262–271. https://doi.org/10.1016/j.iotcps.2023.05.004 (accessed on 17th October 2025).
23. Hussain, F., Hussain, R., Hassan, S. A., & Hossain, E. (2020). Machine learning in IoT security: Current solutions and future challenges. *IEEE Communications Surveys & Tutorials, 22*, 1686–1721. https://doi.org/10.1109/comst.2020.2986444 (accessed on 17th October 2025).
24. Johnson, C. (2016). Securing the participation of safety-critical SCADA systems in the Industrial Internet of Things. https://core.ac.uk/download/46664188.pdf (accessed on 17th October 2025).
25. Kulbacki, M., Chaczko, Z., Barton, S., Wajs-Chaczko, P., Nikodem, J., Rozenblit, J. W., Klempous, R., et al. (2024). A review of the weaponization of IoT: Security threats and countermeasures. *2024 IEEE 18th International Symposium on Applied Computational Intelligence and Informatics (SACI).* https://www.semanticscholar.org/paper/6353fffc96460f2e159590b13cbc1c9ea90f4a7c (accessed on 17th October 2025).
26. Lee, Y. J., Hwang, J. Y., Park, J., Jung, H., & Suhr, J. (2024). Deep neural network-based flood monitoring system fusing RGB and LWIR cameras for embedded IoT edge devices. *Remote Sensing, 16*, 2358. https://www.semanticscholar.org/paper/d7c5fb0f2cbd825b261148b7527ab0eddfb77a8d (accessed on 17th October 2025).
27. Lim, W. Y. B., Luong, N. C., Hoang, D. T., Jiao, Y., Liang, Y. C., Yang, Q., Niyato, D., et al. (2020). Federated learning in mobile edge networks: A comprehensive survey. *IEEE Communications Surveys & Tutorials, 22*, 2031–2063. https://doi.org/10.1109/comst.2020.2986024 (accessed on 17th October 2025).

28. Mendez, D. M., Papapanagiotou, I., & Yang, B. (2017). Internet of Things: Survey on security and privacy. http://arxiv.org/abs/1707.01879 (accessed on 17th October 2025).

29. Nguyen, D. C., Ding, M., Pathirana, P. N., Seneviratne, A., Li, J., & Poor, H. V. (2021). Federated learning for Internet of Things: A comprehensive survey. *IEEE Communications Surveys & Tutorials, 23*, 1622–1658. https://doi.org/10.1109/comst.2021.3075439 (accessed on 17th October 2025).

30. Nguyen, D. T., Xuan-Ninh, H., & Le, K. H. (2022). MidSiot: A multistage intrusion detection system for Internet of Things. *Wireless Communications and Mobile Computing, 2022*, 1–15. https://doi.org/10.1155/2022/9173291 (accessed on 17th October 2025).

31. Nguyen, T. T., & Reddi, V. J. (2021). Deep reinforcement learning for cyber security. *IEEE Transactions on Neural Networks and Learning Systems, 34*, 3779–3795. https://doi.org/10.1109/tnnls.2021.3121870 (accessed on 17th October 2025).

32. Pinto Neto, E. C., Dadkhah, S., Ferreira, R., Zohourian, A., Lu, R., & Ghorbani, A. A. (2023). CICIoT2023: A real-time dataset and benchmark for large-scale attacks in IoT environment. *Sensors, 23*, 5941–5941. https://doi.org/10.3390/s23135941 (accessed on 17th October 2025).

33. Pritika, P., Shanmugam, B., & Azam, S. (2023). Risk assessment of heterogeneous IoMT devices: A review. *Technologies, 11*, 31–31. https://doi.org/10.3390/technologies11010031 (accessed on 17th October 2025).

34. Raoof, M. M., Aldaghmi, N., & Aljuaid, H. (2025). IoT security in healthcare: A recent trend and predictive study of SQL injection attacks. *The Journal of Engineering.* https://www.semanticscholar.org/paper/9c99a57d6680a69116a1eba90aee35bb8bdef0a6 (accessed on 17th October 2025).

35. Rasheed, A., San, O., & Kvamsdal, T. (2020). Digital twin: Values, challenges and enablers from a modeling perspective. *IEEE Access, 8*, 21980–22012. https://doi.org/10.1109/access.2020.2970143 (accessed on 17th October 2025).

36. Rey, V., Sánchez Sánchez, P. M., Huertas Celdrán, A., & Bovet, G. (2022). Federated learning for malware detection in IoT devices. *Computer Networks, 204*, 108693–108693. https://doi.org/10.1016/j.comnet.2021.108693 (accessed on 17th October 2025).

37. Romano, N. (2019). Securing our future homes: Smart home security issues and solutions. https://core.ac.uk/download/213463704.pdf (accessed on 17th October 2025).

38. Sarker, I. H. (2022). AI-based modeling: Techniques, applications and research issues towards automation, intelligent and smart systems. *SN Computer Science, 3.* https://doi.org/10.1007/s42979-022-01043-x (accessed on 17th October 2025).
39. Sengar, H. S. (2024). An ECC based secure authentication protocol for M2M communication in industrial IoT edge device. *International Journal for Research in Applied Science and Engineering Technology, 12*, 30–40. https://doi.org/10.22214/ijraset.2024.62939 (accessed on 17th October 2025).
40. Serror, M., Hack, S., Henze, M., Schuba, M., & Wehrle, K. (2020). Challenges and opportunities in securing the Industrial Internet of Things. *IEEE Transactions on Industrial Informatics, 17*, 2985–2996. https://doi.org/10.1109/tii.2020.3023507 (accessed on 17th October 2025).
41. Sinha, S., & Sindhu, B. (2021). Impact of DoS attack in IoT system and identifying the attacker location for interference attacks. *2022 7th International Conference on Communication and Electronics Systems (ICCES).* https://doi.org/10.1109/icces51350.2021.9489041 (accessed on 17th October 2025).
42. Slupska, J., & Tanczer, L. M. (2021). Threat modeling intimate partner violence: Tech abuse as a cybersecurity challenge in the Internet of Things. *Emerald Publishing Limited eBooks.* https://doi.org/10.1108/978-1-83982-848-520211049 (accessed on 17th October 2025).
43. Udoh, E., & Udoh, E. (2019). An energy aware and secure MAC protocol for tackling denial of sleep attacks in wireless sensor networks. https://core.ac.uk/download/305119264.pdf (accessed on 17th October 2025).
44. Wang, C. X., You, X., Gao, X., Zhu, X., Li, Z., Zhang, C., Wang, H., et al. (2023). On the road to 6G: Visions, requirements, key technologies, and testbeds. *IEEE Communications Surveys & Tutorials, 25*, 905–974. https://doi.org/10.1109/comst.2023.3249835 (accessed on 17th October 2025).
45. Wang, Y., Su, Z., Zhang, N., Xing, R., Liu, D., Luan, T. H., & Shen, X. (2022). A survey on Metaverse: Fundamentals, security, and privacy. *IEEE Communications Surveys & Tutorials, 25*, 319–352. https://doi.org/10.1109/comst.2022.3202047 (accessed on 17th October 2025).

CHAPTER 4

NETWORK AND COMMUNICATION PROTOCOLS

Contents

INTRODUCTION

The realm of network and communication protocols is at the heart of modern digital communications, facilitating unhindered interaction among systems, devices, and users. At its core, the field underscores the need for structured and standardized procedure through which data may be communicated over networks. With increases in the number of devices linked, the relevance of robust protocols increases as a way to manage such complexity. Here, protocols are the collections of rules defining how data packets are created, transmitted, and decoded in a manner that information reaches its destination intact and uncorrupted. Both wired and wireless media are governed by these sophisticated systems preserving the integrity and security of communications and enabling hence applications ranging from simple internet browsing to sophisticated vehicular networks. In the past few years, the need for dedicated communication protocols has grown exponentially with the advent of new technologies such as vehicular ad-hoc networks (VANETs). With the increasing number of cars filling the urban streets, efficient vehicle-to-vehicle communication has been a pressing issue. Annu et al. (2017) adds that traditional routing techniques have a tendency to fail short of what is required under the dynamic environments common in VANETs and therefore propel the initiatives towards developing more adaptive alternatives. An example is the GEOCROSS routing protocol that has been developed to outsmart the limitations of existing practices by optimizing the effectiveness of routing data packets even in complex scenarios such as cross-links. The exploration of such emerging protocols is not only an insight into communication technology's past but also highlights the research that aims to enhance and simplify vehicular communication systems. Additionally, handling data in a large-scale wireless sensor network has its own set of challenges, namely concerning energy constraints and knowledge of the network topology. Albano et al. (2015) elucidates how these have led to the establishment of geographic routing protocols that do not depend on in-depth knowledge of the network. These protocols, such as the Enhanced Greedy Perimeter Stateless Routing (EGPSR), facilitate effective data transmission by utilization of a sensor's geographical location to navigate through the network. This is an important breakthrough in optimizing sensor networks' lifespan at lower energy consumption. The interaction between technological innovation and protocol development is typical of the evolving nature of the industry and points to the vital role of network and communication protocols in shaping the future of digital communication.

Definition of Network Protocols

Network protocols is a term that encompasses a set of rules and conventions that are in standardized form to direct the receipt and sending of data across a network. Network protocols act as core frameworks that enable the coordination of proper communication among different devices, platforms, and systems. Critical at the center of network protocols is interoperability and reliability of data exchange. Each protocol handles single aspects of network communication, for instance, error control, data format, and sending. For instance, the Internet Protocol (IP) is critical in addressing and sending packets of data, and the Transmission Control

Protocol (TCP) sends data accurately and in order. The cooperative working of these protocols provides the ability for different systems to communicate fluently, thereby enabling the sophisticated network of global connectivity. In the dynamic environment of digital communication, protocols are then classified into different categories based on functionalities and layers where they operate. An essential networking model, Open Systems Interconnection (OSI) model, explains a multi-layered approach towards encapsulating such protocols. The layers range from physical data transmission level to application level where end-user function occurs. Protocols such as the Hypertext Transfer Protocol (HTTP) and File Transfer Protocol (FTP) operate at higher layers, enabling web traffic and file transfer, respectively. Protocols at lower layers, such as the Point-to-Point Protocol (PPP), handle the inherent information of data link layer communications. This kind of hierarchical arrangement not only enables the analysis of protocols but also allows easier troubleshooting and upgrading procedures within networking systems, ensuring ongoing improvements in communication effectiveness.

Figure 4.1. The term network protocols encapsulate a set of standardized rules and conventions that dictate how data is transmitted and received across a network.

Source: https://www.auvik.com/wp-content/uploads/2024/06/common-network-protocols-scaled.jpg.

As increasingly large networks become more complex, network protocol security has taken a priority position. Ensuring data carried is kept confidential and intact is crucial in environments under threat of attack. Most protocols employ cryptography methods to secure data, but research indicates that these methods alone might not be effective against sophisticated threats. For instance, routing protocol research in wireless sensor networks highlights the needs of intrinsically robust designs that accept malicious intrusion despite having a portion of network nodes compromised. These protocols are often made robust because of their topological and behavioral properties that adapt to real-time dynamic threats. With the knowledge and creation of these characteristics, network designers are able to enhance security measures, thereby enhancing safe communication across a variety of varying platforms and devices, which remains an essential objective within network and communication protocols (Erdene-Ochir et al., 2010; Lanotte et al., 2018) (Figure 4.1).

Importance of Communication Protocols in Networking

Communication protocols are networking building blocks whereby the organized exchange of information among devices takes place. Protocols play a crucial role in the establishment of commonly acceptable standards that govern the transport of data, such as data integrity, reliability, and maximum bandwidth utilization. In the absence of protocols, heterogeneous devices cannot interpret and manage information effectively, resulting in a heterogeneous communications environment. The complexities of modern networks, particularly those involving multiple technologies and standards, identify the imperative need for trustworthy communication protocols to synchronize the interactions. Furthermore, as networks advance to incorporate advanced technologies like wireless vehicular cooperative systems, there is a greater need for end-to-end protocols. These networks are based on real-time information sharing among infrastructure and vehicles, demonstrating how communication standards translate to operation efficiencies and promote safer traffic management in smart city projects (Cartolano et al., 2008). Security and energy efficiency interaction within network protocols is essential, more so in Mobile Ad hoc Networks (MANETs).

Multicast routing protocols in such environments represent the significance of unambiguously defined communication standards. These protocols enable efficient data dissemination among several users and support the dynamic topologies of wireless environments. Balancing energy consumption against security requirements for forwarding the data is difficult, hence the necessity to engineer sophisticated solutions tailored to specific network demands. Indeed, multicast routing can leverage the wireless communication broadcast nature to maximize bandwidth efficiency, in most instances bounded in the mobile context. The continuous evolution of multicast routing technologies signals the dynamic nature of communication protocols and how they enhance network optimization and security (Meghanathan et al., 2010). Essentially, as much as communication protocols are mere carriers of data transmission, their significance goes beyond that. Compatibility and the potential for future improvements in network technology are made possible by them. As the interconnectedness and complexity of networks grow, the necessity of robust communication protocols for smooth interconnection between varying devices becomes starkly highlighted. Additionally, with new wireless technologies and standards ongoing to develop, the necessity exists to develop and transform existing protocols to keep them ongoing and effective. The ongoing advancement is not merely enhancing the experience of users through faster, more reliable connections but also reinforcing the foundation in order to meet new applications. As the world is calling for seamless communication over everything else, understanding and implementing effective communication channels will be critical in our pursuit of innovative networking mechanisms that are effective and secure (Figure 4.2).

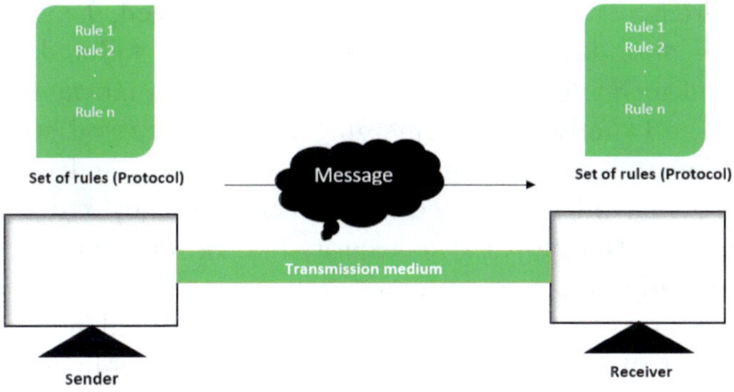

Figure 4.2. Communication protocols serve as foundational components in networking, facilitating the orderly exchange of data among devices.

Source: https://media.geeksforgeeks.org/wp-content/cdn-uploads/20200625134316/1118.png.

4.1. TYPES OF NETWORK PROTOCOLS

In the context of network protocols, classifying them based on their use and function can be used to comprehend their significance in facilitating communication between networks. A primary class of network protocols is the TCP, which is executed at the transport layer. TCP facilitates reliable, in-order, and error-checked data transfer of a data stream between applications on the hosts. Such reliability is achieved with the help of handshaking mechanisms; therefore, TCP is traditionally utilized in applications where accuracy is needed, such as web browsing and email sending. There also exists the UDP that differs from TCP through its emphasis on speed at the cost of reliability by sending messages without establishing a connection first. This makes UDP most appropriate for applications where some data loss is acceptable, such as on-line video games or audio and video streaming in real time, illustrating the diverse functionality of these essential protocols. Furthermore, on a higher layer in the network, various application-layer protocols manage the transfer of data between systems, reinforcing the topic of interoperability of various applications. For instance, HTTP forms the foundation of web communications, giving access to web pages from servers. Similarly, SMTP defines the email transfer, while FTP offers the file transfer through networks. All protocols are guided to a specific use case, allowing applications to communicate effectively. This variety demonstrates the necessity of specialized network protocols for diverse kinds of data transfer; thus, the correct protocol is applied in accordance with the requirements of an individual application. Indeed, the variation among different application-layer protocols demonstrates the tailored ways to meet user needs and technological demands. Additionally, innovations in network protocols are still motivated by emerging technologies and security threats. With increasing usage depending on cloud computing and mobile devices, newer protocols have been devised to enhance efficiency and security across various platforms. Transport Layer Security (TLS), for example, is a protocol devised specifically to secure communication over a computer network in order to protect data integrity and privacy in transit. As indicated in recent literature, the development of privacy-preserving neural network inference models has necessitated efficient communication protocols to preserve the user information without sacrificing high performance values (Bi et al., 2024). Concurrently, the simulators that verify different functionalities of network protocols are critical sources of network behavior and optimization insights (Oikonomou et al., 2024). All these advances emphasize the changing nature of network protocols, which continuously mature to respond to the increasing complexity and demands of networked systems.

4.1.1. Transmission Control Protocol (TCP)

TCP is one of the foundational components of the Internet Protocol Suite, enabling reliable application-to-application communication across connected networks. TCP is a connection-oriented protocol and ensures successful delivery of data in the right order and error-free condition, primarily through techniques such as flow control, error detection, and retransmission of lost packets. This level of dependability is vital for application in applications with guaranteed data integrity such as file transfer and exchange via email. Moreover, the intrinsic nature of TCP allows it to adapt with network situations, dealing with congestion through control of rate of data transmission. These features have led to its extensive application, making TCP a central protocol in internet communication resilience and accommodating various types of applications (Haryono, 2025). Unlike its expected behavior, TCP does produce greater latency due to its advanced mechanisms in order to highlight error recovery and state management. Such latency becomes troublesome for delay-sensitive applications like real-time gaming or live audio and video streaming. For such applications, UDP is typically employed, as it is connectionless in nature, resulting in faster data transfer with lower overhead. But it comes at the expense of reliability, and that can lead to data corruption and packet loss. Whether TCP or UDP would be used, therefore, depends on the application's needs. Programmers must weigh the need for reliability against speed and determine which protocol is better suited to the application's functionality and with which they can deliver maximum performance (Mishra et al., 2024). Recent TCP optimization advancements are important, as they reflect the ongoing enhancement of network protocols to meet increasing internet traffic and diverse application demands. New approaches, such as decision tree-based congestion control algorithms, have been proposed to drastically enhance TCP performance. Such algorithms utilize prediction-based algorithms to dynamically tune data transmission parameters based on real-time network conditions, ultimately reducing congestion and increasing bandwidth utilization. These developments demonstrate the changing dynamics of network communication, in which protocols like TCP can be augmented to support modern problems, allowing efficient data transmission despite congested or high-latency environments. With further development in network architectures, the resiliency and tuning of TCP will remain essential in coping with the demands of today's digital communication (Mishra et al., 2024) (Figure 4.3).

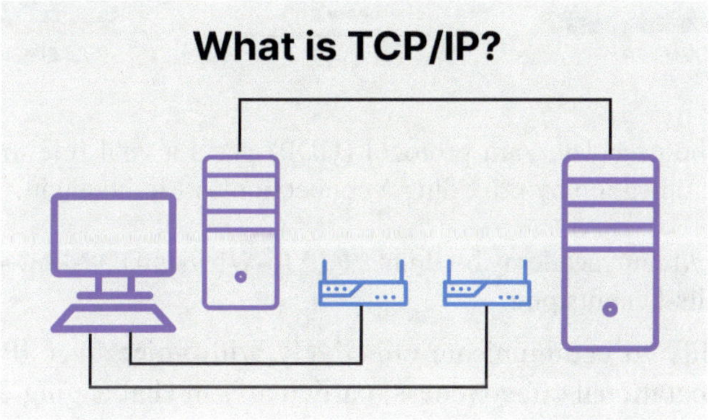

Figure 4.3. Transmission Control Protocol (TCP) is a critical component of the Internet Protocol Suite, establishing reliable communication between applications across interconnected networks.

Source: https://www.fortinet.com/content/dam/fortinet/images/cyberglossary/tcp-ip.jpg.

4.1.2. Internet Protocol (IP)

The IP is the backbone of modern network and communication protocols, providing for data exchange among connected systems. IP in its simplest function is committed to addressing and routing packets of data, having data sent from one device reach its destination. The dynamic nature of the Internet necessitates protocols that are capable of operating under changing circumstances, and IP facilitates this by means of IPv4 and IPv6 standards. The transition from IPv4 to the bigger IPv6 was largely driven by the need for expanded address space and improved network efficiency. This step highlights the central role IP plays in being capable of handling massive networks without sacrificing effective communication even while the number of devices on the Internet keeps growing exponentially. Within battlefield contexts, the requirement for reliable VoIP communications has given rise to such specialized protocols as the SIP. SIP is designed for the creation and management of voice sessions within IP networks and is hence central to push-to-talk communications and situational awareness sharing among troops.

Figure 4.4. The user datagram protocol (UDP) plays a vital role in the realm of network communication by providing a connectionless, lightweight.

Source: https://bunnyacademy.b-cdn.net/F7AJp-What-Is-UDP-how-does-it-work-and-what-are-its-benefits.png.

The ability to communicate effectively with voice over IP networks is essential to operational effectiveness, particularly in challenging environments such as forested battlefields. The development and deployment of SIP underpin the significant advancements in communications protocols that are oriented around performance and price, proving IP's ability to support tactical operations through upgraded connectivity and coordination (Sabila et al., 2021). Besides, multiple IP protocol performance critically affects voice and video transmission quality over the Internet. Comparing VoIP traffic for various configurations such as IPv4, IPv6, and IPv4 with NAT offers extremely critical observations regarding operating behaviors and performance across various bandwidth regimes. Such testing is crucial to optimize communication systems, especially in situations where voice and video streaming are used simultaneously. Understanding the interaction of different IP protocols enhances our ability to design robust communication systems based on specific operational constraints. Lastly, ongoing evaluation of IP and associated protocols is still essential in order to attain safe and high-quality multimodal communications in both civilian and military applications (Kovacik et al., 2021) (Figure 4.4).

4.1.3. User Datagram Protocol (UDP)

The UDP plays an essential role in the world of network communication by providing a connectionless, lightweighther to the TCP. Unlike TCP's establishment of a reliable connection through handshakes and acknowledgments, UDP allows datagrams or packets of data to be sent without direct connection establishment. It is this characteristic that makes UDP particularly desirable for applications requiring speed and efficiency over reliability, such as online gaming, streaming media, and real-time voice. The protocol design achieves optimal performance via the minimization of latency, a critical factor for user experiences involving immediate response and minimal delay durations. Hence, its inherent speed-reliability trade-off provides good scenarios of usage where transmission speed of the data is given higher priority than error correction and data integrity. The streamlining of UDP, however, has its price tag. The absence of any inherent error detection or correction mechanism implies that any loss or data corruption has to be dealt with at the application level. For instance, protocol design for applications based on UDP typically involves measures to deal with packet loss, such as through use of sequence numbers or duplicate information. Furthermore, this may be preceded by increased application complexity because the programmers must anticipate and avoid issues from packet loss. Nevertheless, UDP's performance advantages are typically deemed worth the risks involved. This has resulted in it being used extensively in situations where performance is paramount, even though such usage may require additional error-recovery mechanisms. Its use in real-world applications has served to demonstrate the special place that UDP holds among network protocols. Domain Name System (DNS) queries, streaming media services, and VoIP programs are some of the applications that highlight its uses. For example, in the case of streaming, slight delays in providing data might be acceptable to maintain a seamless streaming process. Similarly, in DNS lookups, rapid response of queries without the overhead of setting up the connection can significantly boost web browsing performance. UDP's instability is also illustrated by its usage in real-time applications where even minimal delays would destroy user experiences. Against this backdrop, researchers and developers continue to advocate for fine-tuning UDP implementations in the construction of resilience against the character of its constraints. Measures to expand usage scenarios have been documented, fortifying the argument for UDPs' continued relevance in network and communication protocols (Brunstrom et al., 2016; Eggert et al., 2008).

4.2. LAYERS OF NETWORK PROTOCOLS

Network protocols are typically developed to an architecture envisioned in a layer model, which segments the complex functions necessary for network communications into usable parts. These layers commonly include the application, transport, network, data link, and physical layers, each playing distinct roles in data transmission. The application layer communicates directly with end-user software, allowing protocols like HTTP and FTP to define how programs on the network send messages. The second level of transport ensures data packets are delivered consistently across the network via protocols such as TCP and UDP, specifying rules for error detection and flow control. This formal procedure enhances manageability and interoperation between network systems so that various technology stacks can communicate easily with each other, which is critical in meeting modern communications needs. For mobile ad hoc networks, the protocol layers of the network are tested in a way that differs from fixed networks, primarily concerning the establishment of peer-to-peer trust among nodes. Ad hoc networks lack such an environment compared to fixed infrastructures in traditional networks, and nodes have to rely on each other to relay and deliver messages. Decentralization complicates the authentication procedure necessary for secure communication. As postulated in the literature, nodes will find it difficult to understand whether they can trust their neighbors or not and if they are merely forwarding incorrect information. Therefore, security protocols must be well designed to protect the data link and network layers from potential threats, and various authentication mechanisms have been proposed. These include challenge-response protocols and zero-knowledge proofs, both of which are intended to ensure the integrity and confidentiality of communications in these sorts of dynamic and often dynamic environments (Douligeris et al., 2007). Quality of Service (QoS) is another important aspect of network protocols, particularly where bandwidth and latency can play a large role in affecting performance. Protocol architecture improvements, such as in the Multi-mission Advanced Communications Hybrid Environment for Test and Evaluation (MACHETE) system, set the stage for incorporating QoS on network and data link layers. The MACHETE system emphasizes the development of virtual channels that support multiple streams of data with provision for sustaining levels of priorities. This provides finer-grained management of data traffic and resource allocations to enable maximum performance in a variety of operational environments. By mapping IP streams onto virtual channels, the framework transcends limitations of traditional QoS classifications and allows for advanced queuing and scheduling policies. Thus, on the basis of these layered protocols, there is better performance along with overall reliability of communication networks under mission-critical usage (Jennings et al., 2025) (Figure 4.5).

Figure 4.5. Quality of service (QoS) is another critical aspect of network protocols, particularly prominent in environments where bandwidth and latency can significantly impact performance.

Source: https://www.fita.in/wp-content/uploads/2024/02/Quality-of-Service-QoS-Services.jpg.

4.2.1. OSI Model Overview

The Open Systems Interconnection (OSI) model serves as a guide book to be used to explain and standardize the intricate functions that occur in the communication of networks. The International Organization for Standardization (ISO) created it because it specifies seven distinct layers each responsible for some tasks that are responsible for making data transfer between systems effective. OSI models impose order on the complex processes that are inherent in networking, ranging from carrying signals physically to application-level interactions. Therefore, it provides different systems and technologies to communicate easily, establishing a level of interoperability that is most essential in the current multi-aspect digital era. It is important for network specialists to comprehend this layered approach because it enables troubleshooting, design, and improving the functionality of the network. The first three layers of the OSI model, physical, data link, and network, are of most significance in ensuring effective communication among devices. The physical layer ensures the transmission of raw bits via a physical medium, setting the foundation for data exchanges. The data link layer then provides error correction and detection mechanisms, ensuring data going over the physical layer is valid and properly transferred. The network layer subsequently ensures the routing of data packets over multiple paths to their destination, effectively addressing traffic management and addressing.

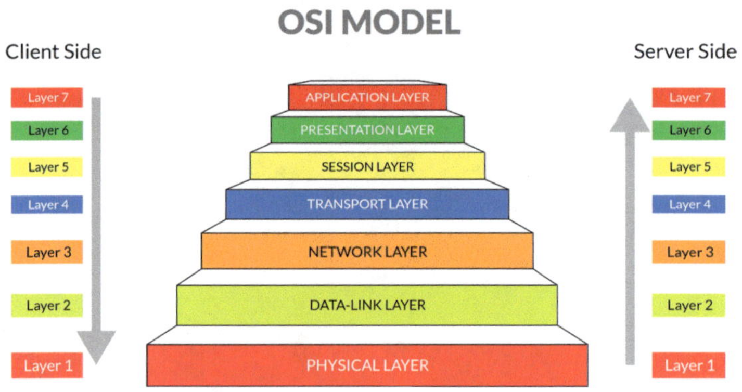

Figure 4.6. The open systems interconnection (OSI) model serves as a foundational framework for understanding and standardizing the complex interactions that occur within network communication.

Source: https://eshielditservices.com/wp-content/uploads/2024/05/OSI-Model.png.

These layers inspire one another to form a harmonious system of communication with each one playing an integral part in data integrity and performance optimization. Looking at these layers makes practitioners value classical networking issues as well as modern issues. In application today, such as small satellite systems, the implications of the OSI model are carried to leading-edge frontiers. As described in recent research, the OSI model directs the design of inter-satellite communications to support complex missions in navigation, remote sensing, and science exploration. The small satellite constellations need reliable inter-satellite communications, advanced routing, and dynamic network configurations to achieve mission objectives. For instance, support for operations by both the physical and data link layers has been improved through the adoption of the OSI model. Not only does this demonstrate the adaptability of the OSI model, but it also illustrates its ongoing relevance in addressing new technologies and changing landscape of network and communication protocols, as provided in Afghah et al. (2016) (Figure 4.6).

4.2.2. TCP/IP Model Overview

The Transmission Control Protocol/Internet Protocol (TCP/IP) model is the internet infrastructure and specifies how data is transmitted between networks. TCP/IP is made up of four layers: application layer, transport layer, internet layer, and link layer, with differing functionalities crucial for facilitating the interaction between devices. The application layer allows user-level programs to communicate, employing protocols such as HTTP and FTP to receive and send information. On the other hand, the transport layer provides the reliable delivery of data through protocols like TCP and UDP, taking care of error detection and correction. Packet routing across multiple networks falls in the internet layer's scope, while direct connection and transfer of data across physical media is delivered by the link layer. All these layers combined offer a robust foundation for diverse network communication and illustrate how layered protocols can simplify complex interaction between systems. In the TCP/IP model, encapsulation of data is a pivotal process utilized for controlling and organizing data as it moves through all of the various layers. The process of encapsulation involves each layer adding its own header information, which is utilized to send data packets correctly and reconstruct them at their point of destination. For example, at the transport layer, a TCP segment wraps data packets and required information for reliable communications like sequence numbers and acknowledgment fields.

Then, at the internet layer, the segment is translated into an IP packet along with routing information. This systematic process not only assists in data integrity but also becomes more efficient, allowing multiple connections and types of data streams to be processed at the same time. The non chunky dialogue between layers is a classic representation of the complexity of the TCP/IP model and speaks to its centrality in today's networking. Not only is TCP/IP the backbone of the internet architecture but it also governs the design and deployment of several security and analytical tools. Network analyzers, as noted in Takács et al. (2010), utilize the capability of the TCP/IP model to monitor network traffic and identify communication protocols operating at the application layer. By analyzing the payload of TCP and UDP packets, these analyzers obtain information about the health of the network and the performance of applications. Furthermore, its widespread use transcends the mere communication of data; the level of impact extends to the way organizations budget for network security protocols and optimize performance. This TCP/IP model's adaptability makes it a benchmark in the universe of network and communication protocols, with room for even more innovation and improvement in the data communications standards.

4.2.3. Comparison of OSI and TCP/IP Models

The comparison of OSI and TCP/IP models is the basis of understanding current network and communication protocols because the two models offer frameworks for the understanding of data transfer over networks. The OSI model that was developed by the International Organization for Standardization (ISO) consists of seven layers—Application, Presentation, Session, Transport, Network, Data Link, and Physical. On the other hand, the TCP/IP model is a more streamlined model which functions on four layers: Application, Transport, Internet, and Network Interface. Layer separation in both models simplifies it to troubleshoot and build but the OSI models greater number of layers exercises finer control over network interaction while the TCP/IP model is more concerned with real-world application than adherence to conceptual layers (Bebek et al., 2015). One of the major points of comparison between the OSI and TCP/IP models is in how they handle protocol specification. The OSI model is a theoretical framework that describes how protocols communicate but does not specify implementation. This opens up room for multiple protocols to be accommodated by the OSI layers such that a larger range of applications can be supported in various systems. On the other hand, the TCP/IP model is being developed from the ground up using real protocols, the Transmission Control Protocol and Internet Protocol, that authenticate its focus on operational networks.

The architecture of the TCP/IP model is a product of the requirements for interoperability and efficient communication, hence the preferred framework for most internet-based applications today (Bebek et al., 2015). Furthermore, the theoretical differences between the two models also manifest at their network functionality and scope. The OSI model provides a total layered model that not only maps the multiple processes involved in data transmission but also outlines how these processes connect to each other. This entirety can be an advantage in the classroom because it outlines a tidy, systematic view of networking. TCP/IP is the functional standard now, however, due to its simplicity and efficiency in facilitating internet communications. With numerous protocols being developed on top of it, TCP/IP has managed to adapt to evolving requirements of global networking, anticipating its relevance in theoretical as well as practical contexts. Understanding these models' strengths and weaknesses is crucial for future network and communication protocol development (Bebek et al., 2015).

4.3. FUNCTIONS OF COMMUNICATION PROTOCOLS

Effective communication protocols are essential to facilitate the exchange of data between varying types of networks, hence facilitating compatibility between devices. The protocols carry out a number of operations, including establishing, managing, and closing down communication sessions. Protocols determine rules that govern data exchanges and provide a formalized means of handling errors and controlling data flow, which becomes crucial in instances of high traffic or unreliable connections.

For instance, in the IoT scenario, heterogeneous devices' convergence mandates that they support standardized communication protocols such as MQTT and AMQP. Such protocols have been identified as key in the development of robust architectures that can efficiently handle the varying needs of various IoT components, as outlined in Pielli et al. (2015). A disciplined communication technique can drastically improve the effectiveness and reliability of data transmission across networks. Additionally, developments in communication networks, particularly with the advent of technologies like 5G, bring into focus the increasing demands on communication protocols to support low-latency and high-throughput services. As the services that require real-time data exchange have become more numerous, the role of protocols becomes even more important to ensure the required factors without compromising the network integrity.

Low-latency communication is required in services such as self-driving cars, telemedicine, and online gaming, where latency will have consequential effects. Thus, network operators are faced with the challenge of upscaling their infrastructure to keep up with these new demands, as indicated in Cuevas et al. (2017). Upgrading in such a way is an indicator of the critical function of communication protocols in facilitating the emerging ecosystem of digital connectivity and innovative services. In addition to enhancing the effectiveness and reliability of communication, protocols also facilitate the secure transfer of information from one network to another. This is more critical today with the digital age, where data exposure and unauthorized access could potentially have far-reaching consequences.

Communication protocols are built with security features that make data encrypted during transit, with confidentiality and integrity being assured. Protocols like HTTPS and TLS are prime examples of this function, offering secure communication over possibly insecure networks. The importance of such security protocols is also emphasized in the context of international data protection law, with its stringent controls on individual data. Therefore, communication protocols not only dictate information transit but also protect the information against external attack, adding to their double-edged role within network systems designed to service an increasingly globalized world (Figure 4.7).

Figure 4.7. Effective communication protocols are essential for facilitating the transmission of data across various network types, thereby ensuring interoperability among devices.

Source: https://agilevision.io/_astro/5.BB0JrbAV_pSOng.webp.

4.3.1. Data Encapsulation

Data encapsulation is the basis for the functioning of network and communication protocols and is a process of data wrapping and passing through a network. Data encapsulation merely involves data being wrapped with protocol information necessary in every level of the OSI (Open Systems Interconnection) model. This not only maintains data integrity but also enables unimpeded communication between heterogeneous systems by representing data in a predefined format. The appended header or trailer at each layer conveys vital information such as source and destination addresses or error-detecting digits. Therefore, data encapsulation ensures interpretation of data by the sending and receiving devices in the right way, and hence facilitates transparent communication between heterogeneous networks, a fundamental necessity in today's computing environments with heterogeneity. Encapsulation of data also provides security and efficiency in network communication. By dividing the data into layers, encapsulation eliminates exposure to potential vulnerabilities because each layer can implement its own set of security solutions for known vulnerabilities. For example, in the transport layer, protocols like TCP (Transmission Control Protocol) carry out error detection to ensure safe data transmission, while the network layer is responsible for routing data packets in the best possible manner.

This layering not only helps secure the entire system, but it also optimizes bandwidth usage so that various types of traffic (e.g., video, voice, data) can be supported on the same infrastructure. Consequently, the encapsulation process plays a pivotal role in tackling data transport complexities to ensure effective interaction among devices. Moreover, active network development offers promising ways of enhancing data encapsulation procedures. Compared to the static method of using networks, where the user may not run code via networks, active networks offer potential for dynamic running of user code by nodes in the network, changing the way data is received and sent. This programmability enables more sophisticated processing of information in the encapsulation, enabling nodes to behave responsively in varying network conditions and also user loads. This responsiveness increases the efficiency of data transfer and also promises future breakthroughs in resource-sharing models, hence facilitating a broad range of applications. With ongoing advancements in active network research, the implications for data encapsulation and network performance as a whole increase ever more, paving the way for a new generation of smart communication protocols that can better service the needs of current networking environments (Brunstrom et al., 2016; Fatta et al., 2001).

4.3.2. Error Detection and Correction

Error detection and correction are essential components of communication and network protocols, particularly where data integrity is the highest requirement. Data, as it is being transmitted across several networks, will be subject to interference, and hence could become corrupted. Checksum, cyclic redundancy check (CRC), and error-correcting codes (ECC) are a few such protocols that have important roles in error detection that can occur due to transmission. These processes enable systems not only to identify inconsistency but also to correct it, ensuring that the information received is identical to the information sent. For instance, in the case of satellite communication, as outlined in the NUTS reliable protocol design (NRP), effective error detection and correction mechanism plays a vital role in providing a reliable communication channel between the satellite and ground stations, especially in environments susceptible to cosmic radiation, which alters electronic data integrity (Jahren et al., 2015). The design of robust communication protocols often incorporates redundancy as a fundamental technique of error management. Redundancy may be manifested in many forms, like redundant data packets or spare bits utilized in the form of parity checking, in a way that enables systems to verify sent data integrity. In highly adaptive network architectures, as proposed in recent technology, dynamic adaptation of error control schemes becomes imperative in response to varying traffic patterns and network states. This flexibility ensures sustained quality of service (QoS) along with optimal bandwidth and energy consumption (Havinga et al., 2000). Employing such adaptive mechanisms helps to manage different kinds of data and maintain the network operational even under unfavorable conditions, hence ensuring overall communication protocol dependability. Furthermore, application of error detection and correction protocols influences network and communication system efficiency more broadly. While data transmission needs increase for use in applications ranging from satellite communications to live video streaming, these processes must be optimized. The successful demonstration and deployment of the NRP for the NUTS CubeSat mission demonstrate how pragmatic benefits are achieved by including improved error management capabilities in the protocol stack. Lastly, these skills enhance the user experience quality by minimizing disturbances and also enable communications technologies to continuously advance to meet the stringent conditions of contemporary applications. As more wireless network deployments are made and applications require more reliable data transfer, error detection and correction will remain a critical factor in deciding on future network protocols (Figure 4.8).

Figure 4.8. Error detection and correction are essential components of network and communication protocols, particularly in scenarios where data integrity is paramount.

Source: https://bluegoatcyber.com/wp-content/uploads/2024/03/img_65f7464c884ce.webp.

4.3.3. Flow Control Mechanisms

Flow control mechanisms are integral parts of communication and network protocols that regulate the rate at which data is transmitted between the receiver and sender. These mechanisms regulate the flow of data packets to ensure that the receiver is not congested and thus may not lead to packet loss and network degradation. Stop-and-wait, sliding window, and credit-based flow control are some of the techniques implemented to enable effective communication. Both of these strategies are different according to the specific needs of the network environment, highlighting the necessity of adaptive methods in various circumstances. Real-time programs, for instance, may favor reduced latency using methods allowing greater amounts of packets to be in transit, and computers with high requirements for reliability may focus on long acknowledgment protocols to avoid loss of data. In the context of IoT, flow control mechanisms are challenged by the resource-constrained environments that are prevalent and dynamic network conditions characteristic of such systems. The Constrained Application Protocol (CoAP) is one of the protocols that have been designed with the explicit goal to enable efficient communication in such an environment. CoAPs support of congestion control mechanisms is extremely essential in the context of group communication because it protects against multicast requests overwhelming the network and thereby conserving bandwidth and power efficiency. Support of such mechanisms becomes critical when numerous devices collaborate with each other, necessitating innovative techniques for efficient data flow control. These performance metrics, such as packet delivery ratio and energy consumption, provide critical insights into the performance of these flow control mechanisms, which can be continually optimized with advancing technology (Fonovi et al., 2024). In addition, information about information flow among various agents in decision-making processes can inform the design of flow control mechanisms tailored for urban transport conditions. In social network analysis, researchers have observed how information is disseminated and maintained as a function of people's position in decision networks. The analysis shows differences in influence and access to resources, which have direct implications for document and communication management. Understanding this is significant for developing protocols that enhance information sharing, thereby facilitating more effective decision-making in complex networks. Identifying influencers and understanding communication barriers can activate the design of efficient flow control systems maximizing the sharing of information among stakeholders. Ultimately, these findings can guide the design of protocols allowing cooperation and strategic interaction between decision-makers in urban transport systems (Alhassan, 2024).

4.4. PROTOCOL STANDARDS AND ORGANIZATIONS

In network and communication protocols, protocol organizations and standards play a central role in bringing about interoperability among disparate systems and consistent practices. International institutions, for instance, the Internet

Engineering Task Force (IETF) and the International Organization for Standardization (ISO), develop and spread these standards. By providing a clearly defined structure to protocol development, such organizations dictate everything from data transport through to security protocols. Their recommendations therefore guarantee that the different technologies cooperate well and efficiently, thereby fostering innovation and the potential to incorporate future technologies in a seamless manner. The complexities that are associated with the Internet's governance and issues surrounding it require these organizations to continually update their protocols, plugging holes in existing standards to meet changing needs of stakeholders and users, as highlighted by Klein et al. (2004). Moreover, the increased application of interconnected devices highlights the importance of robust protocol standards, particularly in the IoT. With billions of devices being connected, protocol standards implication extends beyond connectivity to security, privacy, and reliability. Device interconnectivity requires strong authentication and access control to ensure no cyber-attacks as they become the order of the day with increasingly more devices becoming connected. Standards currently in place must evolve to address the particular challenges of IoT, including vulnerability brought about by poor security solutions. This evolution is imperative not only for the protection of individual devices but also for ensuring the integrity of entire networks—a critical factor in maintaining the trust of users and facilitating large-scale adoption of IoT solutions, as noted in Ali et al. (2019). Generally, the relationship between protocol standards and organizations is fundamental to ensuring network and communication protocol sustainable evolution. As global reliance on technology continues to grow, such forward-thinking posture of these companies will keep protocols modern and functional. The dangers resulting from emerging technologies such as IoT necessitate sustained emphasis on innovation in keeping standards up-to-date and security-and-interoperability centered. Sustained development of protocol standards will continue to combat existing cybersecurity threats and embed innovative solutions that are adapted to suit various needs of users. This self-reinforcing process of improvement is the pillar for effective governance in the era of information, justifying the archaic role of mature organizations as the determinants of the future of network communications by collective means, as evidenced by Klein et al. (2004).

4.4.1. Internet Engineering Task Force (IETF)

The Internet Engineering Task Force (IETF) plays a key role in the development and creation of protocols that are employed to enable network communication. Founded in 1986, the IETF is an open community of engineers and researchers dedicated to the creation and publication of voluntary Internet standards, namely those that pertain to the Transmission Control Protocol/Internet Protocol (TCP/IP) suite. By creating Request for Comments (RFC) documents—critical works offering methodologies, processes, and protocols—the IETF enables open innovation and technological development. Open development ensures that the underlying architecture of the internet is strong, robust, and responsive as well as facilitating future development while at the same time maintaining backward compatibility with technologies that are now available. Among the critical domains addressed by the IETF is developing communications protocols for specific applications and environments.

Figure 4.9. The internet engineering task force (IETF) plays a pivotal role in the establishment and evolution of protocols essential for network communication.

Source: https://media.licdn.com/dms/image/v2/C4D1BAQEtQ2IMw04cPA/company-background_10000/company-background 10000/0/1583329272528?e=2147483647&v=beta&t=7kgkLCAMNvNVFjSALR0O0fBZNcfn5sY1uqiI4HL8ktI.

In particular, the IETF has created the 6TiSCH protocol, a wireless communication stack to support low-power and high-reliability communication in industrial settings. While 6TiSCH provides basic functionalities, significant security issues remain open. The protocol has been criticized for poor inter-device authentication and key management, which is a possible cause of such weaknesses as key leakage or malicious attacks. These weaknesses need to be overcome, and the proposed SAKMS scheme makes use of better elliptic curve cryptography to improve computational efficiency without compromising secure authentication and dynamic updating of keys, a hopeful remedy to secure 6TiSCH-based networks (Yang et al., 2024). Furthermore, IETF is also assisting in harmonizing incompatible communication protocols in the emerging Internet of Things (IoT) market. With numerous different technologies operating in silos, a common framework becomes more important than ever before. IETF achieves interoperability by employing standardized protocols like the eXtensible Messaging and Presence Protocol (XMPP). Not only does the protocol standardize messaging among heterogeneous devices, but it also enhances data ownership as well as trust management on IoT networks. With its capacity to host multiple standards simultaneously and facilitate seamless integration, XMPP serves as a bridge to unite heterogeneous systems, facilitating the vision of an integrated networking architecture. The work of the IETF shows how protocol engineering can lead to an integrated and secure IoT environment where devices talk across each other seamlessly while preserving user privacy and data integrity (Waher et al., 2024) (Figure 4.9).

4.4.2. Institute of Electrical and Electronics Engineers (IEEE)

The Institute of Electrical and Electronics Engineers, or IEEE, is an essential enabler of network and communication protocol advancement and standardization necessary to the contemporary technology ecosystem. Founded in 1884, IEEE is a leading professional association with the task of promoting innovation within a number of different fields but most importantly electrical and electronic engineering. Its focus on standard development ensures that devices will be interoperable, crucial to the growing IoT economy. Through efforts such as the IEEE 802 standards, the organization has developed widely accepted protocols that control wired and wireless networking, enabling devices made by different companies to communicate with each other seamlessly in all types of environments. The standardization is technical but also shapes user experiences and encourages new technology adoption in a wide range of industries. With increased expansion in the IoT, communication overhead and power usage become increasingly important problems, particularly in wireless sensor networks (WSN). The IEEE solves these problems through its research and recommendations, which emphasize the necessity of the creation of lean and light-weight communication protocols that are imperative in battery-powered devices. The organizational devotion to R&D leads to innovation in industrial solutions that are critical in managing sensor-imbedded entities in real-world applications. By promoting a standard network infrastructure that is friendly to various WSN applications, IEEE facilitates the implementation of scalable and sustainable communication networks. This not only demonstrates IEEEs frameworks flexibility but also the reactivity of its frameworks to the evolving technology needs (Leung et al., 2015). Security and privacy issues add to the complexity of the network and communication protocol environment, especially for the IoT. The more devices get connected, the greater the need to ensure the integrity and confidentiality of the data. IEEE's role extends beyond contributing towards resolving these security problems related to different layers of communication in the IoT ecosystem. With a focus on data confidentiality, integrity, and availability principles, IEEE formulates a model to understand and counter vulnerabilities inherent in IoT devices and networks. Through conducting exhaustive surveys and literature review, the organization provides valuable insights into the security landscape with solutions crucial to the broad acceptance and trust of IoT technologies (Mendez et al., 2017). The IEEEs proactive stance on these issues indicates its commitment to not only driving technology forward but also safeguarding users and information in the digital era (Figure 4.10).

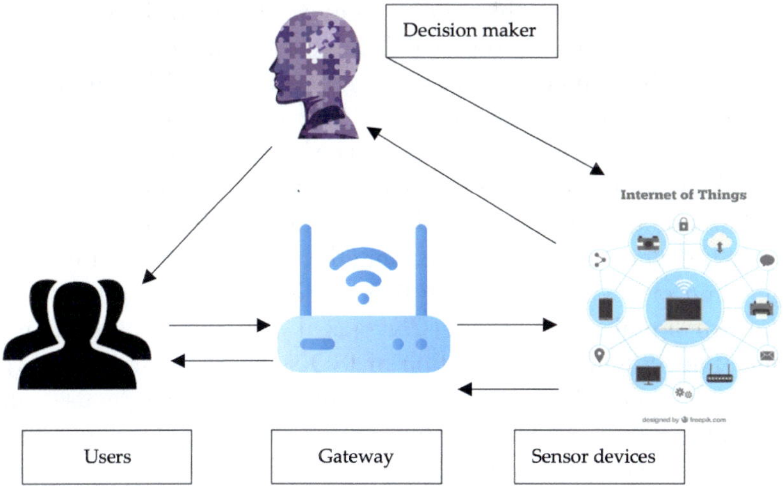

Figure 4.10. As the IoT continues to expand, challenges such as communication overhead and power consumption become increasingly relevant, particularly in wireless sensor networks (WSN).

Source: https://dfzljdn9uc3pi.cloudfront.net/2024/cs-2091/1/fig-1-full.png.

4.4.3. International Organization for Standardization (ISO)

The International Organization for Standardization, or ISO, is a principal organization for standardizing all types of protocols and frameworks for communication and network technologies. ISO was established in 1947, and it encourages international cooperation by developing and issuing standards that facilitate interoperability and quality in industries such as information technology. The success of network protocols depends on simple standards; for instance, the ISO/IEC 27000 series address information security management systems that are essential in safeguarding data in transit. Through the guarantee that organizations will follow standardized procedures, ISO prevents inconsistencies that would arise from disparate technical deployments and enables free flow of information throughout international communications. This congruence not only heightens security but also increases user trust in networked situations, highlighting the deep influence of ISOs in establishing a secured and optimized digital landscape. Cooperation between ISO standards and communication protocols plays a significant role in handling the complexity of quality and interoperability. With various digital systems becoming increasingly interconnected, ensuring smooth interoperation among diverse technologies is a key challenge. Standardization by ISO brings a situation where different systems are able to communicate freely without any potential obstacles arising due to technological incompatibility. The existing research points out the quality dimension as an operational aspect of digital libraries and interoperability, closely connected with ISOs emphasis on maintaining strict quality management across its guidelines. The EU-sponsored project DL.org's Quality Working Group is an example of how to achieve quality interoperability, which includes models consistent with ISOs strategic objectives. These efforts are part of a broader effort towards pushing the standardization of network and communication protocols practice so that quality interoperability is a natural part of modern digital environments (Clavel et al., 2010). In the current network communication setting, the application of ISO standards ensures that systems are dynamic and scalable in an ever-changing technological landscape. With increased international data flows, the contribution of ISOs input into data management protocols is even more crucial. For instance, the use of effective interoperability frameworks, founded upon the DELOS Reference Model, provides a structured approach to enhancing communication quality between systems. The value of this systematic approach is echoed in the development of the Quality Core Model and Quality Interoperability Survey, which examine digital library interoperability complexity (Clavel et al., 2010). Not only do such approaches ease linking systems, but they also facilitate the general goal of building stable communication infrastructures. Lastly, the ISO creates a fundamental foundation upon which communication and network protocols can be built, tested, and implemented to meet the demands of an increasingly changing digital age.

4.5. SECURITY IN NETWORK PROTOCOLS

Security remains a top concern in the evolving networking world, particularly with communications becoming increasingly more wireless in nature. The inherent nature of wireless networks, such as their common data transmission medium, makes them open to attacks that their wired equivalents are immune to. According to Brima (2018), the deployment and design of wireless security protocols have been ridden with serious weaknesses that can be exploited by attackers. The variety of attacks against such weaknesses underscore the need for an extensive investigation of wireless system weaknesses. Through acknowledgment of these flaws, network administrators can fortify wireless protocols better and minimize possible security breaches, making protection of valuable data a top objective for companies reliant on wireless networks. The use of advanced security mechanisms in controlling the sophistication of current networking necessitates adapting to cater to ever more advanced threats. As witnessed in Faezipour et al. (2012), the interplay of rising rates of advancement in communication technologies has led to sophisticated network conditions in which data security and integrity are of utmost importance. Network security does not only apply to protecting data being transmitted, but it is also employed to enhance the performance of distributed systems in general. Implementing high-level algorithms like encryption, authentication, and access controls would considerably minimize the risks from unauthorized access as well as information leakage. With the additional growth of wireless networks, stakeholders must give significance to the formulation of dynamically scalable security protocols to address new threats. Moreover, the integration of new algorithms and methodologies is necessary in developing network security. A technique like the one outlined in the proposed access point check algorithm, as presented in Faezipour et al. (2012), has the potential to make security enhancements without compromising network performance. By using techniques like checksums for message integrity protection, network protocols can authenticate messages and avoid interception of unauthorized messages. As businesses move toward secure wireless communications, empirical evidence from novel approaches can provide actionable advice, ensuring that security measures not only meet current requirements but are also racing with evolving technology. Constant refinement of security measures will make it possible for users and administrators to cope with the complexities of networking with greater confidence.

4.5.1. Importance of Secure Communication

Secure communication in the modern age of digital communication is the building block of network and communication protocols that have a direct impact on all sectors, from personal interactions to organizational operations on a large scale. The necessity of secure communication cannot be overemphasized, particularly when data tampering and cyberattacks are becoming more alarmingly frequent. Ensuring information exchanged between networks is securely passed ensures sensitive data is kept out of unauthorized reach and misuse. Integrity of communications enhances trust between users, especially in sectors like finance, healthcare, and government, where data sensitivity is paramount. Consequently, incorporating robust encryption and authentication procedures in communications protocols is fundamental to individual and corporate data safety, which enhances stakeholders to engage and transact securely without incessant fear of information loss. Besides reminding one of the necessities of secure communication is its relevance to the advancement of emerging technologies like Vehicular Ad-Hoc Networks (VANETs). In VANETs, cars share information real-time to enhance road safety and traffic surveillance. The dynamic and open characteristic of VANETs qualifies them as excellent potential targets for malicious people eager to affect and manage lines of communication.

Figure 4.11. Ensuring that data exchanged across networks is transmitted securely protects sensitive information from unauthorized access and exploitation.

Source: https://www.ibm.com/content/dam/connectedassets-adobe-cms/worldwide-content/stock-assets/adb-stk/ul/g/ac/98/adobestock_876865630.component.crop-2by1-xl.ts=1754067397145.jpeg/content/adobe-cms/us/en/think/topics/data-security/jcr:content/root/leadspace_container/leadspace_article.

Therefore, the implementation of encryption schemes and authentication is important to protect vehicle identities and ensure data integrity being exchanged between vehicles. Authentication of a secure message eliminates the threat of data tampering, thereby enhancing information reliability transmitted over these networks. All these efforts like pseudonym changing tactics, which conceal the identities of users, indicate the focus on protection and privacy, providing a safer platform for car communications (Rajasekaran et al., 2024). Moreover, the development of adaptive security products, such as exemplified by new protocols like GRandLine, depicts the ongoing innovation in secure communication processes. The development of high-impact randomness beacons exemplifies the need for effective yet straightforward measures to dynamic security challenges. These beacons support secure key generation and provision of randomness, critical to guaranteeing compliance with security parameters in a changing network environment. These innovations not only address the technical requirements of secure communication but also compensate for the growing complexities posed by adaptive attackers. As secure communication technologies evolve, so will their integration in current protocols be more important, offering robust protection mechanisms that will adapt to the users' needs as well as create technological models (Bacho et al., 2024) (Figure 4.11).

4.5.2. Common Security Protocols (SSL/TLS)

The expansion of web-based communication necessitates robust security measures to safeguard sensitive information. Normal security procedures, namely Secure Sockets Layer (SSL) and its successor, Transport Layer Security (TLS), play a major role in enabling secure online connections. They function by encrypting data exchanged between servers and clients such that all data taken will be unintelligible to unauthorized users. SSL was first designed to protect online transactions, and it added the factor of security for the personal data exchanged in credit card transactions and other shielded communications. Nowadays, TLS is employed predominantly due to the fact that it addresses some of the vulnerabilities inherent in SSL, and thus enhances the security context of online interactions. While they have been highly developed, there are intrinsic weaknesses in implementations that lead to insecure deployments, which need constant monitoring and betterment of these security controls (Amann et al., 2016). The SSL/TLS infrastructural model relies on the establishment of encrypted sessions, which entails a handshake between communicating parties. This authentication validates the server and optionally the client via cryptographic keys and certificates signed by trusted entities. X.509 Public Key Infrastructures enhance the authentication process to enable users to check whether their communication counterparts are valid or not. Since the environment of cyber-attacks constantly changes, it is difficult to keep these protocols secure. Misconfigurations and the usage of older versions reveal weaknesses that are exploitable by malicious users. Therefore, the community's investment in making SSL/TLS more scalable and resilient is critical in mitigating threat risks that arise due to insecure deployments (Davis et al., 2017). Second, the role of SSL/TLS protocols transcends traditional web deployment; it has a role in protecting mobile communications for various applications. With mobile phones as the dominant computing platform for so many, with functionality ranging from mobile transactions to directions, the potential for taking advantage of insecure connections is there. The current security standards must adapt in this mobile-centric world and emphasize the use of robust security practices that balance usability and security. The evolving requirements of mobile computing mean that future versions of TLS will need to balance high-level security capabilities with easy-to-use experience. By improving these security measures to anticipate and act against likely hazards, developers are able to ensure mobile interactions remain secure and user trust is upheld within a highly connected society (Davis et al., 2017).

4.5.3. Vulnerabilities and Threats in Network Protocols

The inbuilt weaknesses of the network protocols are monumental challenges in the cybersecurity arena. All the layers in the communication protocol stack, i.e., the physical, link, network, transport, and application layers, possess unique vulnerabilities that are susceptible to attacks from the attackers. For instance, the physical layer attacks may be radio frequency interference and jamming based, while the link layer is prone to man-in-the-middle attacks. It is essential to understand these vulnerabilities because they cumulatively form the security profile of wireless networks. Gupta et al. (2013) offers a holistic view of these vulnerabilities by presenting possible attacks at various layers. The narrative highlights the imperative requirement for efficient security measures that will counter these weaknesses without compromising user privacy and guaranteeing effective communication. Attack vectors for network protocols are vast and continually evolving, reinforcing the necessity for thorough defense strategies. Wireless mesh networks (WMNs), in particular, are vulnerable to a multitude of attacks due to their decentralized nature. As an example, attackers have been known to exploit vulnerabilities in key management and user authentication protocols to acquire unauthorized access to network resources. Such effective violations can result in severe data leaks, unauthorized communications, or service impairment. In addition, as noted in Brima (2018), the implementation of cryptographic techniques in wireless security protocols has not necessarily assured the sought-after levels of protection because of design weaknesses and operational failures in widely used systems. This sophistication necessitates multi-dimensional security that not only looks at preventive measures but also effective response mechanisms. In response to the persistent attacks on network protocols, there is a growing emphasis on developing sophisticated security measures. Existing measures need to be extensively tested to ascertain their effectiveness against potential attacks. Gupta et al. (2013) raises the fact that comparative analysis of various security schemes can elucidate their vulnerabilities and strengths, and aid in the selection of appropriate defenses for various applications. In addition, reputation and trust-based schemes are becoming increasingly popular in the context of WMNs as they provide more security through community-based monitoring and accountability. Lastly, strong cryptography, robust risk analysis, and dynamic security will become crucial in safeguarding network protocols from their changing vulnerabilities and risks as well as ensuring secure communication over disparate platforms (Figure 4.12).

Figure 4.12. The vulnerabilities inherent in network protocols present significant challenges in the realm of cybersecurity.

Source: https://cyberexperts.com/wp-content/uploads/images/satellite-cyber-attacks-lyG.jpeg.

4.6. EMERGING TRENDS IN NETWORK PROTOCOLS

The topology of network protocols is evolving very rapidly with advancements in computing capabilities and the general requirement for high-performance applications. As processors become more powerful and storage capabilities increase, the requirements for these to be able to communicate seamlessly increase. New network protocols are developed to cater to the needs of these innovations, particularly for the scenario that requires high bandwidth and low latency. One such notable development is the Axon architecture that integrates hardware, operating systems, and communication protocols for improved performance in high-demand applications. The architectural style is centered on fair division of tasks between software and hardware to enable end-to-end protocol optimization to leverage the capabilities of next-generation high-speed networks in transcending limitations of traditional host-network interfaces (Parulkar et al., 1989). At the same time, the IoT is driving a paradigm shift in network protocols, redefining the engagement rules among devices and communication. As a growing network of connected objects, including RFIDs, sensors, and smart devices, IoT presents new scalability and compatibility challenges. The heterogenous set of IoT solutions presented by various entities suggests a trend towards innovative, application-oriented protocols designed to introduce functionality and usability. Some examples include protocols such as MQTT and CoAP, which have been optimized for communication in constrained environments and facilitating the effective transfer of data without overwhelming network resources. Such developments attest to a growing realization that special protocols are necessary to support many smart applications, and much can be said for the scope of IoT technologies to facilitate interconnected ecosystems that enhance day-to-day life (Jayawardena et al., 2015). Moreover, the implementation of these new protocols is not without its challenge and implication. As networks continue to become more complicated, security and stability are of fundamental importance. New protocols must include advanced security measures designed to contend with the growing list of vulnerabilities of interconnected devices. The transition towards the embrace of greater encryption standards and authentication procedures will not only beef up network defenses but also enhance user trust in smart technology. Looking forward, it is essential that protocol designers remain vigilant to new threats and vulnerabilities and have the capability to adjust their designs according to an ever-changing security environment. This combined approach will play a vital role in the forthcoming development of secure and effective network protocols that are capable of supporting the demands of future applications and technology.

4.6.1. Software-Defined Networking (SDN)

Software-Defined Networking or SDN is a paradigm shift in managing network resources by, in effect, unbundling the control plane and the data plane, a radical departure from traditional networking practices. With this unbundling, it is possible to have the network centrally managed where administrators can configure network services through software applications rather than physical hardware constraints. The effect of this architecture extends beyond the conventional wired networks, as significant effort has been spent to include SDN principles in cellular and wireless networks. In particular, SDN is a key facilitator of the development of 5G communication systems, demonstrating its adaptability to emerging technology demands. Consequently, SDN not only enhances the operational efficiency but also enhances the process of deploying new network services, thereby addressing the growing complexity of the modern digital infrastructures and their multivariant communications requirements

(Alzahrani et al., 2025). The merge of SDN also naturally accompanies the evolution of Information-Centric Networking (ICN), which improves content delivery by focusing on the data rather than the geographical or physical location in which the data resides.

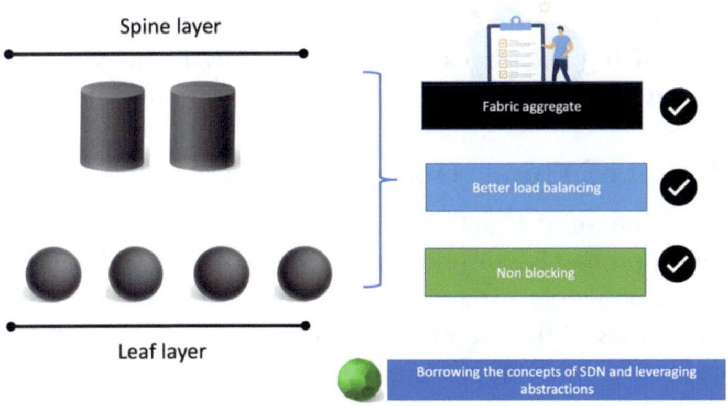

Figure 4.13. Software-defined networking (SDN) represents a transformative approach to managing network resources, effectively decoupling the control plane from the data plane, which marks a significant departure from traditional networking paradigms.

Source: https://network-insight.net/wp-content/uploads/2022/08/rsz_ciso_aci_1-1200x675.png.

This becomes particularly relevant in ultra-dynamic environments, where data needs to be accessed and delivered efficiently and quickly. ICNs capacity to disentangle data from specific transport means positions it as an effective resource for conveying massive sets of data, particularly in application contexts like video streaming and content delivery networks. The marriage of this approach with SDN optimizes the overall efficiency and speed of content distribution within mobile contexts and could transform how end-users' access and interact with data. These new technologies are timely as they respond to the increasing user demand for convenient access to real-time data and quality content from diverse sources (Alzahrani et al., 2025). Furthermore, the incorporation of future technologies like blockchain into the scenario of SDN presents huge potential for the improvement of security and management of the networks. Decentralized and tamper-proof blockchain technology can be employed to address problems of vulnerabilities associated with centrally controlled networks. Blockchain facilitates secure and verifiable transactions between members of the network, hence building trust, openness, and immunity to various forms of cyberattacks like Distributed Denial of Service (DDoS) attacks. The intersection of blockchain and SDN not only streamlines the provisioning of resources as well as network coordination but also strengthens the overall security architecture by the sharing of control as well as evading the risks of points of failure. As research into this intersection progresses, it is paramount that scalability challenges be addressed as well as implementing efficiency-optimizing consensus protocols to allow for maximum leverage of the promise that blockchain can deliver in SDN platforms (Figure 4.13).

4.6.2. Internet of Things (IoT) protocols

The dissemination of the IoT necessitated the development of specialized communication protocols with designs specific to the needs of the connected devices. These protocols offer capabilities for data exchange and sustained connectivity across different environments, from home automation smart homes to industrial-scale applications. Specifically, two important protocols prevail in IoT environments: Message Queuing Telemetry Transport (MQTT) and Constrained Application Protocol (CoAP). MQTT, a lightweight protocol, functions effectively over low-bandwidth, high-latency links, suitable for use in resource-limited devices. CoAP, a protocol specifically developed for constrained environments, is a RESTful protocol that can easily be integrated with prevalent web services. The protocols are representative of the flexibility inherent in IoT communication, demonstrating their intrinsic role in enabling seamless communication across devices. Security is also a top priority in the deployment of IoT protocols because of the interconnectivity threat between devices. With devices communicating sensitive information to each other, unauthorized access and data breaches become a looming threat over them. It is thus a requirement to have strong security measures installed within communication protocols. Knowing the potential attacks makes it possible to design protocols not only for communication but also defense against various attacks. For instance, both MQTT and CoAP have employed several layers of security such as transport layer security and token-based authentication to ensure data integrity and confidentiality. Furthermore, IoT security research is also ongoing with researchers emphasizing the need for strong security specifications as well as interdisciplinary collaboration among cybersecurity experts, network architects, and device manufacturers. The search for a secure IoT infrastructure is not simply technological; it is about addressing pragmatic implications that impact user trust and system efficiency (Tariq et al., 2023). The integration of new technologies, namely blockchain, with IoT protocols has introduced new prospects for solutionizing security threats in industrial uses. The fusion of such technologies holds promise to enhance data integrity and enable secure transactions among the interconnected devices. However, the industrial IoT landscape is endangered with significant issues related to the constraints of resources as well as performance demands of blockchain platforms. Specifically, the speed and scalability of transactions in blockchain must align with the operational demands of IoT devices, which are often bereft of sufficient computing resources. Purposed architectures, such as those derived from Hyperledger Sawtooth, are geared to bridge such gaps by delivering an effective model for data processing and transaction verification in resource-constrained environments. As such, continued research in IoT protocols in the blockchain environment represents a critical research area with the potential to redefine industrial IoT potentials and improve results of service delivery (Khan et al., 2022).

4.6.3. 5G and Its Impact on Communication Protocols

The advent of 5G technology is a significant change in the protocols of communications, the hallmark of which is its ability to support an unprecedented number of devices and applications that require enhanced connectivity. 5G supports higher data rates, improved capacity, and significantly reduced latency, which are required by applications such as the IoT and smart cities. The technology advancements brought about by 5G also necessitate existing communication protocols to be updated to ensure compatibility and deliver optimal performance. Protocols such as those developed by the 3rd Generation Partnership Project (3GPP) are being updated to incorporate the historic achievements of 5G, not merely data transfer speeds but also security features essential for safeguarding sensitive communications across various sectors. In particular, the URLLC program under 5G infrastructure highlights the paradigm shift in protocol development with low-latency applications in perspective. URLLC is designed to support mission-critical communications in verticals like healthcare, automotive, and industrial automation, where latency must be minimized to achieve optimal performance. But many legacies Operational Technology (OT) protocols such as IEC-61850 GOOSE present challenges due to the past design constraints, which are biased more towards higher payloads and higher latency tolerance. This incompatibility of legacy protocols with 5G-directed URLLC parameters highlights the need for a protocol flexibility study in the context of 5G frameworks so that legacy systems can accommodate the stringent demands arising in an environment driven by 5G (Boeding et al., 2024). Moreover, 5G also introduces new security problems that need to be addressed in the communication protocol field. For instance, the 5G Proximity-based Service (ProSe) enables distant user equipment to access the network even at the edge of coverage using relay systems that need to be securely authenticated as well as data integrity. Recent studies of 5G ProSe Authentication and Key Agreement (AKA) protocols have revealed some serious security gaps that must be filled to ensure network integrity. Formal verification of the protocols by comparison with models and through the use of automated verification tools such as Tamarin can help identify weaknesses and guide refinement in security measures without causing much disturbance to existing standards (Ren et al., 2025). With 5G continuing to evolve, it is increasingly necessary that protocols are not only useful but also resilient to new and emerging threats (Figure 4.14).

Figure 4.14. 5G facilitates higher data rates, improved capacity, and significantly reduced latency, which are critical for applications such as the Internet of Things (IoT) and smart cities.

Source: https://cloudgate.ie/wp-content/uploads/2024/07/5g-Connectivity-And-Communication-scaled.jpg.

4.7. CONCLUSION

In concluding an investigation of communication and network protocols, it is apparent that design and implementation of systems are indispensable to facilitating efficient and trustworthy information interchange between diverse applications. Network architectures have been developed such that scaling of technologies that enhance communications as well as integration into improved systems is facilitated. For instance, the research here presents wireless network management methods in healthcare centers, including segmented networks applicable to the nature of the applications. Segmentation allows for better measurement of performance and bandwidth management, leading to a more productive environment of operation. Thus, an explicit realization of structuring and optimizing network resources stands forth as the key finding of this analysis, particularly in busy places such as healthcare, where having the capability to retrieve clinical information in a timely manner will have a causal impact on patient health (Auccahuasi et al., 2025). Furthermore, establishing consensus on protocols within decentralized networks shows growing complexity and the necessity of strong standards of communication. As more industries are adopting blockchain technologies, the importance of high-performance consensus protocols cannot be overstated. The research on Byzantine Fault Tolerant (BFT) protocols shows how variations in network topology can have a significant impact on performance outcomes. In particular, the focus of the paper on protocols like Istanbul BFT and HotStuff illustrates the relationship between protocol performance and network topology. Such observations indicate that not only do networks need to be built for high performance, but they must also evolve to counter the issues presented by real-world applications, where errors and latency can halt the information flow. Therefore, making these protocols efficient becomes necessary in order to achieve efficient consensus in distributed systems (Chan et al., 2024). Lastly, the study of network and communication protocols emphasizes the interdependence of technology, efficiency, and requirements specific to an application. It is necessary while concluding this discussion that it is essential to note that network innovation has a direct impact on the functionality of applications ranging from healthcare to finance. Network segmentation, as explained in the context of healthcare applications, highlights the requirement for bespoke solutions to accentuate maximum efficiency and performance. Therefore, the complexities of consensus protocols similarly indicate the necessity of understanding the underlying structure and what they mean for workability. Thus, future research should remain geared to the finer adjustment of these networks and protocols so that they can respond to the emerging needs of an increasingly dynamic technological environment and yet encourage innovation and collaboration (Auccahuasi et al., 2025; Chan et al., 2024).

4.7.1. Summary of Key Points

In communication and network protocol areas, security is the utmost necessity. Multiple vulnerabilities exist in the communication protocol stack, and particularly in wireless mesh networks (WMNs) where the device convergence exposes more surface area for possible attacks. A detailed examination discovers multiple layers where weaknesses may be located: physical, link, network, transport, and application. Every level has its own security and privacy risks, illustrating the significance of robust defense systems. Examination of these risks highlights the pressing need for continuous research and development of security systems, since even sophisticated systems are at risk of being compromised by emerging threats if they are not refreshed from time to time and protected against potential intrusions (Gupta et al., 2013). Furthermore, the security discussion also encompasses significant topics of user authentication and privacy preserving protocols. Attacks on key management protocol showcase the vulnerable nature of safeguarding user data in network architecture. Strategies for managing these attacks have been developed with the degree of success varying normally based on cryptographic methods and key management techniques employed. The comparison studies presented during different security frameworks provide critical details regarding their trust-based entities and operational costs. The integration of trust management and cryptographic security is essential for the overall dependability of communication protocols in order to promote users' trust in next-generation network technology (Gupta et al., 2013). Examining innovative alternatives in secure communication, integrating visual channels within authentication processes is a promising prospect. This technique facilitates information verification using visual means, and this can enhance user experience and security in real-life applications such as Kiosk computing and multi-factor authentication. Examining the role of visual signals and augmented reality constructs, researchers have offered protocols that are designed to counter potential replay attacks and provide straightforwardly usable verification mechanisms. The concept points out that although both systems are unreliable, they could function effectively without colluding, thereby presenting new means of secure communication that cater to various user needs and situations. The debate is still propelling the discussion of the introduction of new technologies into existing protocols to introduce additional security and user experience.

4.7.2. Future of Network and Communication Protocols

The communications and network protocols of the future will be revolutionized as technologies further develop the interface between devices and systems. One of the most important areas for technology to innovate is in the inclusion of wireless communication in robotic systems. Scientists have demonstrated that implementing wireless networking capabilities into robots does not just improve efficiency but creates larger collaborative efforts within multi-robot systems. Whereas existing techniques tend to lack expert focus on robotic applications, a new opportunity arises in mapping techniques from vehicular ad hoc networks (VANET) into robotic ad hoc networks (RANET). This cross-pollination is capable of propelling quick progress of protocols particularly tailored for robotic applications, as shown by recent studies highlighting the RANET's special requirements in supporting high-throughput multimedia streaming in contrast to the lower throughput messaging requirements of VANET protocols

(Demeester et al., 2012). Another factor of relevance to protocol development facilitated by the necessity for building networked control systems (NCSs) is also of interest. The interaction between communication processes and system performance necessitates accurate planning of sampling procedures and protocol settings. Current research has been more focused on developing knowledge pertaining to the impact of different sampling methods—time-driven and event-driven—on control dynamics. By systematically investigating static and dynamic protocols, researchers are attempting to develop a better insight into how such constituents interact within NCSs. Such work is significant since it develops control protocols that react dynamically to changing network conditions, ultimately enhancing communication integrity in critical systems (Dong et al., 2014). As the area of study expands, it will provide the foundation for future network and communications protocols in dynamically responsive networks. In the future, the potential to incorporate artificial intelligence (AI) into network and communications protocols is yet another significant frontier. AI technologies can significantly enhance the flexibility and efficiency of communications protocols to enable real-time optimization within a more sophisticated digital ecosystem. Machine learning algorithms, for instance, can be employed to track traffic patterns, predict bandwidth usage, and dynamically allocate resources among devices within the network. AI can, in addition, enable more savvy decision-making in network management, reducing latency and security challenges. The successful application of AI in networking protocols will not only speed up communication but also provide opportunities for novel applications across other sectors, including the IoT and smart cities. These advancements are likely to transform the future of connectivity into more robust and efficient communication networks.

4.7.3. Final Thoughts on the Importance of Understanding Protocols

In distilling the research of network and communication protocols, one would need to emphasize the basic significance of understanding such structures not only for technical deployment but also for its purposes towards secure and effective exchanges on the internet. Protocols are literally the backbone of digital communication, dictating how information is being transmitted and compatible between systems. This understanding is particularly significant in a world where data security and confidentiality are more crucial than ever before. Understanding protocol complexities allows specialists to foretell potential vulnerabilities and utilize preventive measures, ultimately leading to a more secure and trusted Internet society. Moreover, as technology advances, such understanding of the building blocks allows individuals and organizations to respond to new challenges rapidly, with resistance in the ever-expanding digital landscape. In addition, the repercussions of inadequate protocol knowledge can be vast, leading to data leakage and consequent reputational loss for organizations. For instance, during the COVID-19 pandemic, the implementation of digital communication protocols for quarantine and contact tracing imposed the impact of ill-understood frameworks. Public authorities were forced to deal with public refusal due to insufficient information on the function and purpose of the protocols. As hinted by studies, providing transparency and rationale for taking such measures greatly enhances public compliance and belief, thereby proving the worth of open communication protocols in sensitive situations (Brooks et al., 2020). Organizations therefore must continue to prioritize thorough training and education on processes so that each respective stakeholder is aware of their roles and risks involved, eventually creating a culture of security and alertness. Besides the overt benefit of protocol understanding, there exists a hidden potential for innovation in frameworks such as federated learning. This framework encourages collaboration over distributed networks while keeping privacy in mind. However, as research has now revealed, understanding the subtlety of client privacy leakage is an important task that must be tackled systematically in such paradigms (Wei et al., 2020). With business houses increasingly likely to employ distributed platforms for machine learning, a sound knowledge of communication protocols becomes integral in ensuring secure data and also smooth learning procedures. On balance, the call for comprehensive protocol understanding goes beyond business technicality; it is about being held accountable for data security and confidentiality, which ultimately determines the future of secure digital communication.

REFERENCES

1. Afghah, F., Burleigh, S., Edmonson, W., Pinto, M., et al. (2016). Survey of inter-satellite communication for small satellite systems: Physical layer to network layer view. https://core.ac.uk/download/148688059.pdf (accessed on 17th October 2025).
2. Albano, M., Cerqueira, T., & Chessa, S. (2015). A module for data centric storage in ns-3. https://core.ac.uk/download/47141586.pdf (accessed on 17th October 2025).
3. Alhassan, A. (2024). Social capital and information flow in decision making: A social network analysis of actors in a road expansion project in Kristiansand, Norway. *International Journal of Politics, Culture, and Society*. https://www.semanticscholar.org/paper/93ee0a5489fc845a1e452465e77eaa95157af098 (accessed on 17th October 2025).
4. Ali, I., Sabir, S., & Ullah, Z. (2019). Internet of Things security, device authentication and access control: A review. http://arxiv.org/abs/1901.07309 (accessed on 17th October 2025).
5. Alzahrani, B., Logothetis, M., Moscholios, I., Vasilakis, V., et al. (2025). Toward information-centric software-defined cellular networks. https://core.ac.uk/download/84338502.pdf (accessed on 17th October 2025).
6. Amann, J., Holz, R., Kaafar, M. A., Mehani, O., et al. (2016). TLS in the wild: An Internet-wide analysis of TLS-based protocols for electronic communication. http://arxiv.org/abs/1511.00341 (accessed on 17th October 2025).
7. Annu, A., & Reema, M. (2017). Performance evaluation and study of routing protocols: MANET vs VANET. https://media.neliti.com/media/publications/237140-performance-evaluation-and-study-of-rout-38d28eee.pdf (accessed on 17th October 2025).
8. Auccahuasi, W., Agustini-Paredes, L., Gamonal-Montoya, J., Costa-Torres, A., Landa-Rojas, M., & Sosaya-Rodriguez, L. (2025). Method for the management of wireless networks in health care facilities. *2025 4th International Conference on Sentiment Analysis and Deep Learning (ICSADL)*. https://www.semanticscholar.org/paper/bbb62b51672feb074d9b799a984d76b63eeab7d1 (accessed on 17th October 2025).
9. Bacho, R., Lenzen, C., Loss, J., Ochsenreither, S., & Papachristoudis, D. (2024). GRandLine: Adaptively secure DKG and randomness beacon with (log-)quadratic communication complexity. *Proceedings of the 2024 on ACM SIGSAC Conference on Computer and Communications Security*. https://www.semanticscholar.org/paper/

bd5a45c017955d7ecc9865d014d9ac7eeba7a21c (accessed on 17th October 2025).

10. Bebek, M. (2015). Analysis of function of the OSI and TCP/IP model layers. https://core.ac.uk/download/197889853.pdf (accessed on 17th October 2025).
11. Bi, R., Xiong, J., Luo, C., Ning, J., Liu, X., Tian, Y., & Zhang, Y. (2024). Communication-efficient privacy-preserving neural network inference via arithmetic secret sharing. *IEEE Transactions on Information Forensics and Security, 19*, 6722–6737. https://www.semanticscholar.org/paper/b3477c252ee5ec14f48307b6a1d29c49ebc8e50b (accessed on 17th October 2025).
12. Boeding, M., Scalise, P., Hempel, M., & Sharif, H. (2024). Evaluating the latency impact for time-critical operational technology applications of transitioning IEC-61850 GOOSE operations to 5G. *2024 IEEE 21st Consumer Communications & Networking Conference (CCNC)*. https://www.semanticscholar.org/paper/83ad4bb9699beac1427ba75a5bd6a54d17e6ab30 (accessed on 17th October 2025).
13. Brima, K. (2018). Authentication problems and access optimization to information WiFi networks. https://core.ac.uk/download/168415159.pdf (accessed on 17th October 2025).
14. Brooks, S. K., Webster, R., Smith, L., Woodland, L., Wessely, S., Greenberg, N., & Rubin, G. J. (2020). The psychological impact of quarantine and how to reduce it: Rapid review of the evidence. *The Lancet, 395*, 912–920. https://doi.org/10.1016/s0140-6736(20)30460-8 (accessed on 17th October 2025).
15. Brunstrom, A., Damjanovic, D., Fairhurst, G., Grinnemo, K. J., et al. (2016). De-ossifying the internet transport layer: A survey and future perspectives. https://core.ac.uk/download/80685935.pdf (accessed on 17th October 2025).
16. Cartolano, F., Filali, F., Gozalvez, J., Krajzewicz, D., et al. (2008). iTETRIS: An integrated wireless and traffic platform for real-time road traffic management solutions. https://core.ac.uk/download/11140413.pdf (accessed on 17th October 2025).
17. Chan, J., Tay, Y., & Yen, B. (2024). A performance analysis of BFT consensus for blockchains. https://www.semanticscholar.org/paper/cdcf81976ee616b06ea5969d0372b628e834e8ca (accessed on 17th October 2025).
18. Chang, E. C., & Fang, C. (2010). Securing interactive sessions using

mobile device through visual channel and visual inspection. http://arxiv.org/abs/1003.0723 (accessed on 17th October 2025).

19. Clavel, G., Ferro, N., Higgins, S., Horstmann, W., et al. (2010). Quality interoperability within digital libraries: The DL.org perspective. https://core.ac.uk/download/10490.pdf (accessed on 17th October 2025).
20. Cuevas, M., Dohler, M., Laya, A., Lema, A., et al. (2017). Business case and technology analysis for 5G low latency applications. https://core.ac.uk/download/96762095.pdf (accessed on 17th October 2025).
21. Davis, V. A. (2017). Internet security for mobile computing. https://core.ac.uk/download/211343997.pdf (accessed on 17th October 2025).
22. Demeester, P., Moerman, I., & Vandenberghe, W. (2012). Adoption of vehicular ad hoc networking protocols by networked robots. https://core.ac.uk/download/55755080.pdf (accessed on 17th October 2025).
23. Di Fatta, G., & Lo Re, G. (2001). Active networks: An evolution of the internet. https://core.ac.uk/download/9469.pdf (accessed on 17th October 2025).
24. Dong, H., Gao, H., Liu, Y., Wang, Y., et al. (2014). Time- and event-driven communication process for networked control systems: A survey. https://core.ac.uk/download/30339590.pdf (accessed on 17th October 2025).
25. Douligeris, C., Komninos, N., & Vergados, D. D. (2007). A two-step authentication framework for mobile ad hoc networks. https://core.ac.uk/download/16272194.pdf (accessed on 17th October 2025).
26. Eggert, L., & Fairhurst, G. (2008). Unicast UDP usage guidelines for application designers. https://core.ac.uk/download/19915619.pdf (accessed on 17th October 2025).
27. Erdene-Ochir, O., Kountouris, A., Minier, M., Valois, F., et al. (2010). Resilient networking in wireless sensor networks. https://core.ac.uk/download/50103688.pdf (accessed on 17th October 2025).
28. Faezipour, M., & Odeh, A. (2012). Secure wireless infrastructure network using access point checking. https://core.ac.uk/download/52955860.pdf (accessed on 17th October 2025).
29. Faruk, H., & Jobair, M. (2023). GR-342 integration of blockchain in computer networking: Overview, applications, and future perspectives for software-defined networking (SDN), network security and protocols. https://core.ac.uk/download/572713940.pdf (accessed on 17th October 2025).
30. Fonović, D., & Kusek, M. (2024). Congestion control performance analysis of CoAP multicast group communication in 6LoWPAN network.

2024 47th MIPRO ICT and Electronics Convention (MIPRO). https://www.semanticscholar.org/paper/9ea5c66d2449f25521c28ba9d6d9785b9e3fc45c (accessed on 17th October 2025).

31. Gupta, A., Mishra, A., Naveed, A., Perrig, A., Shamir, A. A., Franklin, A. D., Wood, A. D., et al. (2013). Security and privacy issues in wireless mesh networks: A survey. http://arxiv.org/abs/1302.0939 (accessed on 17th October 2025).
32. Haryono, W. (2025). Comparative analysis of TCP and UDP protocol performance in sending text messages using chatting applications. *Jurnal Inotera*. https://www.semanticscholar.org/paper/7d2546060d2621220920172c3d6d52c9d36f010b (accessed on 17th October 2025).
33. Havinga, P. J. M. (2000). Energy-efficient wireless communication. https://core.ac.uk/download/pdf/11460969.pdf (accessed on 17th October 2025).
34. Jahren, E. R. (2015). Design and implementation of a reliable transport layer protocol for NUTS. https://core.ac.uk/download/646193810.pdf (accessed on 17th October 2025).
35. Jayawardena, S., Liu, C. H., & Perera, C. (2015). The emerging Internet of Things marketplace from an industrial perspective: A survey. https://core.ac.uk/download/327950098.pdf (accessed on 17th October 2025).
36. Jennings, E. H., & Segui, J. S. (2025). CCSDS advanced orbiting systems virtual channel access service for QoS MACHETE model. https://core.ac.uk/download/pdf/10565275.pdf (accessed on 17th October 2025).
37. Khan, A. A., Laghari, A. A., Shaikh, Z. A., Dacko-Pikiewicz, Z., & Kot, S. (2022). Internet of Things (IoT) security with blockchain technology: A state-of-the-art review. *IEEE Access, 10*, 122679–122695. https://doi.org/10.1109/access.2022.3223370 (accessed on 17th October 2025).
38. Klein, H., Mathiason, J., Holitscher, M., & Mueller, M. (2004). Internet governance: The state of play. https://core.ac.uk/download/71343500.pdf (accessed on 17th October 2025).
39. Kovacik, C. F., & Bugár, G. (2021). Analysis of operational properties of VoIP network. *Acta Electrotechnical et Informatica*. https://www.semanticscholar.org/paper/c4b9435fe06b4918b4c1466e27442437f311b7d6 (accessed on 17th October 2025).
40. Lanotte, R., Merro, M., & Tini, S. (2018). Equational reasonings in wireless network gossip protocols. https://core.ac.uk/download/217583005.pdf (accessed on 17th October 2025).
41. Leung, V. C. M., Mahapatra, C., Sheng, Z., Zhu, Q., et al. (2015).

Recent advances in industrial wireless sensor networks towards efficient management in IoT. https://core.ac.uk/download/30611701.pdf (accessed on 17th October 2025).

42. Meghanathan, N., & Olagbegi, B. S. (2010). A review of the energy efficient and secure multicast routing protocols for mobile ad hoc networks. http://arxiv.org/abs/1006.3366 (accessed on 17th October 2025).
43. Mendez, D. M., Papapanagiotou, I., & Yang, B. (2017). Internet of Things: Survey on security and privacy. http://arxiv.org/abs/1707.01879 (accessed on 17th October 2025).
44. Mishra, K., Jain, N., & Bhutani, S. (2024). Modeling and analysis of the decision tree-based transmission control protocol. *2024 Second International Conference Computational and Characterization Techniques in Engineering & Sciences (IC3TES)*. https://www.semanticscholar.org/paper/f1ff3e2ec9239da1b066d342d6800e2f59a073f5 (accessed on 17th October 2025).
45. Oikonomou, N. V., & Oikonomou, D. V. (2024). Educational applications and comparative analysis of network simulators: Protocols, types, and performance evaluation. *Journal of Engineering Research and Sciences*. https://www.semanticscholar.org/paper/0c09ab030ee8da518cd94fd7eeee07d8fcf4c39a (accessed on 17th October 2025).
46. Parulkar, G. M., & Sterbenz, J. P. G. (1989). Axon: A high-speed communication architecture for distributed applications. https://core.ac.uk/download/233234192.pdf (accessed on 17th October 2025).
47. Pielli, C., Vangelista, L., Zanella, A., Zorzi, M., et al. (2015). Platforms and protocols for the Internet of Things. https://core.ac.uk/download/53529521.pdf (accessed on 17th October 2025).
48. Rajasekaran, A., Danda, N. T. R., Shilpi, M., Shaik, S., & Kota, Y. (2024). A secure wireless communication in vehicular ad-hoc network system. *2024 5th International Conference on Intelligent Communication Technologies and Virtual Mobile Networks (ICICV)*. https://www.semanticscholar.org/paper/460b94c2a6cbf5e840b46f2a2b9bd97670963bd6 (accessed on 17th October 2025).
49. Ren, X., Cao, J., Niu, B., Gan, L., Zhang, Y., Xiong, L., Luo, Y., et al. (2025). A formal analysis of 5G ProSe AKA protocols for U2N relay communication. *IEEE Transactions on Dependable and Secure Computing, 22*, 2909–2924. https://www.semanticscholar.org/paper/297146a6bc39715bbdeb92e769edbb7c04310cb2 (accessed on 17th October 2025).
50. Sabila, S. H., Mustika, I., & Selo, S. (2021). Implementation for soldier

communication based on session initiation protocol: A systematic literature review. *Volume, 4*, 9043–9048. https://www.semanticscholar.org/paper/c16f5d13b5f2fcef73b9913b6cf7b28aa547ecb4 (accessed on 17th October 2025).

51. Takács, T. (2010). Network protocol analyzer. https://core.ac.uk/download/44393046.pdf (accessed on 17th October 2025).
52. Tariq, U., Ahmed, I., Bashir, A. K., & Shaukat, K. (2023). A critical cybersecurity analysis and future research directions for the Internet of Things: A comprehensive review. *Sensors, 23*, 4117. https://doi.org/10.3390/s23084117 (accessed on 17th October 2025).
53. Waher, P., & Brama, R. (2024). Achieving IoT harmonization using XMPP in the IEEE P1451.99 context. *IECON 2024–50th Annual Conference of the IEEE Industrial Electronics Society*. https://www.semanticscholar.org/paper/1c36fca20958e34c9ae4ec1ccaa9d36523df43b2 (accessed on 17th October 2025).
54. Wei, W., Liu, L., Loper, M. L., Chow, K. H., Gürsoy, M. E., Truex, S., & Wu, Y. (2020). A framework for evaluating gradient leakage attacks in federated learning. *arXiv (Cornell University)*. https://doi.org/10.48550/arxiv.2004.10397 (accessed on 17th October 2025).
55. Yang, W., Hou, C., Wang, Y., Zhang, Z., Wang, X., & Cao, Y. (2024). SAKMS: A secure authentication and key management scheme for IETF 6TiSCH industrial wireless networks based on improved elliptic-curve cryptography. *IEEE Transactions on Network Science and Engineering, 11*, 3174–3188. https://www.semanticscholar.org/paper/97eb760278a6278f61a1ece2674f7bc0215bde4c (accessed on 17th October 2025).

CHAPTER 5

CRYPTOGRAPHY FOR IOT DEVICES

Contents

INTRODUCTION

The Internet of Things (IoT) is a connectivity evolution, with a wide variety of devices networked together, enabling the uninterrupted sharing of data. Interconnectedness opens the door to an intelligent environment, with influence on everything from everyday living to industrial processes. With the projected launch of sixth generation wireless networks (6G) approaching, the scope of IoT is likely to grow considerably, with billions of devices connected. However, the very essence of wireless communications is substantial openness that creates enormous security problems. The probability of new security breaches requires unyielding security measures that can deliver secure information under the presence of vast networks. Preventing such vulnerabilities is paramount in fostering trust in IoT use, hence incurring cryptographic solutions as an on-the-spot necessity within this continuously growing digital world (Illi et al., 2023). Cryptography is an essential discipline in ensuring safe communication in IoT systems, but difficulties are encountered due to the resource constraints of the majority of IoT devices. Traditional cryptographic methods, while being effective on resource-rich platforms like smartphones and computers, do not effectively move to resource-constrained environments such as RFID tags and sensors. Hence, lightweight cryptography (LWC) has become an unavoidable alternative, specifically designed for devices with limited processing capacity and memory. The LWC design considers the trade-offs between performance, security, and resource utilization, bearing in mind the inherent nature of IoT devices. Through new approaches, researchers are presenting optimized substitution boxes (S-boxes) that ensure the maximum nonlinear activity of cryptographic operations without cost and inefficiency (Thakor et al., 2023). Thorough understanding of cryptic methods specially designed for IoT implementation is essential to overcoming security challenges posed by this interconnected world. The use of lightweight cryptography not only attempts to provide robust security but also attempts to enhance the overall efficiency of IoT systems. Recent advances in physical layer security (PLS) add support to these efforts by providing secure transmission with low complexity while reducing the demand for advanced cryptographic resources. This multi-pronged security leverages the practices of lightweight cryptography and cutting-edge PLS techniques to create a more secure IoT device infrastructure. As the demand for secure IoT applications continues to increase, examining these innovative solutions will be crucial to overcome the underlying vulnerabilities that accompany mass device interconnectivity and ensure the secure operation of IoT ecosystems (Illi et al., 2023).

Role of Cryptography in Securing IoT Devices

The sudden development of IoT devices has brought into focus the requirement for robust security measures to counterpoint weaknesses in these systems. Cryptography plays a pivotal role in this context, ensuring that sensitive data transmitted over networks remains confidential and inaccessible to malicious elements. As IoT devices proliferate, the ad-hoc nature of connectivity enlarges the attack surface, and it becomes imperative to embed strong cryptographic solutions within such devices. Authenticity and integrity of data should be the most important; in the absence of cryptographic solutions, data can get altered or tapped, negating the very purpose of IoT solutions. Thus, the use of cryptography not only protects devices but also inspires trust among users in the fast-interconnected world of IoT technology, which is crucial for extensive use and adoption of such devices (Mendez et al., 2017). In addition, cryptography provides mechanisms that enhance data integrity and facilitate identity authentication in the context of the IoT. Through the application of cryptographic techniques, IoT devices can ensure that the information that is communicated is neither intercepted nor altered during transmission, thereby making the system more trustworthy.

Figure 5.1. Cryptography plays a pivotal role in this context, ensuring that sensitive data transmitted across networks remains confidential and is not readily accessible to malicious entities.

Source: https://www.institutedata.com/wp-content/uploads/2023/08/Cryptography-and-network-security.png.

Integrity in this context is particularly crucial because it can have cataclysmic consequences when data is lost or altered, most notably in essential systems such as healthcare, transport, and energy management. Employing cryptography offers room for the creation of secure communication channels and protects information from unauthorized eavesdropping. Thus, the basic characteristics of confidentiality, integrity, and availability can be readily ensured, demonstrating the deep relationship between cryptographic methods and a secure IoT framework

(Mendez et al., 2017). For the broader context of IoT device security, blockchain technology is an innovative approach founded on cryptography. As a decentralized and tamper-evident record book, blockchain inherently offers enhanced security against adversarial data manipulation and accountability in the form of open books on transactions. This technology makes use of asymmetrically encrypted transactions to secure and semi-anonymous the interaction of devices with users. Having a peer-to-peer network also contributes to this security via the dispersal of data storage, better warding off central attacks. With more IoT devices becoming everyday fixtures in life, the application of blockchain and its cryptographic roots can actually set the security bar high, establishing an environment in which technological innovation and strong-strength cryptographic mechanisms lead to trust (Figure 5.1).

5.1. TYPES OF CRYPTOGRAPHIC TECHNIQUES

Cryptographic techniques need to be understood at a fundamental level to secure IoT devices because they are commonly utilized in numerous industries. Essentially, symmetric and asymmetric cryptography are two primary types of cryptographic techniques. Symmetric cryptography employs a single key for both encryption and decryption and consequently supports faster processing and less computational overhead, making it extremely handy for resource-constrained IoT devices. However, the issue is key distribution because secure sharing of the key between communicating parties should be guaranteed in order not to ensure unauthorized access that is particularly problematic in dynamic environments. Asymmetric cryptography, as opposed to this, uses a pair of keys—a public key to encrypt and a private key to decrypt. This ensures that even when the public key is disseminated, the private key is unknown, thereby enhancing security in data transfer in IoT applications. Besides traditional cryptography practices, the advent of quantum computing has sparked a need for new approaches. Quantum cryptography offers a thrilling option through practices such as Quantum Key Distribution (QKD), providing secure key exchange through quantum mechanics properties. Infusing QKD with blockchain technology creates a new paradigm for the security of IoT networks. As noted in recent literature, this approach not only ensures decentralized trust via untouchable records but also provides security protocols against the potential vulnerabilities introduced by quantum advancements against classical algorithms. Integrity of data achieved by blockchain can augment the robust security offered by quantum cryptography to safeguard against threats in classical as well as quantum threat spaces, especially keeping in mind the resource constraints of IoT devices (Adeoye, 2025). Moreover, with evolving quantum technology, adapting to new standards becomes ever more critical. The National Institute of Standards and Technology (NIST) is already involved in the standardization of Post-Quantum Cryptography (PQC) to mitigate the danger of quantum attacks against traditional public key infrastructures. Algorithms highlighted in recent studies, such as CRYSTALS-Kyber and SABER, stress lightweight implementation and are perfect for IoT environments. These algorithms have been extensively validated in actual situations to ensure their efficiency against major parameters such as throughput and power consumption. As imminent quantum computing threats loom on the horizon, the implementation of such advanced PQC algorithms is a crucial move towards protecting IoT devices from likely vulnerabilities, ultimately ensuring the integrity and confidentiality of the sensitive data they handle (Sandanamudi et al., 2025).

5.1.1. Symmetric Encryption

Symmetric encryption is at the forefront of cryptography, particularly in IoT security. Symmetric encryption relies on a single key that is used for both decryption and encryption processes. The majority of IoT devices are resource-constrained, so symmetric encryption is a feasible option. Its processing efficiency makes it feasible to process rapidly, a requirement for devices that could have low processing capabilities or limited battery life. Furthermore, symmetric encryption algorithms like Advanced Encryption Standard (AES) are highly prized for their ability to withstand all manner of attacks. This aspect is especially critical in IoT, where devices continuously confront threats due to their connected state and exposure in potentially hostile environments. Thus, effective deployment of symmetric encryption becomes a matter of paramount importance to guaranteeing confidentiality and integrity of communications between IoT devices. However, while its advantages, symmetric encryption also poses certain challenges, primarily related to key management. The need to exchange the encryption key between trusted devices in a secure manner creates vulnerabilities, primarily within a large-scale IoT infrastructure. If an attacker compromises a key, they are not only breaking one line of communication but all communications that are secured with that key. In cases where devices are being inserted or removed from the network, this is particularly a concern and requires very special handling of keys to ensure security levels are being kept. Further, IoT deployments also involve a set of devices that are sourced from various manufacturers each of whom implements various capacities and security models. Therefore, it is essential to develop a comprehensive strategy for symmetric key management and distribution to guard against exploitation of cyber threats. The solutions to these problems are of prime importance in keeping the secure nature of IoT ecosystem communication intact. The future evolution of symmetric encryption mechanisms must also consider growing scale and complexity of IoT networks. As adoption of IoT devices expands through other areas, including healthcare and smart cities, the security issues associated with them grow likewise. New threats such as advanced persistent threats (APTs) and vulnerabilities unique to IoT necessitate existing cryptographic best practices to evolve. Machine learning and AI-driven deployments can provide a path through dynamic encryption pattern adaptation against recognized anomalies and emerging threat vectors. Such methods can go hand-in-hand with traditional techniques to enhance the effectiveness as well as the robustness of encryption mechanisms in IoT. Consequently, security frameworks must evolve along with the technology they aim to protect. Symmetric encryption will form a critical part in this space, though only if used as part of a security paradigm focused on the specific challenges of IoT deployment (Hussain et al., 2020; Wang et al., 2022) (Figure 5.2).

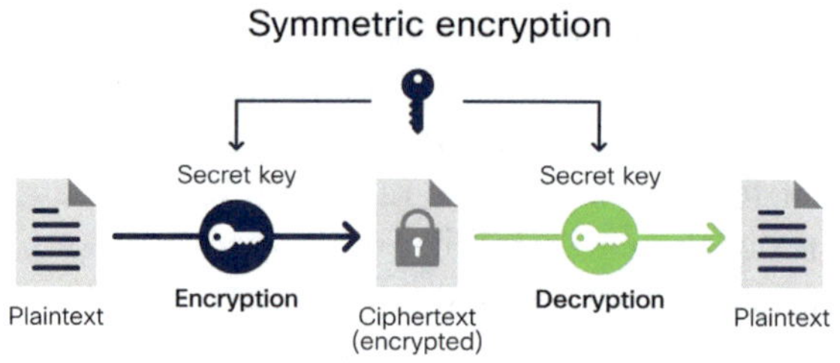

Figure 5.2. Symmetric encryption.

Source: https://miro.medium.com/v2/resize:fit:1400/1*62blCQs9eJ9MPxY7q27aCg.jpeg.

5.1.2. Asymmetric Encryption

Asymmetric encryption, or public-key cryptography, plays a key part in communications protection in IoT devices. Asymmetric encryption is a cryptographic technique based on a pair of keys, an encryption key for public use and a decryption key for private use. The technology is used to further provide confidentiality and integrity of data, whereby data is transmitted securely across potentially insecure networks. IoT, where devices constantly produce and transmit user data, confidentiality of data is a matter of utmost concern. Asymmetric encryption also offers a means of identity verification, which is required to prevent unauthorized access to IoT devices and networks. With the sharing of usage of IoT, the use of robust encryption techniques is important to maintain user privacy as well as create trust in such technologies

(Mehrotra et al., 2022). Practicality of asymmetric encryption on IoT devices is brought about by its ability to cope with the specific limitations of such environments. Unlike traditional symmetric encryption involving the sharing of a common secret key, asymmetric encryption alleviates this deficiency. This is particularly relevant to IoT devices, which typically lack the computation capabilities for secure handling of secret keys. Using key pairs, devices can securely communicate without the disadvantages of key distribution. In addition, the approach to encryption is scalable—a feature that the rapidly expanding IoT environment with millions of connected devices requires. Asymmetric encryption allows secure connections to be made even when the devices are growing in numbers, and data is safe during network operation (Chowdhury et al., 2020). However, the application of asymmetric encryption in IoT systems has its own challenges. One of these is achieving the appropriate balance of strong security capabilities and constrained IoT devices' capacity. As much as asymmetric encryption is more secure, it can require greater computation and processing capability than symmetric encryption like Advanced Encryption Standard (AES). This can result in bottlenecks in low-resource environments. Thus, using the optimal encryption algorithms is of supreme importance. As indicated in existing studies, techniques such as Elliptic Curve Cryptography (ECC) provide a reliable solution, with smaller key size but high security. Thus, proper encryption, therefore, remains one of the major areas of concern in IoT security discussions, with innovations being compelled to achieve maximum performance without compromising data integrity and confidentiality of users (Mehrotra et al., 2022) (Figure 5.3).

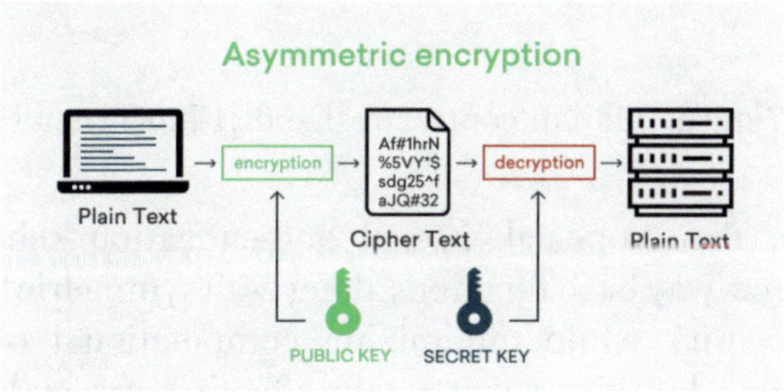

Figure 5.3. Asymmetric encryption.

Source: https://www.clickssl.net/wp-content/uploads/2019/12/asymmetric-encryption.jpg.

5.1.3. Hash Functions

The advent of the IoT has necessitated the development of secure cryptographic protocols, and more importantly, hash functions, which form an essential role in data verification and integrity. Hash functions accept variable-length input data and generate fixed-length hash codes, and therefore they are best employed to verify the integrity of messages among devices. Because IoT devices typically operate in resource-constrained environments, energy efficiency and processing capacity for the aforementioned cryptographic processing are of particular concern. Therefore, employing efficient hash functions makes secure communication possible without subjecting the limited resources of IoT devices to unnecessary overhead. Such an aspect is particularly essential given the pervasiveness of IoT applications, which can involve numerous devices needing authentication as well as guarding against leakage of sensitive data transmission. Aside from their critical role in data integrity, hash functions are also keystone components in most authentication protocols employed within IoT systems.

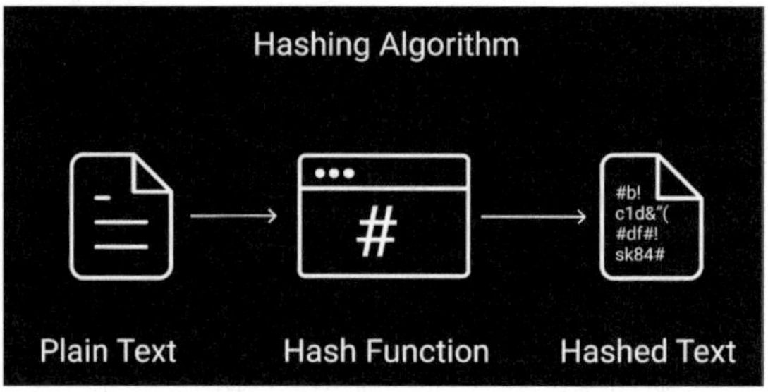

Figure 5.4. Hash functions convert variable-length input data into fixed-size hash codes, making them suitable for validating the integrity of messages exchanged between devices.

Source: https://miro.medium.com/v2/resize:fit:1400/1*uewfVLwd_UIWBUo-3HCe1KA.png.

For instance, the proposed mutual authentication scheme in IoT-Fog networks entails one-way hash functions along with symmetric key cryptography for enhancing security while minimizing computational overhead. By the use of light-weight algorithms that retain effectiveness under computational constraints, such methods ensure that authentication processes do not drain device resources excessively. Such initiative is vital in the context of the vast amount of IoT applications, from home automation to infrastructure monitoring, where device interaction needs to be secure and timely. Therefore, the adaptive and resource-conscious character of hashing algorithms is crucial in reducing the intrinsic security challenges faced by IoT devices in interconnected ecosystems (Jain et al., 2022). Furthermore, a significant emphasis has been put on designing lightweight cryptographic algorithms appropriate for the special requirements of IoT frameworks. Because standard cryptographic guidelines are not typically suited to the limited capabilities of hardware and software in IoT devices, researchers indicate the importance of sophisticated strategies. Light-weight hash functions not only provide the necessary security features, such as collision resistance and pre-image resistance but also meet performance efficiencies required by limited devices. As highlighted by recent studies, application of these algorithms in IoT systems is paramount in safeguarding traded data and thus enhancing system integrity and trust by users. This focus on light mechanisms is not merely an intellectual problem, but a broader industry imperative to incorporate robust, effective security mechanisms that satisfy the urgent imperatives of privacy and data protection in the IoT's new world (Jebrane et al., 2021) (Figure 5.4).

5.2. CHALLENGES IN IMPLEMENTING CRYPTOGRAPHY IN IOT

The rapid expansion of IoT devices poses significant issues in securing these systems based on cryptographic protocols. The majority of IoT devices happen to be resource-constrained, with low processing power and energy budgets that are not enough to support the traditional cryptographic methods that demand much computation effort. For instance, conventional algorithms like RSA and DSA exhibit high energy and latency demands, which are inappropriate for low-power devices in changing environments. Such a constraint necessitates the exploration of lightweight alternatives that will provide adequate security without affecting device performance. The challenge is in identifying cryptographic algorithms that not only confer data confidentiality and integrity but also accommodate the varied capabilities of various IoT systems concurrently (Awasthi, 2025). Another challenge, as things are currently in the cryptographic environment for IoT systems, is the looming quantum computing threat, which compromises the fundamental security of widely used cryptographic algorithms. With advancements in quantum technology further down the line, encryption mechanisms that are used now to secure vast networks of IoT devices can become obsolete and leave systems vulnerable to attacks that have never been seen before. The need for quantum-resistant cryptographic tools brings an added layer of complexity to deployment, particularly with the heterogeneity of IoT networks under which devices normally operate under multiple different protocols and standards. Mechanisms that utilize light-weight, modulus-based models, such as lattice-based and hash-based cryptography, are investigated to achieve a balance between security resilience and constraints on device resources (Awasthi, 2025). Thus, the incorporation of quantum resistance demands strategic re-designing of all existing cryptographic protocols. Finally, the governance and compliance side pertaining to IoT security renders it even more complicated to deploy cryptography. Organizations must struggle with a range of regulatory requirements that may differ significantly within geographic and industry-specific contexts. The lifecycle of IoT devices is usually marked by more than one stakeholder, which means fragmented efforts towards security and variability in the cryptographical procedures utilized. Moreover, the practical implications of integrating these systems into existing infrastructures raise issues about compatibility and operational efficacy. It is paramount for organizations to create integrated governance frameworks that enable timely implementation of security controls without compromising operational integrity. Resolving these governance issues not only enables effective cryptographic solutions but also provides a basis for long-term security in the evolving IoT environment (Choubisa et al., 2025).

5.2.1. Resource Constraints of IoT Devices

The ubiquity of IoT devices has introduced a new world of networked systems, with uses in smart cities and industrial applications. Although the devices have a vast array of benefits, they are typically presented with broad resource constraints that pose genuine challenges to the deployment of effective cryptographic solutions. The majority of IoT devices are well known to have low processing power, memory, and battery life, which compromise their ability to deploy strong security measures. As Ibrahim et al. (2025) argues, the susceptibility of IoT devices to cyber threats has the potential to bring forth disastrous implications on critical infrastructures, emphasizing the acute need for lightweight protection mechanisms that do not compromise performance. Consequently, these resource limitations are significant to consider while developing encryption algorithms that will ensure data integrity and yet remain within these devices' performance realms. Mitigation of the security vulnerability in resource-constrained IoT devices calls for reconsideration of traditional cryptography techniques. Lightweight cryptography presents itself as a focused solution to the problem, utilizing low-complexity algorithms which are both efficient and secure. As an illustration, investigation proposed by Kaur et al. (2024) cites advancements in lightweight hash-based message authentication codes and encryption models specifically designed for energy-restricted contexts. Through the optimization of cryptographic techniques to work within the limitations of bounded computational power, researchers have begun demonstrating practical means of enhancing security with low overhead. These lightweight schemes not only enhance the resilience of security for IoT systems against targeted attacks but also enable mass use of IoT applications across numerous industries where security is an essential factor. The challenge of applying efficient security measures to constrained-resource IoT devices is one of innovation, namely in the design of circuits and algorithmic efficiency. Novel architectures aimed at the optimization of hardware efficiency with the feature of performing cryptographic work are central to enabling the inclusion of security features within such devices. The inclusion of specialized hardware implementations, including the finite-field multiplier for operation on constrained resources, is a significant step toward the realization of this goal. As suggested by Ibrahim et al. (2025), the focus on reducing energy consumption and improving performance via optimized designs can be an essential factor in the overall security posture of IoT devices. With a focus on security capabilities and functional performance, developers can efficiently bridge the gap between needed data protection and the internal limitations symbolized by resource constraints, thereby allowing for the secure deployment of IoT technologies in various applications (Figure 5.5).

Figure 5.5. Many IoT devices are characterized by limited processing power, memory, and battery life, which hinder their ability to support robust security protocols.

Source: https://cdn.prod.website-files.com/643517340ef584b23a15a944/65e6f25a0658a9adef83b72f_constrained-iot-devices-and-the-smooth journey-to-the-cloud.webp.

5.2.2. Scalability Issues

Because the IoT continues to expand, scalability of the cryptographic solutions becomes increasingly relevant. IoT devices are usually noted to possess lesser computing power and varying levels of processing power, which makes it challenging to undertake secure cryptographic algorithms. Traditional methods of cryptography are likely not to be able to meet scaling demands in possibly millions of devices, introducing substantial delay and inefficiency in data processing. Scalability issues arise when large groups of devices require secure communication simultaneously, as key management and encryption overhead can bog down system performance. To address these issues, new cryptographic architectures able to scale with network size increases and heterogeneity of devices are required. Any solution presented must not only enhance security but enable encrypted communication to be efficient and manageable as the IoT grows. To remedy such scalability problems, there have been advanced solutions proposed, including post-quantum cryptographic schemes specifically designed for lightweight IoT deployments. For instance, the QRC_BIKAES framework includes a Bit-Flipping Key Encapsulation scheme along with AES-128 encryption and displays good performance characteristics when employing numerous simulated IoT devices.

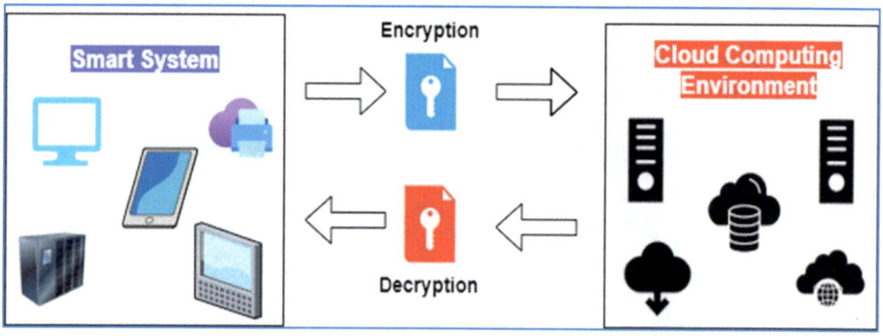

Figure 5.6. By focusing on resource-efficient methods, researchers are paving the way for the development of cryptographic systems that are both secure and capable of scaling with technological advancements.

Source: https://pub.mdpi-res.com/symmetry/symmetry-14-00695/article_deploy/html/images/symmetry-14-00695-g001.png?1648465266.

The performance results indicated that BIKE key encapsulation and decapsulation would have taken approximately 0.001 seconds, whereas AES encryption and decryption occurred in milliseconds. These advances indicate the way in which newer forms of cryptography can offer scalable solutions that can effectively protect large IoT networks without compromising on speed or efficiency. Through highlighting the application of resource-efficient methods, scientists are paving the way for the development of cryptographic systems that are scalable and secure as technology advances (Shilppaa et al., 2025). Another promising field of research to address scalability issues in IoT cryptography is implementing novel encryption methods that borrow from DNA computing principles. The proposed HD-FHE architecture utilizes fully homomorphic encryption in combination with improved elliptic curve cryptography, allowing secure data processing without the requirement for decryption and thereby lowering susceptibility. The new approach significantly enhances efficiency in key generation while simultaneously minimizing resource consumption. Experimental analysis has shown significantly decreased encryption and decryption times and hence attested to the fact that the HD-FHE model does not merely solve scalability but also performance, at least in dynamic settings. With the growth in complexity and scale of IoT networks, success in such hybrid cryptographic techniques will be imperative in securing the data and safeguarding against mounting threats (Sawlikar et al., 2025). The new frameworks, therefore, play a central role in sustaining the security of current and future IoT infrastructures (Figure 5.6).

5.2.3. Complexity of Key Management

The complexity of key management in IoT devices is an emergent problem due to the special nature of such environments. In IoT applications, resources in devices are limited, with defects in processing capability, storage capacity, and power supplies. Consequently, the traditional key management protocols, founded on high computations and heavy storage requirements, cannot be implemented in these environments. The requirements for lightweight cryptographic schemes have pushed researchers to seek alternatives that are sensitive to IoT constraints. Specifically, key management is especially problematic when attempting to maintain rigorous security protocols while ensuring that the devices can effectively work in their resource-restricted environments, hence the endless controversies around the strike rate between security and performance in IoT systems. Moreover, the increased interconnectivity between IoT devices raises the key management complexity because it creates diverse threat vectors. The structure of an IoT system generally involves many devices exchanging data over possibly insecure channels, raising the risk for key exposure and unauthorized access to sensitive information. Key distribution and revocation are therefore the main issues in this case. These processes must confirm keys are securely passed and automatically expire if a device is suspected of being breached. Complexity in managing keys between numerous devices in distributed systems necessitates new solutions to ensure keys are refreshed and rotated effectively without overwhelming the capacity inherent in IoT devices. This is addressed by sophisticated mechanisms that find a balance between security and operational efficiency. Finally, the emergence of advanced cryptographic techniques especially designed for IoT has led to highly promising technologies for the intricacy of key management. Research has thus far indicated that elliptic curve cryptography (ECC) is a viable option since it provides shorter keys and lower computational overhead and is therefore suitable for use on low-power devices. ECC-based protocols, in addition to techniques like blinded signing and zero-knowledge proofs, can offer high security with the requirements of

IoT systems in consideration. These frameworks not only facilitate efficient key management but also address significant areas of concern like data minimization and unlikability, as noted by recent studies (Ciss et al., 2019). With the redesign of generation, distribution, and management of keys, scientists are developing the groundwork for safer and more efficient IoT systems and thereby ensuring the reliability of applications that require close protection of sensitive information (Baig et al., 2014).

5.3. CRYPTOGRAPHIC PROTOCOLS FOR IOT

The expansion in IoT devices has resulted in increased reliance on cryptographic protocols to offer robust security in a wide range of applications. The devices, typically characterized in terms of their limited computational capabilities and heterogeneous environments, are of grave security concern. Traditional cryptography methods may prove unfeasible due to resource constraints, and hence novel lightweight algorithms that are tailored for the environment of IoT have been created. As these devices become more omnipresent in both industry and consumer applications, the employment of cryptographic protocols that can provide authentication, data integrity, and confidentiality becomes imperative. Without such security measures, IoT systems remain vulnerable to every kind of attack, ranging from unauthorized access to systems to data breaches, which present a major threat not only to individual users but also to larger networks and infrastructure. The evolution of cryptographic methods for IoT has been further complicated by the looming danger of quantum computing. As explained in recent studies, traditional encryption methods such as RSA and ECC are sure to fail under the power of quantum algorithms, which can effectively sabotage these systems. Thus, researchers have begun suggesting the adoption of quantum-resistant security mechanisms, such as lattice-based and hash-based cryptography. Such a shift not only mitigates existing security concerns but also future-proofs IoT ecosystems for challenges. By leveraging modular architectures that accommodate such next-generation cryptographic protocols, companies can develop scalable and secure IoT solutions. It is thus critical to have a visionary strategy to security that preemptively addresses the impact of future technologies in an effort to harden IoT environments against advanced threats (Awasthi, 2025). Besides, an end-to-end security solution for IoT devices must consist of multiple layers of defense mechanisms. Organizations must undertake a defense-in-depth method that integrates cryptographic technologies with secure communication protocols as well as hardware security components. With the integration of the above elements, organizations can be in a position to prevent the risks of unauthorized access and data leakage. Practical implementation of such a framework includes robust authentication infrastructure and lifecycle management practices to ensure that security stays ahead of technological advancements. With the IoT security complexities, it is through learning from various industries that the development and deployment of effective strategies can be informed. This integrated approach not only handles current threats but also bolsters security against future risks, ultimately providing integrity of devices in harmony in different environments (Sebastian, 2025) (Figure 5.7).

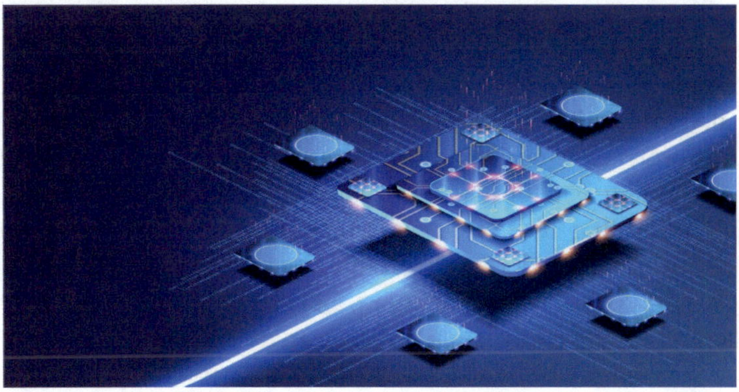

Figure 5.7. The evolution of cryptographic protocols for IoT has been further complicated by the looming threat of quantum computing.

Source: https://www.keyfactor.com/wp-content/uploads/iStock-1211223669-scaled.jpg.

5.3.1. Transport Layer Security (TLS)

TLS deployment on IoT devices is a critical aspect in data confidentiality and integrity. TLS operates through establishing secure sessions between devices and servers, thereby creating a secure channel for communication of data. TLS is structured in layers with cryptographic algorithms that facilitate encryption and authentication, which protects against malicious actions such as eavesdropping and man-in-the-middle attacks. With the growing application of IoT devices, which are more likely to handle sensitive information, inclusion in their communication processes is vital in maintaining user trust as well as compliance with data protection policies. Such protections not only provide security but also render entire IoT ecosystems more dependable, ranging from immunity to various cyber threats prevalent in the current interconnected world. Apart from its robust security aspects, the functional application of TLS must be able to consider that most IoT devices are characterized by a lack of resources. They are frequently executed on low processing power and memory, which may negatively impact the performance of computationally intensive security protocols. Consequently, the optimization of TLS application on these resource-limited devices must be a compromise between security and efficiency. Current studies have proposed the use of lightweight cryptography that preserves the fundamental security properties of TLS but with minimal overhead. Optimizing the handshake protocol and employing algorithms that utilize resources efficiently, IoT devices can then benefit from TLS-enforced security without impacting functionality and performance. Optimization is required as continued expansion of the potential attack surface for cyber-attacks accompanies the increasing proliferation of IoT devices. The evolution of TLS is also directed by the evolution of post-quantum cryptography (PQ) as a solution to protect communications from potential threats caused by future quantum computing capabilities. As quantum technology evolves, classical cryptographic building blocks can be vulnerable to unknown computational power. Thus, efforts are underway to identify how TLS can utilize PQ algorithms for enhancing the security of IoT devices. Current studies, for example, on TLS performance when new key encapsulation mechanisms (KEMs) and digital signature schemes are introduced, are carried out to ascertain the most effective solutions that work in IoT environments. The study is centered on the selection of efficient PQ algorithms that, besides being compatible with existing TLS systems, will render IoT devices secure against upcoming challenges, hence capturing the dynamicity of cryptography as it evolves to address new network security challenges (Iqbal et al., 2023; Bozhko et al., 2023) (Figure 5.8).

Figure 5.8. As quantum technology advances, traditional cryptographic algorithms may become vulnerable to unprecedented computational power.

Source: https://media.licdn.com/dms/image/v2/D4E12AQFSz1TQ2ywPug/article-cover_image-shrink_720_1280/article-cover_image-shrink_720_1280/0/1729182439851?e=2147483647&v=beta&t=vIDPcxhJPR_5Ygzt3RCU5_dt29jPGoJvcaT-vL3sqHuc.

5.3.2. Datagram Transport Layer Security (DTLS)

The pervasiveness of IoT devices necessitates strong security, particularly because these devices are used to operate in environments with constraints. Datagram Transport Layer Security (DTLS) is an applicable solution in establishing secure communication over untrusted networks. DTLS is designed to provide similar levels of security assurances as its equivalent, Transport Layer Security (TLS), but it is optimized for use with connectionless protocols like UDP. This kind of adaptation is literally a necessity for IoT applications in which preserving reliable, real-time communication is crucial. With encryption, data integrity, and authentication, DTLS ensures that data communicated between devices remains secure and tamper-proof, safeguarding against security problems prevalent in IoT scenarios in which data leaks would result in massive-scale breaches of privacy (Nabavirazavi et al., 2022).

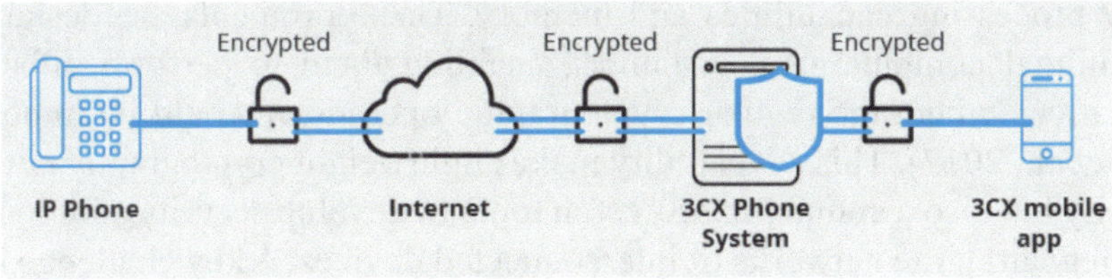

Figure 5.9. Datagram transport layer security (DTLS).

Source: https://www.3cx.com/wp-content/uploads/2020/11/dtls.png.

In IoT environments, where devices are usually power-constrained, the lightness of DTLS is particularly advantageous. The protocol employs a efficient authenticated key exchange (AKE) protocol to enable devices to authenticate each other securely and share a common session key without demanding computations. This is significant because most IoT devices are powered by finite battery power, and thus require security protocols that do not compromise their operational efficiency. More resource-efficient AKE replacements have been proposed for implementation, but DTLS remains a foundation technique that balances security with efficiency in resource-limited environments. The use of DTLS ensures that the traffic encrypted keeps data leakage to a minimum, a very important consideration given the increasing cyber-attacks on smart devices (Nabavirazavi et al., 2022). Further, the extension of DTLS to IoT environments aligns with the general desire for end-to-end security of sensitive data transmission. Since IoT applications are continuously changing—between smart homes and industrial automation—the attack surfaces also vary, generating a demand for strong protocols to defend against outside attacks. The advent of energy-efficient hardware accelerators for DTLS instrumentation presents a promising path towards enhancing IoT device performance without compromising security. These developments allow for easier interaction between low-power devices and cryptographic operations, preventing the risk of energy depletion during the task of operation. Therefore, the use of DTLS in IoT networks is a major step towards guaranteeing the secure and resilient infrastructure that can support the future of connected devices (Figure 5.9).

5.3.3. Lightweight cryptographic protocols

The accelerated expansion of the IoT has created an insistent need for enhanced security mechanisms, which are typically hindered by the built-in vulnerabilities of the devices. Lightweight cryptographic protocols have emerged as a significant answer to delivering data integrity and confidentiality without jeopardizing the limitations typically inherent in IoT devices, such as low processing capabilities and memory. These protocols are designed to use minimal computational resources, enabling them to perform effectively in situations where the regular cryptographic operations would be impossible (Chen et al., 2017). This adaptability makes lightweight cryptography not just a necessity but also a compelling research topic to develop security solutions that can safeguard large networks of interconnected devices. A key challenge in IoT security is dealing with effective key management and computation. Advances in lightweight cryptographic architecture have been working to bypass these challenges through innovative approaches, such as edge computing-based reconfigurable security architecture.

Such systems, employing near-user edge devices, render the complexities of key management simple and move the computational burden of security algorithms from resource-constrained IoT devices. This design adjustment not only optimizes performance but also supports the flexibility needed for on-demand deployment of next-generation cryptographic primitives (Chen et al., 2017). The integration of such frameworks indicates the potential for enhancing IoT security while making provision for the varied and dynamic nature of IoT ecosystems. Further, the performance of a number of lightweight cryptographic protocols, such as Attribute-Based Credentials (ABC), is paramount to their feasibility for IoT use. Protocols such as I2PA and U-Prove have proven to be promising in terms of both memory consumption and computation time, and therefore are especially suitable for devices that lack resources. Conversely, options such as Idemix have proved to be less than optimal in terms of computation time (Ciss et al., 2020). Therefore, analyzing these protocols under their respective environments proves indispensable to determining their real-world applications and deficits. As the IoT ecosystem continues to evolve, ongoing optimization and testing of lightweight cryptographic protocols will be necessary to give strong security to connected devices and balance performance constraints (Figure 5.10).

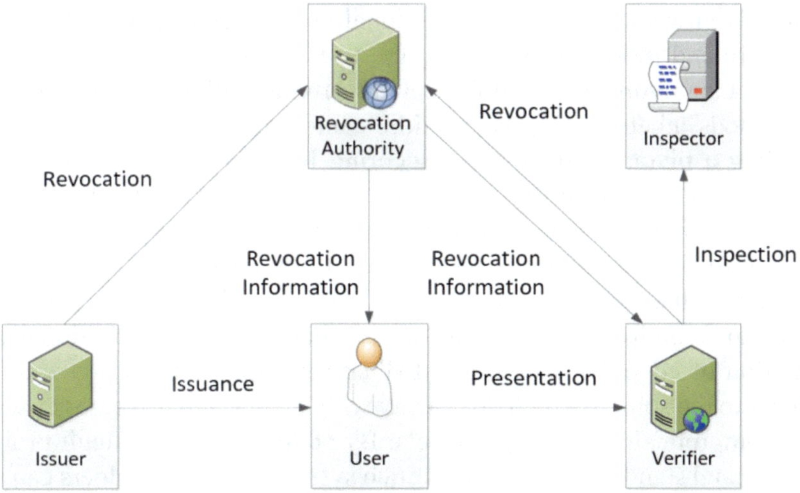

Figure 5.10. Attribute-based credentials (ABC).

Source: https://www.researchgate.net/publication/283672143/figure/fig1/AS:669382460059650@1536604623075/Attribute-Based-Credentials-System.png.

5.4. FUTURE TRENDS IN IOT CRYPTOGRAPHY

The future of cryptography in IoT will change radically as the requirement of secure communication among networked devices increases. As IoT applications increase in areas like healthcare and smart cities, the demand for lightweight cryptographic protocols is crucial. Conventional encryption algorithms have extremely high computation needs, which restrict their application in resource-constrained IoT devices. Later schemes, such as signcryption schemes, give a two-in-one function through the integration of digital signatures and encryption schemes to minimize overhead but enhance security. This shift towards lightweight cryptographical methods not only speeds up data processing but gives robust security solutions tailored to the limitations of IoT devices, allowing one to enable reliable communication in emerging technological setups (Sreedevi et al., 2025). In addition, emerging trends in cryptography have the potential to reshape security norms for IoT devices. Zero Trust Architecture places a focus on robust authentication methods and continuous verification, making network access inherently more secure. This is particularly significant in light of the distributed and heterogenous nature of IoT environments, which are generally exposed to virtually all types of attacks. Secondly, advancements in quantum-safe cryptography have the prospect of balancing the threats to quantum computing's power to subvert conventional cryptosystems. As IoT networks handle more and more sensitive data, the use of privacy-protective methods, such as data anonymization and federated learning, will also gain momentum. These methods enhance user privacy without undermining information integrity, representing a pivotal shift towards securing IoT ecosystems from emerging threats (Mutyal, 2025). In the future, the integration of artificial intelligence (AI) into cryptographic mechanisms presents new avenues to enhance IoT security. Intrusion detection systems based on AI and adaptive security platforms have the capability to recognize patterns and anomalies in real-time, which is an evolving defense mechanism against threats. Additionally, the combination of edge computing and IoT cryptography allows processing the data closer to the source, which does away with latency and increases efficiency without compromising security controls. By addressing the difficult problems of usability and standardization across such systems, the stakeholders can usher in a new era of secure, scalable, and privacy-preserving IoT environments. Envisioning these trends will not only guide upcoming research but inform industry practice as we endeavor to secure the vast networks that make up the Internet of Things (Mutyal, 2025) (Figure 5.11).

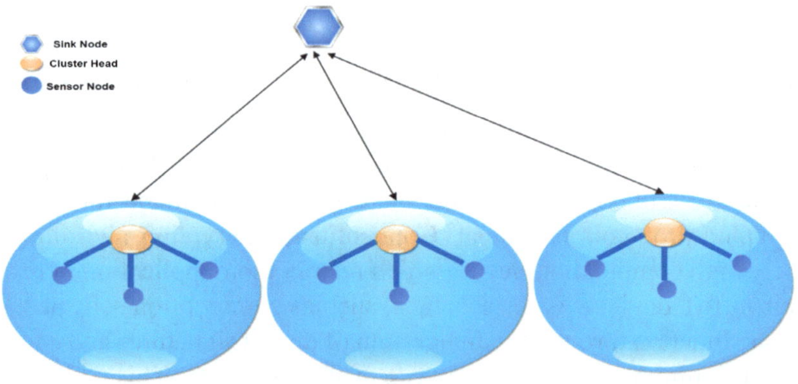

Figure 5.11. Newer mechanisms, such as signcryption techniques, offer a dual solution by integrating digital signatures with encryption processes, thereby minimizing overhead while enhancing security.

Source: https://media.springernature.com/full/springer-static/image/art%3A10.1038%2Fs41598-025-95836-8/MediaObjects/41598_2025_95836_Fig1_HTML.png.

5.4.1. Quantum Cryptography

The arrival of quantum cryptography introduces paradigm-shifting methods in securing communications in the IoT. Traditional cryptographic systems relying on complex mathematical puzzles are extremely vulnerable in the development of quantum computing technologies. Quantum cryptography, or Quantum Key Distribution (QKD), offers a secure solution anchored on the principles of quantum mechanics to ensure data transmission security. This groundbreaking technique enables two parties to share encryption keys securely impossible with conventional approaches. As more IoT devices get networked, the integration of QKD can provide a grass-root security against potential quantum attacks, avoiding threats associated with conventional public-key schemes easily decrypted by quantum algorithms (Ehsan et al., 2025).

But the applied use of quantum cryptography in IoT networks does present some challenges. In particular, the hardware requirements and environmental limitations that are present within most IoT devices, e.g., limited processing capacity and high energy requirements, make it difficult to deploy quantum key distribution systems. The wide variety of IoT devices makes it so that not all devices can support the advanced technology needed for efficient quantum cryptographic strategies. To address these needs, the existing discussions have moved towards lightweight cryptographic approaches in combination with post-quantum cryptography (PQC) solutions. These solutions aim to achieve maximum cryptographic performance while being compatible with the unique requirements of resource-constrained devices within IoT applications to provide adequate security controls without compromising the operational capabilities of the devices (Althobaiti, 2025).

With our advancement towards a quantum technology-dominated age, the use of post-quantum cryptography with quantum cryptographic protocols will be critical in securing IoT infrastructures. Utilizing protocols such as CRYSTALS-Kyber and NTRU provides cryptographic security even in the face of quantum attacks, securing key exchange processes that are fundamental for communication. Such post-quantum key encapsulation mechanisms are formatted to satisfy stringent efficiency needs simultaneously with strong security, thereby improving their application in resource-limited environments. Emphasizing ongoing studies on their integration into IoT networks will be key to the deployment of future generations of interrelated devices being able to successfully counteract future threats in an environment dominated by quantum technology through the marriage of new security methods with realistic implementation dynamics for IoT applications (Ehsan et al., 2025; Althobaiti, 2025) (Figure 5.12).

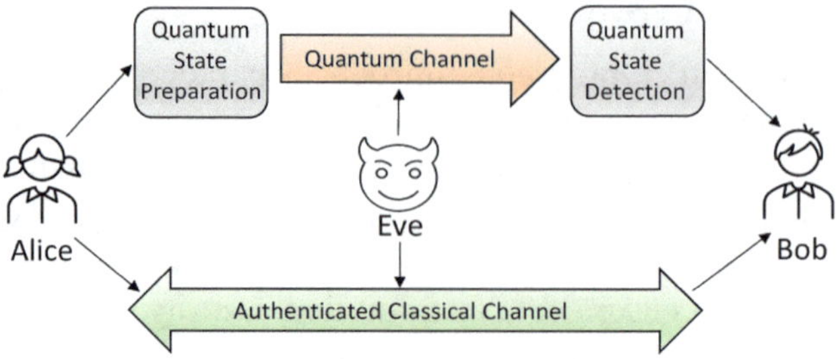

Figure 5.12. Quantum cryptography, particularly Quantum Key Distribution (QKD), offers a robust solution by leveraging the principles of quantum mechanics to ensure secure data transmission.

Source: https://www.researchgate.net/publication/361443234/figure/fig1/AS:11431281179421549@1691188862672/Schematic-of-a-general-quantum-key-distribution-QKD-protocol.png.

5.4.2 Blockchain Technology

The development of blockchain technology has revolutionized cryptography, particularly for Internet of Things (IoT) devices. IoT devices have become omnipresent and a part of our day-to-day life, and the need for effective security systems to protect sensitive data grew manyfold. Blockchain follows a decentralized ledger system that speeds up security by encrypting transactions in an immutable form. This potential is of the utmost significance for IoT applications, where unauthorized entry and data breach can have dire consequences. Through the integration of blockchain solutions, IoT data management can achieve levels of transparency and trust hitherto unimaginable as all transactions are retained in a verifiable and tamper-evident manner, thus bypassing the incuriosity's of traditional centralized systems. In addition, the compatibility of blockchain with other emerging technologies makes it more efficient in IoT security. For instance, the combination of blockchain with artificial intelligence and machine learning enhances its ability to identify anomalies and validate transactions in real-time. These technologies can cooperatively operate to create a smart system that not only identifies possible threats but also initiates countermeasures autonomously. The immersive character of the metaverse, according to Wang et al. (2022), leads to the significance of advanced security technologies given that IoT devices interact in such large virtual worlds. In this context, blockchains ability to preserve user confidentiality while securing data integrity takes center stage in facilitating secure interaction among different platforms, thus raising the bar higher for cybersecurity processes in IoT. However, applying blockchain technology to IoT systems is not without challenges.

Scalability remains the biggest problem because increasing numbers of devices generate massive amounts of data that have to be processed efficiently. Current blockchain networks are not sufficient to support the volumes of transactions required for real-time IoT use, particularly in environments of high frequency. Troublingly, interoperability problems also come up when different IoT devices utilize different blockchain protocols. Researchers have pinpointed the need to overcome these challenges for the mass use of blockchain on IoT systems. As cited in Dwivedi et al. (2022), a reflection on the socio-economic aspects of adopting these technologies can provide insight into creating a future of change. It is imperative that all stakeholders collaborate in considering remedies that balance scalability and interoperability without sacrificing the high standards of security blockchain foresees (Figure 5.13).

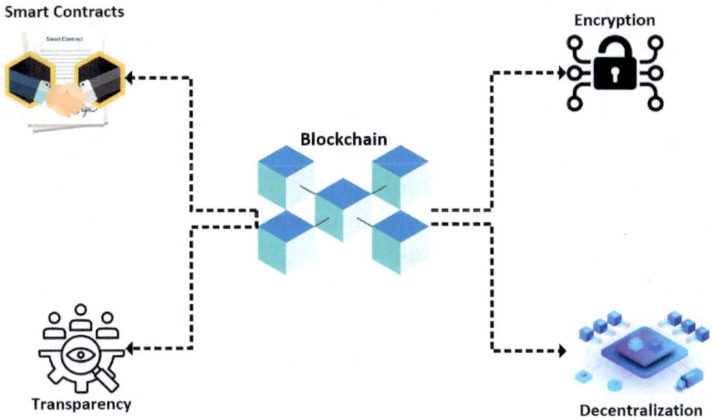

Figure 5.13. Blockchain utilizes a decentralized ledger system that enhances security by cryptographically securing transactions in an immutable format.

Source: https://www.mdpi.com/applsci/applsci-14-07007/article_deploy/html/images/applsci-14-07007-g001.png.

5.4.3. AI and Machine Learning in Cryptographic Solutions

The application of AI and machine learning in cryptographic solutions is a paradigm change to enhancing the security of IoT devices. Traditional cryptography rests on pre-known algorithms and key management schemes that may not be sufficient to deal with the dynamic nature of cyber-attacks. With machine learning, cryptographic systems can become adaptive to changing threats in real time. For instance, AI can monitor patterns of behavior of IoT device traffic, detecting anomalies that may indicate potential security breaches and allowing for proactive response. Such adaptability not only protects IoT devices against known threats but also enhances their immunity to emerging attack vectors. Furthermore, the potential benefits of utilizing AI and machine learning extend to encryption algorithms themselves. As the demand for secure data transfer grows, so does the complexity require in cryptographic methods. Machine learning is capable of improving algorithm use through means such as dynamic key generation and in-real-time assessments of cryptographic resilience. By utilizing AI, cryptographic systems are able to adapt encryption procedures to the capability of a specific device or level of sensitivity of data such that even constrained IoT devices can maintain a high-security level without losing performance. Customization is key to ensuring that cryptographic mechanisms not only remain highly secure but also optimized, thus making mass IoT adoption of secure communication protocols a reality. Security and privacy concerns inherent in the IoT domain require innovative solutions to cryptography, where emerging technologies like blockchain again come into contact with machine learning. Specifically, as mentioned in recent work, uses of blockchain technology alleviate fundamental issues of data integrity and decentralization in IoT systems essential for security risk mitigation. The uniform integration of these technologies can enhance user privacy through the provision of permanent records of interactions and transactions with open handling of data. Furthermore, the integration of AI-based analytics in blockchain protocols can enable operational efficiencies by enabling adaptive feedback to unauthorized access, providing deep insights into potential vulnerabilities on heterogeneous devices. By combining these merged technologies, next-generation cryptographic devices for IoT can be more efficient, resulting in a safer digital world (T-The et al., 2023; Wang et al., 2022) (Figure 5.14).

Figure 5.14. Machine learning can optimize algorithm performance through techniques such as dynamic key generation and real-time assessments of cryptographic strength.

Source: https://www.techmagic.co/blog/content/images/2024/05/cover-AI-Anomaly-1.png.

5.5. CONCLUSION

In summary, the use of cryptography in IoT devices is a critical evolution towards ensuring the security and privacy of large networks of connected devices. As the scale of IoT deployment becomes even larger, so does the need for robust security mechanisms to protect sensitive data. With emerging communication technologies such as 5G and the scheduled introduction of 6G, the security landscape continues to evolve at an increasingly rapid rate. Such evolution necessitates the application of sophisticated cryptographic methods that can safeguard vast amounts of information while providing low latency and high performance. Effective cryptography, in addition to hardening device integrity, constructs user trust, hence driving IoT uptake in industries ranging from homes to industry. In addition, as environments become more complex, the combination of cryptography and emergent technologies presents opportunities and threats. Technologies such as Digital Twin technology leverage IoT and big data analytics to create digital replicas of real-world things, enabling real-time monitoring and decision-making. However, these technologies underscore the paramount importance of robust cryptographic systems to protect sensitive information from possible breaches. Ensuring data integrity and confidentiality in such an environment requires a full understanding of the specific challenges posed by both the physical and cyber realms of such technology. Therefore, researchers and implementers must tackle the challenge of designing cryptographic frameworks that are not only scalable but also are easily compatible with other technologies for maximum effectiveness in diminishing security risks. Cryptography in IoT devices will need constant research and development to adapt to a shifting technology landscape. The imminent deployment of 6G and facilitating technologies is set to usher in a new age of communication that provides greater capacity, enhanced security features, and lower latency rates. However, as discussed in readily available literature, there are significant challenges still to be addressed. Most notable among these are the matters of making future technologies, i.e., blockchain and advanced artificial intelligence systems, and cryptographic approaches work hand-in-hand, so to speak, to secure IoT infrastructures. As we progress towards achieving a safe and resilient IoT space, it is essential that researchers lead the exploration of novel cryptographic solutions that address today's and tomorrow's challenges to data integrity and privacy and, consequently, open the door to a safer interconnected world.

5.5.1. Summary of Key Points

When looking at the horizon of cryptography in IoT devices, it is essential to grasp the two-pronged aspect of security vulnerabilities posed by such connected devices. The widespread use of IoT devices has given rise to vulnerabilities that compromise data integrity and authentication schemes, provided primarily by the limited computational capacities of such devices. Traditional security paradigms, relying on centralized authentication mechanisms and traditional cryptography, are wanting against these threats. As outlined in the literature, these solutions have single points of failure and are increasingly at risk from emerging threats, including quantum computing breakthroughs. There is thus an imperative for novel cryptographic solutions tailored for the particular limitations and needs of IoT architectures.

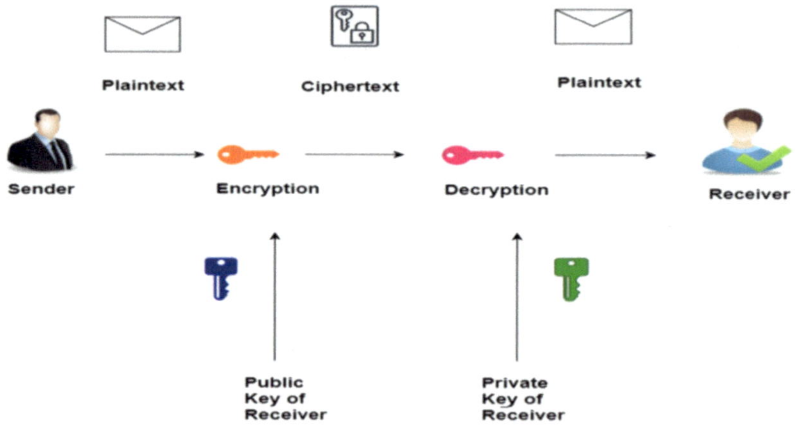

Figure 5.15. The introduction of decentralized Public Key Infrastructure (PKI) systems customized for IoT applications is another critical area of focus.

Source: https://media.springernature.com/lw685/springer-static/image/art%3A10.1007%2Fs11042-023-16970-x/MediaObjects/11042_2023_16970_Fig5_HTML.png.

One significant innovation for securing IoT devices is the integration of blockchain with quantum cryptographic methods. Leveraging the decentralized nature of blockchain, this new method has built-in advantages for data integrity and tamper-protection. Quantum Key Distribution (QKD) is employed by the proposed solutions to enable secure key exchanges, thereby giving interception-free communication channels even under quantum computational attacks. As the research proposes, the integration of these technologies creates a robust security framework that not only keeps IoT networks secure against conventional attacks but also prepares them to counter the new threats posed by quantum computing. With the progression of IoT, this combination of blockchain and quantum cryptography presents an effective means of enhancing security in existing implementations. Moreover, the presence of decentralized

Public Key Infrastructure (PKI) solutions optimized for IoT use cases is also a domain of vital significance. Traditional PKIs reveal their vulnerability when implemented in resource-constrained environments typical of IoT devices—scalability and authentication certificate management being significant issues. The zone design proposed eliminates these complexities by introducing zone masters that streamline certificate management at groups of IoT devices, thereby minimizing single points of failure considerably. In addition, utilization of light-weight cryptographic algorithms, such as Elliptic Curve Cryptography (ECC), enhances performance without compromising security. Combined, these developments emphasize the imperative for new cryptographic solutions suited to the IoT ecosystem to allow security frameworks to keep up with technological advancements and increasing interconnectedness of devices (Adeoye, 2025; El-Hajj et al., 2024) (Figure 5.15).

5.5.2. Importance of Ongoing Research

Further studies on cryptography for IoT devices are instrumental in enhancing the security ecosystem of a rapidly interconnected world. As the universal development of IoT devices increases, with it increase the weaknesses of these systems in vulnerability, so cryptographic solutions will have to secure sensitive data. Scientists are faced with the unique problems presented by the resource constraint environments of IoT devices, which generally provide minimal processing capabilities and battery life. By exploring newer paradigms and methodologies such as federated learning, developers can design cryptographic solutions that not only prioritize security but also reduce resource usage. The interactive nature of security protocols and device performance thus makes it a focal point for scholars to research, calling for continuous inquiry into adaptive and efficient methods of cryptography (Li et al., 2020). Besides, the realization of the potential of integrating breakthrough technologies, such as IoT-based Digital Twin solutions, shines a light on the need to conduct ongoing research. The concept of the Digital Twin is an interactive model of physical devices, which can help optimize operational efficiencies and predict failures. New security concerns that accompany this innovation have to be solved through robust cryptographic algorithms in order to ensure the confidentiality and integrity of data being sent. As the industry, particularly manufacturing and smart city implementations, adopts Digital Twin technology, researchers must also learn its intersections with IoT security standards. To overcome such intricacies through ongoing research efforts allows it to develop application-specified cryptographic solutions not just for protecting sensitive information but also to facilitate trust in newly adopted technologies (Fuller et al., 2020). Apart from fighting current weaknesses, ongoing research drives the development of adaptive solutions that can counter subsequent threats yet to emerge. As cybercriminals continue to develop further, there is an ever-growing need for dynamic cryptographic techniques that will also self-advance according to rising threats. It is up to researchers to pursue ongoing exploration, assessing how current frameworks can be refined or substituted because vectors of attack evolve with time and are normally seen on IoT infrastructure. By promoting the spirit of ongoing learning and adaptation within the cryptographic world, the technology is able to adjust rapidly to current challenges and challenges yet to arise, rendering the IoT devices resistant to the changing technological and threat landscape. The timeliness of ongoing research thus not only helps in safeguarding current systems but also serves as a stepping stone for the creation of future innovations in cryptography for IoT devices.

5.5.3. Future Outlook for Cryptography in IoT Devices

With the topology of the IoT changing, the future of cryptography for IoT devices will become increasingly paramount in keeping data secure and intact. With billions of devices connected and each able to collect and transmit sensitive data, the use of robust cryptographic processes is a must to avoid unauthorized entry and data breaches. Encryption techniques, for example, symmetric and asymmetric cryptography, are key to safeguarding data when it travels across networks to provide confidentiality. As the elaborate summary illustrated, the sharing of sensitive information accentuates the need for stronger encryption techniques specifically tailored to meet the particular constraints and requirements of IoT setups, which are commonly defined by inferior processing capabilities and power constraints (Fayayola et al., 2024). Besides, next-generation tech innovations will drive the development of sophisticated cryptographic technologies for IoT devices. Quantum computing innovations and advancements in blockchain technology bring new possibilities for strengthening security measures, creating stronger systems against evolving cyber threats. Implantation of artificial intelligence within cryptographic settings can also support adaptive security solutions that evolve to respond to current threats, consequently enhancing IoT environments' defense mechanisms. By embracing such cutting-edge technologies, developers are able to create a safer infrastructure that not only avoids threats but also creates confidence regarding the use of IoT devices across different sectors, including smart homes, healthcare, and industrial applications. The need for stronger security solutions in a world of increased interdependence is evident (Zhao et al., 2023). Still, the future of cryptography within IoT devices is threatened by serious challenges that need to be addressed in order to ensure successful security solutions. The ever-faster development of cyber threats, such as advanced malware and ransomware attacks, calls for continued research and advancements in cryptographic methods. In addition, compliance with regulatory frameworks, such as GDPR and HIPAA, makes security measures development challenging because companies must balance effectiveness in business operations against strict compliance with data protection regimes. As the IoT expands further, stakeholders must come together and create industry standards and guidelines for deploying cryptography solutions not only addressing security requirements but also fulfilling compliance requirements. Lastly, a robust approach to cryptography in IoT can lead the way to a secure internet world that encourages trust and reliability among connected systems (Fayayola et al., 2024).

REFERENCES

1. Adeoye, S. (2025). Securing IoT devices: A novel approach using blockchain and quantum cryptography. *Cognizance Journal of Multidisciplinary Studies*. https://www.semanticscholar.org/paper/5dee571ad54b67660c207d14146282a054191e6a (accessed on 17th October 2025).
2. Al Khatib, I., Shamayleh, A., & Ndiaye, M. (2024). Healthcare and the Internet of Medical Things: Applications, trends, key challenges, and proposed resolutions. *Informatics, 11*, 47. https://doi.org/10.3390/informatics11030047 (accessed on 17th October 2025).
3. Allioui, H., & Mourdi, Y. (2023). Exploring the full potentials of IoT for better financial growth and stability: A comprehensive survey. *Sensors, 23*, 8015. https://doi.org/10.3390/s23198015 (accessed on 17th October 2025).
4. Althobaiti, F. A. (2025). Lightweight cryptography for IoT: A comprehensive survey of algorithms, implementations, and standardization. *World Journal of Advanced Engineering Technology and Sciences*. https://www.semanticscholar.org/paper/6380a53c15b217693a8979b260596033218c3798 (accessed on 17th October 2025).
5. Awasthi, A. (2025). Quantum-resistant security for IoT systems: Challenges and implementation strategies. *International Journal of Scientific Research in Computer Science, Engineering and Information Technology*. https://www.semanticscholar.org/paper/1793a771fdde668348fcc1930bd1994518806a64 (accessed on 17th October 2025).
6. Baig, Z. A. (2014). Securing the Internet of Things infrastructure–Standards and techniques. https://core.ac.uk/download/41537076.pdf (accessed on 17th October 2025).
7. Bera, B., Das, A. K., & Sikdar, B. (2025). Quantum-resistant secure communication protocol for digital twin-enabled context-aware IoT-based healthcare applications. *IEEE Transactions on Network Science and Engineering, 12*, 2722–2738. https://www.semanticscholar.org/paper/bfcbd8323bac3e0ef3b7ff470567282038b174fa (accessed on 17th October 2025).
8. Bozhko, J., Hanna, Y., Harrilal-Parchment, R., Tonyalı, S., & Akkaya, K. (2023). Performance evaluation of quantum-resistant TLS for consumer IoT devices. https://doi.org/10.1109/ccnc51644.2023.10060762 (accessed on 17th October 2025).
9. Chen, J. C., Hsu, R. H., Lee, J., Quek, T. Q. S., et al. (2017). Reconfigurable security: Edge computing-based framework for IoT. http://arxiv.org/

abs/1709.06223 (accessed on 17th October 2025).

10. Choubisa, M., & Jajal, B. (2025). Lightweight ECC and token-based authentication mechanism for IoT. *International Journal of Scientific Research in Computer Science and Engineering*. https://www.semanticscholar.org/paper/00f2c982bc37af51c9a1a972016aac27a4d16a62 (accessed on 17th October 2025).
11. Chowdhury, M. Z., Shahjalal, M., Ahmed, S., & Jang, Y. M. (2020). 6G wireless communication systems: Applications, requirements, technologies, challenges, and research directions. *IEEE Open Journal of the Communications Society, 1*, 957–975. https://doi.org/10.1109/ojcoms.2020.3010270 (accessed on 17th October 2025).
12. Ciss, A. A., Mattern, F., Veseli, F., Sene, I., Camenisch, J., Koblitz, N., Vullers, P., et al. (2020). I2PA, U-prove, and Idemix: An evaluation of memory usage and computing time efficiency in an IoT context. http://arxiv.org/abs/1904.08331 (accessed on 17th October 2025).
13. Ciss, A. A., Niang, O., & Sene, I. (2019). I2PA: An efficient ABC for IoT. https://core.ac.uk/download/226789165.pdf (accessed on 17th October 2025).
14. Dahiya, R., Kumar, A., Dahiya, V. K., & Agarwal, N. (2023). Facilitating healthcare sector through IoT: Issues, challenges, and its solutions. *EAI Endorsed Transactions on Internet of Things, 9*, e5. https://doi.org/10.4108/eetiot.v9i4.4317 (accessed on 17th October 2025).
15. Dwivedi, Y. K., Hughes, L., Baabdullah, A. M., Ribeiro-Navarrete, S., Giannakis, M., Al-Debei, M. M., Dennehy, D., et al. (2022). Metaverse beyond the hype: Multidisciplinary perspectives on emerging challenges, opportunities, and agenda for research, practice and policy. *International Journal of Information Management, 66*, 102542. https://doi.org/10.1016/j.ijinfomgt.2022.102542 (accessed on 17th October 2025).
16. Ehsan, M. A., Alayed, W. M., Rehman, A. U., Hassan, W. U., & Zeeshan, A. (2025). Post-quantum KEMs for IoT: A study of Kyber and NTRU. *Symmetry*. https://www.semanticscholar.org/paper/4d83611571847fdb065f45cf95dc42bff953e6ea (accessed on 17th October 2025).
17. El-Hajj, M., & Beune, P. (2024). Decentralized zone-based PKI: A lightweight security framework for IoT ecosystems. *Inf., 15*, 304. https://www.semanticscholar.org/paper/1223f89e2290b6fec3ec2cf1b041955f1de74cac (accessed on 17th October 2025).
18. Fayayola, O. A., Olorunfemi, O. L., & Shoetan, P. O. (2024). Data privacy and security in IT: A review of techniques and challenges. *Computer Science & IT Research Journal, 5*, 606–615. https://doi.org/10.51594/

csitrj.v5i3.909 (accessed on 17th October 2025).

19. Fuller, A., Fan, Z., Day, C., & Barlow, C. (2020). Digital twin: Enabling technologies, challenges and open research. *IEEE Access, 8*, 108952–108971. https://doi.org/10.1109/access.2020.2998358 (accessed on 17th October 2025).
20. Hussain, F., Hussain, R., Hassan, S. A., & Hossain, E. (2020). Machine learning in IoT security: Current solutions and future challenges. *IEEE Communications Surveys & Tutorials, 22*, 1686–1721. https://doi.org/10.1109/comst.2020.2986444 (accessed on 17th October 2025).
21. Huynh-The, T., Gadekallu, T. R., Wang, W., Yenduri, G., Ranaweera, P., Pham, Q. V., Benevides da Costa, D., et al. (2023). Blockchain for the metaverse: A review. *Future Generation Computer Systems, 143*, 401–419. https://doi.org/10.1016/j.future.2023.02.008 (accessed on 17th October 2025).
22. Ibrahim, A., & Gebali, F. (2025). Enhancing security for resource-constrained smart cities IoT applications: Optimizing cryptographic techniques with effective field multipliers. *Cryptography*. https://www.semanticscholar.org/paper/7bf8f0ba9142435daa79ea61c57c6445a9cfd726 (accessed on 17th October 2025).
23. Illi, E., Qaraqe, M., Althunibat, S., Alhasanat, A., Alsafasfeh, M., de Ree, M., et al. (2023). Physical layer security for authentication, confidentiality, and malicious node detection: A paradigm shifts in securing IoT networks. *IEEE Communications Surveys & Tutorials, 26*, 347–388. https://doi.org/10.1109/comst.2023.3327327 (accessed on 17th October 2025).
24. Iqbal, M., Laksmono, A. M. A., Prihatno, A. T., Pratama, D., Jeong, B., & Kim, H. (2023). Enhancing IoT security: Integrating MQTT with ARIA cipher 256 algorithm cryptography and mbedTLS. https://doi.org/10.1109/platcon60102.2023.10255171 (accessed on 17th October 2025).
25. Ismail, S., Mehannaoui, R., Hunde, E. T., & Reza, H. (2025). Among the DLTs: Holochain for the security of IoT distributed networks—A review and conceptual framework. *Sensors (Basel, Switzerland), 25*. https://www.semanticscholar.org/paper/d17b3cec8d46f36f73838e2bbfffad21c4bcd449 (accessed on 17th October 2025).
26. Jain, U., Pirasteh, S., & Hussain, M. (2022). Lightweight, secure, efficient, and dynamic scheme for mutual authentication of devices in Internet-of-Things-Fog environment. *Concurrency and Computation: Practice and Experience, 35*. https://doi.org/10.1002/cpe.7428 (accessed on 17th October 2025).

27. Jebrane, J., & Lazaar, S. (2021). A performance comparison of lightweight cryptographic algorithms suitable for IoT transmissions. *General Letters in Mathematics, 10*, 46–53. https://doi.org/10.31559/glm2021.10.2.5 (accessed on 17th October 2025).

28. Kaur, B., Rakhra, M., Singh, D., Singh, A., & Shruti. (2024). Advancements in lightweight cryptography: Secure solutions for resource-constrained environments in IoT, WSNs, and CPS. *2024 11th International Conference on Reliability, Infocom Technologies and Optimization (Trends and Future Directions) (ICRITO)*. https://www.semanticscholar.org/paper/7b845cb33f8b5b10088e87f59613a4b9e2276246 (accessed on 17th October 2025).

29. LeBlanc, N. (2020). An analysis and enumeration of the blockchain and future implications. https://core.ac.uk/download/322850883.pdf (accessed on 17th October 2025).

30. Li, T., Sahu, A. K., Talwalkar, A., & Smith, V. (2020). Federated learning: Challenges, methods, and future directions. *IEEE Signal Processing Magazine, 37*, 50–60. https://doi.org/10.1109/msp.2020.2975749 (accessed on 17th October 2025).

31. Maqsood, T., Hameed, K., Junaid, M., & Tahir, N. (2025). Enhancing IoT healthcare security with post-quantum cryptography: A performance and case study analysis. *2025 6th International Conference on Advancements in Computational Sciences (ICACS)*. https://www.semanticscholar.org/paper/b954642151968f9723e135caf47c6bd23dc549d9 (accessed on 17th October 2025).

32. Mehrotra, U., Mehta, N., Agarwal, P., Gupta, S., & Shrivastava, P. (2022). Methodology to test optimal encryption algorithms for IoT applications. https://doi.org/10.1109/ic3i56241.2022.10073291 (accessed on 17th October 2025).

33. Mendez, D. M., Papapanagiotou, I., & Yang, B. (2017). Internet of Things: Survey on security and privacy. http://arxiv.org/abs/1707.01879 (accessed on 17th October 2025).

34. Mutyal, M. R. (2025). Security and privacy challenges in IoT: A review of threats, solutions, and future trends. *International Journal for Research in Applied Science and Engineering Technology*. https://www.semanticscholar.org/paper/c59ba2016798a9e16434ac2e8733094312a56284 (accessed on 17th October 2025).

35. Nabavirazavi, S., & Iyengar, S. (2022). LAKEE: A lightweight authenticated key exchange protocol for power constrained devices. *ArXiv, abs/2210.16367*. https://www.semanticscholar.org/paper/118a1ee95be08b90d8c2455040af884a9fec1cb6 (accessed on 17th October 2025).

36. Rahman, M. A., & Laskar, A. N. (2024). Securing IoT networks: Challenges and solutions for next-generation smart devices. *Journal of Information Technology and Sciences*. https://www.semanticscholar.org/paper/4652fd57a0ffa7b2fe46182beddd00b2a4008c79 (accessed on 17th October 2025).
37. Rangaree, P., & Marshell, J. M. (2025). Enhanced lightweight cryptographic protocols for secure IoT-based sensor and ad hoc networks. *ICTACT Journal on Communication Technology*. https://www.semanticscholar.org/paper/3f900252049ccc5c10f8fcbc4432b9f831620702 (accessed on 17th October 2025).
38. Rejeb, A., Rejeb, K., Treiblmaier, H., Appolloni, A., Alghamdi, S., Alhasawi, Y., & Iranmanesh, M. (2023). The Internet of Things (IoT) in healthcare: Taking stock and moving forward. *Internet of Things, 22*, 100721. https://doi.org/10.1016/j.iot.2023.100721 (accessed on 17th October 2025).
39. Sai, S., Kanadia, M., & Chamola, V. (2024). Empowering IoT with generative AI: Applications, case studies, and limitations. *IEEE Internet of Things Magazine, 7*, 38–43. https://www.semanticscholar.org/paper/ba1d100c72e1e6d331aafbe402014d77bd3e3c80 (accessed on 17th October 2025).
40. Sandanamudi, P. K., Agrawal, N., Tripathi, N., & Kumar, P. B. N. (2025). Securing UAV communications: A comparative performance analysis of post-quantum cryptographic techniques. *2025 17th International Conference on COMmunication Systems and NETworks (COMSNETS)*. https://www.semanticscholar.org/paper/39875bcc0a4bc111a14b3af9b29a66e39156fb88 (accessed on 17th October 2025).
41. Sawlikar, A. P., Raich, D., Ganguly, B. S., & Yadav, L. N. (2025). An enhanced encryption scheme for IoT-based wireless sensor network using DNA enclosed fully homomorphic approach. *Transactions on Emerging Telecommunications Technologies, 36*. https://www.semanticscholar.org/paper/b0fa09be3eba1b0a597cedbe5a4144525ae9d0e6 (accessed on 17th October 2025).
42. Sebastian, M. (2025). Securing IoT devices: A comprehensive technical framework. *World Journal of Advanced Research and Reviews*. https://www.semanticscholar.org/paper/67c980f20695e337c87409e47b725927b583199e (accessed on 17th October 2025).
43. Shilppaa, K., & Kallam, S. (2025). A quantum-resistant cryptography for secure IoT communication using novel QRC_BIKAES framework. *2025 IEEE 5th International Conference on VLSI Systems, Architecture,*

Technology and Applications (VLSI SATA). https://www.semanticscholar.org/paper/ecdae03ec5f3667eb6e7f5036e8c512cd49a8243 (accessed on 17th October 2025).

44. Sreedevi, T. P., & Shastri, V. H. (2025). Evolving trends in lightweight cryptography for secure IoT: Overcoming challenges and delivering solutions. *International Research Journal on Advanced Engineering and Management (IRJAEM)*. https://www.semanticscholar.org/paper/057712d9cdd1929cd02a4ba66b031ee77778ddb5 (accessed on 17th October 2025).
45. Subhashini, R., & Jyothi, D. G. (2024). Broken-stick regressive lightweight Speck cryptographic constrained application protocol for data security in IoT aware smart home. *International Journal of Computer Networks and Applications*. https://www.semanticscholar.org/paper/5f6d926ed2fff1fb6f274ef54d6e98abcef6d238 (accessed on 17th October 2025).
46. Subhashini, R., & Jyothi, D. G. (2024). Optimized constrained application protocol for IoT smart home data security: A novel lightweight approach. *2024 International Conference on Recent Advances in Science and Engineering Technology (ICRASET)*. https://www.semanticscholar.org/paper/9fb2ed16e1189982b9fd2a6fab7f620188759a01 (accessed on 17th October 2025).
47. Thakor, V. A., Razzaque, M. A., Darji, A. D., & Patel, A. (2023). A novel 5-bit S-box design for lightweight cryptography algorithms. *Journal of Information Security and Applications, 73*, 103444. https://doi.org/10.1016/j.jisa.2023.103444 (accessed on 17th October 2025).
48. Thangavel, S., Kotiyal, A., Thomas, A., Patil, H., Kulkarni, S., et al. (2024). Robust authentication protocols for IoT devices in high-density networks. *2024 International Conference on Distributed Systems, Computer Networks and Cybersecurity (ICDSCNC)*. https://www.semanticscholar.org/paper/9634668cc89b6cc2e37dba5a4dc90c818772af00 (accessed on 17th October 2025).
49. Wang, Y., Su, Z., Zhang, N., Xing, R., Liu, D., Luan, T. H., & Shen, X. (2022). A survey on metaverse: Fundamentals, security, and privacy. *IEEE Communications Surveys & Tutorials, 25*, 319–352. https://doi.org/10.1109/comst.2022.3202047 (accessed on 17th October 2025).
50. Yu, S. J., Lee, Y. C., & Yang, C. H. (2021). A 1.18mW double ratchet cryptographic processor with backward secrecy for IoT devices. *2021 IEEE Asian Solid-State Circuits Conference (A-SSCC)*. https://www.semanticscholar.org/paper/ecfd4f47cf5a0a90aded01138f2983318c45ed2b (accessed on 17th October 2025).

CHAPTER 6

PRIVACY AND DATA PROTECTION IN IOT

Contents

INTRODUCTION

The Internet of Things (IoT) represents a transformative shift in the manner in which devices communicate, interact, and share information, revolutionizing day-to-day life in various aspects of smart cities, smart homes, and industrial applications. The massive interconnected network enhances efficiency and convenience via real-time monitoring and automatic control. However, this advancement in technology raises a lot of issues regarding privacy as well as data protection. Because these devices are continuously collecting and transmitting information, oftentimes without explicit user consent, the danger of unauthorized entry and data breach escalates. An effective comprehension of these privacy issues is a key to effective data protection policies that can safeguard user information as well as sustain trust in IoT technology. This chapter will address the issues and procedures that need to be followed to address privacy and security in the context of this very dynamic world. In order to comprehend the sophisticated relationship between IoT, data protection, and privacy, it is crucial not to merely focus on the vast amount of data generated but also on the broad variety of applications and environments where IoT pervades. From healthcare monitoring systems of patient health to smart grids for effective energy utilization, the range of uses presents unique challenges for secure data storage and processing. The application of advanced technologies such as blockchain holds the promise for enhancing security, especially in advanced environments like smart cities and industry, where accountability and trust are critical issues. By studying these technologies, it is possible to discover their potential in evading risks of data manipulation and misuse. Through this chapter, the methods and models of security needed to maintain individual privacy in IoT applications will be investigated. Edge computing emerges as an essential component for addressing the privacy and data protection challenges embedded in IoT systems. By addressing data closer to where it is created, edge computing reduces reliance on cloud-based central infrastructures, thereby providing lower latency and greater application responsiveness for applications such as intelligent energy grids and power monitoring apps. Furthermore, it enables real-time data analysis while maintaining closer privacy control because sensitive information does not have to be transported to distant servers. This capability not only benefits to solve the immediate issues of security but also fulfills the provisions mandating strict data protection guidelines. It will be looking at the implications of adopting edge computing in the IoT system throughout this chapter and how it can offer pathways towards improved data security that lead towards a space where the trust of users is preserved in this increasingly connected world.

Importance of Privacy and Data Protection in IoT

With the continuing growth of IoT devices that continue to change the nature of our daily lives, data security and privacy cannot be overstressed. The IoT ecosystem typically consists of a vast population of connected devices, from home smart devices to wearables tracking health metrics. Each such device captures and exchanges sensitive personal data, which can create a number of vulnerabilities if not secured well. For instance, IoT technology use in environmental parameter measurement, i.e., air quality, points towards actual need for robust mechanisms of data protection. In a system that is supposed to send temperature and humidity measurements, the presence of security measures like AES-128 encryption and effective access control becomes imperative in the attempt to safeguard individual and sensitive data that is collected by these devices. Hence, following strict privacy protocols is critical towards upholding user trust and integrity of IoT solutions. Further, research also pinpoints some critical vulnerabilities in current IoT infrastructures that compromise user privacy and data integrity. Ineffective handling of credentials, susceptibility to network attacks, and ineffective encryption methods highlight the critical need for an enhanced security framework.

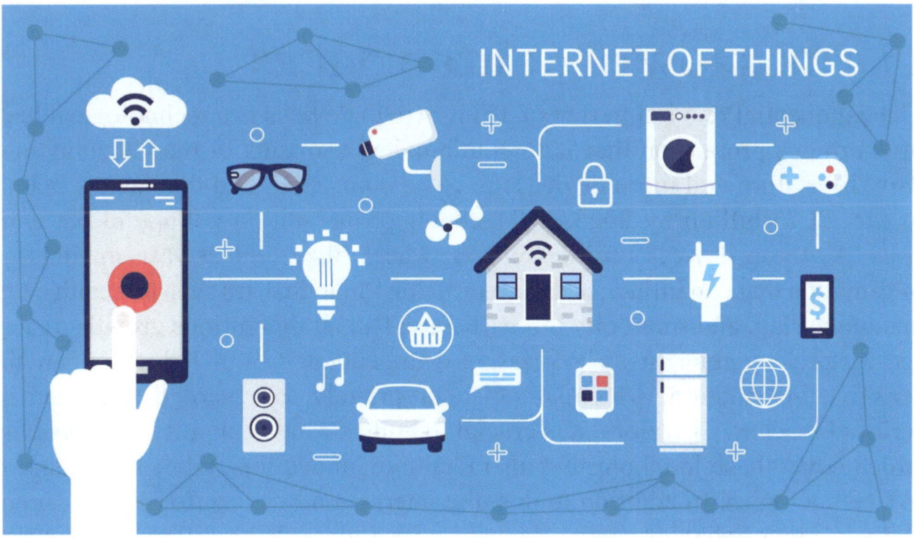

Figure 6.1. The IoT ecosystem often encompasses a vast array of interconnected devices, from smart home appliances to wearables that track health metrics.

Source: https://network-insight.net/wp-content/uploads/2017/10/AdobeStock_150511712-scaled.jpeg.

Despite technological advancements in IoT security, many systems continue to expose their users to malicious threats. The reality is that unchecked vulnerabilities could lead to unauthorized access, data leakage, and the irreversible compromise of user privacy. As illustrated in high-profile case studies, the effects of weak data protection can far outreach individual users to involve organizations and society at large. The strategies, therefore, encompass preventive and rapid response measures that must be developed and implemented to guarantee a safer IoT environment (Ahmad et al., 2024). In order to overcome these threats, all the major stakeholders must come together. Organizations, governments, and civil societies must come together to develop best practices and regulatory policies that guarantee data protection in the IoT environment. This effort should also be directed towards raising awareness and education for the users regarding potential threats and ensuring protection of their personal information. Furthermore, security technology research and development should go on to address new threats and risks. By creating a culture of cooperation and vigilance, it is possible to buffer against the IoTs widespread data aggregation features. Finally, making sure that privacy and data protection remain strong is not a matter of technology alone, but one of shared responsibility that calls for the sustained efforts of all stakeholders (Figure 6.1).

6.1. THE GROWTH OF IOT DEVICES

The exponential rise in Internet of Things (IoT) devices is a technological leap of enormous proportion that is revolutionizing segments of the economy and daily life. More and more devices are to be connected, and the pace is bound to exceed 75 billion by 2025. IoT technology integration is hopeful but with risks. As these devices proliferate everywhere, they collect vast amounts of information that can influence decision-making in industries such as health care, manufacturing, and smart city infrastructure. But all this furious growth creates serious privacy concerns. The massive data generated by IoT devices contain sensitive information, which, if not appropriately safeguarded, can lead to serious breaches. Therefore, it is crucial to build strong data protection systems which cover these loopholes but also facilitate innovation and development of IoT technologies. In addition to this, the interaction between IoT development and consumer behavior cannot be emphasized more. With different industries utilizing data that is derived from connected devices, the marketing strategy used has changed significantly. Personalized marketing experiences are more aimed at individual consumers by analyzing data in real-time, facilitating greater customer engagement and loyalty. The strategy also presents opportunities for ethical controversies over consumers' privacy. The issue arises whenever businesses exploit the fine line between personal services and intrusiveness that may turn consumers off. Additionally, while business organizations aim to capitalize on their huge data reservoirs, regulatory compliance is equally important to maintain the trust of consumers in the future. With data-driven pressures and protecting individual privacy in counterpoise, issues of ethics regarding consumer data usage in the growing IoT sphere arise, and hence it is ever so important to have continuous discourse and legislation. Lastly, the potential social impact of widespread adoption of IoT extends beyond being convenient; they reflect profound issues of trust and security. More connectivity brings more danger from cyber-attacks on IoT devices that can be a threat to users' personal data. For instance, as smart home devices get more popular, the vulnerabilities in these devices can be exploited as portals by hackers. This is compounded by new innovations such as augmented reality ads, which, while boosting engagement, also raise implications of user privacy of their information (Dwivedi et al., 2022). Further, as companies like marketing firms evolve through the application of AI and data from IoTs, there are ethical concerns brought up regarding consumer rights and autonomy over their virtual identities (Dwivedi et al., 2020). In order to see that the expansion of IoT devices continues to remain sustainable and positive, it is important to deal with these privacy and security issues upfront, promoting a balance between innovation and safeguarding the rights of the individual (Figure 6.2).

Figure 6.2. Personalized marketing experiences are increasingly tailored to consumers based on real-time data analysis, resulting in enhanced customer engagement and loyalty.

Source: https://cdn.onix-systems.com/uploads/Will_AI_help_build_stronger_customer_connections_6dd443a9d3.webp.

6.1.1. Statistics on IoT Device Proliferation

The deployment of IoT devices has scaled unprecedented heights, significantly altering the design of data consumption and creation across all sectors. The estimate puts the number of IoT devices connected at over 30 billion by the year 2025, building a vast network that has become intertwined with day-to-day life as well as many commercial processes. This rapid adoption not only improves operational effectiveness and productivity but also raises serious concerns related to data protection and privacy. As organizations more and more depend upon IoT solutions to automate operations and drive better decision-making, they are confronted with an onslaught of sensitive data that must be safeguarded with enhanced care. With a robust IT infrastructure necessary to handle the continually expanding amount of data, organizations are confronted with the problem of how to ensure that the architectures they establish can effectively safeguard user privacy in this dynamic digital world, and thus the urgent need for stronger data protection legislation (Allioui et al., 2023). Wherever IoT devices expand, the medical field is a mixed picture of both possible gains and inherent risks with this techno-rush. With greater reliance on networked devices to track patients, collect data, and perform advanced diagnostic procedures, healthcare providers now must manage enormous quantities of sensitive patient information.

Figure 6.3. With an increasing reliance on interconnected devices for patient monitoring, data collection, and advanced diagnostic processes, healthcare providers are now managing vast amounts of sensitive patient information.

Source: https://www.philips.com/c-dam/corporate/innovation-and-you/global/dec-2023/top-10-most-read-header.jpg.

A bibliometric analysis revealed that academic attention to IoT applications in healthcare has grown exponentially, with topics like blockchain technology and artificial intelligence embedding being at the forefront (Rejeb et al., 2023). Although this boom has its advantages, it also presents new challenges in data privacy. With the possibility of unauthorized access to individual health data, there is a growing need for robust security architecture. With healthcare institutions using IoT technologies, they must put data privacy first to ensure compliance with relevant laws and regulations while maintaining public trust in the management of personal data. Finally, while the benefits of IoT growth are evident, so too are the pressing concerns involving privacy and data protection. With every new gadget, there are new points of exposure, and it is becoming increasingly difficult for institutions to have adequate barriers against potential breaches. It calls for the realization that the devices' architecture in an IoT environment must be accompanied by security aspects at every level of deployment. Organizations need to adopt a proactive approach by updating their data protection methods based on increasing threats due to device proliferation. With such a dynamic area, establishing standards for data governance will be essential to the extent that the inherent benefits of IoT will not be bought at the expense of individual privacy. In the future, balancing technological advancement with rigorous protection of data will be part of unleashing IoTs full potential without undermining users' privacy (Allioui et al., 2023) (Figure 6.3).

6.1.2. Types of IoT Devices and Their Functions

The IoT is a wide range of devices with varying functionalities across industries, transforming daily life and industries themselves at large. Among the most common types of IoT devices are sensor-based smart home systems with smart thermostats, lights, and security cameras. These technologies are more convenient as they offer remote control via smartphones, optimize energy consumption, and improve security via enhanced surveillance capabilities. But the convergence of such systems raises fundamental questions regarding privacy and data security because they forever collect and process personal data. Such interconnectivity refers to an essential aspect of IoT: although it improves functionality and functionality, it necessarily involves challenges around possible data leakage and unauthorized access to confidential data, necessitating urgent attention to privacy policy and data protection policies (Dwivedi et al., 2020). In addition to smart home devices, wearables are also a significant category, with several health and fitness features. Wearable devices such as fitness trackers and smartwatches are designed to monitor vital signs, body activity, and general well-being, thereby promoting healthier lifestyles. These wearables gather a range of personal health data, which can be incredibly valuable in medical diagnostics and personalized health guidance. Yet collection and utilization of health data raise serious privacy issues. Third-party vendors' potential misuse of confidential health data or data leaks exposing individuals to privacy risks are fears evoked. The data handling is further complicated by this sector's technological innovation, through the implementation of Mobile Edge Computing, inducing an urgent need for wide-ranging data privacy regulation (Lim et al., 2020). Industrial IoT devices are yet another significant category, responsible for the efficiency and safety of industries like manufacturing, agriculture, and logistics. Industrial IoT devices provide real-time monitoring and control of operations, including the tracking of equipment performance and environment levels through sensors. Through predictive maintenance and optimization of supply chain operations, industrial IoT systems increase overall productivity and reduce operating expenses. However, their integration into major infrastructure has certain significant security implications. As industries become more integrated, the stakes of data security escalate with possible ramifications not only for a single organization but also for public safety and economic welfare. Hence, it is important to address the particular privacy and data protection challenges raised by industrial IoT deployments using robust security measures and compliance with relevant regulation (Dwivedi et al., 2020).

6.1.3. Implications of Widespread IoT Adoption

The impact of IoT wide-scale adoption is profound, particularly with respect to data security and privacy. With more devices connected to each other, vast amounts of personal data are being generated and shared on a daily basis. Such expansion poses serious challenges to data security as the connectivity of IoT devices provides numerous points of vulnerability to cyber-attacks. Organizations should realize that while IoT technologies have the potential to maximize operation effectiveness and decision-making procedures, as has been seen in recent research, it also requires setting up effective data management systems to ensure sensitive data are safeguarded. Poor protection of user data can result in significant legal penalties and loss of organizational reputation, thus influencing trust in IoT technologies. Therefore, comprehensive privacy and data security measures are essential in this new digital world of exchange (Allioui et al., 2023). Besides, the implications are not entirely technical; they also entail ethical and social ones. With IoT sensors sensing private details about people's lives, matters of consent, openness, and the risk of surveillance present themselves. The transformation to a more interconnected way of life puts a burden on both users and developers to know the privacy threats that come with IoT adoption. The continuous debate on responsible digitalization points towards the need for the enforcement of ethical principles and standards to ensure technology is used in the best interests of society without infringing on human rights. The urgency of such dialogue is proportional to the universal drive towards confronting climate change, as urged in the UN COP26 conference, highlighting the symbiotic relationship between society and technology. There needs to be an equilibrium response where the benefits of IoT are derived without impinging on individuals' privacy liberty (Dwivedi et al., 2021). Lastly, the challenge of accomplishing successful data protection for IoT deployment is also elevated by the speed of technological advancement. Organizations and businesses must be agile in adapting their security infrastructure as new threats evolve. This agility does not necessarily require sophisticated technology solutions but also constant spending on cybersecurity training and awareness among employees and users. The integration of IoT into critical infrastructures necessitates a prioritization of enhanced encryption, secure data communication protocols, and real-time monitoring to actively spot threats. In trying to gain from IoTs possibilities for enhanced productivity and efficiency, corporations also need to concurrently create comprehensive frameworks outlining data usage, management, and privacy policies to ensure compliance with relevant regulations. Ultimately, the mastery of those complexities will shape the future of IoT implementation, finding harmony between innovation and the demands of privacy and data security (Allioui et al., 2023) (Figure 6.4).

Figure 6.4. Failure to adequately protect user data can result in significant legal penalties and damage to organizational reputation, thereby affecting trust in IoT technologies.

Source: https://www.adnovum.com/hs-fs/hubfs/IMAGES/04_Insights/Blog/2021/3%20Ways%20Organisations%20Can%20Ensure%20Data%20Protection.jpg?width=1088&name=3%20Ways%20Organisations%20Can%20Ensure%20Data%20Protection.jpg.

6.2. PRIVACY CONCERNS IN IOT

The nascent field of the IoT presents a host of privacy problems that are deserving of severe examination, particularly as this technology involves the integration of personal data collection into everyday objects. Privacy is traditionally a static construct; however, contemporary research reveals that it is dynamic and context-dependent. Users tend to adopt varying levels of data protection depending on the provided technology and environment, a phenomenon that compels it to be more challenging for us to comprehend privacy in the rapid digital world. Such vagueness in user expectations in IoT environments can raise distrust, an aspect that can hinder the adoption of health-enhancing technologies. Thus, researchers have begun to suggest a more sensitive and nuanced conceptualization of privacy that is aware of these complexities and addresses the one-issue causalities surrounding cutting-edge technologies such as IoT, particularly in areas of sensitive nature such as digital health and informatics (Herriger et al., 2025). Another significant additional layer to the problem of privacy associated with IoT is the problem of data security in and of itself, particularly for the healthcare sector. As more and more devices begin collecting sensitive health data, inadequate protection mechanisms can have the ability to lead to abuses or invasion of privacy. Even as there are obvious advantages of IoT solutions—i.e., improved healthcare efficiency and improved patient outcomes—the advantages are supplemented with escalating threats in connection with personal data safety. A lack of effective regulatory mechanisms, particularly in nations like Indonesia, increases patient information's vulnerability to third-party and healthcare provider misuse and leakage.

Governments, therefore, need to implement robust legislation that guarantees the first priority be given to protecting personal information in IoT healthcare systems to build users' confidence and promote ethical use of such technologies (Rohmah, 2024). Finally, IoT privacy solutions must converge as a joint endeavor of stakeholders, including policymakers, technology developers, and deliverers of healthcare. All of these stakeholders must contribute towards crafting an ecosystem that respects the privacy of users while leveraging IoT innovation. For instance, technology developers must accord utmost priority to secure design practices that incorporate privacy protections from the outset, having encryption of data, ethical processing of data, as well as open user consent procedures. At the policy level, devising overall regulation and guidelines will make users aware of their rights and the potential repercussions of data sharing. Likewise, healthcare providers must ensure truthful communication with patients about the use of their data, forming informed consent in line with ethical best practices. Cumulatively, these steps may lay the ground for building a trust that is requisite for embedding IoT into everyday life sustainably, especially in sectors where privacy is concerned.

6.2.1. Types of Personal Data Collected by IoT Devices

The explosion of IoT devices has changed the landscape of personal data collection, and a careful consideration of the nature of data collected and the effect on privacy and data protection is merited. IoT devices, such as smart home appliances, wearables, and health-monitoring devices, collect generally an immense quantity of personal data, including biometrics, location data, and usage patterns. For instance, wearable fitness trackers collect information related to an individual's physical activity, heart rate, and sleep quality automatically every day. Such continuous monitoring can be highly enlightening for individuals but is at the same time raising serious issues related to privacy. As the public continues to rely more and more on such technology, the volume and scope of personal data accumulated increase the opportunity for misuse or unauthorized exploitation, and the imperative for good privacy policies and structures is all the more urgent. In addition, the interaction between IoT devices and other technologies further increases the various kinds of personal data available for collection. When combined with smart environments, they communicate with each other, creating a massive network that collectively collects information on people's habits, likings, and even routines. For example, a smart thermostat can track people's temperature likings based on their activities while simultaneously taking in data from a fitness tracker for tracking activity levels.

This linking can result in complex data profiles not only characterizing personal tastes but also subjecting them to sophisticated analytical instruments for advertisement or even monitoring. Thus, as has been laid down in the data protection and privacy discourse, the risk of personal data being manipulated and analyzed by them without consent is an important legal and ethical concern that has to be addressed (Bormida, 2021; Dwivedi et al., 2022). Finally, the types of personal data collected by IoT devices extend beyond technical readings or usage behaviors; they increasingly entail data that can be attributed to the identities of individuals, and hence, have the potential to lead to stigmatization and discrimination. The majority of IoT devices collect private data regarding health, such as blood glucose levels from diabetic's trackers or heart rates from smartwatches. Compilation of such data seems to be able to unintentionally reveal factors of vulnerability that can be abused. Additionally, the threat of re-identification from de-anonymized data sets reinforces the problem, as described by recent studies on "group privacy" and data profiling. Hence, while IoT devices are capable of enhancing the standards of private and public life with personalized services, they also, in the process, challenge the society-accepted norms of privacy and individual independence and necessitate a robust regulatory mechanism for protecting the rights of users (Bormida, 2021; Dwivedi et al., 2022) (Figure 6.5).

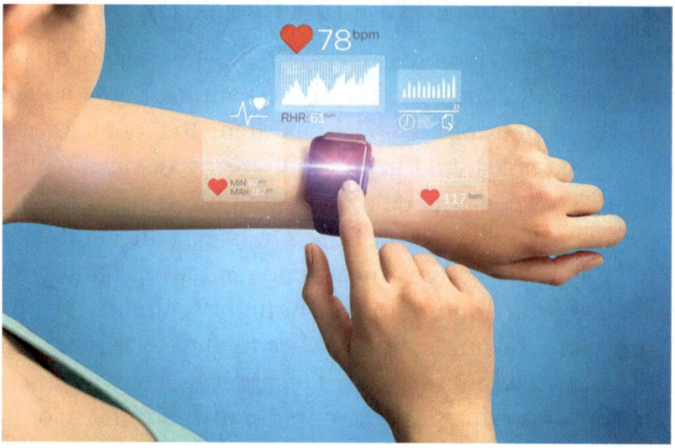

Figure 6.5. Wearable fitness trackers continuously collect data related to an individual's physical activity, heart rate, and sleep quality.

Source: https://hospitalsmagazine.com/wp-content/uploads/2023/01/wearable-devices-.jpg.

6.2.2. Risks Associated with Data Breaches

The large number of IoT devices significantly raises the level of risk of data breaches, ushering in a complex landscape of privacy concerns. Since numerous devices take in and transmit sensitive information, vulnerabilities in the security systems they use can compromise personal details to unauthorized parties. Data breaches occur when malicious individuals exploit such vulnerabilities, the most common of which are either weak authentication systems or unsecured communication protocols. The implications of these invasions can be severe, invading individual privacy and making it easier for identity theft, monetary frauds, and illegitimate surveillance. As IoT products are expanding their horizons, solutions for these vulnerabilities become more and more essential to secure sensitive information and maintaining trust of users in virtual environments. Inadequate consideration of security in such networked devices may cause extensive harm, the logic of which reinforces the need to deliver sound data protection measures throughout IoT networks (Fayayola et al., 2024). Direct financial loss and privacy violations, besides, data breaches have organizational liability and loss-of-reputation consequences. Companies that are the victims of data breaches can be legally penalized, particularly in instances where there is a violation of pre-set standards such as the General Data Protection Regulation (GDPR). Conformity with such standards emphasizes accountability since it compels organizations to carry out proactive measures for protecting data. Besides, violations lead to the loss of consumer trust since users are more hesitant to provide their data to firms that have themselves indicated vulnerability. Therefore, organizations should not only defend against breaches but also cultivate an open and transparent culture that defends against threats to establish stakeholder trust in their data management practice. This regulatory compliance eventually leads to more stringent privacy and security protocols in the IoT environment (Fayayola et al., 2024). Furthermore, the issue of data privacy in IoT systems is further complicated by the dynamic nature of cyber threats. As cybercriminals continue to develop and improve, existing levels of security have a tendency to fail to counter future forms of attack such as incentivized ransomware or sophisticated phishing attacks. The interconnectivity of IoT devices provides a means for the attackers to attack many points of entry, which increases the impact of one attack. Additionally, most IoT devices lack heavy computation capabilities and no enhanced security features, which exposes them to being exploited. This reality calls for a two-pronged effort of device architecture security enhancement and enhancing users' awareness of potential threats. Effective privacy protection in the IoT space requires not just technical means but also holistic methods for user consent, transparency, and lawful collection of data, and thereby making the digital space more secure for all parties involved (Haris et al., 2023).

6.2.3. User Awareness and Consent Issues

For the case of the IoT, user identification and consent are big concerns due to the pervasive nature of data collection and processing. Users are not able to have a wide overview of how their data is processed, leading to the violation of privacy and trust. This is additionally compounded by the numerous devices that constitute the IoT system and can collect different types of data, from apparently innocuous location tracking to more in-depth personal information. With ever-more ubiquitous IoT devices, it is imperative that there be a robust framework to ensure that users are adequately informed of their rights, dangers, and what the implications are of consenting to the collection and processing of data. Implementing these protection measures is essential to enhancing user trust and fostering a culture of responsible data stewardship in the IoT environment (Cunche et al., 2018). IoT consent issues are more than a matter of recognizing individual users; they necessitate a more advanced mechanism that appreciates the transient nature of data exchange. The conventional model of informed consent is insufficient in a world where information may be obtained and utilized in perpetuity for multifarious purposes. Users unwittingly grant consent to extensive data collection practices without full understanding of the attendant repercussions. This call to reform necessitates anew evaluation of mechanisms of consent, encouraging transparent, user-oriented interfaces that facilitate users to make informed decisions about their information. Apart from that, with IoT devices becoming increasingly powerful at manipulating and sharing data in real-time, there is a requirement to devise mechanisms for revocation of consent through which the users maintain control over their digital identities as circumstances evolve (Perera et al., 2015). Adherence to principled consent processes guarantees that data harvesting becomes less enigmatic and promotes an equitable relationship between users and service providers. Addressing the problem of user consent and awareness is not only an ethical issue but also a legal imperative, particularly in terms of regulations such as the General Data Protection Regulation (GDPR). The GDPR puts in place strict requirements for user consent, whereby it must be explicit, informed, and clear. This background sets the stage for why IoT companies should put in place informed consent procedures that are regulatory compliant and user-centered. Technology advancements should be harnessed to craft accessible privacy controls and detailed consent statements so that users may understand their data rights. Moreover, an open debate regarding users' expectations of privacy can ensure IoT providers' heightened responsibility. As organizations strive to address compliance requirements, they also must weigh that effort against the need for user engagement and education to build trust and ensure that consent is not mere formality but an expression of user autonomy in the new digital landscape (Cunche et al., 2018) (Figure 6.6).

Figure 6.6. Users often lack a comprehensive understanding of how their data is being utilized, leading to potential breaches of privacy and trust.

Source: https://blogs.idc.com/wp-content/uploads/2021/02/02.22.21_AP_Featured-scaled.jpg.

6.3. DATA PROTECTION REGULATIONS

Increased utilization of IoT devices has witnessed increased levels of regulation of data protection legislation, given the sensitive details the devices typically collect. As IoT technology has become a staple in daily life, from smart home gadgets to pet health tracking devices, user privacy concerns impose the necessity for strict regulatory standards. Legal initiatives like the General Data Protection Regulation (GDPR) in the EU and the California Consumer Privacy Act (CCPA) in the US have become significant instruments in establishing standards for data treatment and getting the consent of users. These laws impose strict standards on data collection practices, educating consumers regarding their individual data rights and enhancing data processing practice transparency, thereby promoting a culture of accountability among makers of IoT devices and providers of services. Compliance with these data protection acts is challenging but also offers opportunities to the ever-evolving world of IoT. As has been observed in analysis that takes into account the implications of regulations like GDPR and CCPA, there is a critical need for automated compliance solutions to manage the fast-growing volume of sensitive data generated by IoT devices. The intricacy of integrating privacy compliance into existing frameworks necessitates innovative solutions, particularly given the pace at which technology evolves. The application of advanced techniques like deep learning offers feasible solutions to enable automation of compliance monitoring and checking and thereby ease some of the burdens placed on organizations. Solutions that offer functionalities like anomaly detection as well as dynamic policy updating not only enhance compliance but also enhance the overall data security, making it more resilient to counter IoT threats. Specifically, the development of machine learning-driven automated compliance frameworks is a groundbreaking approach to addressing data protection regulation in IoT settings. Through embracing deep learning techniques, researchers have made systems capable of offering real-time threat detection and compliance check, showing how regulatory compliance and technological development intersect. The study proves high threat detection and compliance levels, identifying the strengths of such frameworks in providing complementary data protection mechanisms for IoT systems. Emphasizing such automated technologies not only enables organizations to navigate through the intricacy of the compliance of regulations but also shapes a future in which the privacy of the users is secured amid intensifying challenges by increasingly interconnected devices and the gargantuan quantities of data that they generate (Eleyan et al., 2025). The relationship between regulations and technological advancements will ultimately determine the effectiveness of protecting privacy in the evolving era of IoT.

6.3.1. Overview of GDPR and its Relevance to IoT

The General Data Protection Regulation (GDPR), which came into force in May 2018, has proven to be a seminal framework for data protection within the European Union. The GDPR aims to fortify the privacy rights of individuals by placing stricter compliance obligations on organizations that handle personal data. Such a regulatory environment is particularly relevant to the IoT, which is characterized by ubiquitous data gathering and networked devices. GDPR dictates the principle of data transparency, security, and users' consent on which IoT manufacturers and service providers are under an obligation to ensure personal data are processed lawfully and fairly. The principles of data minimization and limitation of purpose directly address the structure and functionality of IoT devices, and hence businesses are prompted to introspect on how they gather, store, and process sensitive information. In addition, GDPR's extraterritorial application reaches across EU boundaries and forces international IoT companies to fall into line with its strictures if they handle data from EU citizens. This requirement has made people more conscious of data protection tenets within most industries, and IoT applications have come under the spotlight since most of them involve real-time data capture and analysis. Requirement that organizations appoint a Data Protection Officer and carry out Data Protection Impact Assessments merely underscores regulatory challenge for IoT stakeholders. As IoT devices continue to spread, the imperative to minimize potential risks to personal data becomes increasingly significant, necessitating compliance-oriented approach to IoT deployment and design. Companies must not only be GDPR compliant but also incorporate privacy-by-design principles into their IoT offerings to sustain user trust and protect consumer interests. While addressing privacy concerns in the use of IoT, organizations must ensure that they implement stringent data protection measures in accordance with GDPR guidelines. Techniques such as encryption and pseudonymization can be core to maintaining the privacy of personal data, especially given that IoT gadgets have a propensity to accrue sensitive information that can lead to privacy breaches when mishandled. The concerns surrounding algorithmic discrimination and data integrity presented in earlier studies demonstrate the necessity of a holistic approach towards data management within IoT settings (Williamson et al., 2024). Additionally, companies need to consider moral aspects, such as transparency of data usage and selling practices and the adequacy of obtaining user consent. It is important that the stakeholders of IoT remain proactive to the evolving regulation and technology by forging an interdisciplinary dialogue and encouraging joint governance to supplement GDPR compliance in addressing the critical intersection of privacy, data protection, and the very rapidly evolving face of IoT (Aldboush et al., 2023) (Figure 6.7).

Figure 6.7. The general data protection regulation (GDPR), implemented in May 2018, has emerged as a fundamental framework for data protection within the European Union.

Source: https://www.axistechnolabs.com/images/gdpr/gdpr-approach-img.png.

6.3.2. Other International Data Protection Laws

The international data protection laws environment is evolving extremely quickly, with states trying to strike a balance between technology that is moving ahead and people's privacy. A few jurisdictions, like the General Data Protection Regulation (GDPR) in the European Union and California's Consumer Privacy Act (CCPA), prescribe the standard for strong data protection practices. Others, however, are beginning to establish their own data protection regimes that are attuned to local culture and governance systems. For instance, Brazil's Lei Geral de Proteção de Dados (LGPD) captures the GDPR's attention to consent and rights of the individual, but also incorporates factors that are more context-specific. Familiarity with these disparate legislative approaches is paramount, particularly as the IoT expands. As IoT devices continuously churn out and transmit personal information, having access to these foreign laws matters significantly to international privacy standards and transborder information flows. Interestingly, the West African continent is currently facing a growing need for having strict data protection legislation that addresses emerging digital challenges. Countries like Nigeria have begun developing national laws to govern data protection based on user consent and data protection procedures. The same applies in other African nations where lack of response to prepare general regulations has resulted in weaknesses to be exploited against personal data. The African Unions Convention on Cyber Security and Personal Data Protection, adopted in 2014, presents a continental framework for member states to enhance data governance. As IoT devices increasingly become the norm in African countries, the merging of these new laws with indigenous cultures and economic conditions is an area of highest priority. This heightened awareness and regulatory response are significant in safeguarding user privacy and establishing trust within technological spaces.

Figure 6.8. The African Unions Convention on Cyber Security and Personal Data Protection, adopted in 2014, provides a continental framework for member states to enhance their data governance practices.

Source: https://fpf.org/wp-content/uploads/2024/11/shutterstock_2053032029-scaled.jpg.

The metaverse is a primary frontier that intersects with international data protection regimes as it is a blend of social networks, virtual reality, and augmented reality. As the metaverse evolves, so too are fears for user privacy, ownership of data, and security risks involved with such immersive spaces born. The very essence of mass gathering of data and greater interaction in virtual realms poses new challenges to existing paradigms of data protection. Research has shown that the merging of metaverses into everyday life distorts boundaries between actual and virtual interactions, and it becomes imperative to redefine international laws to address these subtleties. Privacy concerns, particularly for vulnerable groups of actors engaging in virtual interactions, necessitate policymakers across the globe to move with speed. Enacting global data protection legislation in a manner that is responsive to the distinctive challenges posed by new technologies, including the metaverse, is essential to protecting users' rights and creating a secure digital future (Figure 6.8).

6.3.3. Compliance Challenges for IoT Manufacturers

The rise of IoT devices has revolutionized many industries but has also amplified compliance challenges within the realms of privacy and data protection. IoT manufacturers generally grapple with the complexity of compliance with stricter regulatory frameworks. The regulations, such as the General Data Protection Regulation (GDPR) and the California Consumer Privacy Act (CCPA), provide exacting requirements for handling, storing, and processing of data. Therefore, the producers have to implement robust data management standards both in accordance with the law but also in response to the transparency and accountability expectations of the consumers. Failure to be in accordance with the regulatory scheme can result in heavy financial penalties, loss of customer confidence, and reputational damage to the business, which reinforces the utmost importance of proactive compliance strategies in the IoT market. In addition to compliance as an external regulatory burden, IoT creators are also saddled with inherent challenges of function heterogeneity and architecture of the devices. The dynamic composition of IoT ecosystems in terms of connected things and unbroken data flow complicates compliance. Individual devices generate enormous quantities of personal data, and the associated data protection has to be tailored with respect to various forms of data and usage contexts. Manufacturers must balance demands of functionality and innovation against demands of privacy. On top of this, technological advancements happen so rapidly that they outpace regulations, making manufacturers unsure of future compliance needs. Thus, organizations must be agile to adapt their compliance strategy to shifting regulatory landscapes in addition to increasing threats of IoT deployments. For the purpose of efficiently fighting such compliance problems, IoT manufacturers are now using sophisticated technologies such as artificial intelligence (AI) and automated compliance verification software. Integration of AI tools provides a valuable platform to progress compliance efficiency and precision. For instance, Chintoh et al. (2025) cites the application of AI in transforming privacy risk analysis through offering innovative solutions that can assist in addressing complex compliance problems. These technologies can facilitate real-time monitoring of data flow and provide insights into the regulatory needs. Furthermore, with the arrival of automated structures, such as in Echenim et al. (2025), producers are able to streamline the procedures for ascertaining compliance, thus ensuring that they are well-positioned to meet their legal obligations while streamlining oversight. This adoption of technology not only facilitates the risk mitigation but also fosters a compliance culture that is tuned into the ever-evolving digital landscape.

6.4. SECURITY MEASURES FOR IOT DEVICES

With the rise of IoT devices defining everyday life, securing IoT devices is a prime concern. The interconnected nature of IoT ecosystems exposes them to the risk of cyberattacks, which can render user privacy and data at risk. Strong encryption technology is one of the key avenues for extending IoT security. Advanced encryption measures can offer security for data exchanged between devices and measures for reducing risk from unauthorized access. Aside from that, the encryption protocols must be adaptive to the evolving threat, thus making resilience for IoT networks more immune to potential intrusion. By positioning encryption as a fundamental security solution, users can best protect user data and trust the deployment of IoT technology that is critical to its wider adoption and integration in sectors (Kumar et al., 2025). In addition to encryption, employing AI for detecting anomalies is an essential solution for managing security threats in IoT environments. AI can analyze vast volumes of data gathered by IoT sensors to identify unusual patterns that may signify imminent security risks, such as DDoS attacks. This is a proactive measure that enables organizations to rapidly identify and address possible breaches, minimizing the impact on user privacy as well as the overall system efficiency. Through ongoing learning from new data, AI systems can react to changing threats and improve threat identification. Given the complexity of IoT networks, integrating AI solutions into security systems offers the potential for more adaptable and effective protection against unauthorized access and data breaches (Fatima et al., 2024). Lastly, involving blockchain technology offers a viable platform for enhancing IoT device security features. Through decentralized and tamper-evident ledger, blockchain can potentially improve authenticity and integrity of data generated by IoT devices. With this technology, secure transactions will be facilitated and data exchanged between devices will be ensured intact and credible. Further, the transparency of blockchain has the potential to promote greater accountability among the involved parties in IoT systems. As more and more industries adopt the capabilities of IoT, integrating blockchain solutions with traditional security methods can fortify resilience against various cyber threats. By integrating these new technologies, businesses can create a secure end-to-end security framework that not just safeguards the user data but also fosters consumer trust in IoT applications (Kumar et al., 2025) (Figure 6.9).

Figure 6.9. Emerging encryption methods can safeguard the data transmitted between devices and mitigating risks of unauthorized access.

Source: https://blog.ishosting.com/hubfs/blog/data-encryption/encryption.png.

6.4.1. Best Practices for Securing IoT Devices

Securing IoT devices is increasingly so with proliferation threatening individual privacy and data security. One of the practices necessary is the use of strong, multifactor authentication mechanisms. These mechanisms strengthen security by requiring more than a single method of verification before granting access. Under the IoMT security study, adopting a four-factor authentication mechanism would prove to significantly improve protection against intrusion and data breach. By incorporating the utilization of knowledge, possession, inherence, and device uniqueness factors, this model further strengthens the security posture of IoT devices that often operate in resource-constrained environments. By prioritizing robust authentication techniques, users and companies can effectively minimize threats created by device vulnerabilities, thereby securing sensitive data (Byeon, 2025). Periodic firmware updates of IoT devices is also a best practice. The majority of security breaches are due to antiquated software, so it is crucial for users to update their devices. Manufacturers typically release updates that not only introduce new functionality but also patch flaws. A proactive approach includes the setting of reminders or the utilization of automated tools to make certain that patches are applied the instant that they become available. It is also important to employ secure coding practices at the development level in order to avoid such prevalent vulnerabilities as those involving inadequate input validation and error handling. By creating a culture of regular maintenance and safe development, stakeholders ensure a general framework to protect the security and stability of IoT systems from future threats (Nutalapati, 2024). Finally, by employing encryption techniques on data stored in and carried by IoT devices, it is imperative in securing a communications setup. Data encryption both in transit and at rest protects against unauthorized access and ensures confidential information remains confidential. This is particularly crucial when dealing with personal identifiable information or other sensitive data that, in the event of a breach, could cause serious privacy violation. Moreover, secure communication protocols such as TLS ensure secure against man-in-the-middle attacks, which are prevalent in IoT networks. Collectively, the encryption acts and secure communications assure an invincible layer of defense, safeguarding user privacy amidst the complexities of digitality in IoT (Byeon, 2025; Nutalapati, 2024).

6.4.2. Role of Encryption in Data Protection

Encryption technologies integration is a fundamental aspect of data protection in the IoT. As devices are increasingly interconnected, the quantity of sensitive data being transmitted across networks grows exponentially, enhancing the risk of malicious access and data losses. Encryption represents a line of defense that encrypts plaintext data into an unreadable format, which can only be accessed by authorized staff. This ensures that even if data packets are intercepted in transit, they cannot be accessed by would-be attackers. Encryption's role in the IoT ecosystem cannot be overstated, as it not only protects individual privacy but also builds trust in digital environments where data sharing is vital to function and innovate. Thus, deployment of robust encryption mechanisms is of utmost importance in providing privacy and data integrity in a more connected world. Also, the power of encryption in protecting data within IoT devices is augmented by advancements in cryptographic techniques. Since technology is advancing at a very high speed, technologies deployed for encrypting data are themselves getting more sophisticated with enhanced resistance to contemporary threats. Encryption technologies such as AES (Advanced Encryption Standard) and RSA (Rivest-Shamir-Adleman) have become powerful systems of security for safeguarding sensitive information. However, as encryption technologies advance, so do the mechanisms of cybercrime, which implies that there is a constant demand for innovation in the practice of encryption. The application of encryption in IoT devices also has to be accompanied by an overarching security strategy, comprising regular updates and the implementation of encryption in hardware. This all-encompassing strategy holds encrypted data secure from attacks that are exploitable by malicious individuals and ultimately safeguards user data integrity and diminishes breaches. Finally, the regulatory landscape of safeguarding information further underscores the significant importance of encryption in the IoT sector. Given the imposition of regulation such as the General Data Protection Regulation (GDPR), businesses are being made more responsible for the safety of personal data. In this respect, encryption is seen as best practice and also commonly used as a compliance measure. This is not only to emphasize the importance of encryption in ensuring confidentiality of users but to invoke a legal interest in organizations employing secure forms of encryption. With an increased public consciousness of data privacy issues emerging, there will be a growing demand for open encryption policies that will drive innovation and advancement in this area. In this context, encryption not only signifies a technical means but also the foundation of ethical accountability in the big data and IoT era, yet safeguarding users' personal information as private and unapproachable to unauthorized entities (Bormida, 2021; Dwivedi et al., 2022) (Figure 6.10).

Figure 6.10. Encryption serves as a critical line of defense, transforming plaintext data into an unreadable format that can only be decrypted by authorized parties.

Source: https://www.sealpath.com/wp-content/uploads/2024/02/asymmetric-encryption.png.

6.4.3. Importance of Regular Software Updates

The need for regular updates of software cannot be overstated when it comes to IoT devices, particularly privacy and data protection. IoT technologies are increasingly penetrating various areas of our everyday lives and critical infrastructures and therefore are likely to become top priorities of cyber-attacks. Each software update typically has bug fixes, performance optimizations, and most significantly, necessary security patches designed to counteract vulnerabilities that malicious actors can exploit. Regular updates thus constitute a first line of defense, safeguarding personal and business-sensitive information from unauthorized intrusions and access. As IoT studies have established, understanding what drives software functions is essential to businesses employing IoT devices to maintain information under control and enhance operation efficiency (Allioui et al., 2023). Consequently, neglecting update can lead to significant risks, undermining the very privacy protection that organizations strive to achieve. In addition, artificial intelligence employed in data handling increases the significance of software updates. AI systems rely heavily on clean and high-quality data in order to generate actionable insights. Old software, however, can disrupt the purity of such data, making AI-based decision-making processes unreliable (Aldoseri et al., 2023). Software update frequency enhances functionality as well as imposes data handling mechanisms in line with evolving privacy standards and regulatory requirements. As increasingly more organizations rely on AI systems embedded in IoT devices, software updates become a priority in an effort to minimize opportunities for biases caused by inadequate data processing. This task of software update is a critical function since it influences the reliability of data and thus the efficiency of organizations in leveraging AI technologies and also remaining compliant with data privacy laws. Finally, service continuity within IoT ecosystems is contingent upon the freshness and health of their software foundation. As dangers in the cyber environment evolve, so must the regulations under which IoT device's function. Current software ensures security functionality remains aligned with new technical countermeasures, an integral component in guaranteeing the continuity of service and protecting user confidence. Additionally, an active update strategy demonstrates an organization's dedication to being a good data steward—a perspective increasingly held to be critical by consumers and stakeholders alike in today's digital environment. By having a culture that puts a priority on software updates, business enterprises are able to strengthen their security position while building themselves up as ethical keepers of data privacy, hence gaining consumer trust in the IoT solutions they deploy (Allioui et al., 2023). This approach eventually results in IoT usage that is sustainable in such a way that these technologies realize their promise while sufficiently safeguarding personal and business data.

6.5. ETHICAL CONSIDERATIONS

With the rise of the IoT, the moral implications regarding privacy and data protection become increasingly complex and multi-dimensional. The connecting features of IoT devices provide functionality for continuous gathering of individual information, even without express knowledge or approval in some cases. This raises severe ethical issues regarding ownership of such information and abuses. Ethical guidelines must consider the consequences of data commoditization and surveillance, which push stakeholders to move beyond legal compliance to considering ethical responsibility to users. Emphasizing a user-centric approach can help to create guidelines that focus on the privacy of individuals but promote an open and transparent ethos for data practices. Such an ethical base is essential in order to provide user trust and ensure technological advancement does not come at the cost of human rights and freedoms. In addition, the ethical scenario is further complicated by global variations in privacy requirements and regulation. Various governments, such as the European Union's General Data Protection Regulation (GDPR) and California Consumer Privacy Act (CCPA), necessitate strict rules on data treatment that differ based on various cultural attitudes towards privacy. These laws highlight the tension between promoting innovation and protecting people's rights and one of the major ethical considerations emerges in relief: how can the standards of the world be harmonized so that everyone everywhere is safeguarded? Ethical dialogue is required in crossing this terrain, since it can shape policies that recognize and respect the inherent dignity of individuals without preventing technological progress.

Figure 6.11. Ethical frameworks must engage with the implications of surveillance and data commoditization, urging stakeholders to consider not only legal compliance but also moral responsibilities toward users.

Source: https://www.isaca.org/-/media/images/isacadp/project/isaca/tiles/search/privacy-6.png?mw=550&hash=AAA1850053F204663715933DDD221D80.

The dialectic between innovation and regulation must be made with a thoughtful appreciation of the ethical stakes involved in cross-border data flows. In addressing such ethical concerns, the responsibility of technology creators and commercial organizations in promoting ethical behavior in IoT environments is becoming more prominent. Companies are being forced to be proactive about implementing ethical measures into their design and operational plans. This involves leveraging technologies that enhance data security, such as encryption and anonymization, and fostering ethical awareness culture among developers and engineers. Besides, incorporating feedback and consent mechanisms into product design aligns ethical issues with user empowerment. As underscored in recent scholarship, including research on AI and IoT convergence, the imperative to balance innovation with ethical responsibility further underlines the criticality of identifying solutions that are adaptable yet prioritize privacy and security. Thus, the work is not just compliance but in building a sound ethical basis which will direct future progress in the speedy context of IoT (Figure 6.11).

6.5.1. Ethical Implications of Data Collection

The emergent addition of the IoT into the daily life also raises major ethical implications around data collection processes. With billions of devices continuously amassing personal information, stakeholders—consumers, businesses, and policymakers—must contend with complex issues of consent and privacy. Individuals typically remain unaware of the extent and nature of gathered data, resulting in a wide gap in consent. Moreover, consumers may unwittingly agree to terms favoring expansive data usage and exchange that has ethical concerns towards autonomy and ownership of personal data. As more data dictates business strategy and decision-making, organizations must contend with their moral responsibilities towards consumers, particularly in issues of transparency of data usage and consequential implications accompanying such actions (Allioui et al., 2023). The ethical implication of information collection is exacerbated by power relation discrepancies between large firms and single consumers. Large firms with advanced algorithms and gigantic databases often have disproportionate influence on consumer behavior and social norms and therefore raise issues about possible manipulation and exploitation. In addition, the asymmetry can create biased outcomes, particularly for minority groups whose data are disproportionately collected and profiled. Algorithmic decision-making bias is another ethical dimension, since biased data could perpetuate systemic inequalities. The need for equitable data management solutions becomes critical for solving such problems, thus opening doors for calls for regulation standards that ensure fairness, accountability, and responsible data stewardship within sectors involved in IoT (Dwivedi et al., 2022). Moreover, the probability of data abuse grows with the expansion of data collection in IoT environments. Permanent storage poses moral issues regarding observation and privacy erosion. If effective protection for data is not put in place, individuals become vulnerable to various types of exploitation, including identity theft and unapproved observation. In addition, the capacity of the government to enter the lives of citizens through IoT devices poses serious ethical concerns surrounding civil liberties and personal freedoms. With debates regarding data ethics arising, it is more important than ever before that governments and companies respect user privacy and implement good data protection measures. Such commitment lies at the heart of creating trust among consumers and balancing technological advancement with moral obligations (Allioui et al., 2023) (Figure 6.12).

Figure 6.12. Corporations, equipped with powerful algorithms and vast datasets, often hold overwhelming influence over consumer behavior and societal norms, thereby raising concerns about the potential for manipulation and exploitation.

Source: https://indian-retailer.s3.ap-south-1.amazonaws.com/s3fs-public/2021-11/big-data-technology-business-finance-concept.jpg.

6.5.2. Balancing Innovation with Privacy Rights

The increasing interconnectivity of the IoT in everyday life is promising but also problematic, particularly concerning the right to privacy. As IoT devices proliferate, they collect gigantic amounts of personal data—from shopping habits to health information. This collection of data may allow new solutions that will simplify and organize people's lives in innovative ways. But with the lack of robust frameworks to govern how this information is utilized come valid concerns about privacy. Individuals have their information commodified without their overt consent, and it creates a gap between the potential of innovation and the rights of people to maintain control of their personal data. The thin line between innovation and privacy should be walked; therefore, the regulatory systems should evolve with the pace of technological advancements to mitigate these challenges effectively without inhibiting innovation in the IoT sector (Singh, 2024). Furthermore, the evolving regulatory landscape should address the inherent tension between technological advancement and privacy protection. Existing privacy laws have been drafted for the pre-digital age and thus struggle to match the increased speed of development due to IoT. For instance, the EU's General Data Protection Regulation (GDPR) and the U.S.'s California Consumer Privacy Act (CCPA) aim to safeguard individual rights while also fostering an innovation culture simultaneously. But the issue is always to make sure that such regulation does not stifle technological progress or impose too onerous a compliance burden, that dampens investment in new technology. This gap has to be filled by a flexibility and agility of regulation strategy so that individual rights are not compromised as new innovation emerges (Singla, 2024). Moreover, the balance between innovation and privacy also translates to ethical issues surrounding data collection and use. As companies develop new technologies that utilize data from Internet of Things devices, they must be compelled towards responsibility and openness in their data activities. Consumers must be empowered so they can understand what data is collected, how and from whom, and what threats are inherent. By doing so, not only are businesses upholding privacy rights but also creating a trust relationship with their users towards an ethical environment. It is beneficial to consumers as well as companies, as an aware user base can engage with innovative products with more ease while having the control lever over their personal data. Demand for ethical frameworks that come before technological advancements is crucial in developing a platform upon which privacy rights and innovation are able to coexist in harmony (Singh, 2024).

6.5.3. The Role of Companies in Protecting User Data

With the rise of the IoT period, companies have an important responsibility to safeguard users' data from hackers and unauthorized access. IoT devices contribute to a geometric explosion of data generation, triggering privacy and data protection issues. As custodians of such sensitive data, companies must incorporate strong security measures and policies that prioritize users' privacy. By integrating privacy considerations into IoT device functionality and design—usually referred to as Privacy by Design—companies can anticipatively mitigate risks. Moreover, scientists are beginning to examine the socio-economic effect of such technology, as a coherent data protection strategy facilitates ethical requirements and regulatory conformance and fosters consumer trust and loyalty (Dwivedi et al., 2022). Besides, businesses are now more critically examined for their data processing methods, thus transforming the way they approach consumer privacy. Regulation of laws, such as the General Data Protection Regulation (GDPR), puts greater emphasis on the duty of companies to ensure that user data is collected, processed, and stored ethically and lawfully.

Accordingly, companies are required to obtain consent from users legally, thereby enhancing transparency as well as trust. Disobedience will attract very heavy financial penalties as well as reputational damage, which in turn leads organizations to strengthen their data protection systems. By adopting robust data governance patterns as well as applying advanced technologies such as encryption and secure access control, organizations can create a secure data environment for all users and stay in compliance with regulatory demands (Bormida, 2021). Second, the concept of user empowerment also arises as a core principle in the data protection conversation. Companies can facilitate user interaction through the provision of open access to personal data management functionalities, allowing users to control their own data. Offering functionalities such as data portability and user-oriented privacy settings empowers consumers and boosts their trust in the brand. This shift from a traditional model of data ownership to one of user control is an actualization of greater recognition of ethical implications present in the data collection processes. As highlighted by contemporary industry debates, incorporating ethical dimensions into business strategies can translate into sustainable practices that protect consumer rights as well as create peaceful coexistence between businesses and consumers to ultimately serve society as a whole (Bormida, 2021) (Figure 6.13).

Figure 6.13. The proliferation of IoT devices leads to an exponential increase in data generation, raising concerns over privacy and data protection.

Source: https://www.hostduplex.com/blog/wp-content/uploads/2024/01/IoT-Device-vulnerabilities.webp.

6.6. FUTURE TRENDS IN IOT AND DATA PROTECTION

As the IoT increases its footprints in consumer and industrial space, new trends are bound to have a significant impact on data protection endeavors. Of prime concern is introducing AI in IoT technology to enhance the analysis of data and security measures. The intersection of these technologies offers not only improved operational efficiency but also a foundation for safer data privacy measures. IoT devices, by processing machine learning algorithms in real-time, can better predict future security risks and be pro-active about it accordingly. With growing complexity and scale of data collected through IoT devices, organizations must adopt innovative data protection strategies that leverage AI capabilities. This shift promises not only increased security but also a greater ethical approach to practice, ensuring that IoT advances do not compromise citizens' rights to privacy (Marengo, 2024). Healthcare is among the most essential domains to benefit from advancements in IoT technology. Future advancements lean towards a strong shift towards intelligent healthcare systems aimed at safeguarding information through increased observation and analysis. Healthcare IoT use cases such as remote monitoring are enabling secure delivery of real-time information, greatly enhancing patient care but, simultaneously, also creating privacy concerns. A systematic review of IoT-based healthcare systems displays that, while these technologies strengthen the quality of care, they also expose sensitive health information to breaches. Hence, future use cases will likely need an intense focus on encryption and secure data-sharing mechanisms as per strict privacy legislation. This is an important step towards establishing confidence among patients and healthcare professionals and realizing the full potential of IoT innovations to improve health outcomes (Abdulmalek et al., 2022). The regime of compliance under IoT and protection of data will likely shift as there is development with alterations in technology. With data privacy concerns becoming increasingly important, regulatory frameworks will be compelled to adapt, offering greater protections to the consumer. This future trend might lead to the establishment of extensive regulations that insist on data encryption standards, user permission, and clarity on data usage. The firms will also be compelled to incorporate data protection from the outset of IoT product design, embedding a culture of privacy by design. The crossroads of increasing regulatory control and technological advancement presents challenges as well as opportunities for firms. The success of creating a safe IoT future that promotes innovation while protecting data will depend on effective collaboration between the actors such as policymakers, technology firms, and citizens (Marengo, 2024).

6.6.1. Emerging Technologies and Their Impact on Privacy

Emerging technologies, particularly in the context of the IoT, are reshaping the privacy landscape and data protection. As more devices are connected, more data is exchanged, elevating the vulnerability of unauthorized access and abuse of personal information. Interconnectedness can facilitate unprecedented innovation in healthcare, home automation, and urbanization. However, it also comes with great vulnerabilities, as data diffusion in numerous platforms has a tendency of exposing people. Increased ease in collecting, analyzing, and disseminating confidential information has frightened consumers and policymakers regarding their practices for data security and rights to privacy, making it a challenging situation for enacting severe deterrents for potential infringement and misuse. The concept of the metaverse represents the next stage of emerging technologies and shows the need for robust privacy regimes. Virtual and augmented reality technologies are gaining pace, and the blurring of the physical and digital worlds raises basic questions regarding user privacy. Immersive space users do not even know that they are exposing very large amounts of personal data, which can be aggregated and utilized by corporations as well as malicious players. This coming together of technologies not only reconfigures social interactions but also brings new challenges on the trust, privacy, and data integrity questions. Users are placed in a position where they find themselves as agents navigating in interactions where the threat posed by their virtual avatars and data profiles becomes increasingly opaque, calling for an evaluation of the privacy regulations and moral norms that regulate these new environments (Dwivedi et al., 2022). With the advancements in IoT, the union of blockchain technology can also resolve future privacy challenges despite its practical limitations. While blockchain supplies a decentralized mechanism for securing and maintaining data intact, there is some doubt over its use in industrial IoT networks concerning scalability and resource availability. The intensive computational needs demanded by blockchain systems will contradict the resource limitation of IoT devices to hinder privacy provision with secure communication. There is a need to look for innovative frameworks that integrate blockchain capabilities into IoT infrastructure to improve data protection without compromising performance. By examining these dynamics, we can strive to develop more efficacious solutions considering privacy among the many challenges brought about by new technologies in the sphere of Industry 5.0 and beyond (Khan et al., 2022).

6.6.2. Predictions for IoT Security Advancements

As the IoT continues to expand, security technologies also need to evolve in step to meet new security threats. The most critical of these to develop is making more robust encryption technology and authentication protocols. Industry experts forecast that due to the interconnectivity of IoT devices, current security models will need to be re-written to include advanced cryptography tools that can protect large amounts of data transferred between devices. In line with this, use of AI for IoT security will gain momentum, allowing real-time threat detection and response. As underscored in a common observation by various researchers, digital marketing challenges and prospects will reflect these technology changes, bringing into focus the need for ethical consideration in implementing new security measures (Dwivedi et al., 2020). Moreover, as IoT networks become increasingly advanced, utilization of the Digital Twin is anticipated to pick up pace in enhancing security infrastructures.

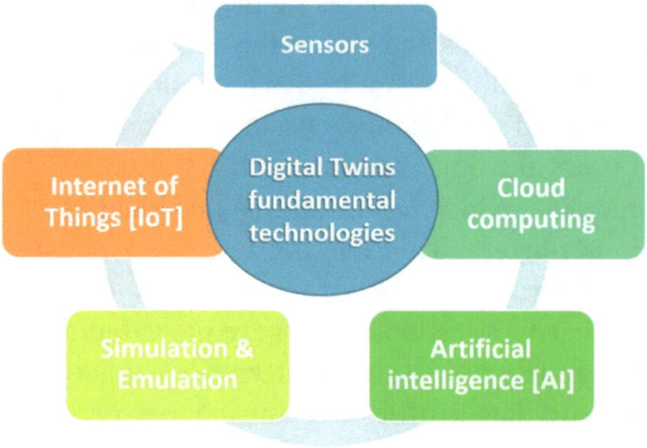

Figure 6.14. The digital twin, defined as the integration of data between a physical and a virtual machine, serves as a powerful tool for simulating and monitoring IoT environments.

Source: https://images.prismic.io/encord/Z_kxZOvxEdbNO7db_image4.png?auto=format,compress.

The Digital Twin, or the link of data between a physical and a virtual machine, can serve as a good agent for simulating and monitoring IoT systems. Researchers say that by leveraging the Digital Twin technology, organizations can create virtual models of their IoT systems so that flaws can be identified before they can be used against them. This proactive approach not only facilitates risk assessment but also allows for timely release of updates and patches for security loopholes, thereby enhancing overall data security. The strides that this technology is taking reflect the falls that have been experienced by other sectors, as can be seen from recent research emphasizing the necessity of continuous growth and assessment within the realm of IoT security (Fuller et al., 2020). As IoT security picks up pace, governments, manufacturers, and consumers will need to collaborate in shaping an impenetrable ecosystem. Future forecasts predict regulatory climates will shift to demand stronger security measures, thus spurring manufacturers to create more secure products. In addition, public campaigns for data protection and privacy are likely to propel consumers into adopting security best practices. This collaborative approach may lead to more robust IoT infrastructures, weighing security against convenience. Ultimately, the collective inputs of various stakeholders are expected to decide the future of IoT security, highlighting the importance of an integrated approach that focuses on privacy but is responsive to technological advancements (Dwivedi et al., 2020) (Figure 6.14).

6.6.3. The Evolving Landscape of User Expectations

The intersection of user expectation and technology innovation is becoming increasingly complex as the IoT continues to grow. User expectations have been altered irreparably by unprecedented rates of technological change, summoning greater demands for transparency and control of personal data. The more users become knowledgeable about the threats from IoT devices, the stronger their demand for robust privacy protection becomes. The explosion of data breaches and misuse of personal data has raised awareness regarding individual rights, compelling users to anticipate businesses and developers adhering to stricter data privacy policies. This shift is embodied by legislation such as the GDPR that gives power to the people by establishing robust guidelines on data handling and consent. With increasing technology and growing user expectations, the first task is how best to reconcile existing frameworks to effectively accommodate these changes, ultimately maintaining privacy as the priority of a data age. With rising user expectations regarding the protection of data and privacy, regulatory frameworks also need to change. The challenge lies in creating legislation that is capable of keeping up with the rapid rate of technological advancement, which is prone to leave existing legal structures behind. Though the GDPR and related regulation represent a significant step forward, their application can be inconsistent, with issues around real compliance and application. Additionally, the new challenges represented by emerging technologies such as artificial intelligence and big data analytics require rethinking regulatory strategies. By critically examining the effectiveness of existing data privacy laws, policymakers and scholars can assist in mitigating technology's ethical consequences. For instance, with the demand for blanket regulations on matters that do not have any protocols, such as in Indonesia, there is an urgent need to act when protecting user information adequately, especially in the realm of IoT and e-health technology advancements (Rohmah, 2024). As users more and more want more accountability and transparency from organizations, user empowerment is more important. Such development necessitates deeper insight into not only technical potential but also ethical consequences of user consent and trust. Users in IoT scenarios don't know that devices harvest huge amounts of data, which leads to declining trust in technological systems. Organizations must therefore lay importance on educating the users and engaging in open communication concerning data collection, use, and data protection. In such interaction lies a critical element of making users aware of their rights clearly and encouraging informed consent. By adopting such a culture of openness, organizations are not only able to align with evolving user expectations but also enhance their public reputations in a competitive market. Finally, an effective resolution to user issues is essential in developing a sustainable and trust-aware IoT system (Ehimuan et al., 2024).

6.7. CONCLUSION

The search for privacy and data protection in the era of IoT highlights not only the tremendous opportunities of networked devices but also the catastrophic vulnerabilities they create. With growing data collection, the necessity for firm security controls is increasingly evident. Having confidentiality, integrity, and availability of the vital data in place is now a point of starting necessities for any business embracing IoT technology. Systems must be implemented that not only secure unauthorized access but also follow regulatory frameworks, such as the GDPR. Compliance with regulations is necessary because it gives confidence to users, whose private and sensitive information is typically at stake. Hence, it is important to continuously evaluate existing strategies to ensure data privacy while maintaining pace with new threats and technological advancements that characterize the digital world (Fayayola et al., 2024). Convergence of IoT with healthcare systems is an evident example of the delicate balance between innovation and privacy. As digital health applications become more mainstream, they pose unique questions regarding the privacy safeguarding of individuals' health information. Applications of state-of-the-art technology, such as blockchain with homomorphic encryption, promise solutions to these issues. Not only do such new technologies secure data storage and sharing, but they also maintain users' privacy when processing information. Such a system allows patients to empower themselves by bestowing control over their individual health information while facilitating medical professionals to access and utilize the information responsibly. The continued research and development in this area represent a progressive measure to address the dangers presented by data breaches and make both patients and healthcare providers feel secure (Ali et al., 2023). Generally, as the IoT environment evolves, embracing effective data and protection measures remains essential to preserve user confidence and safeguard sensitive information. More varied technologies bring risks and opportunities demanding deeper strategies for data integrity and privacy. Organizations must remain vigilant, crafting robust strategies that can firmly counter dynamic cyber threats while satisfying strict regulatory requirements. One can create a strong framework by training emergent technologies and newly adopted security protocols that not only facilitates the growth of IoT applications but places utmost importance on protecting individual privacy. With the upcoming convergence of technology and personal data, the commitment to enhancing privacy and data security will ultimately characterize the IoT future (Ali et al., 2023; Fayayola et al., 2024).

6.7.1. Summary of Key Points Discussed

The rapid inclusion of IoT gadgets in our everyday lives also brings enormous privacy and data concerns. With an increasing number of households adopting smart appliances, security devices, and wearable technology, the volume of data that can be generated is gargantuan. Most of this data contains personal information, which, if poorly managed, can become the victim of breaches and abuses. Expectations of consumer privacy are evolving; individuals no longer just want to protect their data but also understand how the service providers utilize it. Loopholes of current regulations necessitate an integrated approach to deal with these challenges with greater transparency and accountability towards data usage. Researchers emphasize an equitable approach that encourages innovation as well as safeguards individual privacy in the process. User consent and agency is a common theme in the privacy argument within the context of IoT. The majority of consumers are able to unintentionally give their personal information with no clear understanding of the entire scope of what they are agreeing to when utilizing smart devices. Simple and cogently structured consent mechanisms are essential but fail in current technology landscape. Furthermore, IoT devices more and more collect information in streams, which makes well-informed consent more and more challenging. Such a state implies a deep convenience-privacy trade-off that requires a forum for more discussion on how users can maintain control of their data. Market data show that a firmer regulatory system, combined with technological safeguards, can bridge the divide between consumer trust and the actions of IoT companies and establish a more trustworthy arena for consumers. Besides, convergence of technology advancements and moral issues in IoT encompasses complex challenges. As devices become increasingly interconnected, risks of ownership and third-party sharing of data increase. Companies have a tendency to gather data from a wide range of sources, and questions regarding ownership of data and how the data can be sensibly secured become relevant. All these are compounded by the complex ethical issues of vulnerability and exploitation, particularly on vulnerable communities that do not necessarily possess the resources to secure their personal data. The growing reliance on data analysis in sectors such as healthcare and education calls for rigorous examination of the ethical elements of data use, particularly bias and discrimination. Addressing these ethical concerns not only requires compliance with the law but also organizations' active initiative to prioritize ethical considerations as their first priority in designing and implementing IoT technologies, ultimately leading to an ethical data environment.

6.7.2. The Importance of Ongoing Vigilance in Data Protection

In the rapidly evolving IoT ecosystem, the necessity for continuous vigilance in data security cannot be overstated. With devices proliferating and getting more networked, massive amounts of personal data are in the process of being generated, stored, and exchanged continuously. This ecosystem is a desired target for cyber attackers, who take advantage of vulnerabilities in IoT device design and implementation. Therefore, it is imperative for firms to adopt an assertive data protection stance in terms of regular security audits, upkeep, and proper risk management procedures. By staying alert, corporations can minimize potential breaches and ensure compliance with changing laws, safeguarding their property as well as public confidence. Further, the dynamic nature of cyber threats necessitates a dynamic platform for information protection that keeps pace in tandem with technological advancements and shifts in criminal tactics. The implications of careless data protection measures extend beyond individual organizations to impact consumer safety and privacy at large. Since personal data becomes increasingly attached to devices used for many aspects of daily life—from smart home appliances to body-worn health monitors—the danger of extensive privacy intrusion due to any failure is exacerbated. The integration of cutting-edge technologies such as blockchain and AI in IoT platforms is imperative in providing safe data sharing, anomaly detection, and privacy for the users. With tools capable of enhancing data integrity at a decreased risk factor, organizations can establish an ongoing vigilance platform that not only complies with regulatory requirements but also reflects their commitment towards ethical technology implementation. Ongoing vigilance in this instance translates into an enhanced defense against subsequent intrusions, which reinforces the consumer protection infrastructure. Second, fostering a culture of vigilance within an organization entails continuous training and awareness programs that engage employees at all levels. Engaging staff in the details of data privacy practice, potential threats, and the importance of attentive monitoring heightens the overall security position of the organization. At the same time, employing cutting-edge protection measures, such as Differential Privacy, says a lot about keeping patients' and customers' data secure from malicious and accidental disclosure. As businesses innovate and respond to the complexities of the IoT ecosystem, maintaining a strong focus on data protection fosters consumer confidence and loyalty. This trust then becomes a deciding factor in the long-term fortunes of the organization, echoing the requirement of an ongoing, vigilant mindset towards data security to adequately cope with the complexities of current technological landscapes.

6.7.3. Call to Action for Consumers and Manufacturers Alike

This intersection of privacy and data protection in the IoT is a call to action for consumers and producers alike. Consumers increasingly rely on networked devices that, for the most part, collect enormous amounts of personal data, with few being aware of the harms at stake from such convenience. This is precisely why consumer awareness needs to be fostered. Individuals must learn about implications of data sharing and questioning privacy policies. Such a shift in consumers would lead to a greater demand for open practices from manufacturers, which would encourage them to make it their topmost priority to protect customers' information and put in place more secure practices. Lobbying for informed decisions means that individuals can exert influence, which could ultimately create a marketplace that cares about privacy and safety. Manufacturers are stuck, though, as they attempt to find their way through the shifting landscape of privacy laws and consumer pressure. The requirement to meet stringent data privacy laws necessitates additional spending on security technologies and techniques. This transformation is driven mainly by the ongoing digitalization of their business models and the influence of the Industry 4.0 revolution with an emphasis on trust in consumer relations. Hence, manufacturers need to include privacy by design within their product development processes, such as conducting thorough risk assessments and responding to proactive communication on data usage. As stated, the shift to this more ethical practice is not only a question of regulation but also a critical component for the provision of competitive advantage in a market that is progressively marked by ethics and transparency (Sima et al., 2020). In combination, the combined effect of consumers and producers can usher in the era of an ethical data privacy ecosystem in the IoT. This coexistence can take the shape of public campaigns, wherein customers express their right to privacy and producers respond with individual solutions to address these concerns. There must be an awareness on both sides regarding their role and responsibility in this interactive situation. Producers must remain attuned to customer concerns, but customers must take it upon themselves to demand ethics and accountability.

REFERENCES

1. Abdulmalek, S., Nasir, A., Jabbar, W. A., Almuhaya, M. A. M., Bairagi, A. K., Khan, M. A. M., & Kee, S. H. (2022). IoT-based healthcare-monitoring system towards improving quality of life: A review. *Healthcare, 10*, 1993–1993. https://doi.org/10.3390/healthcare10101993 (accessed on 17th October 2025).

2. Ahmad, A., Maulana, R., Akmal, K., et al. (2024). Data privacy and security in the age of IoT: A comprehensive study on information system vulnerabilities. *Journal Informatic, Education and Management (JIEM)*. https://www.semanticscholar.org/paper/c666a819b11052bb358b8637926 1e0208668be41 (accessed on 17th October 2025).

3. Aldboush, H. H., & Ferdous, M. (2023). Building trust in fintech: An analysis of ethical and privacy considerations in the intersection of big data, AI, and customer trust. *International Journal of Financi al Studies, 11*, 90–90. https://doi.org/10.3390/ijfs11030090 (accessed on 17th October 2025).

4. Aldoseri, A., Al-Khalifa, K. N., & Hamouda, A. M. S. (2023). Re-thinking data strategy and integration for artificial intelligence: Concepts, opportunities, and challenges. *Applied Sciences, 13*, 7082–7082. https://doi.org/10.3390/app13127082 (accessed on 17th October 2025).

5. Ali, A., Al-Rimy, B. A. S., Alsubaei, F. S., Almazroi, A. A., & Almazroi, A. A. (2023). HealthLock: Blockchain-based privacy preservation using homomorphic encryption in Internet of Things healthcare applications. *Sensors, 23*, 6762–6762. https://doi.org/10.3390/s23156762 (accessed on 17th October 2025).

6. Allioui, H., & Mourdi, Y. (2023). Exploring the full potentials of IoT for better financial growth and stability: A comprehensive survey. *Sensors, 23*, 8015–8015. https://doi.org/10.3390/s23198015 (accessed on 17th October 2025).

7. Byeon, H. (2025). Vulnerability analysis of privacy-preserving four-factor authentication for medical IoT environments and sustainable development goals. *Journal of Lifestyle and SDGs Review*. https://www.semanticscholar.org/paper/6fc274fb928642db1add182e1f9ad940c2684990 (accessed on 17th October 2025).

8. Chintoh, G. A., Segun-Falade, O. D., Odionu, C. S., & Ekeh, A. H. (2025). Challenges and conceptualizing AI-powered privacy risk assessments: Legal models for U.S. data protection compliance. *International Journal of Frontline Research in Multidisciplinary Studies*. https://www.

semanticscholar.org/paper/1d47aced0634995ffc0dfd32689405245a57b584 (accessed on 17th October 2025).

9. Cunche, M., Morel, V., & Le Métayer, D. (2018). A generic information and consent framework for the IoT. https://core.ac.uk/download/162948483.pdf (accessed on 17th October 2025).

10. Da Bormida, M. (2021). The big data world: Benefits, threats and ethical challenges. *Advances in Research Ethics and Integrity*. https://doi.org/10.1108/s2398-601820210000008007 (accessed on 17th October 2025).

11. Dwivedi, Y. K., Ismagilova, E., Hughes, D. L., Carlson, J., Filieri, R., Jacobson, J., Jain, V., et al. (2020). Setting the future of digital and social media marketing research: Perspectives and research propositions. *International Journal of Information Management, 59*, 102168–102168. https://doi.org/10.1016/j.ijinfomgt.2020.102168 (accessed on 17th October 2025).

12. Echenim, K. U., & Joshi, K. P. (2025). Automating IoT data privacy compliance by integrating knowledge graphs with large language models. *IEEE Access, 13*, 118438–118451. https://www.semanticscholar.org/paper/44ce69a5b1ad07987f4d028ecac8cebbe3ac5fef (accessed on 17th October 2025).

13. Ehimuan, B., Chimezie, O., Akagha, O. O., Reis, O., & Oguejiofor, B. B. (2024). Global data privacy laws: A critical review of technology's impact on user rights. *World Journal of Advanced Research and Reviews*. https://www.semanticscholar.org/paper/c8d22231abb3824442bcbf54c48ca078be3f842c (accessed on 17th October 2025).

14. Eleyan, A., Ahmed, H., & Bejaoui, T. (2025). Leveraging a deep learning-based privacy compliance framework for IoT applications. *2025 5th IEEE Middle East and North Africa Communications Conference (MENACOMM)*. https://www.semanticscholar.org/paper/290ffa57bd7c19d1e3f1fd13ebb282ca86e9d5eb (accessed on 17th October 2025).

15. Fatima, M., Ali, A., Rana, M. T. A., Ahmad, M., Un Nisa, F., Khan, H., Farooq, H. U., et al. (2024). Enhancing the resilience of IoT networks: Strategies and measures for mitigating DDoS attacks. *Journal of Mechanics of Continua and Mathematical Sciences*. https://www.semanticscholar.org/paper/2fc6fc4b351af192de13b4e3a8b70533065d5c48 (accessed on 17th October 2025).

16. Fayayola, O. A., Olorunfemi, O. L., & Shoetan, P. O. (2024). Data privacy and security in IT: A review of techniques and challenges. *Computer*

Science & IT Research Journal, 5, 606–615. https://doi.org/10.51594/csitrj.v5i3.909 (accessed on 17th October 2025).

17. Fuller, A., Fan, Z., Day, C., & Barlow, C. (2020). Digital twin: Enabling technologies, challenges and open research. *IEEE Access, 8*, 108952–108971. https://doi.org/10.1109/access.2020.2998358 (accessed on 17th October 2025).
18. Gowda, D., Kawale, S. R., Prasad, K. D. V., Kumar, N. A., Reddy, N. S., & Ashreetha, B. (2023). Technologies for comprehensive information security in the IoT. *2022 International Conference for Advancement in Technology (ICONAT)*. https://doi.org/10.1109/iconat57137.2023.10080332 (accessed on 17th October 2025).
19. Haris, M. A. H. B., Yahya, M. I. H. B., & Ibrahim, M. N. B. (2023). Security and privacy issues in Internet of Things (IoT). https://doi.org/10.36227/techrxiv.23512389.v1 (accessed on 17th October 2025).
20. Herriger, C., Merlo, O., Eisingerich, A., & Arigayota, A. (2025). Context-contingent privacy concerns and exploration of the privacy paradox in the age of AI, augmented reality, big data, and the Internet of Things: Systematic review. *Journal of Medical Internet Research, 27*. https://www.semanticscholar.org/paper/6e9f908ef0ef945035b8b6a7c10321a8d8d6ea37 (accessed on 17th October 2025).
21. Khan, A. A., Laghari, A. A., Shaikh, Z. A., Dacko-Pikiewicz, Z., & Kot, S. (2022). Internet of Things (IoT) security with blockchain technology: A state-of-the-art review. *IEEE Access, 10*, 122679–122695. https://doi.org/10.1109/access.2022.3223370 (accessed on 17th October 2025).
22. Kumar, M., Kumar, K., Verma, R., Sharma, H., & Kumar, S. (2025). Addressing IoT privacy and security: A comprehensive perception into challenges and improvement strategies. *Advances in Nonlinear Variational Inequalities*. https://www.semanticscholar.org/paper/4579f2682a7cd80a4a3eb528e80147ed88040651 (accessed on 17th October 2025).
23. Lim, W. Y. B., Luong, N. C., Hoang, D. T., Jiao, Y., Liang, Y. C., Yang, Q., Niyato, D., et al. (2020). Federated learning in mobile edge networks: A comprehensive survey. *IEEE Communications Surveys & Tutorials, 22*, 2031–2063. https://doi.org/10.1109/comst.2020.2986024 (accessed on 17th October 2025).
24. Liu, D., Liang, H., Zeng, X., Zhang, Q., Zhang, Z., & Li, M. (2022). Edge computing application, architecture, and challenges in ubiquitous power Internet of Things. *Frontiers in Energy Research, 10*. https://doi.org/10.3389/fenrg.2022.850252 (accessed on 17th October 2025).
25. Marengo, A. (2023). The future of AI in IoT: Emerging trends in

intelligent data analysis and privacy protection. https://doi.org/10.20944/preprints202312.2184.v2 (accessed on 17th October 2025).

26. Marengo, A. (2024). Navigating the nexus of AI and IoT: A comprehensive review of data analytics and privacy paradigms. *Internet of Things, 27*, 101318–101318. https://doi.org/10.1016/j.iot.2024.101318 (accessed on 17th October 2025).

27. Nutalapati, V. (2024). Essential security practices for fortifying mobile apps. https://www.semanticscholar.org/paper/404e0897c1cce017e6d46db6fe1941a65f5f51b1 (accessed on 17th October 2025).

28. Odimarha, A. C., Ayodeji, S. A., & Abaku, E. A. (2024). The role of technology in supply chain risk management: Innovations and challenges in logistics. *Magna Scientia Advanced Research and Reviews, 10*, 138–145. https://doi.org/10.30574/msarr.2024.10.2.0052 (accessed on 17th October 2025).

29. Perera, C., Ranjan, R., & Wang, L. (2015). End-to-end privacy for open big data markets. https://core.ac.uk/download/327950102.pdf (accessed on 17th October 2025).

30. Rejeb, A., Rejeb, K., Treiblmaier, H., Appolloni, A., Alghamdi, S., Alhasawi, Y., & Iranmanesh, M. (2023). The Internet of Things (IoT) in healthcare: Taking stock and moving forward. *Internet of Things, 22*, 100721–100721. https://doi.org/10.1016/j.iot.2023.100721 (accessed on 17th October 2025).

31. Rohmah, N. Q. (2024). Health data protection and privacy in the Internet of Things era: The new legal challenges in Indonesia. *Leges Privatae*. https://www.semanticscholar.org/paper/84cb5bfc2b38082744d18f061b19778fd0c291bd (accessed on 17th October 2025).

32. Sima, V., Gheorghe, I. G., Subić, J., & Nancu, D. (2020). Influences of the Industry 4.0 revolution on the human capital development and consumer behavior: A systematic review. *Sustainability, 12*, 4035–4035. https://doi.org/10.3390/su12104035 (accessed on 17th October 2025).

33. Singh, B. (2024). *Cherish Data Privacy and Human Rights in the Digital Age*. Advances in Human and Social Aspects of Technology book series. https://doi.org/10.4018/979-8-3693-3334-1.ch007 (accessed on 17th October 2025).

34. Singla, A. (2024). The evolving landscape of privacy law: Balancing digital innovation and individual rights. *Indian Journal of Law, 2*, 1–6. https://doi.org/10.36676/ijl.v2.i1.01 (accessed on 17th October 2025).

35. Thu, M. L. L., & Makararpong, D. (2025). Analyzing the appeal of IoT devices in pet care: A study of applications and user adoption. *2025 IEEE*

International Conference on Cybernetics and Innovations (ICCI). https://www.semanticscholar.org/paper/60c659152f6d96c7dddb9f07347552cb53c7e396 (accessed on 17th October 2025).

36. Wang, Y., Su, Z., Zhang, N., Xing, R., Liu, D., Luan, T. H., & Shen, X. (2022). A survey on metaverse: Fundamentals, security, and privacy. *IEEE Communications Surveys & Tutorials, 25*, 319–352. https://doi.org/10.1109/comst.2022.3202047 (accessed on 17th October 2025).
37. Williamson, S., & Prybutok, V. R. (2024). Balancing privacy and progress: A review of privacy challenges, systemic oversight, and patient perceptions in AI-driven healthcare. *Applied Sciences, 14*, 675–675. https://doi.org/10.3390/app14020675 (accessed on 17th October 2025).

CHAPTER 7

ACCESS CONTROL AND IDENTITY MANAGEMENT

Contents

INTRODUCTION

The growth in digital technologies within contemporary society has necessitated the proper use of access control and identity management procedures as a requirement in cybersecurity. As more organizations implement connected systems, the protection of sensitive information from unauthorized access becomes more critical. Access control gives an interface through which users are permitted to engage with resources based on their identity, role, and organizations' policies. This setup not only protects precious information but also maintains legal compliance. With cyber-attacks changing constantly during the current era, robust access control practices are necessary to keep threats in check and organizational stability against incursions intact. Identity management, part of access control, entails identification, verification, and user identity administration in computer networks. As highlighted in disruptor technology discourses, businesses are encouraged to utilize sophisticated identity management systems to counter privacy and security threats. The use of cutting-edge authentication technologies—such as biometrics, multi-factor authentication, and contextual access control—makes the verification process of identities more trustworthy. By granting access to sensitive resources only to authentic users, organizations can strengthen their immunity to cyber-attacks. The intersection of these two fields allows for an integrative approach to security that is required to safeguard digital assets in today's interconnected world. With the ongoing cybersecurity debate, fresh challenges and opportunities continue to arise, especially given technologies such as AI and the metaverse having a profound impact on traditional paradigms for access management and identity management. The virtual threat environment is being redesigned by advanced tools, which also introduce solutions and threats. Application of AI in identity verification processes enhances efficiency but introduces serious ethical considerations regarding biases in the training dataset. In addition, as businesses consider integrating metaverse-based immersive technologies into their processes, the importance for user access and verifying identities is huge. Therefore, researchers and professionals must clinically examine such themes rigorously, cultivating knowledge that informs good security practice and addresses the evolving nature of cybersecurity threats, as seen in today's controversies over generative AI and its double-edged ability to bring productivity value and create vulnerabilities (Dwivedi et al., 2023; Koohang et al., 2023).

Definition of Access Control

Access control is an essential aspect of cybersecurity that provides structures and methods to manage who may have access to resources within an established system. Access control can be described as the act of defining and applying the rules that define what authorities end users possess pertaining to access to critical data and systems. It spans various methods such as user authentication, authorization, and accountability to ensure that only legitimate users have access to confidential information. As frequency in cyber-attacks increases, the enforcement of robust access controls has become imperative to organizations who desire to safeguard their digital resources and be compliant with regulations.

Developing an integrated access control system enhances security, maintains data confidentiality and integrity, and consequently minimizes data breaches that could compromise user information and institutional trust. Furthermore, deployments of access control systems are intrinsic to identity management in cybersecurity practice. Identity management encompasses identification, authentication, and authorization of users accessing company resources, and in doing so, establishes a critical synergy with access control. This relationship is key in enforcing multi-factor authentication, role-based access controls, and periodic audits to maintain access permissions aligned with organizational policies.

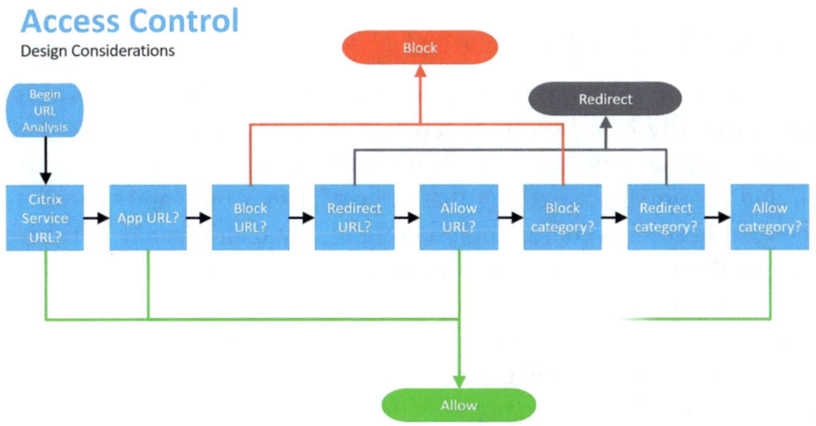

Figure 7.1. Access control serves as a foundational component of cybersecurity, providing structures and methodologies to manage who is authorized to access resources within a given system.

Source: https://i.ytimg.com/vi/1X9XUadVju8/maxresdefault.jpg.

With cyber-attacks growing more advanced on a daily basis, organizations must develop their access control policies to accommodate ongoing monitoring as well as adaptive access controls that take into account real-time user behavior and context. This flexibility allows organizations to deflect risks of unauthorized access, achieving a more dynamic approach to cybersecurity that responds before the fact to threats and vulnerabilities actual in the digital space. Access control also plays a role in regulatory compliance and governance in the model of cybersecurity. Organizations are typically faced with a variety of legislative rules and industry standards that oblige them to embrace stringent access control procedures to protect personally identifiable information as well as sensitive organizational data. Failure to adhere to these guidelines is likely to result in huge penalties and loss of reputation. For instance, issues of data breaches underscore the importance of robust access control mechanisms, especially following the failure of current legal frameworks to adequately clamp down on such threats. As intimated in cybersecurity practice discourse, anticipatory action in the form of national data security legislation could be required to augment existing standards, ensuring safe protection of user information, and fostering trust in online environments (Anglano et al., 2018; Marcus et al., 2018). It is hence imperative to revisit and redefine access control definitions within the broader context of identity management to establish a secure cyber environment that respects privacy and security (Figure 7.1).

Importance of Identity Management

The concept of identity management is the keystone in the world of cybersecurity, primarily based on its function as a gatekeeper of access. This system of management will only grant approved users access to sensitive information and resources, something that is crucial in a time and era where data breaches are becoming increasingly common. By continuously verifying the identities of the users, organizations can protect their digital assets, and identity management is a critical component of effective cybersecurity practices. Further, reliance on good identity management principles ensures that organizations enhance regulatory compliance, thereby reducing legal exposures associated with data privacy violations. This regulatory environment puts prominence on ensuring that identity management practices are compliant with existing legislation and data protection best practices (Anglano et al., 2018). In addition to risk handling, identity management also plays a key role in establishing user trust and confidence. Users are more likely to engage with digital systems and share sensitive information where they can be certain that their personal information is properly safeguarded. That security is what makes life simpler for businesses that rely on user interaction to thrive, as has been illustrated in the boom in mobile app development. With this growth, however, comes the risk of user data becoming more exposed, which is why it is so vital that identity management systems are strong. It is not merely a matter of protecting proprietary information; it is also about controlling how user data is collected, used, and transferred. The practice analysis of ubiquitous mobile applications presents the image of an entangled coexistence between trust by the user and personal information management (Fathaigh et al., 2018). In addition, the evolving nature of technology necessitates adaptive management of identity. With cybersecurity threats continuing to evolve, organizations must continuously enhance their identity management practices to address arising weaknesses. Such flexibility can take different forms, such as the addition of multi-factor authentication, utilization of biometric systems, and utilization of artificial intelligence in conducting real-time identification. Besides improving security, these technologies also allow for user experiences that are more secure and faster to access resources. As the online environment becomes increasingly complex, identity management will only grow stronger in demand, and thus it is necessary for organizations to invest in cutting-edge solutions that protect identities without undermining the effectiveness of the digital space (Anglano et al., 2018) (Figure 7.2).

Figure 7.2. As cyber threats evolve, organizations must continuously refine their identity management practices to address new vulnerabilities.

Source: https://cdn.prod.website-files.com/6622e518d7c98f7c26fd28c4/678c0f9b2ca5e8ace4b3f5d1_ID%20Threats.png.

7.1. TYPES OF ACCESS CONTROL

Access control is a fundamental principle of cybersecurity that determines who may access specific resources within an organization. Among the modes of access control mechanisms, Discretionary Access Control (DAC) allows users to administer and control access to their resources. In a DAC model, resource owners grant or deny permission for accessing resources for other users, giving a personalized and flexible mechanism of security. This mode, while easy to work with, can pose serious threats if not managed with caution because individuals may inadvertently open the door to attackers or lose permissions granted over time. Organizations resort to using DAC together with robust identity management procedures that monitor and log access so users are constantly aware of privileges and responsibilities, thereby mitigating risks associated with unauthorized access and data leaks (Anglano et al., 2018). Another popular model is Mandatory Access Control (MAC), which operates on a more strict protocol by imposing access rules set up by a central authority and not by a user. Access privileges in MAC environments are decided based on pre-set security policies, taking into account information sensitivity and users' security clearances. This type of access control will often be prevalent where security needs are very high, i.e., government and military facilities, where the effect of unauthorized access will be catastrophic. Inflexibility in MAC systems will offer much added security but may result in less user flexibility, usually resulting in trouble during collaboration. As such, schemes that use MAC need to reconcile operational effectiveness with uncompromised security policies, creating a situation where information integrity is maximized without compromising productivity (Ani et al., 2020). Role-Based Access Control (RBAC) is another important method, wherein user authorization is granted according to pre-defined roles in an organizational hierarchy. This model allows uninhibited access control administration through role mapping to job duties, thus eradicating unnecessary exposure to sensitive information. By defining roles such as Administrator, Employee, or Guest, organizations can automate the provisioning and deprovisioning of access, which is highly relevant for large organizations. Additionally, RBAC supports compliance with regulation by providing a clear audit trail of privileges associated with a specific role, making it easier to manage and monitor risks. The ability to quickly alter access as a response to role modifications such as employee promotions or departmental transitions provides organizational flexibility without diminishing the safety of sensitive data (Anglano et al., 2018).

7.1.1. Discretionary Access Control (DAC)

Discretionary Access Control (DAC) is a core access control method in cybersecurity that grants users autonomy to make decisions about who has access to their data or resources. In the DAC system, the owner of an object, such as a file or resource, is given the autonomy to make access decisions, delegating them to other users at their discretion. This client-based philosophy facilitates flexibility and cooperation, allowing tailored rights of access based on personal requirements. This autonomy, however, can also present significant drawbacks in the shape of unauthorized data transfer and potential cascading permits, which can lead to security risks. Achieving the ideal blend between accessibility and security is critical in correctly implementing DAC measures across various organizational environments. One of the notable aspects of DAC is its applicability to emerging technologies, particularly the IoT. With the increase in interconnecting devices, access control becomes a daunting task, as traditional DAC systems may not be capable of coping with the dynamic nature of IoT. As quoted in recent literature, the several vulnerabilities of IoT systems need robust access control mechanisms to mitigate potential attacks. For instance, enhancing physical security, employing encryption, and employing secure messaging protocols are foundational security elements that can be integrated into DAC. Through this, organizations are able to ensure that the possibilities of IoT innovation are not nullified by security breaches that exploit weaknesses in access control.

The integration of DAC with modern technologies emphasizes the urgent need for organizations to adopt end-to-end cybersecurity practices that integrate these developments (Pourrahmani et al., 2023). Furthermore, organizations have to overcome legal requirements and data privacy issues when applying DAC as an access control component. Immediate security requirements are complemented by regulatory directives that guide organizations in how they should manage and protect sensitive information. Access Control mechanisms, including DAC, must be designed to prevent unauthorized access, thereby aligning organizational practices with compliance requirements. In light of the rapidly changing cyber threat landscape, adopting a zero-trust approach that incorporates DAC principles could significantly bolster an organizations defense against potential breaches. The analysis of current access control techniques and their application across various sectors, such as cloud computing and software-defined networks, reflects the ongoing enhancement of DAC systems in meeting present-day cybersecurity needs and ensuring data confidentiality and integrity (Golightly et al., 2023) (Figure 7.3).

Figure 7.3. Discretionary access control (DAC).

Source: https://cyberhoot.com/wp-content/uploads/2020/02/653239-637074661640011299-16x9-1.jpg.

7.1.2. Mandatory Access Control (MAC)

Mandatory Access Control (MAC) is a rigorous access control method applied in cybersecurity systems. As opposed to discretionary access control systems in which users have the ability to allow permissions for their data, MAC has system-level policies that are characterized by set parameters restricting users' levels of ability to see or manipulate data. Such a model is particularly useful in information environments where confidentiality is most important, such as governmental and military environments, since it categorizes information based on pre-established clearance levels. By eliminating subjectivity in access rights, MAC enhances security by ensuring that sensitive information can only be accessed by authorized users, thereby eliminating possibilities of human mistakes or malicious intent. The use of MAC systems is often reliant upon a formalized classifying system that is needed to regulate access. Users are assigned unique labels that are equated with the sensitivity of the data involved, and access decisions are solely made on the basis of these labels and not user identity or role.

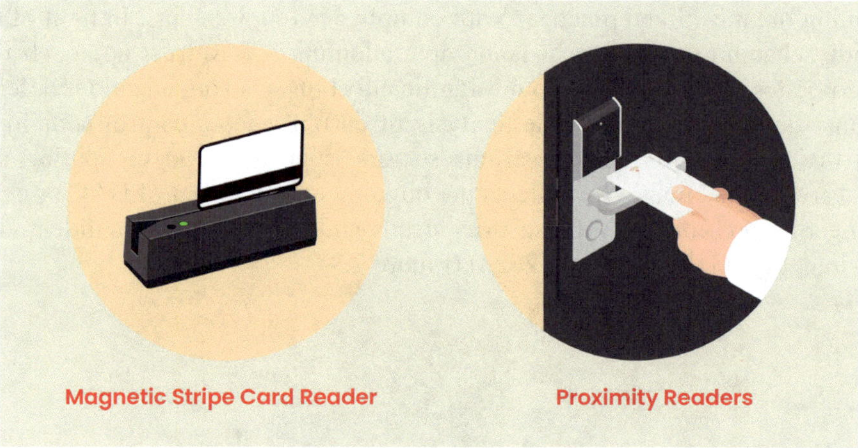

Figure 7.4. Mandatory access control (MAC).

Source: https://doswljnolqe2s.cloudfront.net/sep-3-1.png.

This rigid framework is preferable in order to protect highly sensitive data, especially where breaches of data would have severe consequences. Additionally, as highlighted in existing proposals of next-generation cybersecurity strategies, MAC integration with emerging technologies, such as Software-Defined Networking (SDN), can further strengthen the security stance through dynamic routing of data flows based on adherence to configured security policies, thereby overcoming the vulnerabilities of current data handling systems (Moura et al.,

2015). As a high-security technology, MAC poses challenges to be resolved by organizations. The complexity involved in managing access in systems using MAC can significantly hinder user mobility and cooperation. For instance, the use of higher-level permissions for seemingly routine tasks can enrage users and slow down productivity. Moreover, the static character of MAC policy typically leads to rigidity that fails to adapt to the high rate of change that occurs in dynamic organizational environments. Organizations need to balance between having stringent access controls and allowing users to actually get the job done. With the changing nature of cybersecurity threats, the flexibility of access control mechanisms will play a key role in responding to these new threats and protecting critical information assets (Burstein et al., 2011) (Figure 7.4).

7.1.3. Role-Based Access Control (RBAC)

Role-Based Access Control or RBAC is an important feature of access control to sensitive information and systems in organizations. In its method of delegating authorization based on roles played by users rather than individual identities, RBAC simplifies managing security policies for large groups of users. The model allows for a more precise demarcation of power in the sense that users have access to only that information required for their own roles. As cyber threats are constantly changing, the method for restricting access based on thoroughly documented roles can serve to reduce risks associated with unauthorized usage and data breaches. In those systems where many users can be required to access at varying levels, RBAC provides an administers and scalable approach to access management that supports security as well as organizational efficiency. The advantages of RBAC are most profoundly felt in the sort of environment of finance and healthcare, where there is a tremendous amount of sensitive data. In healthcare, for instance, hospital staff may need to be able to access patient information germane to their specific role but not view unrelated data. This principle of least privilege not only enhances security but also aids compliance with regulations such as HIPAA, which mandates patient information confidentiality. As organizations increasingly move towards cloud solutions, incorporating RBAC becomes increasingly crucial to effectively manage access in various systems. These technologies like vendor-independent repositories (Bastião et al., 2020) can utilize RBAC methods in order to guarantee data integrity when they enforce necessary access controls that are adapted depending on organizational processes in multi-repository systems. Despite having numerous benefits, RBAC also has some disadvantages. Issues are potential concerning the rigidity of access rights since roles of users and hence the resultant responsibility may get altered with time. This necessitates periodic review and refreshing of the role assignments to prevent privilege creep, where users accumulate more privileges than they require to perform their duties. Also, increasing organizational complexity may lead to ambiguous definition of roles. Studies reveal that while RBAC offers solid models of access control, it can fail to keep up with changing business processes (Khetani et al., 2025). Therefore, organizations must be vigilant and utilize more controls such as frequent auditing and dynamic access controls to complement RBAC and surmount its limitations and mount a good defense against new attacks (Figure 7.5).

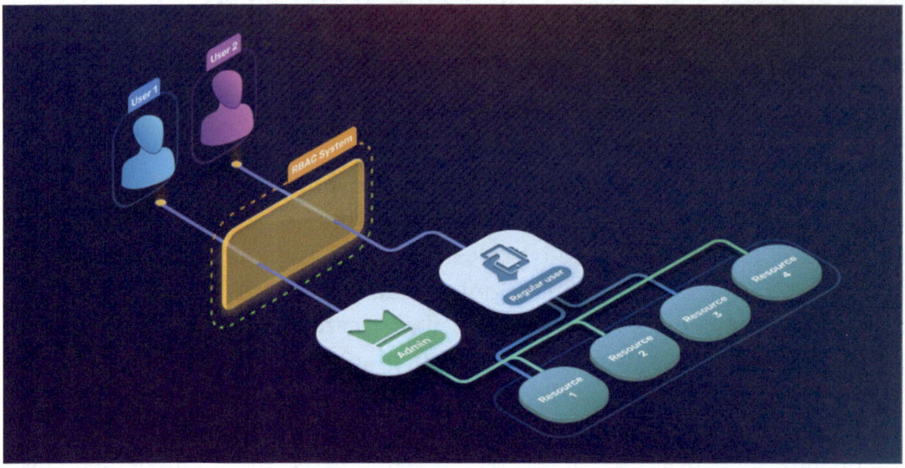

Figure 7.5. Role-based access control (RBAC).

Source: https://supertokens.com/covers/what-is-rbac-cover.png.

7.2. IDENTITY MANAGEMENT SYSTEMS

The cybersecurity space has increasingly placed IMS at the center of effective access control frameworks. IMS facilitates the administration of users by implementing technologies that provision, authorize, and authenticate securely. An effective IMS not only streamlines user administration but also protects sensitive information from unauthorized access by ensuring its confidentiality. With multifactor authentication and role-based access control, organizations can significantly minimize the risk of identity theft as well as cyber-attacks. IMS is also important in enabling compliance with several regulatory mandates to safeguard organizational integrity as well as users' trust in online platforms. In the scenario of healthcare and other such vital sectors, this is even more important, since a single settlement would lead to severe legal repercussions and loss of public confidence, giving greater emphasis to the imperative for stringent identity management processes (Eswaran, 2024). The emergence of advanced technologies such as blockchain has also revolutionized Identity Management Systems by introducing decentralized methods. Traditional identity management relies on vulnerable central databases, but blockchain provides a secure and open method of managing identities. Organizations with this technology have the ability to create unalterable ledgers that track all identity transactions, enhancing transparency as well as accountability. Most significantly, decentralized management of user identity with blockchain has the ability to reduce the overhead of operation required for validating user credentials, which eventually eases service provision while providing necessary security. These systems free users by providing them with greater control of digital identities, which is critical in ensuring that organizations and their stakeholders have confidence in trusting one another. Hence, utilizing blockchain-enabled identity management is a best practice and a strategic advantage for companies seeking to enhance their cybersecurity model (Subramaniyan et al., 2023). In the broader cybersecurity landscape, the implementation of Identity Management Systems in the overall security strategy is imperative. These systems not only facilitate access control but also serve as the foundation for overall security governance. Through the integration of attributes like encryption of data, real-time surveillance, and incident response mechanisms, organizations can be made cyber-threat resilient. The growing capability of cyber attackers necessitates an active stance for identity management in such a way that continuous monitoring and adjustment of access policies are in consonance with organizational risk appetites and regulatory principles. Apart from this, establishment of a culture of security where staff is regularly educated on identity management and cybersecurity threats is inevitable. As companies go through digital transformation, the reliance on effective Identity Management Systems will further increase, making their adoption an imperative sector of concentration to build overall cybersecurity resilience (Eswaran, 2024).

7.2.1. Components of Identity Management

Identity management is the cornerstone in cybersecurity for establishing robust access control policies. Identity provisioning, authentication, and identity governance are three key components of effective identity management. Identity provisioning involves creating, modifying, and removing user accounts and privileges on various systems. It ensures that proper privileges are granted to users based on their roles in an organization. Another significant one is provisioning automation to minimize human error and improve efficiency. Through optimizing the identity management, organizations ensure security loopholes that may be developed by obsolete or unwanted permissions are removed to make the overall security architecture more robust. The other segment of identity management is authentication as it verifies the identity of individuals who are seeking to access sensitive systems and information. The application of multi-factor authentication (MFA) significantly enhances security by requiring more than one type of verification, i.e., passwords and biometric data or security tokens. With this multi-tiered approach, even if a password is compromised, the unauthorized access remains extremely unlikely. Furthermore, the application of advanced technologies like adaptive authentication allows organizations to assess risk in real time and provide context-sensitive controls for access. Since businesses continue to experience evolving cyber threats, authentication process optimization is the solution to protecting sensitive information and maintaining user trust in digital environments. Identity governance entails the rules and regulations tasked with enforcing compliance and security within the identity management practices. This aspect calls for regular audit and review of user identities, roles, and permissions to enable organizations to maintain the art of data security based on best practices. A well-designed identity governance program allows organizations to address regulatory compliance and industry requirements, e.g., GDPR and HIPAA, lowering legal liabilities. Good governance also guarantees that privacy concerns are handled, e.g., in the cybersecurity logs example. The logs must achieve a balance between reporting the incident and preserving privacy, particularly for critical infrastructures. Therefore, the inclusion of privacy policies and anonymization procedures within identity governance systems is paramount to guaranteeing a secure, privacy-conscious ecosystem (Eénez et al., 2019) and promoting proactive risk management strategies that enhance organizational security postures (Anglano et al., 2018) (Figure 7.6).

Figure 7.6. Identity provisioning involves creating, modifying, and deactivating user accounts and access rights across various systems.

Source: https://www.conductorone.com/images/understanding-identity-and-access-provisioning-lifecycle-1.jpg.

7.2.2. Authentication Methods

The world of cybersecurity is constantly evolving, particularly with regards to authentication methods, which are the first line of security in identity management and access control. The conventional username-password credentials, although prevalent, are increasingly inadequate with their susceptibility to exploits like phishing and password guessing. As threats grow more sophisticated and the volume of sensitive data increases, organizations must resort to more secure authentication practices. Multi-factor authentication (MFA) is now a standard innovation that applies knowledge-based factors (passwords) together with possession-based factors (security tokens or phones) or inherence factors (biometrics) to create a multi-layered security mechanism. The method tremendously minimizes the threat of illegal access while being in line with best practice in the safeguarding of sensitive information, particularly in the event of sensitive sectors like finance and healthcare where the breach of data can be disastrous (Anglano et al., 2018). Also, the utilization of biometric authentication methods, including fingerprint recognition and facial recognition, is a significant move towards ease of use and safety against illegal access. Such technologies exploit unique physiological characteristics, making unauthorized copying extremely hard. Apart from enhancing security, biometric systems also ease the user experience by the reduced need for complex passwords, which are major causes of user frustration and bad security practice. With the inclusion of biometric data are critical ethical and privacy concerns, because unauthorized access to such personal information can have significant implications for human rights and freedoms.

Therefore, caution has to be exercised in organizations such that strict policies on data storage and processing are complementary to biometric system deployment. The enforcement of strict standards around the handling of such sensitive data is critical to maintaining trust among users as well as complying with regulatory standards (Marcus et al., 2018). Finally, the future of authentication methods is inextricably linked to how technology such as artificial intelligence and machine learning develops, which can be applied to enhance existing systems as well as create new models of identity authentication. These technologies are capable of reviewing user context and behavior and identifying anomalies, providing an additional layer of protection with the application of continuous authentication methods. For instance, a system could inspect trends in user actions, including geospatial positions and device utilization, to detect possible fraud in real-time. While the use of such sophisticated methods promises to enhance security protocols, it also provokes the demand for careful examination of the accompanying risks, which can include potential bias in the algorithms of AI and implications for fairness in access. Equilibrium between increased security and protection of civil liberties will be essential as organizations weigh the evolving dynamics of access control and identity management with cybersecurity (Anglano et al., 2018) (Figure 7.7).

Figure 7.7. Multi-factor authentication (MFA) has emerged as a critical advancement, combining knowledge-based factors (passwords) with possession-based factors (security tokens or mobile devices) or inherence factors (biometrics) to create a layered security approach.

Source: https://cdn.prod.website-files.com/61845f7929f5aa517ebab941/66d6c14aea60d1dc6eb965cb_Multi-Factor%20Authentication-%20How%20It%20Works%20and%20Why%20It%20Matters.jpg.

7.2.3. Authorization Processes

A profound understanding of the authorization process is paramount to ensuring efficient security provision in access control and identity management systems. Authorization dictates the power and privilege levels accorded to users based on their functional positions within an organization, with the aim of preventing unauthorized revelation of sensitive information and systems. In computer security, this process will typically involve various levels of authentication to ensure that users possess the appropriate permission levels for specific tasks. Subsequent to authorization systems are the use of role-based access control (RBAC) systems, which allow for an effective method of managing user permissions coupled with limiting possibilities of privilege escalation. The availability of advanced technologies like Artificial Intelligence elevates the levels of accuracy in such authorization processes, hence allowing for dynamic policy adjustment based on behavior and context of users, which consequently enhances an organization's security stance (Olabanji et al., 2024). In the process of studying educational institution authorization procedures, comparative analysis reveals considerable differences between private and public universities.

User identity, role, and access privilege management is a common thread; however, divergence occurs when these institutions are executing authorization procedures. Surprisingly, private universities encompass contractors and vendors as part of their user group, leading to additional challenges in managing the right of access. Moreover, password habits variation, session closure policy, and check for user status and role frequency show the necessity of tailored authorization strategies that address institutional needs and security concerns. Deploying rigorous verification procedures and dynamic permissions update can significantly enhance the security system, enabling institutions to shield their cyber space from new threats (Mollakuqe et al., 2024).

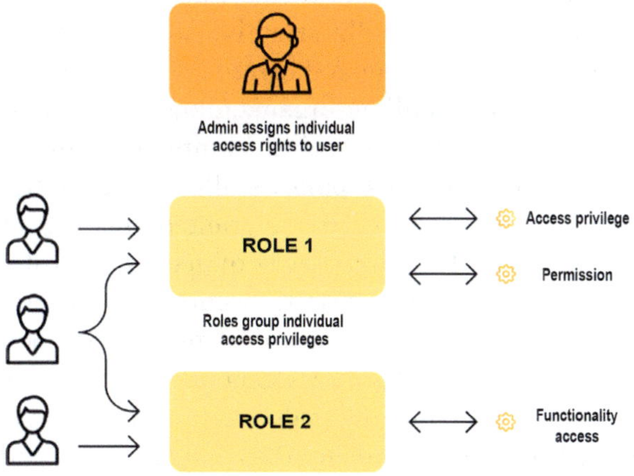

Figure 7.8. Effective authorization frameworks leverage role-based access control (RBAC) systems, allowing for a streamlined method of managing user permissions while simultaneously mitigating the risk of privilege escalation.

Source: https://cerbos.dev/blog-images/2021-05-31_the-hidden-costs-of-user-authorization/image-1.png.

The evolving nature of digital threats necessitates constant reassessment of the authorization processes in order to keep up with new types of cybersecurity threats. Since organizations are putting increasingly sophisticated systems in place, integrating user input into the authorization model is crucial. Adaptive learning algorithms can potentially provide adaptive authorization systems that respond to evolving user behavior or access requests in real-time. Moreover, transparency in authorization grant and in the basis for permission can contribute to user trust and compliance with security measures. Focus on creating dynamic, user-centric authorization systems will allow organizations to prepare themselves more effectively to address a sophisticated threat environment.

These novel approaches signal a requirement not just to safeguard sensitive data but also to improve overall user experience in access control systems as an expression of the conflicting security and usability objectives in modern-day cybersecurity measures (Olabanji et al., 2024) (Figure 7.8).

7.3. THE ROLE OF POLICIES IN ACCESS CONTROL

Policies are crucial in determining access control systems within organizations, providing an orderly framework for controlling who should have access to a given resource and under what conditions. Policies are critical in ensuring only the appropriate staff can handle sensitive information to minimize the opportunity for data breaches and unauthorized access. In cybersecurity, well-defined access control policies allow organizations to apply security controls in an effective manner while remaining compliant with regulations. By defining user roles and permissions, policies allow organizations to apply the principle of least privilege, where users are granted only the access needed to perform their job functions. This first aspect of access control not only guards organizational assets but also gives rise to security culture awareness within the organization, making way for an overall identity management strategy. In addition, enforcing access control policies is not merely a technical imperative but an essential organizational imperative that responds to evolving cyber threats to the organization. With technological advancement more and more altering the digital landscape, access control policies must adapt to newer threats and evolving user demands. Doubt regarding the application of newer technologies such as artificial intelligence and the metaverse emphasizes the necessity of robust policy frameworks. Organizations must consider ethical and legal issues, in particular, the implementation of technologies with important effects on consumer behavior and organizational performance. Notably, the conversation regarding the metaverse emphasizes the requirement of policy amendments to address societal and cultural implications, and therefore it becomes essential that organizations devise agile and forward-looking access control policies that possess the ability to tackle such issues in real-time (Dwivedi et al., 2022, 2023). Secondly, the effectiveness of access control policies depends on continuous analysis and adaptation to maintain pace with internal and external developments. With growing business expansion and new technologies, it becomes essential that their access control mechanisms be current and relevant. This necessitates compliance with periodic audits and reviews of access permissions, which can lead to the identification of vulnerabilities and areas for improvement. Training initiatives also take center stage in confirming worker awareness of access control implementations and the importance of adhering to these policies. By embedding a proactive culture into access control, organizations can build resilience against imminent threats while aligning their practices with industry standard and regulatory requirements. Thereafter, policy intervention in access control not only guides organizational cybersecurity efforts but also shapes overall identity management trends to ultimately produce a further secured digital environment for all parties involved.

7.3.1. Development of Access Control Policies

Evolution of access control policies is the need of the hour in the current cybersecurity landscape where businesses need to match the level of sophistication of digital environments. Traditional access control models that relied on manual and static policy processes cannot keep pace with increasing threats and dynamic user demands anymore. Such evolution necessitates reviewing existing frameworks to add adaptive approaches that can consider real-time incidents and user activity. Using advanced technologies, such as AI, organizations can develop policies that not only remain more responsive in nature but are also capable of performing continuous surveillance and anomaly recognition. The implementation of AI into access control allows for more efficient and secure management of user identities and addresses compliance requirements since the versatility of such systems ensures ongoing synchronization with organizational policy and regulatory requirements, further enhancing overall cybersecurity posture (Hariharan, 2025). In doing so, organizations are increasingly implementing User Identity Management Systems (UIMS) as a bottom-up strategy in the development of access control policies. UIMS not only improve the identification and authentication process but also provide a platform for secure consumption of services by users across various platforms. With growing digital expansion, strong access control becomes indispensable in defending sensitive information against new security threats like identity theft and phishing. UIMS provide sophisticated authentication processes incorporating two-factor authentication that combines classic credentials with biometric attributes. This innovative process of user identity authentication not only improves access security but also mitigates unauthorized access and cybercrime risks. By continuously improving identity management, organizations can meet legal demands and proactively fight the threats present in today's networks (Nonum et al., 2025). Access policy creation also demands a holistic solution to user activity auditing and monitoring. A successful policy system must have the ability to monitor access attempts, authorizations, and actions taken by users to identify patterns that indicate potential security breaches or policy violations. Through the assistance of exhaustive logging and analytics, organizations can generate insights into user activities that form the foundation for ongoing policy enhancement. Such observations make it possible to pre-emptively modify the rights of access and can trigger alerts for unusual behavior, enhancing risk mitigation strategies. In addition, having transparent procedures for conducting periodic reviews of access policies makes it possible for them to remain updated in the event of changing organizational requirements and threat landscapes. Through incorporation of continuous evaluation into developing access control, organizations provide a dynamic security position that does not fall behind emerging attacks while guarding core assets (Hariharan, 2025) (Figure 7.9).

Figure 7.9. Organizations are increasingly turning to user identity management systems (UIMS) as a foundational strategy in the development of access control policies.

Source: https://www.10duke.com/wp-content/uploads/2022/03/PAM-1-300x232.png.

7.3.2. Enforcement of Security Policies

Security policy enforcement is an essential aspect of identity management and access control in cybersecurity, the security shield that stands behind an organization's security posture. Security policies define how to permit access rights, to whom and what systems can connect, and on what conditions should the access be allowed or revoked. Effective policy not only defines user action guidelines but also necessitates the implementation of technical controls to enforce the compliance. Through this, businesses are able to avoid risks from illicit access and loss of data. As with the increase in sophisticated cyber threats, enforcement strategies for such policies have revolutionized to a great extent, leading to the implementation of models like Zero Trust Architecture (ZTA), which emphasizes continuous verification and not trusting solely on the basis of network location. Therefore, a shift towards dynamic enforcement is essential in the safeguarding of precious assets. Identity and access management (IAM) solutions are indispensable for enforcing security policies. IAM not only streamlines user authentication and access authorization processes but also aligns with ZTA principles by ensuring that every access request is authenticated in real-time. This multi-layered deployment of access rights utilizes various technologies, such as multi-factor authentication, role-based access, and encryption, which most effectively enhance organizational security.

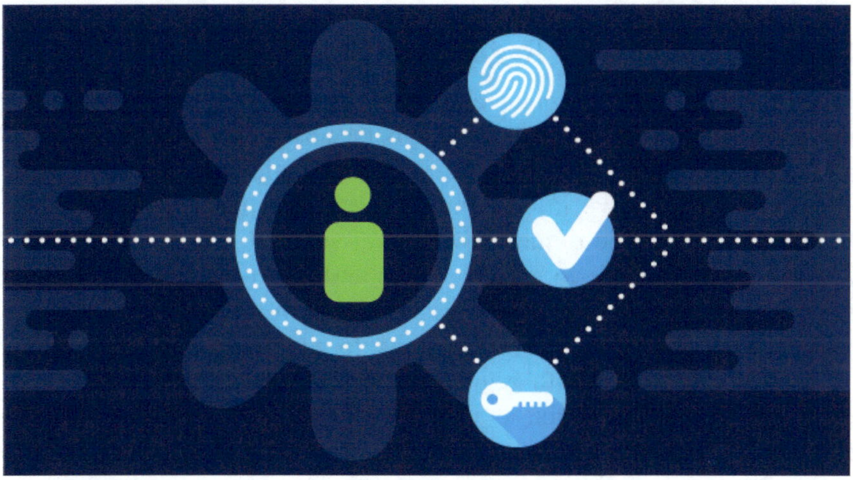

Figure 7.10. Incorporating identity and access management (IAM) solutions is essential for the effective enforcement of security policies.

Source: https://www.cisco.com/content/dam/cisco-cdc/site/images/legacy/assets/swa/img/anchor-info/what-is-iam-banner-628x353.png.

While organizations grapple with consolidating legacy systems, imposing wide security policies becomes a highly challenging endeavor. Issues such as scalability and user resistance have a tendency to bring the deployment of IAM frameworks that are capable of delivering stronger security postures to a grinding halt. Yet organizations that are successful in deploying strong IAM solutions are able to manage user identities more effectively and enforce hard access controls, thereby lowering potential exposures. Improvements in cybersecurity frameworks and awareness of the Zero Trust model emphasize the need for ongoing monitoring and adaptive policy enforcement. With increasingly advanced cyber threat environments, having static policies alone is not sufficient any longer. Organizations must embrace a maturity model approach to developing their security practices over time. This involves actively examining and refining their enforcement controls in order to stay current with evolving threats and compliance requirements. Research indicates that the Zero Trust security market is a testimony to this need for adaptive enforcement and is expected to grow significantly in the foreseeable future, estimated at ∃80.58 billion as of 2028. By layering various enforcement approaches in one adaptive maturity framework, organizations are not just improving existing security infrastructure, but future-proofing against identity management and access control risk as well, with a secure cybersecurity stance in an ever-changing landscape (Alebiosu et al., 2025; Alnoaimi et al., 2025) (Figure 7.10).

7.3.3. Compliance with Regulatory Standards

The need for regulatory compliance in access control and identity management is becoming a norm in the context of cybersecurity. Organizations must deal with a complex domain of local, national, and global regulation with the intent to protect sensitive information and personal data. Without a unified framework for regulation, most firms are vulnerable and are leading to inconsistency in response to data breaches and cyber-attacks. As highlighted by the ongoing prevalence of data breaches, which not only erode consumer confidence but also expose organizations to extreme legal vulnerabilities, the necessity to comply with regulatory requirements becomes paramount. A national data protection act, as discussed in Marcus et al. (2018), may be able to provide minimum standards for data security protocols and therefore a more concrete framework for compliance and enhancing overall cybersecurity cover. Further, regulation compliance is not only about sticking to the rules; it plays a significant role in transforming security into culture in organizations. With robust identity management systems that are compliant with regulatory demands, organizations can insulate themselves from unauthorized access and data breach risks. The employment of comprehensive access control mechanisms ensures that sensitive information is accessed solely by legitimate people, instrumental in safeguarding personal information. The necessity for continuous training and focus brought out in Anglano et al. (2018) also shows that compliance practice has to be ingrained as part of an organization's continuous plan to establish a situation where the security of the organization is paramount. Taking an ongoing proactive stance will enhance the capability of organizations to act constructively to threats, subsequently diminishing the effect of such potential breaches on consumers as well as the business itself. In addition, the evolving cyber threat landscape necessitates regulatory needs to be updated on a continuous basis in a bid to address emerging threats. Models for compliance must be flexible enough to match the level of advancement in current cyber-attacks and developments in identity management technology. A too strict regulation risks dampening innovation but failing to keep abreast of new technologies such as biometrics and artificial intelligence. Regulatory bodies, therefore, must be engaged with the cyber world, taking into account both the recommendations of industry experts and the proposals as outlined in Anglano et al. (2018). The symbiotic method can lead to the development of vibrant standards that not only provide protection for data and privacy but also allow organizations to enhance their cybersecurity posture. In a world where data breaches happen all the time, creation and adherence to suitable compliance regulations are required for creating a secure online society that safeguards individuals' identities and personal information.

7.4. TECHNOLOGIES SUPPORTING ACCESS CONTROL

The access control environment is revolutionized by the arrival of certain technologies with the purpose of ensuring security and simplifying identity management. Biometric authentication is one of them that relies on unique physiological attributes such as fingerprints, retina scan, and facial recognition. By examining these biological markers, biometric systems can provide high security and accuracy along with minimizing the weaknesses of traditional password-based systems. The success of this technology lies not only in its ability to authenticate people but also in its anti-spoofing feature, which makes it a key component of protecting sensitive data in most industries. Additionally, interoperability of biometric technologies with current infrastructure is becoming ever more feasible, thereby making them a candidate solution for access requirements today, as discussed in various sectors and applications laid out in cybersecurity literature (Anglano et al., 2018). The second most critical technology that supports access control is identity management systems based on multi-factor authentication (MFA). MFA utilizes multiple authentication methods, which is far more secure in contrast to single-factor deployments. For instance, an individual may be required to give away something they know (a password), something they have (a smartphone for an offline code), and something they are (biometric authentication). The multi-factor system renders it extremely difficult for unauthorized access since would-be hackers will have to overcome several barriers. With companies adopting cloud environments and distant workspaces, the faith in robust identity management systems takes center stage. The implementation of MFA along with identity management platforms not only defends highly sensitive information but also ensures compliance with data protection regulatory requirements, enhancing the overall security posture of the company (Ani et al., 2020). Finally, the pervasive explosion of

Internet of Things (IoT) devices presents unique challenges and opportunities to access control technologies. As these networked devices become ubiquitous, the requirement for sophisticated security controls to manage their access to various networks comes into focus. Traditional access controls do not address the dynamic and diversified IoT environment. Therefore, innovative technologies based on contextual access control are being put forward to facilitate organizations in defining access privileges according to real-time assessments of the context. Through continuous analysis of variables such as user behavior, device status, and environmental conditions, these high-end systems deliver adaptive access controls that will vary to accommodate the immense diversity of circumstances presented by the IoT environment. This approach not only fortifies the security infrastructure but also significantly reduces any possible weakness associated with such high-speed developmental technologies, highlighting the importance of further research and development on the access control and identity management front (Anglano et al., 2018) (Figure 7.11).

Figure 7.11. As organizations adopt cloud services and remote work environments, the reliance on robust identity management frameworks becomes critical.

Source: https://www.hostduplex.com/blog/wp-content/uploads/2024/01/Secure-Remote-Working-Environments.webp.

7.4.1. Multi-Factor Authentication (MFA)

The increasing rate of cyber-attacks necessitates a strong identity management and access control system in place, with Multi-Factor Authentication (MFA) becoming an important feature. MFA shifts the security paradigm away from the traditional model of username and password by incorporating additional verification factors that significantly enhance security against unwanted access. These may be something one is aware of, like a password; something one owns, like an online token or mobile phone; or something one is, like biometric data. The use of MFA has been shown to reduce the risk of successful cyber-attacks, and therefore it is a main strategy for organizations that are looking to safeguard sensitive data while following regulatory standards. The combination of several security technologies in MFA solutions is an excellent case of foresight required in this era of complex threats. Directive frameworks such as the European Union's NIS2 Directive highlight strong authentication controls, reinforcing MFA as a fundamental access control mechanism. The NIS2 Directive not only highlights the requirement for MFA but also imposes strong requirements on covered entities to change their existing authentication practices. MFA not only serves as a deterrent for unauthorized entry but also assists in ensuring adherence to such evolving legal mandates.

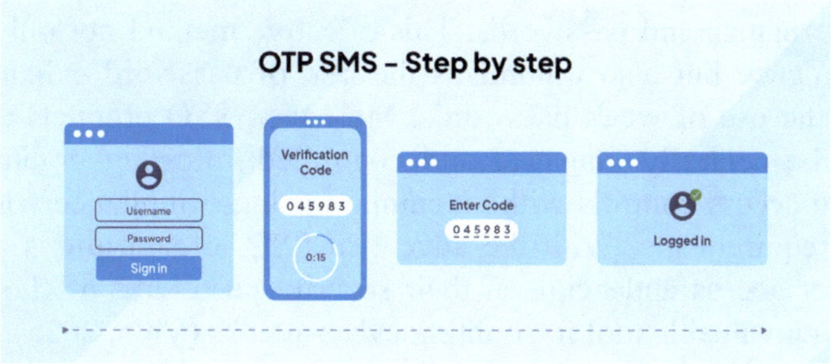

Figure 7.12. SMS-based one-time passwords (OTPs).

Source: https://www.textmagic.com/wp-content/uploads/2024/04/OTP-SMS-Step-by-step.png

As organizations deploy their cybersecurity strategies to address these regulative forces, concern for new technologies moves to the center of attention. This compliance-driven migration to MFA supports a centralized model for identity administration and reduces the threats brought about by substandard authentication guidelines, with promise of adherence to evolving business needs, thereby making overall cybersecurity infrastructure stronger. The choice of MFA products also defines to a great extent the effectiveness of an organization's access control guidelines. Although traditional methods such as SMS-based OTP have been favored in the past, recent studies indicate that they might not be as secure as the high security standards imposed by current legislation like NIS2. With the emergence of more secure options such as FIDO2 passkeys, organizations realize the need to future-proof their authentication measures. These modern solutions not only enhance security against common attacks, including phishing, but also meet the ultimate goal of creating a more secure IT environment. With multi-factor authentication taking place through advanced technologies, organizations can enjoy a balance between security, usability, and compliance, and thus a robust defense against the ever-evolving landscape of cybersecurity attacks (Vartiainen et al., 2025). The pro-active implementation of MFA will considerably improve the overall integrity and confidentiality of sensitive data and also reinforce users' faith in electronic transactions (Figure 7.12).

7.4.2. Single Sign-On (SSO) Solutions

In the rapidly changing world of cyber security, Single Sign-On (SSO) solutions have emerged as an essential component of successful identity and access control solutions. SSO enables individuals to log in once and access multiple applications and services, thus reducing the need of managing multiple usernames and passwords. This effective method not only enhances user convenience but also minimizes the risk of password exhaustion, thus precluding the use of weak passwords. Moreover, SSO products enable user identity to be centrally managed and controlled, allowing organizations to apply strong access controls without compromising compliance with multiple regulatory requirements. With the advent of SSO, organizations are able to simplify user access and heighten their security posture as a whole, thereby making it an invaluable tool for fighting cyber-attacks (Vitla, 2025). Moreover, the integration of Multi-Factor Authentication (MFA) with SSO solutions offers an extra measure of security essential for defending confidential information. MFA requires users to authenticate themselves based on two or more factors, making unauthorized access very difficult. This hybrid approach—combining user convenience inherent in SSO with the robust security of MFA—fixes the critical flaws of one-factor authentication methods. With an increasingly cloud-dependent business world, the need is critical to deploy security solutions that not only protect data but also comply with regulatory environments such as GDPR and HIPAA. By wisely adopting SSO with MFA, organizations can enhance their identity management systems and therefore decrease compliance risks and enhance their resistance to advanced cybersecurity threats (Alam et al., 2024). The deployment of SSO solutions within organizations also demands thorough consideration of implementation plans and technical systems. With changing cybersecurity threats, the need for end-to-end security controls such as role-based access controls (RBAC) and activity audit is more important than ever. A properly architected SSO environment enables organizations to configure user permissions and roles with ease and ensure that the access is given on the basis of least privilege. It not only minimizes the likely attack vectors but also ensures compliance with industry frameworks and regulations. Fundamentally, SSO solutions when combined with robust access control mechanisms create a robust identity management context that not only contributes towards ease of user access but also significantly enhances an organization's management of compliance obligations and cyber threat mitigations (Vitla, 2025) (Figure 7.13).

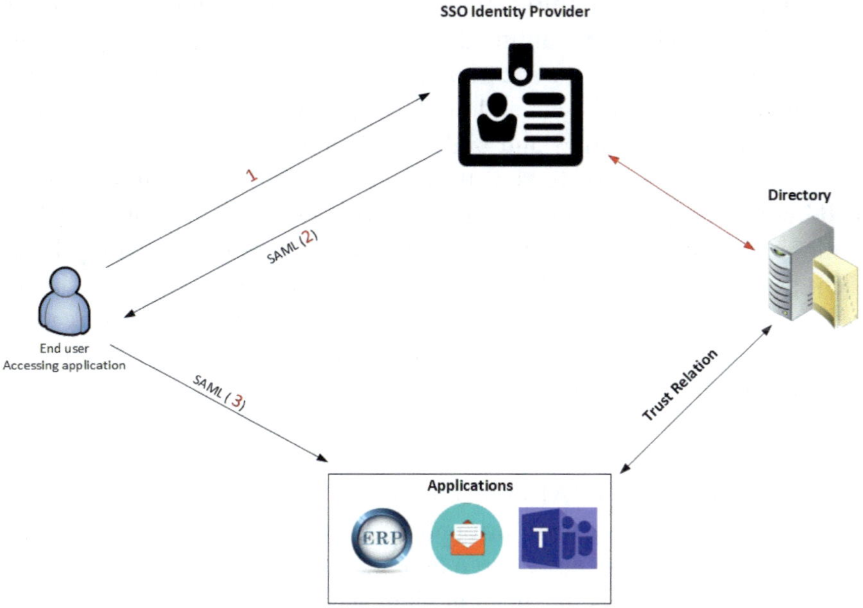

Figure 7.13. Single sign-on (SSO) solutions have emerged as a vital component of effective access control and identity management frameworks.

Source: https://teksalah.com/wp content/uploads/2020/11/Drawing1-1.jpg.

7.4.3. Identity and Access Management (IAM) Tools

With the evolving landscape in cybersecurity, Identity and Access Management (IAM) technologies are leading the way in the security of critical data and guaranteeing that organizations are equipped with robust controls over access. IAM technologies make it easier to manage user identities and their permissions within the digital space. Through the establishment of a single authentication system, IAM solutions enable organizations to implement security policies effectively without the illegal entry of unauthorized users. The functionality of IAM tools extends far beyond compliance; they allow business efficiency with the ability for companies to strike a balance between security and end-user experience. With companies moving increasingly into cloud environments, needs for secure IAM solutions grow, highlighting the importance of adaptive tools with the ability to integrate into heterogeneous systems and services. IAM tools are those various technologies and processes utilized to manage users' identities through their life cycle. From identity management and creation to safe authentication and access, these solutions allow for identity governance on a complete level. Moreover, the implementation of multifactor authentication (MFA) within IAM solutions further increases security by requiring more than one form of verification before granting access to confidential data or applications. This multi-stage approach to security makes organizations more resistant to the potential of break-throughs and credential theft. Thus, organizations need to be proactive in evaluating and updating their IAM practices to align with evolving cybersecurity threats as well as evolving regulatory requirements, and also address privacy and data security concerns. Furthermore, integrating new technologies, such as AI and ML, into IAM systems is transforming the field of identity management. AI-driven IAM solutions can track user behavioral activity and detect anomalies that may indicate potential future security threats. Firms can implement proactive countermeasures to deal with such threats before they become big-time incidents. The inclusion of AI in IAM tools not only enhances security but also emphasizes the imperative of migrating towards a constantly evolving technological landscape. However, ethical and legal aspects for the use of AI in identity management cannot be overlooked, including organizations' growth through complexity with the use of data and privacy rights. There must be research on those areas to develop IAM solutions that are both effective and ethical, taking into account hidden biases and privacy concerns (Dwivedi et al., 2022, 2023).

7.5. CHALLENGES IN ACCESS CONTROL AND IDENTITY MANAGEMENT

Identity management and access control are intimidating tasks in cybersecurity that need to be addressed by organizations to safeguard confidential information. Diversity of user access needs is a significant challenge, as it would complicate the implementation of efficient access controls. Vendors, employees, and third-party partners typically require different access levels to the system and data, necessitating a fine-grained identity management. Furthermore, the evolving nature of organizational environments, such as working remotely and onboarding new workers, increases the degree of complexity in maintaining access permissions current. Due to shifting threat levels, it is presently more important than ever to implement a unified model of access control that is both flexible and secure, wherein only appropriate individuals have access to sensitive systems and information. Regulatory compliance is also a significant issue in the access control and identity management sector, as organizations work with a more stringent regulatory environment. Various regulations and standards enforce mandated practices for protecting organizational and individual data, offering complexities for compliance. For instance, organizations need to deal with different rules in different locations when they install controls conforming to standards such as the General Data Protection Regulation (GDPR) and the Health Insurance Portability and Accountability Act (HIPAA). In addition, compliance is frequently a context of complex negotiations involving stakeholders, rendering it challenging to hasten the deployment of necessary access controls.

Figure 7.14. Employees, vendors, and external partners often require varying levels of access to systems and data, necessitating a granular approach to identity management.

Source: https://www.adnovum.com/hubfs/FILES/04_Insights/Blog/2024/blog_managed_digital_identitiy_image_header.jpg.

As pointed out by Anglano et al. (2018), there is the need for having standardized rules for cyber defense, making it crucial to address these compliance concerns as part of adding complexity to the business environment for organizations seeking to implement effective identity management measures. Moreover, increased cases of identity theft and data breaches makes it more complex to manage access and identity. With increasing complexity in cyber-attacks, organizations become increasingly vulnerable to attacks that target sensitive user information. Current incident response systems have been found lacking in providing comprehensive security against such vulnerabilities.

As proposed in Marcus et al. (2018), flaws in current legal frameworks further exacerbate the problem as they lack a national data security standard. Therefore, organizations must be forward-thinking in their identity-related risk management, from rethinking data gathering practices on personal data to leveraging sophisticated technology to offer robust data protection at all times. Thus, addressing these multifaceted issues is a prerequisite not only for compliance and security but also for building trust through effective identity management in today's era (Figure 7.14).

7.5.1. Insider Threats

In the ever-evolving world of cybersecurity, insider threats have emerged as a growing problem, and most of the time, they are harder to contain compared to external threats. Insider threats can be broadly explained as security threats that originate from within the company via employees or contractors who misuse their access rights to unintentionally or intentionally cause harm to the organization. As opposed to external attacks, with which one can typically deal using robust firewalls and intrusion detection, insiders require an access control and identity management-based solution. The Zero Trust Architecture (ZTA) framework, with emphasis on authentication at every access point and imposition of least privilege access, takes a key role in reducing the insider threat. By giving their users access only to information that is needed for their functions, organizations can effectively minimize chances for malicious or careless actions that will lead to data breaches or significant operation interruption (Nasiruzzaman et al., 2025). The most effective way to combat insider threats is through the implementation of strong identity management systems with biometric and behavioral analytics. Legacy password-based authentication methods are becoming progressively less effective since they are susceptible to easy violations and social engineering attacks. A high-tech solution integrates biomechanical access controls, such as pressure-sensitive floors and biometric interfaces, along with AI-based behavioral analytics. This synchronizes threat identification and removes unauthorized access threats without losing sensitive information. Empirical studies have shown that a multi-modal approach is capable of attaining over 95% accuracy rates in threat detection, significantly improving the security posture of an organization against insider attacks with both physical and cyber data (Ogunmolu, 2025). Organizations must possess an holistic model with emphasis on continuous monitoring and swift responses to anomalies to effectively address insider threats. Installations of differential privacy mechanisms in behavior detection systems guarantee that although analysis is performed, data from individual users are protected and therefore compliant with regulatory needs. This is especially crucial in sectors such as energy, where confidentiality and data integrity are of utmost concern. Hierarchical federated learning frameworks are particularly promising due to their ability to facilitate collaborative learning on different sites without exchanging raw data. With advancements in systems, organizations can implement solutions that not only react to the current threats but also learn from the history and thus make their defense mechanisms against insider threats always stronger in the increasingly complex cyber world (Ogunmolu, 2025) (Figure 7.15).

Figure 7.15. To effectively address insider threats, it is essential that organizations adopt a holistic model that emphasizes continuous monitoring and timely responses to unusual behavior.

Source: https://cdn-cchkmpj.nitrocdn.com/CJXGnJvCvbQYOSNVvxpLvOY-cHhpJDKbH/assets/images/optimized/rev-0d49871/ossisto.com/wp-content/uploads/2024/11/Future-Trends-in-Incident-Response-Services.webp.

7.5.2. Evolving Cyber Threats

The cybersecurity environment is regularly reconfigured by new cyber threats that challenge conventional defensive measures. As organizations become more reliant on digital infrastructure, the prevalence and complexity of cyber-attacks have grown, with attackers employing complicated methods such as phishing, ransomware, and zero-day exploits. Cyber attackers leverage automation and artificial intelligence to make their attacks more sinister and more difficult to detect and defend against. The emergence of the metaverse further complicates this image, as virtual worlds introduce new threats related to user identity and access control. Organizations must adapt their cyber security strategy to not only protect data but protect user interactions in these immersive spaces as well. The ongoing debate about the metaverse makes the greatest need for robust identity management systems that shall be capable of withstanding and keeping up with increased technological advances as well as new threats (Dwivedi et al., 2022). Organizations and businesses are increasingly becoming interested in access control and identity management as key factors in their cybersecurity measures owing to emerging cyber threats. The use of multi-factor authentication and identity verification processes has become critical in preventing unauthorized access to sensitive information. Secondly, zero trust architectures are increasingly being popularized, transforming the centuries-old perimeter-based model of security. Under this system, trust is never assumed; instead, ongoing verification of identities and activities of users is required. This shift is concurrent with global initiatives towards the consolidation of democratic governance, not simply reacting to cyber vulnerabilities but to the broader implications of cybersecurity and its consequences on individual freedom and rights. By taking on these advanced identity management habits, organizations can become more responsive to new threats while making the digital environment safer. With evolving cyber threats, the implication is beyond immediate economic loss or data breach, reaching public trust and organizational integrity. Stakeholders are increasingly aware that the compromise of information could lead to reputational damage, legal issues, and regulatory scrutiny. The organizations therefore have to establish a culture of cybersecurity awareness, where the staff is brought to consciousness about their role in safeguarding sensitive information. Training and education should be focused on identifying probable threats, such as social engineering attacks, and enforcing adherence to defined access controls policies. On top of this, organizations must consider the societal effects of cyber-attacks based on knowledge from ongoing evolution within cybersecurity to guide policies that protect consumer welfare and enhance electronic marketing practice in emerging virtual reality (Dwivedi et al., 2022). Lastly, a knowledgeable workforce and watchful risk management are essential to guiding the challenges posed by emerging cyber threats and ensuring the integrity of access control systems and identity management processes.

7.5.3. Balancing Security and Usability

It is an essential issue to achieve the optimal balance between usability and security in identity management and access control under cybersecurity. Companies are striving to protect valuable information, thus imposing severe security controls that introduce complexity, degrading the user experience. Users are going to face a complex authentication procedure requiring multi-factor authentication or frequent password updates, and it is hard for them to access the information they need immediately. These barriers can cause frustration, decreased productivity, and a potential disregard for security practices.

Therefore, it is necessary to adopt mechanisms that not only enhance security but also address the usability of systems in a manner that security becomes a facilitator rather than an impediment to routine operations. To establish an environment that is conducive to both security and usability, organizations must turn towards adopting user-centered design principles to their access control mechanisms. This is an issue of understanding user behavior and modifying security controls to address it, reducing the cognitive load on users. Using risk-based authentication as an example can illustrate this balance; it can support various security controls depending on the risk factor of the access request. Simplifying authentication flows and removing unnecessary obstacles allows organizations to facilitate compliance with security controls without reducing user experience. As security technologies evolve, so should the practices of implementing them, taking into account the input of end-users in order to better optimize the overall efficiency of access control systems.

Figure 7.16. Users may find themselves navigating a convoluted authentication process that includes multi-factor authentication or frequent password changes, making it difficult to access the information they need efficiently.

Source: https://skillie.co.in/wp-content/uploads/2023/07/image-11.png.

Additionally, the paradigm for implementing security measures must be malleable enough to manage the different demands of different groups of users. For instance, enterprise systems are usually some mix of legacy and new software structures, which results in issues in synchronizing security protocols with user requirements. As established in present arguments on cybersecurity infrastructure, there is a need to emphasize training and awareness initiatives that inform users about security practice applicable to their situation (Anglano et al., 2018). In addition, privacy-by-design may enable organizations to come up with systems that are designed with usability in mind, significantly guarding information yet facilitating friendly access (Beardo et al., 2019). Through the embedding of security into the very texture of system designs, organizations have managed to successfully balance security and usability, creating an environment where users remain secure while being enabled (Figure 7.16).

7.6. BEST PRACTICES FOR EFFECTIVE ACCESS CONTROL

Good access control is a central tenet of cybersecurity that operates on the least privilege principle, which restricts user rights to only what they need to perform their job function. Based on this principle, organizations can significantly reduce the attack surface that would otherwise be open to malicious attackers, enhancing security as a whole. Implementing role-based access control (RBAC) is one of the best practices designed for efficient user permission management. RBAC categorizes users by role in the company, thus simplifying access permission management and modification. It not only simplifies managing users, but also simplifies compliance with regulatory needs by having documentation clearly define who has access to sensitive data. Furthermore, regular access control audits should be performed in order to identify and rectify any discrepancies and ensure that access privileges are aligned with existing business needs and security policies. Use of multifactor authentication (MFA) in access controls is another best practice to improve organizational security controls against unauthorized access. MFA requires users to provide more than one form of verification before systems or data may be accessed, thereby having an additional layer of security compared to using plain passwords. This is critical in guarding sensitive information because it reduces the threats that come with compromised credentials. As cyberspace threats keep changing, so should access control systems; therefore, organizations need to adopt adaptive authentication practices that assess contextual conditions such as the location of the user or the device's trustworthiness. These practices enhance security but also provide a frictionless user experience, limiting friction in legitimate requests for access. Continuity training and education initiatives for the importance of MFA can also allow users to adhere to best practices, inculcating a security culture within the organization. Finally, the implementation of latest technologies such as blockchain-based IAM can transform how organizations implement access control. Blockchain not just boosts transparency and accountability towards user credentials but also supports a decentralized process whereby identity data can be verified without revealing sensitive information. This paradigm shift promotes the adoption of a user-centric strategy where users can gain better control over their digital identities while creating a superior security environment. Further, organizations will also have to remain aware of the ethical aspect and legal concerns associated with revolutionary technologies such as artificial intelligence. By examining the relationship between innovative solutions and the potential impact on security and privacy, organizations can create best practice that enhances access control while also sustaining trust and regulatory compliance. This intersection of policy and technology needs to be examined in-depth as organizations struggle to keep pace with an ever-changing cybersecurity landscape (Dwivedi et al., 2023; Subramaniyan et al., 2023).

7.6.1. Regular Audits and Reviews

The implementation of regular audits and reviews is important in building robust access control and identity management procedures within cybersecurity guidelines. Reviews assist organizations in acquiring the insights they require to analyze the efficacy of their security controls as well as their policy compliance. By carefully reviewing user access logs, authentication types, and permission levels, businesses can identify vulnerabilities that could lead to unauthorized access. Periodic audits are an affirmative step to not just ensure data integrity but also enhance the accountability of users, such that only authorized personnel have access to sensitive information. The audits can also help organizations harmonize their access controls with regulations, hence reducing the risk of accumulated penalties and data breaches, which is against the call of constant watchfulness in a dynamic digital landscape. Moreover, the quickly evolving nature of technological advancements necessitates that organizations re-evaluate their access control systems from time to time. With more and more devices being connected online as the Internet of Things (IoT) and other connected devices come on board, the security boundary has expanded, posing new challenges in managing identities and access procedures. Regular audits can provide insight into the effect of connecting IoT devices, which come with varying levels of risk that normal cybersecurity software might not fully address. For instance, companies must modify their access policies to extend to these devices so that unauthorized agents will not exploit security loopholes. By enforcing frequent updates in access controls through comprehensive audits, companies do not just streamline business operations but protect sensitive data from burgeoning threats, thus enhancing their cybersecurity position in an increasingly interconnected world (Allioui et al., 2023). While companies struggle to stay abreast of the complexities of cybersecurity, the concept of a cycle of continuous improvement remains paramount. Regular review offers the opportunity to strengthen access control policies, making adjustments based on audit findings and incident reports. This cycle of ongoing review facilitates an environment of learning and adaptation. Besides, as such technologies as the metaverse have exposed, augmenting cybersecurity architectures also must shift to support new access management scenarios encountered in such virtual environments. Businesses must reconsider their risk assessments and policies to incorporate the adoption of complexity from handling identities within the metaverse, thus preparing for opportunities and challenges being posed by such technologies (Koohang et al., 2023). In conclusion, regular reviews and audits not only ensure compliance but also drive strategic improvements in access control systems to enable organizations to efficiently combat evolving cybersecurity threats (Figure 7.17).

Figure 7.17. Regular audits serve as a proactive mechanism to not only ensure data integrity but also to enhance user accountability, ensuring that only authorized personnel can access sensitive information.

Source: https://www.v-comply.com/wp-content/uploads/2025/01/https___www.v-comply.com_blog_compliance-audits-a-guide-to-ensuring-regulatory-adherence.png.

7.6.2. User Education and Training

A key element of improving access control and identity management in cybersecurity is users' education and training. Cyber-attacks are mostly attributed to human action, and it is therefore important that companies create a culture of cybersecurity among employees. The training interventions should address a number of issues, including the recognition and reporting of phishing scams, the importance of password security, and the recognition of social engineering tactics. Such education not only enables users but also reduces the level of security risk from human error by a significant margin. As more and more organizations rely on digital platforms, appropriate training ensures that employees know about their part in safeguarding sensitive information and reiterates the fact that cybersecurity is everybody's responsibility. In addition, technology's dynamic nature, as embodied in innovations such as the metaverse and AI, necessitates ongoing education by users. Emergence of new platforms and tools brings with it opportunities and risks to organizational security. For instance, generative AI tools bring improved productivity, but they also bring associated ethical and security concerns that users have to navigate carefully. Hence, cybersecurity training must be adaptable and regularly refreshed to continue keeping pace with technological advancements to make employees fully competent to handle tools they face in their everyday work. By incorporating user training within the company culture, businesses can limit threats and enhance overall security posture, ultimately contributing to a stronger infrastructure. Moreover, the success of user education is evident across various industries, such as banking and healthcare, where identity management is essential. Industry-specific training modules aimed at responding to the particular requirements of each industry can make the relevance and efficiency of educational initiatives more effective. In banks, for instance, where sensitive financial data are handled, employees must be skilled in implementing secure access mechanisms and complying with regulatory requirements. Similarly, health care providers must understand the value of protecting patients' information against unauthorized use. As organizations explore the potential of the metaverse and other new technologies, a robust user training initiative will be essential. This training will not only foster adherence to security protocols but also foster an proactive attitude towards detection and reduction of potential threats in a dynamic cyber world, so that users become the first line of defense against invasions (Dwivedi et al., 2023; Koohang et al., 2023).

7.6.3. Implementation of Least Privilege Principle

The application of the Least Privilege Principle is an important component of effective access control and identity management within cybersecurity protocols. According to the principle, users and entities must be granted the minimum level of access necessary to perform their respective functions. By applying the principle, organizations can reduce risks of unauthorized access as well as potential breaches. One of the largest obstacles to applying this principle is getting the role and permission definition right, especially in deeply hierarchical systems with many classes of users. Having just the right levels of access is important to defending that privileges closely track personal responsibility so overall security position and organizational performance are optimized. Establishing a robust Least Privilege model is also complemented by end-to-end Privileged Access Management (PAM) approaches that address the unique vulnerabilities in privileged accounts. According to recent research, stolen credentials are among the primary drivers of security incidents, and because of this, organizations should put a high value on PAM solutions. The difference between the volume of privileged and standard user accounts exacerbates these vulnerabilities because privileged accounts tend to be an initial cyber-attack target. Effectively applying the Least Privilege Principle thus means organizations must create a comprehensive understanding of their access requirements and constant monitoring and auditing of privileges granted to users. This process will allow the identification and resolution of potential security exposures within the existing infrastructure, thereby fortifying the defenses of the organization. In cloud platforms specifically, the implementation of the Least Privilege Principle involves technical as well as governance controls to allow the mitigation of data breach risks. Cloud providers such as Amazon Web Services (AWS) present unique challenges due to their large-scale infrastructure and shared responsibility models. With corporations perpetuating the transition to cloud platforms, developing sophisticated models of governance that feature legislative oversight of data protection is crucial. Synchronizing multiple levels of data protection technology with current legal requirements guarantees least privilege principles are effectively integrated into an organization's cloud governance framework. This multi-dimensional strategy not only enhances compliance but also enhances security architecture against emerging threats, hence fostering an effective identity management system critical to ensuring organizational integrity in light of evolving cybersecurity threats (Cankaya et al., 2024) (Figure 7.18).

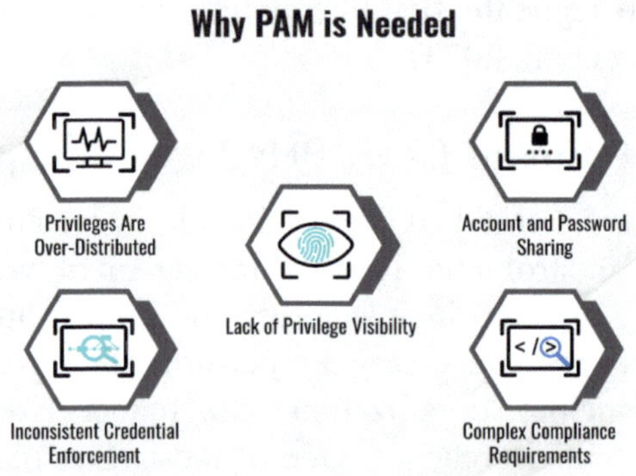

Figure 7.18. Establishing a robust Least Privilege framework also involves comprehensive Privileged Access Management (PAM) strategies that address the unique vulnerabilities associated with privileged accounts.

Source: https://marvel-b1-cdn.bc0a.com/f00000000310757/www.fortinet.com/content/dam/fortinet/images/cyberglossary/pam.jpg.

7.7. CONCLUSION

In short, the security scenario of cybersecurity is evolving at a rapid rate with identity management and access control forming the core components in cyber-attack defense. As companies continue to increasingly use cloud-based solutions, they will necessarily have to deal with problems like unauthorized access and data leakage that undermine their operational integrity. Robust access control, backed by good identity management, helps ensure that users only have access to systems up to their authorized level. This is particularly significant in situations where data sensitivity is high and where the consequence of a breach is catastrophic. The integration of advanced technologies like blockchain, as suggested by recent research, can provide an additional layer of robustness to the systems, allowing for an environment where effectiveness and security coexist (Madu, 2025). Apart from this, the advent of decentralized technology calls for a shift from traditional cybersecurity methods. The employment of centralized databases makes the systems vulnerable to a single point of failure, which exposes organizations to unimaginable vulnerabilities. New architectures using decentralized identity management systems not only address such limitations but also encourage user autonomy through self-ownership of their data. Using decentralized models, organizations are able to significantly improve their cybersecurity status. New patterns should ensure flexible systems combining both organizational policy and technology to mitigate the threat from new cyber threats (Barros et al., 2025). Finally, as we struggle with the complexity of identity management and access control, cooperative research and collaboration will be required to build end-to-end security solutions. Stakeholders from every sector will have to come together in order to establish optimal best practices and regulatory protocols that align with today's reality of digital ecosystems. It is this cooperative approach that will assist us in developing cybersecurity frameworks that are resilient, scalable, and adaptable to emerging threats. It is important that organizations remain proactive with their security practices, examining and revising their access control and identity management infrastructures on an ongoing basis to safeguard sensitive data and maintain user trust. All these efforts combined will bring about a safer digital space in which access control and identity management are a part of long-term cybersecurity resiliency.

7.7.1. Summary of Key Points

In cybersecurity, proper access control and identity management are the critical foundations that safeguard digital resources and infrastructure. Key among the points to be taken into consideration include the requirements of robust authentication methods to validate user identities and judicious use of access controls to mitigate data exposure. Ensuring that only authorized employees have access to confidential information makes organizations more secure against insider threats and external threats. Besides that, the use of advanced technologies such as multi-factor authentication and biometric authentication fortifies existing frameworks, creating a multi-layered security position that significantly reduce the likelihood of unauthorized access. The multi-faceted method prioritizes the use of security measures to adapt to evolving threats and maintaining user confidence in online services. As the cybersecurity environment evolves, understanding the ethical role of identity management and access control becomes increasingly important. The interplay between cybersecurity practice and inherent rights is complex, calling for a balance between privacy rights and security controls. Controls that enhance security, such as complete tracking of data and surveillance, become intrusive on individual freedoms and cause ethical dilemmas. To traverse this terrain, programs such as CANVAS encourage value-oriented cybersecurity that is in line with European standards but also emphasizes the importance of responsible measures that not just safeguard infrastructures but also respect individuals' rights. Therefore, organizations must adopt open policies so that stakeholders are informed of and enabled regarding the data protection systems put in place, encouraging an environment of accountability and trust. Lastly, education and awareness in society and organizations are an utmost priority in the case of effective access control and identity management. Stakeholders like citizens and employees must have a good understanding of the cybersecurity threats and the importance of adherence to procedures that have been established. Educational programs must focus on building a culture of cybersecurity awareness with proactive actions prioritized over reactive actions. This collaborative approach not only increases the security stance overall but also assists in empowering people to take control of their online security. These assets like training and workshops can serve to enhance best practice knowledge in cybersecurity, thereby upholding the collective responsibility for a secure digital world as has been brought out in recent cyber security debates and research papers, such as those in Anglano et al. (2018) and Bangerter et al. (2017).

7.7.2. Future Trends in Access Control and Identity Management

Identity and access management's future is increasingly defined by the employment of Zero Trust Architecture (ZTA), a paradigm shifts which is in opposition to the conventional perimeter security models. Never trust, always verify is the premise of ZTA and is combined with least-privilege access, where users are only granted the minimum privileges necessary for their role. This model helps organizations have more control over potential risks due to insider attacks and lateral movements within their networks. As increasing numbers of organizations move to cloud infrastructures and remote working, the basic ZTA principles such as real-time analysis, incorporation of identity management, and multi-factor authentication (MFA) become key aspects for robust security. In spite of this, implementation of ZTA poses issues including configuration difficulty and performance's influence, in which phased implementation and ongoing improvement are necessary to counter continuously evolving cybersecurity threats (Nasiruzzaman et al., 2025). Strong User Identity Management Systems (UIMS) are essential in assisting security systems in the case of continuously evolving cyber threats. UIMS defies the increasing trend of identity-based cybercrime by providing a comprehensive solution for managing identities in the digital space. With cybercriminals remaining focused on exploiting vulnerabilities in identity systems, it has become essential for organizations to embrace advanced identity solutions that are capable of distinguishing genuine users from criminals. Using multi-factor authentication practices, along with emerging biometric practices, UIMS fortifies the perimeter around sensitive information. Specifically, the employment of biometric identification systems marrying fingerprint biometrics with advanced algorithms for pattern-matching reflects a trend towards more secure authentication that is forward-looking. The trend is essential for organizations seeking to contain risks of data breaches and identity theft and underscores the importance of continuous innovation in identity management technology (Nonum et al., 2025). AI and ML will revolutionize identity management and access control by automating and enhancing security procedures. The technologies can analyze user behavior patterns, detect anomalies, and predict imminent security threats in real-time. Organizations are able to infuse AI-based solutions into access control systems to automate responding to security breaches and make adaptive policy decisions based on evolving threat landscapes. Furthermore, AI and ML can assist in amplifying the output of risk assessments and facilitate anticipatory countermeasures for evolving weaknesses. With maturation, the technologies are likely to be priceless resources for identity management initiatives, facilitating continuous monitoring and enforcement of security controls. The future of access control will definitely be based on the successful integration of AI and ML so that organizations can remain ahead of constantly changing, increasingly sophisticated cyber-attacks (Nasiruzzaman et al., 2025).

7.7.3. Final Thoughts on Cybersecurity Importance

The significance of cybersecurity cannot be overstated in today's digital age. As commerce is increasingly transacted on electronic platforms, it is essential that confidential data is protected. Proper cybersecurity measures, particularly access control and identity management, serve as the first line of defense against any form of unauthorized access. Having robust access controls ensures that only authorized personnel can use, access, or share confidential information. Without strong identity management controls, organizations open themselves up to more potential data breaches with consequential financial loss, legal penalty, and reputational damage. Organizations must recognize that cybersecurity is not only an IT issue, but it is an organizational imperative that requires top-down support to create a culture of security awareness throughout the enterprise. Moreover, the connection between open access and data stewardship reveals complex issues concerning the privacy and protection of data. When research institutions and universities collect tons of data, they must balance protection against transparency. Open access demands could be counterposed to the need for the protection of sensitive data given that institutions increasingly collect and maintain academic and grey data regarding activity on an individual level. The boundaries that separate research data from individual information are thinning out, making it challenging to assess associated risks and responsibilities. This is where critical discourse regarding cybersecurity practices comes in, considering that universities are grappling with the threat of data misuse by third parties and its implications for accountability and transparency in their operations. A cybersecurity-focused holistic approach to data governance is needed for the support of trust and upholding ethical principles in data management. Finally, investing in cybersecurity is inherently a forward-looking investment in an organization's future sustainability and resilience. By putting access control and identity management at the top of the agenda, organizations can shore up their defenses against the constantly shifting tide of cyber threats. Intellectual property protection and protection of personal data must be at the forefront of cybersecurity because the risk implication of a vulnerable defense is catastrophic. As literature has now emphasized, organizations must adopt multilayered cybersecurity that incorporates both technological as well as human aspects like training and sensitization campaigns. Cybersecurity holistically managed will allow organizations to handle the subtleties of the digital age with less risk and greater confidence of stakeholders. Briefly, the commitment to enhance access control and identity management is not just a component of existing security but also the vehicle for the long-term sustainability of organizational business (Anglano et al., 2018; Borgman et al., 2018).

REFERENCES

1. Akhtar, N., Ghamande, M. V., Khatak, S., et al. (2024). Cyber security strategies for protecting health management systems. https://core.ac.uk/download/640070097.pdf (accessed on 17th October 2025).
2. Alam, S., Woods, C. J., Williams, M., Moore, D., Prior, I., Williams, E., Yang-Turner, F., et al. (2024). Federated single sign-on and zero trust co-design for AI and HPC digital research infrastructures. *SC24-W: Workshops of the International Conference for High Performance Computing, Networking, Storage and Analysis*. https://www.semanticscholar.org/paper/4c327b782d3d19aeaa947a8885b7129d14d05e82 (accessed on 17th October 2025).
3. Alebiosu, J. A., Anadozie, C., Ayodele, G. T., Abdulrahman, I. A., & Isaiah, T. A. (2025). Zero trust architecture: Beyond perimeter security–Implementing continuous authentication and least privilege access. *International Journal of Advances in Engineering and Management*. https://www.semanticscholar.org/paper/7f9d001f5aed3eedd3141957ffbe1a9e192be5d8 (accessed on 17th October 2025).
4. Allioui, H., & Mourdi, Y. (2023). Exploring the full potentials of IoT for better financial growth and stability: A comprehensive survey. *Sensors, 23*, 8015–8015. https://doi.org/10.3390/s23198015 (accessed on 17th October 2025).
5. Alnoaimi, S., & Alomary, A. (2025). Zero trust security: A comprehensive comparative analysis of zero trust maturity models. *2024 International Conference on IT Innovation and Knowledge Discovery (ITIKD)*. https://www.semanticscholar.org/paper/beed6a9fc0c04ed194bc7b51ca16f089accaab2d (accessed on 17th October 2025).
6. Anglano, C., Aniello, L., Antinori, A., et al. (2018). The future of cybersecurity in Italy: Strategic focus area. https://core.ac.uk/download/188830442.pdf (accessed on 17th October 2025).
7. Ani, U., Anthi, E., Burnap, P., et al. (2020). Dynamic real-time risk analytics of uncontrollable states in complex Internet of Things systems, cyber risk at the edge. https://core.ac.uk/download/491119431.pdf (accessed on 17th October 2025).
8. Bangerter, E., Gordijn, B., Inversini, R., et al. (2017). *Canvas White Paper 3: Attitudes and Opinions Regarding Cybersecurity*. https://core.ac.uk/download/158610046.pdf (accessed on 17th October 2025).
9. Barros, P., Agupugo, C. P., Ejichukwu, E., Ogunmoye, K. A., & Hayden, M. D. (2025). Decentralized energy security: Cybersecurity challenges and

opportunities in distributed renewable energy. *World Journal of Advanced Research and Reviews*. https://www.semanticscholar.org/paper/792c7a5715eb1bc82f192f4d92fb64da4fe91a9a (accessed on 17th October 2025).

10. Bastião, L., Costa, C., & Lebre, R. (2020). A cloud-ready architecture for shared medical imaging repository. http://arxiv.org/abs/1904.05795 (accessed on 17th October 2025).
11. Borgman, C. L. (2018). Open data, grey data, and stewardship: Universities at the privacy frontier. http://arxiv.org/abs/1802.02953 (accessed on 17th October 2025).
12. Burstein, A. J., Mulligan, D. K., & Wang, L. (2011). Privacy in the smart grid: An information flow analysis. https://core.ac.uk/download/288432753.pdf (accessed on 17th October 2025).
13. Cankaya, E. C., Dye, O., & Heo, J. (2024). Reflection of federal data protection standards on cloud governance. http://arxiv.org/abs/2403.07907 (accessed on 17th October 2025).
14. Dodero Beardo, J. M., Duarte, M. P., Rodríguez García, M. M., et al. (2019). Privacy-preserving reengineering of model-view-controller application architectures using linked data. https://core.ac.uk/download/288159343.pdf (accessed on 17th October 2025).
15. Dwivedi, Y. K., Hughes, L., Wang, Y., Alalwan, A. A., Ahn, S. J., Balakrishnan, J., Barta, S., et al. (2022). Metaverse marketing: How the metaverse will shape the future of consumer research and practice. *Psychology and Marketing, 40*, 750–776. https://doi.org/10.1002/mar.21767 (accessed on 17th October 2025).
16. Dwivedi, Y. K., Kshetri, N., Hughes, L., Slade, E., Jeyaraj, A., Kar, A. K., Baabdullah, A. M., et al. (2023). Opinion paper: "So what if ChatGPT wrote it?" Multidisciplinary perspectives on opportunities, challenges and implications of generative conversational AI for research, practice and policy. *International Journal of Information Management, 71*, 102642–102642. https://doi.org/10.1016/j.ijinfomgt.2023.102642 (accessed on 17th October 2025).
17. Estrada Jiménez, J. A., Forné Muñoz, J., Rebollo-Monedero, D., et al. (2019). Anonymizing cybersecurity data in critical infrastructures: The CIPSEC approach. https://core.ac.uk/download/288625522.pdf (accessed on 17th October 2025).
18. Eswaran, U. (2024). *Fortifying Cybersecurity in an Interconnected Telemedicine Ecosystem*. Advances in Medical Technologies and Clinical Practice book series. https://doi.org/10.4018/979-8-3693-2141-6.ch002 (accessed on 17th October 2025).

19. Fathaigh, R. Ó., van Eijk, N., & van Hoboken, J. (2018). Mobile privacy and business-to-platform dependencies: An analysis of SEC disclosures. https://core.ac.uk/download/220158973.pdf (accessed on 17th October 2025).

20. Golightly, L., Modesti, P., Garcia, R., & Chang, V. (2023). Securing distributed systems: A survey on access control techniques for cloud, blockchain, IoT and SDN. *Cyber Security and Applications, 1*, 100015–100015. https://doi.org/10.1016/j.csa.2023.100015 (accessed on 17th October 2025).

21. Hariharan, R. (2025). AI-driven identity and access management in enterprise systems. *International Journal of IoT*. https://www.semanticscholar.org/paper/8fe91a7ef6cc2a226e5bf96f68d537798a467f1b (accessed on 17th October 2025).

22. Khetani, S. (2025). Data integrity and security: Blockchain vs. traditional databases. https://core.ac.uk/download/657107281.pdf (accessed on 17th October 2025).

23. Koohang, A., Nord, J. H., Ooi, K. B., Tan, G. W. H., Al-Emran, M., Aw, E. C. X., Baabdullah, A. M., et al. (2023). Shaping the metaverse into reality: A holistic multidisciplinary understanding of opportunities, challenges, and avenues for future investigation. *Journal of Computer Information Systems, 63*, 735–765. https://doi.org/10.1080/08874417.2023.2165197 (accessed on 17th October 2025).

24. Madu, V. K. (2025). Blockchain-based cybersecurity models for cloud computing. *Engineering and Technology Journal*. https://www.semanticscholar.org/paper/6e70da284dbb035536962264178970c4f2545852 (accessed on 17th October 2025).

25. Marcus, D. J. (2018). The data breach dilemma: Proactive solutions for protecting consumers' personal information. https://core.ac.uk/download/213020823.pdf (accessed on 17th October 2025).

26. Mollakuqe, E., & Dimitrova, V. (2024). Comparative analysis of identity management, access control, and authorization practices in public and private universities. *Open Research Europe, 4*. https://www.semanticscholar.org/paper/2b0fab650089322c6740c01ad864ffcb6e53ded0 (accessed on 17th October 2025).

27. Moura, J., & Serrao, C. (2015). Security and privacy issues of big data. https://core.ac.uk/download/567653903.pdf (accessed on 17th October 2025).

28. Nasiruzzaman, M., Ali, M., Salam, I., & Miraz, M. H. (2025). The evolution of zero trust architecture (ZTA) from concept to

implementation. *2025 29th International Conference on Information Technology (IT)*. https://www.semanticscholar.org/paper/fe71bc9bfee68cd6c3fe02e5c146b5f480d38c64 (accessed on 17th October 2025).

29. Nonum, E. O., & Ojo, O. D. (2025). Review of secure user identity management systems (UIMS) for preventing and controlling cybercrime. *International Journal of Research and Innovation in Applied Science*. https://www.semanticscholar.org/paper/80ae20071767e30ba281241d00e1701810cdd571 (accessed on 17th October 2025).
30. Ogunmolu, A. M. (2025). Federated detection systems for insider threats in energy facilities using biomechanical access control and AI-based cybersecurity. *Journal of Engineering Research and Reports*. https://www.semanticscholar.org/paper/f335a55e4ebc063e9880aaaad2b98326fd86b6d4 (accessed on 17th October 2025).
31. Olabanji, S., Olaniyi, O. O., Adigwe, C. S., Okunleye, O. J., & Oladoyinbo, T. O. (2024). AI for identity and access management (IAM) in the cloud: Exploring the potential of artificial intelligence to improve user authentication, authorization, and access control within cloud-based systems. *Asian Journal of Research in Computer Science*. https://www.semanticscholar.org/paper/9cddb76c900c4e73de7ae9856ddd8f912d29ed1e (accessed on 17th October 2025).
32. Pourrahmani, H., Yavarinasab, A., Hosseini Monazzah, A. M., & Van Herle, J. (2023). A review of the security vulnerabilities and countermeasures in the Internet of Things solutions: A bright future for the blockchain. *Internet of Things, 23*, 100888–100888. https://doi.org/10.1016/j.iot.2023.100888 (accessed on 17th October 2025).
33. Subramaniyan, S., & Prabhu, S. (2023). The impact of adopting blockchain-based identity access management: Current applications and potential directions. https://doi.org/10.1109/icaaic56838.2023.10140585 (accessed on 17th October 2025).
34. Toropov, R. (2025). Securing privileged access: Best practices for PAM system implementation. https://core.ac.uk/download/638726231.pdf (accessed on 17th October 2025).
35. Vartiainen, R. (2025). Multi-factor authentication under NIS2: Requirements and implementation for regulated entities. https://core.ac.uk/download/657107270.pdf (accessed on 17th October 2025).

CHAPTER 8

INTRUSION DETECTION AND ANOMALY DETECTION

Contents

INTRODUCTION

The rapid development of technology has led to the explosive growth of the Internet of Things (IoT), which has become a part of daily life. The connectivity makes it possible for the devices to share information and communicate with each other with ease, enhancing innovation in fields such as healthcare, transport, and urban infrastructure. However, as the number of devices increases, so do the threats accompany these technologies. The anomaly and intrusion detection systems are now essential components for defending IoT systems, a reaction to growing data security and privacy concerns. It is not enough to detect unauthorized access but also detect patterns of anomalies that may indicate potential threats, which calls for a robust and dynamic network security strategy. An understanding of the intricacies that come with intrusion detection and anomaly detection in the IoT setting requires a balance examination of old and new. Traditional security solutions may not be able to deal with the heterogenous set of devices and the customized setting of the IoT world. Therefore, advanced techniques such as machine learning are being increasingly incorporated into detection systems. Machine learning technologies offer the ability to handle massive data in real time so that potential danger can be discovered speedily. The application of methodologies like Federated Learning (FL) is an excellent example of the shift to decentralized means, where training occurs on-device without needing extensive data sharing. This reduces the vulnerabilities that are linked to central data gathering, thus improving the security position of IoT networks, particularly where data privacy is essential (Nguyen et al., 2021). The ongoing evolution of IoT brings new challenges in implementing effective intrusion and anomaly detection systems. It is the duty of engineers and researchers to keep up with evolving security paradigms in order to counter emergent threats related to the unique factors of IoT, i.e., diversity of devices and varying operating environments. In addition, the convergence of technologies like artificial intelligence needs to go hand-in-hand with ethical considerations in order to ensure privacy as a principle for IoT applications. As these programs progress, becoming acquainted with the principals involved and state-of-the-art methodologies of intrusion and anomaly detection will be vital. To counter effectively against potential cyber-attacks, an interdisciplinary analysis of the security environment with cross-fertilization ideas from various disciplines will be required in fostering resilience in IoT environments and preserving integrity of the vast network of devices (Wang et al., 2022).

Overview of Intrusion Detection and Anomaly Detection

Intrusion detection and anomaly detection are critical building blocks in the Internet of Things (IoT) security infrastructure. While IoT device growth accelerates, from household appliances to industrial sensors, the threat of unauthorized intrusion and data theft has grown exponentially. Intrusion detection systems (IDS) are used to monitor network and system activity for malicious activity or policy violations, hence serving as a filter against intruders. Anomaly detection, on the other hand, is interested in identifying patterns that diverge from a learned baseline, which signals the possibility of security breaches. Through the detection of abnormal behavioral patterns in large datasets, the detection systems fortify the resilience of IoT networks. With an evolution in technology, greater reliance on artificial intelligence and machine learning presents new avenues for improving such detection methods so that more robust responses are able to be issued against sophisticated attacks. Applying machine learning techniques in anomaly detection and intrusion detection has transformed the practice of cybersecurity for IoT environments. Traditional approaches were not successful in managing the dynamic behavior of network traffic and the heterogeneous set of devices. Machine learning techniques, however, can handle vast amounts of data generated by wireless sensor networks (WSNs) and IoT devices to identify anomalies effectively. These techniques are particularly useful since WSN data has been historically noisy and unreliable and hence difficult for direct anomaly detection methods (Haque et al., 2023). With the use of various machine learning techniques, including supervised, unsupervised, and semi-supervised learning, researchers have significantly improved anomaly detection. This improvement not only assists in detecting violations but also enhances the overall reliability of the system, ushering in more secure IoT architectures that can withstand ever-changing cyber-attacks. In addition, federated learning presents an epochal approach to privacy-preserving IoT network anomaly detection.

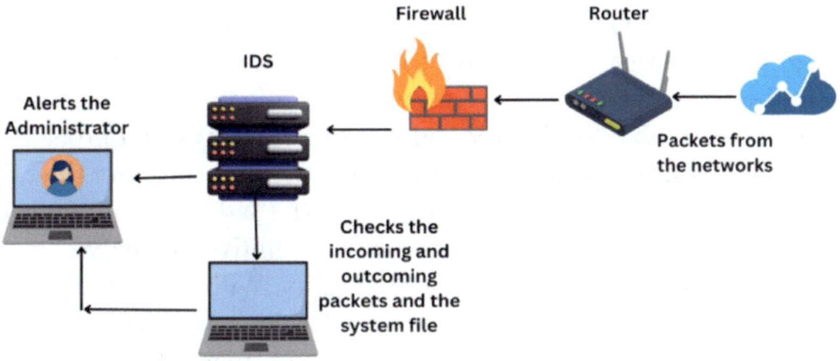

Figure 8.1. Intrusion detection systems (IDS) are designed to monitor network and system activities for malicious activities or policy violations, thereby serving as a barrier against intruders.

Source: https://pub.mdpi-res.com/computers/computers-14-00087/article_deploy/html/images/computers-14-00087-g001.png?1741005090.

Traditional approaches have relied on centralized data aggregation, which is usually responsible for causing privacy and scalability challenges in IoT large-scale systems. Federated learning makes decentralized data training possible, facilitating collaborative model development at the cost of personal privacy (Nguyen et al., 2021). This approach is particularly effective in anomaly detection since it uses the data of several IoT devices without compromising data privacy. The implications are enormous since it enhances the real-time identification of anomalies in a wide range of devices, thus facilitating timely action and detection against the threat. By implementing federated learning in the case of intrusion and anomaly detection, IoT networks can get an efficient security system that balances the needs of data analysis against decentralization and privacy imperatives (Figure 8.1).

8.1. UNDERSTANDING INTRUSION DETECTION SYSTEMS (IDS)

Increasing ubiquity of Internet of Things (IoT) devices in industries has put a premium on reliable Intrusion Detection Systems (IDS) that assist their defense against cyber-attacks. Traditional IDS architectures have been predicated on signature-based methods of detection, which are customized to identify well-known threats but often prove inadequate in the face of fresh avenues for attacks. The emergence of sophisticated cyber threats in IoT networks calls for a dynamic paradigm, and this has seen the application of hybrid IDS that combine rule-based detection and machine learning. These networks have the potential to identify anomalies that suggest potential intrusions, thereby enhancing the security position of IoT environments. Through this twin approach, the systems are not only capable of mitigating the risk of familiar threats but are also able to identify and react to new ones in a proactive way, making them integral components of modern network security routines that are tailored to the unique realities thrown up by IoT (Sadikin et al., 2023). With the hybridization of detection methods comes cognitive anomaly detection as a crucial element in wireless IoT network security. With an increasing number of potential anomalies, traditional signature detection becomes progressively inefficient, forcing the adoption of anomaly-aware methodologies. Cognitive approaches leverage knowledge-based anomaly-awareness gained through data-driven observations to detect abnormal behavior in a network based on established behavioral patterns. By focusing on radio frequency (RF) spectrum activity, scientists were able to develop methods that scan for anomalies like jamming or unauthorized attempt access. These systems monitor the network in real time, having knowledge about patterns that are outside of the norm. The expected behavioral patterns can then trigger alerts for any significant discrepancies, enabling swift action against likely security attacks and industrial IoT and mission-critical communication services resilience (Jauhar et al., 2018). Moreover, the incorporation of machine learning and deep learning methods into IDS is a paradigm shift in anomaly detection on IoT networks. The ability of such advanced algorithms extends well beyond mere pattern recognition; they are capable of adapting to and changing in response to adapting threat patterns. To give an example, using spectral data within RF signals, anomaly detection software can identify typical patterns of interference or breakdown in transmission, illustrating their effectiveness in real-world use. This adaptability not only increases the detection ratio but has the capacity to reduce false alarms significantly, a characteristic vulnerability of traditional IDS architectures. Consequently, their application within the framework of limited IoT architectures represents challenges rather than opportunities for safeguarding sensitive data and maintaining the integrity of mission-critical systems across domains (Jauhar et al., 2018) (Figure 8.2).

Figure 8.2. Cognitive approaches leverage data-driven insights to discern abnormal activity within a network based on learned behavior profiles.

Source: https://www.e-spincorp.com/wp-content/uploads/2021/01/new-jobs-internet-hp-orig-scaled.jpg.

8.1.1. Types of Intrusion Detection Systems

Intrusion Detection Systems (IDS) can be divided into various categories based on their modes of operation, primarily signature-based, anomaly-based, and hybrid systems. Signature-based IDSs work through the detection of recognized patterns of attack like a virus scanner identifies some pre-defined signatures of malicious activity. Such a system is very precise with minimal false positives, and therefore, for known threats, it is the one to use. However, it is less effective against new or unknown attacks, which typically mutate rapidly within IoT networks. Pre-defined signature reliance means that the system has to update often in order to remain efficient, limiting its adaptability in dynamic situations. This reliance also introduces a significant vulnerability, as increased complexity and volume of IoT traffic can outweigh the ability to maintain sufficient signatures, requiring other detection methods to keep up with evolving threats. Anomaly-based Intrusion Detection Systems, however, employ machine learning and statistical approaches to establish a baseline for normal network activity and then identify departures from the standard. These systems offer a promising solution for identifying new, previously unseen attacks, which is particularly crucial in the rapidly changing IoT world. By studying patterns and behaviors, anomaly-based systems can detect malicious activity that diverges from established norms, identifying possible threats prior to their capacity to harm.

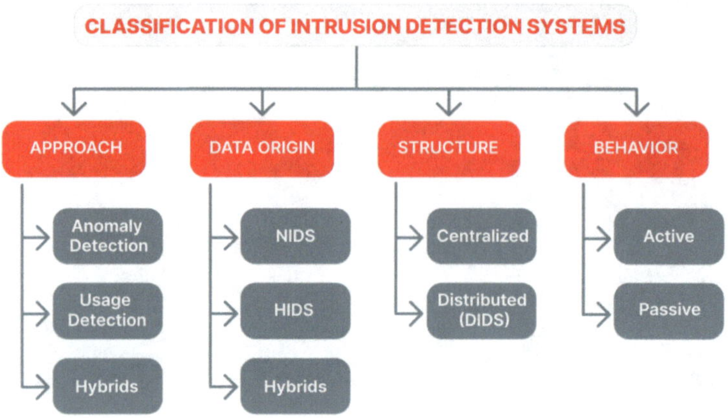

Figure 8.3. Types of intrusion detection systems.

Source: https://storage.googleapis.com/breathecode-asset-images/a4e9a5272c6f96dbad2bd8619c1f896cb0d6170593739b35907dbbe5a5444254.png?raw=true.

But beware, these systems are not problem-free; they generate more false positives since regular activities might be mistakenly perceived as anomalies. Thus, there is a need to refine the detection algorithms, particularly in cases where regular traffic can change significantly (Chen et al., 2022). This compromise between sensitivity and specificity presents ongoing research and application challenges within the development of effective anomaly detection techniques. Hybrid Intrusion Detection Systems combine signature-based and anomaly-based methods to benefit from each technique while eschewing each method's weaknesses. With both of these systems integrated, a hybrid IDS can provide robust defenses against known attacks through signature detection while simultaneously maintaining the capability of spotting fresh, previously unknown attacks through anomaly detection techniques. Such multi-layered strategies are particularly beneficial in the context of the IoT, where diverse threat profiles necessitate adaptive security mechanisms. Emerging advancements have led to new hybrid models that incorporate machine learning to enrich detection features and improve the overall performance of the system. A hybrid model, for example, can dynamically shift the direction of its detection in response to the network traffic condition, thereby optimizing the usage of resources and improving the detection accuracy of threats (Sadikin et al., 2023). In a world where IoT infrastructures must face increasingly sophisticated cyber-attacks, hybrid IDS is a giant leap towards creating a strong security system (Figure 8.3).

8.1.2. Key components of IDS Architecture

Intrusion Detection System (IDS) architecture is a sophisticated system required for security provision in IoT environments. Basically, the IDS is simply comprised of a series of necessary components, including data collection, data analysis, and notification. The data collection module is crucial as it aggregates network traffic and logs from various IoT devices to identify potential threats. This first step is the cornerstone of the subsequent analysis phase, in which advanced algorithms screen the gathered data for anomalies or threats. The effectiveness of the two stages should be of highest priority, as they are the cornerstone of the entire security stance of the system and its operational reliability, particularly within the high-speed context of IoT networks (Alatawi et al., 2022). IDS architecture's second key characteristic is its detection methodology categorization. Anomaly-based is more desired in IoT platforms since it can identify unknown attacks by establishing a baseline of typical behavior. The approach utilizes machine learning algorithms such as ensemble learning to enhance the detection capacity. By using models such as bagging, LPBoost, and RUSBoost, the IDS will be able to classify data flows well and minimize false positives. Apart from that, by applying feature engineering algorithms, e.g., principal component analysis, the system can reduce data dimensionality, becoming more effective. As there are increasingly developing IoT ecosystems, the robustness of such detection methods to learn new threats evolving over time is imperative to maintaining healthy security mechanisms (Alatawi et al., 2022). Finally, the IDS architecture also emphasizes the importance of system deployment and scalability. As IoT devices are heterogeneous in nature, IDS solutions should be universal in applicability across various environments, from edge computing nodes to centralized deployments. Interoperability with fog computing is particularly of interest as it offloads security processing closer to the data's source, minimizing latency and enhancing real-time threat identification. This distributed design enables enhanced efficiency and resilience as security controls are taken to where data is being generated. Furthermore, the IDS model's scalability guarantees that it can handle more and more devices in a growing ecosystem, something required to maintain data integrity, confidentiality, and availability as IoT continues to expand perpetually (Alatawi et al., 2022).

8.1.3. Role of IDS in IoT Security

In the rapidly evolving environment of the Internet of Things (IoT), the role of Intrusion Detection Systems (IDS) has become crucial to ensuring sound security. As IoT devices proliferate, so do their weaknesses and vulnerabilities for attack. Most legacy security controls do not work due to the nature of these networked devices' threats, which are usually installed in dynamic environments with varied security maturity. A good IDS, in addition to analyzing network traffic, analyzes device behavior to detect anomalous patterns that foretell security infractions. With the use of advanced techniques such as machine learning and deep learning, contemporary IDS solutions offer proactive security protection that can adapt to new threats and provide enhanced resilience in IoT environments against hostile attacks. Integration of advanced technologies into the area of IDS significantly enhances its contribution towards IoT security. For instance, petascale processing not only supports massive data analysis but also complex prediction models that can identify latent vulnerabilities even before they are discovered (Latifi et al., 2018). This new paradigm shifts the security model from reactive to proactive by concentrating on real-time monitoring and behavior analysis as opposed to traditional signature-based methods. Furthermore, with more IoT devices generating tons of data, the need for an IDS to properly classify and analyze this data becomes all the more important. Most importantly, IDS must identify benign versus malicious activity, a question of prime importance when it comes to ensuring the integrity of IoT networks. Furthermore, the increasing adoption of fog computing together with IoT solutions brings new prospects for enhancing security via the intelligent positioning of IDS features. Fog computing reduces latency and bandwidth consumption by handling data closer to where they originated, thereby maximizing the performance of threat detection (Butun et al., 2018). The architecture not only enhances data management but also provides real-time anomaly detection across different IoT settings. In that regard, the convergence of fog computing and IDS capabilities has promise to counter security attacks in progressively more advanced IoT ecosystems. Considered collectively, these technologies point to the key role that IDS will play as an IoT ecosystem protector, ultimately instilling greater confidence and trust in the technology that underlies today's networked systems (Figure 8.4).

Figure 8.4. As IoT devices proliferate, so too do the vulnerabilities and potential attack vectors associated with them.

Source: https://media.licdn.com/dms/image/v2/D5612AQGp8dG9v2h6iA/article-cover_image-shrink_720_1280/B56Zg6rUAfHkAI-/0/1753331093089?e=2147483647&v=beta&t=yzdKp99XFicUE6NuHt02kVSYlnJNlKiDFWYloNgpHaI.

8.2. ANOMALY DETECTION TECHNIQUES

The diversified multi-environment of Internet of Things (IoT) devices presents challenging situations for cybersecurity, especially in terms of energy efficiency and effective anomaly detection. Traditional Intrusion Detection Systems (IDS) are inclined to need constant monitoring, which means enormous power consumption. In this situation, the strong need for methods that will guarantee robust security at the expense of saving energy is compelling. Techniques such as the Ensemble Techniques with Sleep Mode Management (ELSM) technique have been suggested to address these issues. ELSM suggests a sophisticated mechanism for waking up the IDS only when there is a probability of anomaly detection, thus conserving energy in normal operating conditions. By enhanced machine learning capability with this paradigm-breaking energy management, the ELSM approach offers overall security without compromising its efficiency in operation, contributing significantly to the long-term sustainability of IoT networks (Al-Naimat et al., 2024). Anomaly detection approaches underlie IDS operation by distinguishing normal and malicious behavior based on systematic analysis of patterns of data. Some of the most significant advances in this field is the development of hybrid feature selection techniques, which enhance classification accuracy by enhancing the input data to learning algorithms. The application of particle swarm optimization, ant colony algorithms, and genetic algorithms has reduced the size of training sets. Optimized features enhance the performance of classifiers at the detection stage. Together with ensemble learning methods, such as those based on rotation forests and bagging, the methods have worked exceptionally well in several datasets, e.g., NSL-KDD and UNSW-NB15. Apart from improving the sensitivity and accuracy of the models, this also adapts to dynamic security attacks, hence the overall resilience of the IoT ecosystem (Comuzzi et al., 2019). Furthermore, the usage of statistical significance tests in the results of anomaly detection adds robustness to IDS performance assessment. While much work simply takes into account accuracy metrics, utilizing statistical testing offers a more detailed perspective of model effectiveness. Utilizing two-stage statistical significance testing, for instance, alongside the classification outcomes is a richer form of validation of the hybrid models in question. This technique helps identify that the improved results are not random but indicate actual improvements in intrusion detection in advanced datasets. By developing a statistical credibility benchmark in IDS research, techniques such as these give weight to findings in the space of anomaly detection, which justifies adopting robust technical frameworks combined with solid statistical analysis in enhancing IoT security solutioning (Comuzzi et al., 2019).

8.2.1. Statistical Methods for Anomaly Detection

One of the significant characteristics of intrusion detection systems (IDS) within the Internet of Things (IoT) is the use of statistical methods for anomaly detection. These traditional approaches are paramount in identifying deviations in normal behavior, particularly in scenarios involving resource constraints and evolving environments. Statistical methods draw on statistical techniques, such as probability distributions and hypothesis tests, to quantify and report anomalies in data streams generated by IoT devices. Statistical methods are distinct from signature-based methods that require extensive databases of known threats. Statistical methods can react to new, unknown attack vectors based on statistical techniques, thereby enhancing the security posture of IoT networks. The ability to identify abnormal patterns not only offers security to sensitive data but also ensures that it is always secure and resistant to potential intrusions for essential IoT systems. Statistically, models may appear in various forms, including regression analysis, clustering, and multivariate analysis. The models help identify normal states of functioning and hence contribute to the identification of outliers that could indicate malicious operations. For instance, with clustering techniques, typical behavior data points can be grouped in a way that detecting such anomalies outside of these clusters will be simpler. More sophisticated methods such as hybrid statistical techniques, where more than one statistical technique is used to improve accuracy, demonstrate encouraging results for specific IDS implementations. From intrusion detection research, two-tier classification with incorporation of statistical significance testing has been proven to perform better than other methods with datasets like NSL-KDD and UNSW-NB15 and achieved high detection and accuracy rates (Comuzzi et al., 2019).

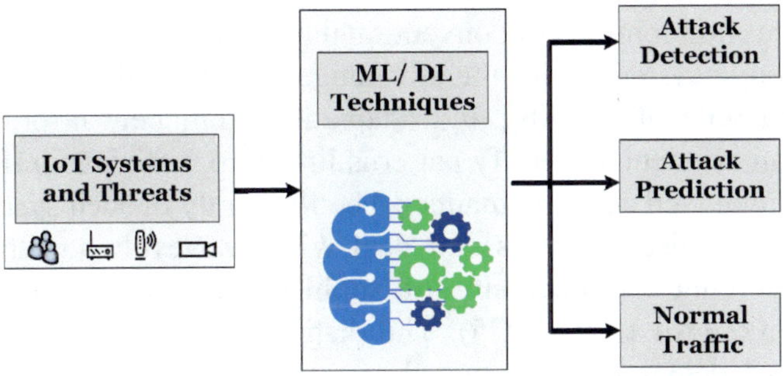

Figure 8.5. A significant aspect of intrusion detection systems (IDS) within the realm of the Internet of Things (IoT) involves the implementation of statistical methods for anomaly detection.

Source: https://www.mdpi.com/electronics/electronics-09-01177/article_deploy/html/images/electronics-09-01177-g008.png.

The evidence proves the effectiveness of using statistical techniques to maximize anomaly detection reliability in IoT. Also, as IoT devices typically have poor processing power and memory resources, application of statistical anomaly detection methods is even more applicable. The challenge lies in designing algorithms that are lightweight yet powerful enough to provide real-time intrusion detection without an excessive performance overhead. It is especially significant because the majority of IoT devices have battery power and cannot provide resource-intensive cryptographic algorithms (Ahmadinia et al., 2016). Scholars have tried various options, including combining machine learning and statistical approaches, to enhance the detection sensitivity of IDS without compromising on efficiency. With the application of random neural networks (RNNs), for instance, it is possible to achieve efficient intrusion detection, as in a study that achieved an accuracy of 97.23% in intrusion detection for identifying aberrant patterns in IoT systems. These developments underscore how statistical techniques are capable of advancing and adapting to guarantee that intrusion detection mechanisms are able to safeguard IoT settings against a wide variety of threats (Figure 8.5).

8.2.2. Machine Learning Approaches

The use of machine learning (ML) methods in intrusion detection systems (IDS) is transforming the cybersecurity landscape, particularly within the realm of Internet of Things (IoT). Traditional security measures cannot address the unique issues within IoT environments that are characterized by their incredibly high numbers of connected devices and heterogeneous structures. Recent studies emphasize the shortcomings of conventional methods to spark a paradigm shift towards adaptive systems with the advantage of ML methods. By employing algorithms capable of learning and adaptation from new information, ML-based IDS can efficiently identify patterns linked to malicious traffic to detect threats in a timely and accurate manner. The flexibility of such systems enables them to counter false positives and deal with ever-evolving attack vectors, thereby reinforcing the necessity of sophisticated cybersecurity solutions in IoT networks (Ali et al., 2025). The distinctive nature and vulnerabilities of IoT devices demand a customized approach towards intrusion detection. ML techniques have been identified to perform particularly well in dealing with the complexities in IoT systems, including their limited resources and heterogeneity. Current literature has focused on some of the numerous ML methods and demonstrated how they can be applied to IoT setups to make them more robust against cyber-attacks. Techniques such as supervised learning, unsupervised learning, and anomaly detection techniques play a crucial role in separating normal and abnormal traffic in a network. Moreover, the real-time processing quality of ML models allows for quick intervention based on identified anomalies, hence minimizing the resulting damage from intrusions. The more complex and voluminous IoT data are, the more ML systems offer a reasonable solution for giving security and stability in such connected ecosystems (Sharma et al., 2025). In spite of the promising innovation of ML methods in intrusion detection, a number of challenges remain inhibiting their general use across IoT security. Such challenges encompass heterogeneity of devices, constrained processing resources, and changing network structures that make it difficult to apply strong ML algorithms. Additionally, the literature calls for continued studies into improving the scalability and effectiveness of ML models specifically designed for use in IoT applications. Future work must overcome these shortcomings and examine emerging solutions such as transfer learning and federated learning, which can potentially achieve revolutionary leaps in performance and plasticity under varying conditions. Evolution of a better comprehension of how to most effectively include ML approaches within existing security frameworks will be key to further evolving the overall security status of IoT environments, eventually toward an increasingly robust and secure digital environment (Ali et al., 2025) (Figure 8.6).

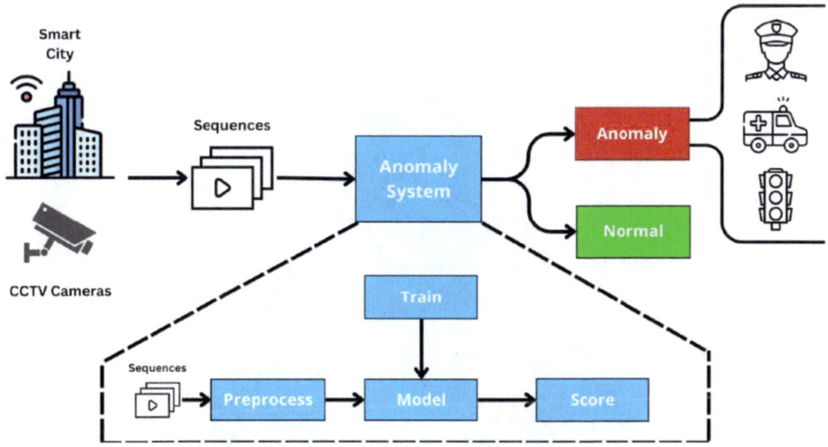

Figure 8.6. Techniques such as supervised learning, unsupervised learning, and anomaly detection algorithms play a critical role in classifying normal versus abnormal behavior in network traffic.

Source: https://www.mdpi.com/applsci/applsci-15-05520/article_deploy/html/images/applsci-15-05520-g001.png.

8.2.3. Challenges in Implementing Anomaly Detection

Their deployment into Internet of Things (IoT) environments also creates multilateral issues that complicate their effectiveness and usage. One significant hindrance is the heterogeneity of IoT devices, with notable differences in hardware resources, communication protocols, and operating environments. Anomaly detection algorithm tailored for a particular device may lack scalability across other diverse devices, thus leading to inefficiencies and an elevated level of false positives. In addition, the huge data volume produced by IoT devices makes it more challenging to detect anomalies because traditional algorithms can barely cope with processing and analyzing the surge in an effective way. Thus, developing personalized solutions that can handle the unique features of each device and network topology becomes essential in making the anomaly detection system more trustworthy (Sharma et al., 2025). The second imperative challenge is the inherent resource constraint of most IoT devices, particularly those intended for low-power applications. Most techniques used for anomaly detection need significant computation and memory, which are not achievable through the limited resources of IoT devices. This limits the development of lean models to perform efficient anomaly detection without compromising device performance.

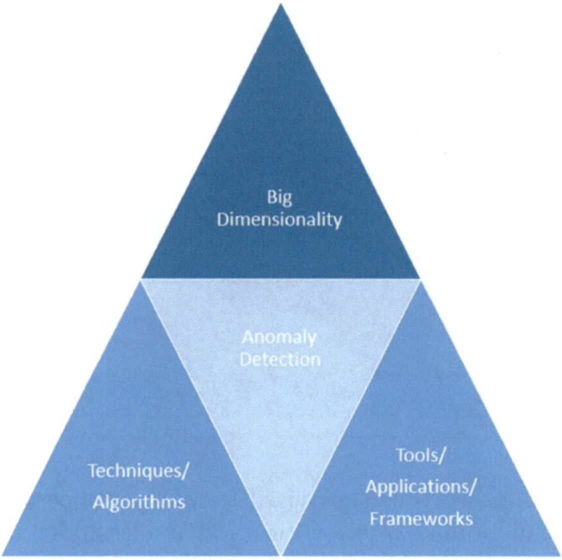

Figure 8.7. Adapting anomaly detection algorithms to rapidly accommodate these changes is essential for maintaining robust security measures.

Source: https://media.springernature.com/lw685/springer-static/image/art%3A10.1186%2Fs40537-020-00320-x/MediaObjects/40537_2020_320_Fig2_HTML.png.

Research initiatives, such as investigations of the Isolation Forest (IForest) algorithm, have begun intervening in this challenge with promising results in distinguishing normal and threatening action with the aim of maximizing resource usage (Gomez et al., 2024). But achieving equilibrium between the detectability complexity of approaches and the performance of IoT devices when operating is a difficult task that needs to be sustained to explore further and innovate. In addition, the dynamic character of IoT networks raises continuous challenges for the installation of anomaly detection systems. The frequent installation and removal of devices, varying network topologies, and changing attack vectors make static detection models obsolete. Anomaly detection algorithms need to be adapted quickly to respond to these fluctuations for sustaining effective security measures. Additionally, dealing with zero-day attacks—where the nature of the threat is unknown—provides additional hurdles, as conventional static models fail to identify such threats. In designing anomaly detection systems, it is necessary that there are mechanisms of adaptive learning integrated that can learn to adapt with the IoT device landscape and the approach of adversaries (Sharma et al., 2025). This flexibility will not only make these systems more effective in general but will also bring us closer to a safer IoT environment (Figure 8.7).

8.3. COMPARISON OF INTRUSION DETECTION AND ANOMALY DETECTION

The difference between Intrusion Detection Systems (IDS) and Anomaly Detection Mechanisms (ADM) is a major aspect of protecting Internet of Things (IoT) environments. An IDS largely relies on pre-defined signatures of known threats, and it can respond to known attack patterns in a timely manner. This signature approach has an advantage in the predictable behavior of traffic. But because IoT ecosystems constantly evolve, fixed signatures may be ineffective against sophisticated or novel attacks. ADMs, however, analyze network behavior to build a baseline of normal activity, so deviations that might represent a potential threat are detected. This adaptability makes ADMs particularly valuable in dynamic ecosystems such as IoT, where variability in such ecosystems complicates threat detection. Therefore, the integration of both systems offers an even tighter security posture, taking advantage of the strengths in each technique while compensating for their weaknesses. While both Intrusion Detection Systems and Anomaly Detection Mechanisms play a critical role in IoT security, both have inherent challenges on both the performance and accuracy sides. IDS is prone to having too many false positives due to the strictness of its signatures, hence causing alert fatigue among security personnel. Conversely, while ADMs are favorable in the sense that they can identify new threats through abnormal behavior detection, they are not exception to false positives and might misinterpret normal activity as malicious. The challenge here is the training phases of ADMs, which consume a large amount of data in order to learn baseline behaviors successfully. In IoT application, where resource deficiency and uncertainty of device behavior are norms, it is critical to reach the best balance between sensitivity and specificity for anomaly detection. Hence, joining both systems as a hybrid might enhance the detecting function while reducing detriments inherent in single systems. New approaches are consistently addressing the limitations of traditional IDS and ADMs in IoT security. With the use of advanced artificial intelligence and machine learning techniques, detection rates and response times have been proved to be improved. For instance, by combining the strengths of both worlds, researchers have proposed anomaly detection systems based on deep learning that can make proactive predictions about security violations, as demonstrated by recent work (Latifi et al., 2018). These systems learn from network traffic on a continuous basis, adapting to evolving threat vectors and reducing the likelihood of attacks to a great extent. Besides, studies like the one in the study on passive network sniffing techniques present concrete solutions for IoT environment monitoring, with detection ratios nearing 99 percent for specific attack vectors (Adebisi et al., 2020). By the implementation of such new solutions, IoT security can be maximized to ensure that the systems are maintained in a position of strength against the ever-changing threats.

8.3.1. Fundamental Differences Between the Two Approaches

The distinction between anomaly detection and intrusion detection in the Internet of Things (IoT) framework is the center to understand their sole purpose and utilization. Intrusion detection systems (IDS) are primarily preoccupied with detecting known attacks and prevention by utilizing pre-programmed rules that define network behavior as benign or malicious. IDS works better under circumstances where attacks are like attacks that have been documented in their databases. Conversely, anomaly detection systems adopt a more inquisitive approach that identifies deviation from well-known patterns of normal behavior without the prior identification of known threats. This is a reflection of methodological core differences insofar as IDS make use of signature-based approaches, whereas anomaly detection makes use of statistical analysis and machine learning to determine anomalous patterns (Comuzzi et al., 2019). The operational complexities of intrusion detection and anomaly detection also support their contrasting approaches. Intrusion detection is typically simpler to deploy, with reference to past attack rule sets, and is deployable in relatively short periods of time in highly characterized environments. This simplicity causes issues, though, like in dynamic IoT spaces where new attacks are unlikely to fall within known signatures. Anomaly detections adaptive learning mechanisms use, in contrast, provides it additional freedom to respond to new attacks. By means of machine learning algorithms, as expounded in a comprehensive review of their application in wireless networks, anomaly detection systems are able to learn dynamically the evolving threat landscape (Chen et al., 2019). This is crucial in IoT, where things constantly join and leave, leading to an ever-changing landscape. While intrusion detection and anomaly detection systems are different in nature, they are equally critical to safeguard IoT environments, with different functions to fulfill. Intrusion detection systems offer an effective line of defense against known attacks, thereby establishing a security baseline, while anomaly detection systems offer a layer of defense against unknown vulnerabilities. Synergism between these types of systems offers an improved overall security system by complementing the deficiencies of one another; e.g., timely identification of emerging threats through anomaly detection can feed and reinforce the intrusion detection rule sets. Thus, a successful security strategy for IoT needs to keep in mind the combination of both methods, amplifying their respective virtues while taking care of the intricate issues arising from the changing threat landscape (Figure 8.8).

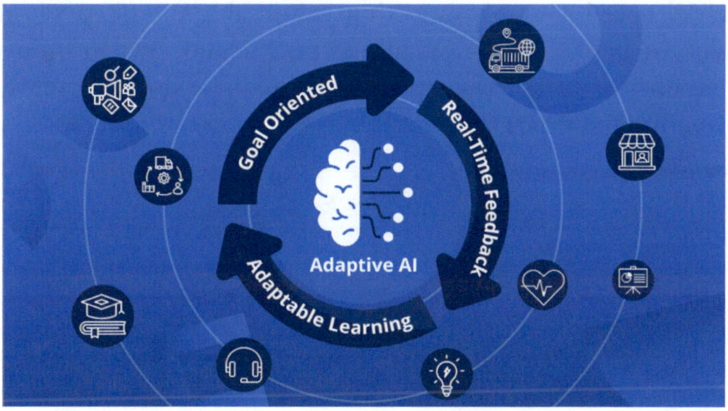

Figure 8.8. By employing machine learning algorithms, as discussed in a comprehensive review of their applications in wireless networks, anomaly detection systems can dynamically adjust to evolving threat landscapes.

Source: https://d3lkc3n5th01x7.cloudfront.net/wp-content/uploads/2023/02/13215346/HOW-TO-IMPLEMENT-ADAPTIVE-AI-IN-YOUR-BUSINESS-Banner-1.png.

8.3.2. Strengths and Weaknesses of Each Method

Intrusion detection systems (IDS) are categorized into signature-based and anomaly-based methods, each having its own advantages and disadvantages. Signature-based IDS is strong in identifying known attacks by analyzing incoming traffic against pre-stored patterns of malicious behavior. The method tends to have low false-positive rates, making it more reliable in well-structured environments. However, its greatest flaw lies in its inability to identify new attacks, which are very lethal in ever-evolving network environments. Hence, such systems often do not identify sophisticated threats that are not compatible with signatures available at present. Anomaly-based methods, however, use machine learning algorithm to create baseline behavior patterns, which allow them to detect anomalies that may represent intrusion attempts. While this approach may identify new attacks, it may give greater false-positive rates in dynamic environments where there are valid traffic changes, which highlights the intrinsic trade-offs between adaptability and precision in IDS offerings (Pawlicki et al., 2023). In IoT environments, the choice of intrusion detection methods must similarly be informed by the particular constraints posed by such connected devices. For example, resource-limited IoT devices frequently curtail the use of advanced anomaly detection algorithms, calling for more straightforward techniques that don't compromise performance. Machine learning model-based anomaly detection, while able to effectively detect new attacks, involves intensive computational power and data to train models to accurately identify anomalies. This can be unrealistic for IoT use cases, which normally have limited processing.

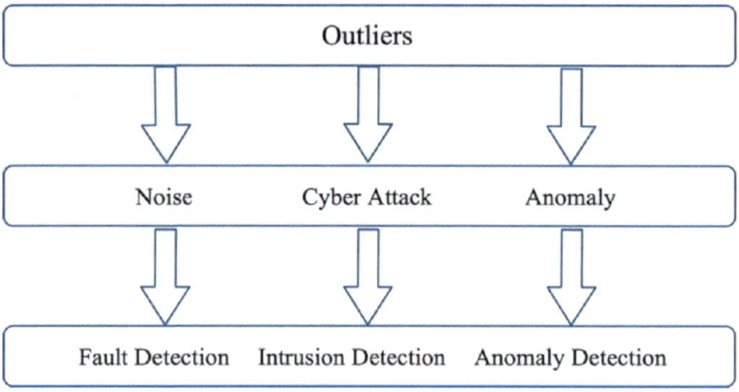

Figure 8.9. Anomaly detection based on machine learning models, while capable of effectively identifying novel attacks, requires substantial computational power and data to train models accurately.

Source: https://pub.mdpi-res.com/applsci/applsci-11-05320/article_deploy/html/images/applsci-11-05320-g001.png?1623138383.

Yet, emerging techniques like distributed or edge-based anomaly detection are being explored to mitigate these weaknesses. By processing data closer to where it is generated, these methods can leverage local knowledge in reducing the resource burden on individual devices and thus compromise detection capability with operational efficiency (Pawlicki et al., 2023). The signature-anomaly hybrid solution, which capitalizes on both signature and anomaly-based methods, is a valid response to the limitations present in intrusion detection for IoT networks. The method leverages the strength of both methodologies in an attempt to better identify known and unknown threats and maybe lower false-positive rates. For example, the hybrid approach can implement signature detection for regular traffic and implement anomaly detection techniques to flag unusual patterns that are typical of emerging attacks. However, this blended mode of application has its weaknesses, including increased complexity in implementation and increased need for computing resources. Additionally, the facilitation of effective communication between the two methods as well as the solving of the problem of conflicting detection outcomes can pose additional challenges to security experts. Yet, recent work in the field suggests that a properly implemented hybrid solution would be able to successfully promote the security posture of IoT ecosystems in accordance with today's efforts at improving machine learning and deep learning-oriented IDS models (Abdullah et al., 2020) (Figure 8.9).

8.3.3. Situational Applicability in IoT Environments

Situational applicability in Internet of Things (IoT) settings is a necessity in developing secure intrusion detection systems and anomaly detection methods. The heterogeneity of IoT applications, ranging from home automation to industrial sensors, necessitates different security processes and detection mechanisms in accordance with their unique operation contexts. As an illustration, a home automation system's security system must learn from user behavior, environment, and connectivity of devices so that alerts and responses are up to the moment for potential intrusions. In addition, IoT's dynamic nature with potentially many devices communicating across diverse networks complicates intrusion detection. It is more and more necessary to deploy adaptive algorithms that are capable of learning from situational data, hence enhancing the precision of security responses and minimizing false alarms. In the case of anomaly detection itself, situational applicability also stresses the importance of robust datasets that represent varied operational conditions commonly found in IoT environments. Recent advances have allowed the construction of large-scale datasets, e.g., the Edge-IIoTset, that enable a wide range of IoT and Industrial IoT (IIoT) applications. The datasets contain various attack patterns and device attack styles, which are required for training machine learning-based detection models. The operational profile of each device defines the baseline of what constitutes normal behavior, thus allowing the fine-grained investigation of anomalies. By leveraging such large datasets, researchers and developers can craft more comprehensive detection mechanisms to meet specific situational contexts, thus enhancing security controls in IoT applications. Moreover, studying situational applicability in IoT settings is more than building datasets; it involves addressing the inherent problems introduced by heterogeneous technologies and architectures employed. The device dependency and the identifying characteristics of IoT settings, such as low power and varying levels of computational capacity, necessitate device-specific detection mechanisms that are able to cater to these constrains. It is extremely relevant in the realm of advanced metaverse applications, where interoperability and scalability concerns undermine secure data processing and transmission (Wang et al., 2022). With demand for converged IoT solutions on the rise comes the demand for intrusion detection systems that are not just robust but as responsive as possible to meet evolving situation parameters in order to gain optimal security across heterogenous IoT scenarios (Ferrag et al., 2022).

8.4. CURRENT TRENDS IN IOT SECURITY

The security landscape for Internet of Things (IoT) has greatly enhanced with the rise in devices and how they are interconnected very elaborately. Trends today reveal a shift from traditional security measures to sophisticated means of addressing the dynamic nature of the networks. Researchers are looking for more sophisticated models, such as deep learning models, to enhance intrusion detection systems (IDS) and anomaly detection systems (ADS) in IoT settings. These systems are essential for real-time threat detection and adaptation based on new forms of cyberattacks. Utilizing large datasets to train prediction models, networks can identify network traffic as being malicious or benign before breaches are even experienced, and thus prevent vulnerabilities within inter-connected devices and networks, as posited in recent research (Latifi et al., 2018). As technology behind IoT becomes more sophisticated, so must measures protecting such environments. The most notable advancement is the emergence of machine learning (ML) approaches that facilitate adaptive learning necessary in guaranteeing security in diverse networks. Through the use of unsupervised and supervised learning methods, ML is capable of handling vast data volumes to identify patterns and outliers that signify potential intrusions. This has become even more relevant with the diverse applications of IoT that spread across sectors like healthcare and manufacturing, each with specific security requirements. The ability of ML algorithms to learn data-driven recommendations creates proactive security, which makes them valuable assets for IoT security solutions in the future (Chen et al., 2019). In addition, embedding these sophisticated security solutions into existing network architecture is a key trend in IoT security. Organizations are now adopting multi-layered security practices that not only focus on perimeter security but also implement rigorous surveillance techniques throughout the system. These broad-based mechanisms ensure security to be maintained at various levels, from device level to application level. Consistent monitoring and anomaly detection provide prompt actions in response to threat, and organizations can react quickly with newly emerging vulnerabilities. The combined application of such tactics, using deep learning platforms alongside machine learning techniques, demonstrates commitment to staying ahead of cyber-attacks and exemplifies a foresighted strategy in the IoT security space (Latifi et al., 2018).

8.4.1. Emerging Technologies in Intrusion Detection

The IDS environment is undergoing significant transformation driven by the escalating depth and heterogeneity of the Internet of Things (IoT) and cyber-physical systems. With each system being interconnected to others, traditional security solutions tend to fall short in countering emerging threats. Recent innovations point to the use of deep learning approaches that leverage enormous quantities of data generated by IoT devices. Such forethoughtful approach allows for continuous monitoring of network trends of data, thereby identifying potential security threats in advance. Such technologies not only enhance detection but also evolve with increasing attack vectors, and therefore are a requirement in safeguarding critical infrastructure. With the use of high computation power, such deep learning models can classify files as benign or malicious, thereby developing a predictive model of intrusion prevention. This technological advancement is a paradigm shift, from being a reactive to a proactive defense system in intrusion detection (Latifi et al., 2018). Further, the innovation of sophisticated frameworks to observe cyber-physical systems, such as SCADA systems, is indicative of the necessity for resilient security protocols in an interconnection scenario. The transition of SCADA systems from isolated networks to networked systems exposes them to an entire range of cyber threats that can undermine national security and economic stability. Accordingly, an in-depth understanding of inter-alia vulnerabilities becomes the order of the day. In a quest to place themselves at the attacker's perspective, security analysts are able to identify loopholes and chinks in existing defenses, which eventually assists in formulating foolproof countermeasures. The integration of advanced intrusion detection technologies is most critical, not only because it demands such systems to recognize attacks in real time but also anticipate potential breaches even before they materialize. The leading position that emerging technologies take in SCADA security cannot be overstated as they present an integrative approach to protecting critical infrastructures (Almalawi et al., 2017). In the rapidly changing landscape of IoT, application of emerging technologies for intrusion detection is important to mitigate the advanced threats that organizations are experiencing. Emerging technologies like AI and machine learning are being increasingly accepted to increase the power of IDS so that they can detect advanced attack patterns and anomalies with high impact. These more intelligent systems can learn from historical data, which makes their sensing more reliable and reduces false alarms. Furthermore, edge computing enables these developments through the analysis of data closer to the sources where it is being generated, thus accelerating responses and decreasing latency. As more IoT devices are being deployed, scalable and dynamic solutions for intrusion detection are needed. With constant evolution and adaptation to emerging threats, the convergence of these emerging technologies ensures a robust security posture, fostering the integrity and reliability of interdependent systems in the contemporary digital age (Almalawi et al., 2017; Latifi et al., 2018) (Figure 8.10).

Figure 8.10. Supervisory control and data acquisition (SCADA) systems.

Source: https://www.e-spincorp.com/wp-content/uploads/2018/09/scadasystem.img_-1024x732.png.

8.4.2. Integration of AI and Machine Learning

Artificial Intelligence (AI) and machine learning (ML) applications in the field of IoT have revolutionized traditional security practices, particularly intrusion and anomaly detection. With their increasing use, IoT devices carry vulnerabilities exposing them to a range of cyber-attacks, thereby necessitating complex security solutions. Traditional security measures generally do not work due to the heterogeneity and dynamic nature of IoT networks, coupled with device limitations that further complicate traditional detection methods. Through AI and ML, practitioners can design models that learn from massive amounts of data generated by IoT devices. Such methods enable real-time detection and adaptive response against likely threats, significantly enhancing overall security positions in increasingly complex digital environments. Moreover, advanced machine learning architectures enable the deployment of anomaly-based intrusion detection systems tailored to IoT usage. As powerful as they are with supervised learning and behavior analysis, such systems can identify normal patterns and anomalous activity typical of cyber intrusions. For instance, models like one-class SVM have been extremely effective, where they have achieved detection accuracy of nearly 99.71% in real-world scenarios, according to recent research. With algorithms to scan massive datasets, such systems can detect impending threats more accurately and with lower operating costs, thus proving particularly valuable in resource-scarce situations. In combination with software-defined networking (SDN) and network function virtualization (NFV), these functionalities add still more resiliency and flexibility in reacting to emerging security threats within IoT ecosystems (Mishra, 2025). Though the innovative advancements create a lot of interest, integrating AI and ML in current cybersecurity systems poses some profound challenges. The implementation of these innovative models into various IoT systems has the tendency to encounter challenges of scalability, interoperability, and data privacy. Organizations must deal with complexities of existing IT infrastructure in making the integration of these intelligent threat defense systems without compromise on performance and security. However, research shows that combining ensembles and machine learning classifiers has a striking impact on the resilience of systems to cyberattacks by anomaly-based detection. Continuous research into AI-driven cybersecurity solutions also continues to attempt to overcome such challenges while pushing the boundaries of what is possible when it comes to IoT security. Future studies are intended to target the continued advancement of such technologies in order to create potent defenses against the burgeoning cyber threat environment (Schmitt, 2023).

8.4.3. Regulatory Frameworks and Compliance Issues

In the area of intrusion detection and anomaly detection in the Internet of Things (IoT), regulatory policy plays a primary role to guide compliance strategies that secure information and uphold system integrity. Increased connectivity of IoT devices, being a virtue, simultaneously amplifies risks of being targeted by malicious actors. This increased risk indicates the importance of applying robust security frameworks in congruence with the prevailing regulation. Regulatory standards, such as Europe's General Data Protection Regulation (GDPR), have necessitated rigorous data handling practices in order to preserve user privacy and security. The influence of such paradigms is of utmost importance as they compel organizations to embrace proactive measures towards the detection of potential security breaches, thereby ensuring greater accountability and compliance with the IoT ecosystem. Developing adequate regulatory environments not only empowers individual organizations, but also increases the overall security of interdependent systems. Furthermore, the regulatory climate of IoT presents unique challenges that demand a sophisticated solution to compliance. Since IoT technologies themselves are in a state of continuous flux, regulatory structures should also be dynamic in order to accommodate emerging threats and vulnerabilities. The use of best practices and standards, such as those advocated by industry associations, can assist in limiting threats from the implementation of anomaly detection systems. Regulator bodies typically require provisions that insist on the use of advanced security controls, such as encryption and routine system audits. For instance, the dynamic nature of cybersecurity may require the implementation of intrusion detection systems compatible with various regulatory needs. Extended exposure to compliance needs makes security controls not only remain current with legal standards but also integrate fresh technology and best practices in risk handling, providing a sound base to withstand cyber-attacks. The amalgamation of artificial intelligence (AI) and regulatory compliance is more evident in the case of IoT security. While advancements in AI technologies can enable organizations to ramp up their ability to identify anomalies, the associated impact on privacy and human rights is also a consideration. For example, utilizing AI-based systems to improve the efficiency of threat detection and mitigation but, in doing so, utilizing such technology involves thoroughly scrutinizing ethics and compliance with existing legislation. As studies by RUSI indicate, the use of AI in national security is to be weighed against frequent review of privacy and human rights concerns in relation to regulation (Babuta et al., 2020). The dual agenda of exploiting new technologies while upholding legal and ethical standards presents a sophisticated challenge to organizations. With changing IoT, adaptive regulatory policies will be a must to maintain the integrity and reliability of systems that work with advanced detection methods (Figure 8.11).

Figure 8.11. As IoT technologies continuously evolve, regulatory frameworks must also adapt to address emerging threats and vulnerabilities.

Source: https://deviceauthority.com/wp-content/uploads/2025/06/Device-Authority-Blog-Post-Banners-2025-06-05T144157.215.jpg.

8.5. FUTURE DIRECTIONS IN IOT SECURITY

The rapid development of the Internet of Things (IoT) generates a contradiction of innovation and exposure, thus calling for swift innovations in IoT security. The future of this trend is shifting increasingly towards innovative machine learning (ML) and deep learning (DL) techniques that can outperform security threats. Recent studies show the potential of federated learning (FL) as a decentralized learning approach that offers enhanced privacy via the capacity of IoT devices to collaborate while not disclosing sensitive data to a central server. By utilizing local data for training, FL has the potential to avoid privacy violations while improving the overall classification accuracy of intrusion detection systems. This advancement is a change in IoT security measures in a strategic direction, focusing on enhancing defenses against more sophisticated attacks and ensuring user data integrity, thus opening the way for additional research in this significant field (Alzuabi et al., 2023). Leveraging the new approaches in IoT security, researchers are increasingly utilizing behavior-based detection mechanisms particular to the unique traffic patterns of IoT devices. By examining particular behavior, for instance, the limited number of endpoint communications and periodic intervals between packet sends, algorithms can effectively determine malicious behavior. Integrating such IoT-specific data into machine learning algorithms has proven to have high accuracy when detecting distributed denial of service (DDoS) attacks, as cited in research demonstrating the effectiveness of the integration of feature selection with state-of-the-art ML algorithms (Apthorpe et al., 2018). This approach not only enhances defense against known threats but also presents a mechanism of how to come up with proactive approaches to predict and mitigate potential future attacks, hence significantly contributing to the evolution of anomaly detection in IoT security. Since the IoT ecosystem of devices is constantly evolving, so are the means of their protection. IoT security research directions in the future will likely be more on how artificial intelligence, edge computing, and anomaly detection methods converge. Edge computing provides real-time processing at the network edge, which reduces latency and can make security systems more agile. Combined with the capabilities of ML and DL, edge devices can execute low-cost, effective anomaly detection algorithms that are able to identify security threats immediately before they are able to become issues. Combination of these technologies, when implemented collectively, not only creates an even stronger IoT environment but also pushes forward with the understanding of how to best manage and decode the large amounts of data that these connected devices produce. This paradigm focuses on an innovative approach in the defense of IoT realms from ever-evolving vulnerabilities and security threats to data (Alzuabi et al., 2023).

8.5.1. Predictions for the Evolution of Detection Systems

The evolution of detection mechanisms in the era of the Internet of Things (IoT) is poised to become much better in reaction to the increased cybersecurity threats. As conventional security systems prove ineffective, the focus is moving towards evolving strategies that take advantage of sophisticated technologies such as machine learning and artificial intelligence. These technologies enable systems to learn from past attacks, adapt to cope with new attack vectors, and increase predictive capability. An adaptive approach can result in real-time anomaly detection with reduced reliance on pre-set signatures, which is critical because IoT environments are dynamic. Smart architectures that not only identify threats but actively counter them are the pressing need of the hour. The use of random neural networks, as discussed in Ahmadinia et al. (2016), is just one of the many examples of how such methods have the potential to work at high levels of precision in detecting anomalies with low performance overhead, setting the stage for much more robust IoT security solutions. As more and more IoT devices become dispersed, effective security management becomes an increasingly difficult issue.

The limitations of conventional security solutions, as described in existing literature, indicate that users cannot have sole responsibility for tallying such risks. Innovations to detection systems must address user ease and ease of installation. A case study of a signature-based monitoring solution for consumer IoT environments demonstrates the viability of using active malicious activity detection via passive network sniffing techniques. Such an approach allows consumers to benefit from sophisticated security features without requiring the significant levels of technical expertise, as determined in Adebisi et al. (2020) through the high detection accuracy reported. Thus, the detection systems of the future will probably concentrate on both efficient and easy-to-use solutions to allow further categories of users to participate and benefit from more robust cybersecurity positions. Shifting into the future, detection solution scalability will be paramount as IoT networks become larger. Forecasting models will need to factor in evolving threat scenarios presented by the increasing variety of devices and what they perform. A future detection system will need to encompass not only anomaly detection but real-time adaptation to counter newly emerging vulnerabilities. The need for a converged solution of device verification, behavior profiling, and ongoing system assessment will propel the development of next-generation detection solutions. Moreover, convergence between cloud computing and IoT offers a bright future for centralized monitoring and analysis to enable greater interconnectivity between systems. While the security environment keeps evolving, embracing these enhancements will be critical to ensuring defenses against growing numbers of cyber-attacks while maintaining performance efficiency demanded by resource-constrained IoT devices as postulated in Ahmadinia et al. (2016) (Figure 8.12).

Figure 8.12. With traditional security measures proving inadequate, the focus is shifting towards innovative strategies that harness advanced technologies such as machine learning and artificial intelligence.

Source: https://images.prismic.io/evalink-website/984c211b-d5e1-4f8c-a54e-f6f87772f791_Frame+1000001223.png?auto=compress,format.

8.5.2. The Role of Blockchain in Enhancing Security

Blockchain technology application to intrusion detection and anomaly detection systems provides a disruptive way of enhancing security within the Internet of Things (IoT). With IoT devices becoming widespread, the attack surface is significantly large and calls for meaningful security. Distributed architecture of blockchains provides a tamper-evident ledger that records transactions and operations, allowing increased traceability and accountability. This attribute proves especially useful in IoT setups where many devices autonomously communicate with one another, and conventional security controls are insufficient. Utilizing blockchain, organizations can guarantee that any malicious access or irregularities in device communication are reported instantly and documented, thus enabling an immediate response to possible threats. Implementation of such systems is with the findings of Yaseen et al. (2020), where it is emphasized that adaptive and resilient security features against dynamic cyber threats are necessary. Furthermore, implementation of machine learning algorithms in combination with blockchain makes it possible for advanced anomaly detection functionality on IoT infrastructures. Machine learning will be used to identify anomalies in patterns in the immutable data on the blockchain that are indicative of potential intrusions or abnormal behavior. For instance, leveraging convolutional neural networks (CNN) as highlighted in Amrullah et al. (2025) allows complex data flow and analysis of user activity between devices. Once the anomalies are detected, the blockchain may automatically trigger response protocols, eliminating threats in real time without the intervention of humans. The integration not only optimizes detection but also reduces the time to respond to incidents, critical in preventing damage from cyber-attacks. Such advancements point to the necessity of a complete approach to cybersecurity in IoT that combines machine learning and blockchain to better secure defense systems.

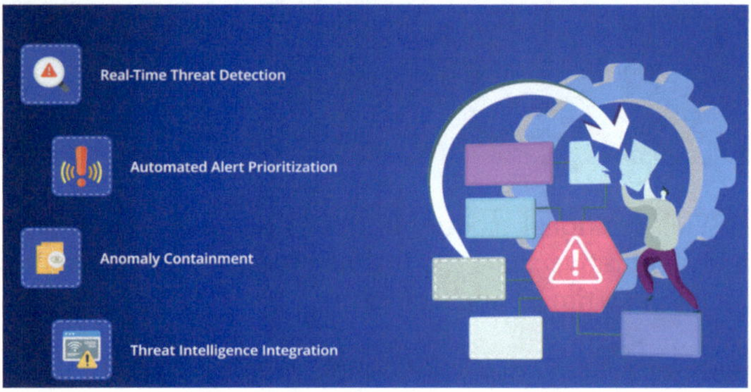

Figure 8.13. When anomalies are detected, the blockchain can autonomously execute response protocols, mitigating threats in real-time without human intervention.

Source: https://d3lkc3n5th01x7.cloudfront.net/wp-content/uploads/2024/05/15034020/AI-in-Incident-Response-1-1.png.

Beyond detecting anomalies, blockchain has the potential to enhance overall cybersecurity systems through its capacity to provide safe data exchange among connected devices. In an IoT environment where compatibility is paramount, the challenge of maintaining data integrity during transactions becomes paramount. Blockchain addresses this by enabling secure encryption of transactions and identity management in a safe way via distributed protocols. This aspect makes it such that only authentic devices can engage in meaningful data exchanges, thus minimizing vulnerability to malicious attacks. Moreover, as found in Yaseen et al. (2020), the combination of behavior-based security models and blockchain can indeed effectively improve detection systems' efficacy against sophisticated threats. By ensuring the availability of a minimum level of security conditionally achieved only by authenticated parties, blockchain does not only secure individual devices but also secures the overall network infrastructure, producing a strong IoT security framework (Figure 8.13).

8.5.3. Importance of User Education and Awareness

The Internet of Things (IoT) pervades ordinary life, providing convenience but compromising security as well. User education plays a critical role in mitigating these weaknesses since the majority of people are not adequately informed about the appropriate usage and security measures in regard to the devices. Massive training programs can potentially increase user awareness about potential attacks, such as unauthorized use and data breaches, enabling users to detect abnormal activities. In addition, promoting an educated user population allows users to perform active measures such as firmware updates and the use of secure passwords that are primordial in guarding against potential intrusions. Lastly, user awareness is the last line of defense in the intricate web of IoT ecosystems, and this emphasizes the necessity of structured education programs and tools implemented especially for IoT security. As fog computing and IoT continue to merge, their implications on cybersecurity heighten. Educated users can appreciate the intricate interactions between their devices and the security infrastructure shielding them. According to research, learning about the working mechanisms of IoT and fog computing increases users' capacity for identifying and neutralizing threats, hence overall system resilience. User education is therefore essential in making people not only mere recipients of technology but active stakeholders in ensuring their environments are protected. Education programs aimed at enlightening users on the potential security concerns brought about by the incorporation of fog computing's can facilitate informed decision-making processes, which are essential in establishing trust and reliability in the IoT environment (Butun et al., 2018). Furthermore, the rapid evolution of artificial intelligence (AI) in network security underscores the importance of heightened user awareness regarding cybersecurity best practices. AI technologies can improve anomaly detection and incident response; yet, the efficiency of such systems is entirely contingent upon user activity and insight. Users must be prepared to work with these sophisticated platforms, for well-informed users are less likely to make decisions that can compromise security by default. Training focused on AI system strengths and weaknesses can significantly enhance the ability of users to navigate and respond to threats. According to recent studies, more effective user training may reduce significantly human-based vulnerabilities, enhancing the performance of AI systems in IoT networks (Karim et al., 2024). Therefore, establishing an atmosphere of awareness ensures that the users are on guard and prepared for the dynamic cyber-attacks.

8.6. CONCLUSION

In short, the more complexity and cyber-attacks frequency in IoT systems demand reconsidering the traditional Intrusion Detection Systems (IDS). The shift towards AI and machine learning technologies has been vital in overcoming the restrictions of traditional systems, which are always behind high-level attacks. With the addition of adaptive AI algorithms, it is possible to make IDS more sensitive and responsive. These advances allow security infrastructures to detect known and emerging attacks with accuracy and force, offering more robust defense tools against an ever-evolving adversary landscape. As mentioned, bridging the divide between legacy IDS and modern AI-based systems is a key research area for making IoT networks more secure (Shaik, 2025). In addition, the design and organization of effective IDS to fit IoT present novel challenges. Heterogeneity of, and resource constraint in, IoT devices presents a challenge in deploying standardized security measures. Therefore, the future direction should be towards lightweight solutions that, besides being effective in anomaly detection, are also feasibly deployable in resource-constrained environments. There ought to be close coordination among scholars, industry stakeholders, and policymakers in tackling challenges, creating efficient security frameworks that secure sensitive data in IoT environments. This joint strategy will enable IDS innovations to keep pace with the rapid proliferation of IoT, strengthening the integrity and security of networked systems (Dinkar et al., 2024). In the long run, the deployment of AI and machine learning in intrusion and anomaly detection in IoT spaces offers a shining road map for enhancing cybersecurity. As the threat landscape keeps evolving, so must our approaches to protecting such valuable networks. Emphasis on continuous learning and model adaptation presents a key element of IDS design, making it possible to achieve real-time threat monitoring flexibility. The future will call for continuous research in further developing these technologies and overcoming challenges such as interpretability and scalability in real-world applications. By fostering an innovation and responsive culture in cybersecurity, we can better prepare and mitigate the challenges presented by the dynamic nature of the cyber threat environment of IoT infrastructures (Dinkar et al., 2024; Shaik, 2025).

8.6.1. Summary of Key Points Discussed

The landscape of IoT security has drastically changed with more devices being on the network. This setup brings about various challenges, particularly given the necessity of efficient intrusion detection and anomaly detection. The creation of full-fledged datasets which can be employed in helping machine learning-based systems is one significant aspect of broadening security. For instance, the Edge-IIoTset dataset has emerged as a valuable resource designed specifically for IoT and Industrial IoT applications that span an array of sensors and devices. Not only does the dataset aid in the detection of different types of attacks but also supports machine learning model performance assessment in centralized and federated learning modes. The use of large datasets in leading the way in innovation for detection techniques cannot be overstated. Underpinning debates for IoT intrusion detection is knowledge about varying attack vectors that brake system integrity. The examination of threats via DoS/DDoS attacks, methods of information gathering, and man-in-the-middle vulnerability highlights the diversification of IoT security (Wang et al., 2022). By categorizing potential threats into separate groups, security researchers can better design more adequate countermeasures to specific categories of attacks. Furthermore, the multi-dimensional nature of IoT environments necessitates a transition towards adaptive anomaly detection mechanisms that would be capable of learning to adapt to evolving patterns of normal behavior. Accordingly, the employment of advanced machine learning techniques, including traditional and deep learning patterns, has now become central to enhancing detection rates and reducing false positives for security systems. Within the midst of developments in detection practices stands the fundamental requirement of interdisciplinary cooperation to address security concerns that are inherent to IoT systems. The convergence of intelligence from disciplines such as artificial intelligence, network security, and privacy engineering can lead to end-to-end security solutions that adapt dynamically to address the increasingly rapid transition in threats. Initiatives such as the examination of privacy and security issues in emerging paradigms, including the metaverse, underscore the imperative role of anticipatory action in protecting virtual platforms (Wang et al., 2022). By addressing both the technical and behavioral aspects of security, future research can make IoT infrastructures resilient. Continued examination of existing schemes, along with fresh methodologies of data analysis and threat assessment, will be essential to maintaining security and effectiveness of IoT deployments in the future.

8.6.2. The Necessity of Robust Security Measures in IoT

The vast landscape of the Internet of Things (IoT) points towards greater security measures, particularly in light of the boom in devices connected to the internet in the majority of industries. The more integrated they become into everyday usage, the greater the vulnerability to abuse, making them prime targets for cybercrime. This situation is compounded by the lack of standardized security protocols in IoT environments, causing vulnerabilities that affect not only individual devices but also global networks. It is compounded by the heterogeneous nature of data generated by IoT devices, which must be processed using sophisticated techniques to effectively detect anomalies. In the absence of strong security mechanisms, risks of data breaches, unauthorized access, and system failures significantly increase the chances of impairing the functionality and dependability of IoT infrastructures. Organizations must adopt a multi-faceted strategy for security involving advanced technology and processes. Intrusion Detection Systems (IDS) are at the core of such a strategy by actively monitoring network traffic for malicious activity. The integration of machine learning techniques further enhances the abilities of IDS by enabling them to learn from data patterns adaptively and improve their detection abilities. This is especially necessary in advanced environments, such as Industrial Internet of Things (IIoT) systems, where volumes of data and potential attack surfaces are extensive. Techniques such as the ones emphasized in recent studies have the potential to detect anomalies, revealing that techniques such as k-nearest neighbors and random forests achieve significant precision and recall in identifying security threats (Zhukabayeva et al., 2025). The development of such technologies emphasizes the need to include resilient security controls in IoT frameworks. Moreover, the development of testbeds and datasets particularly for intrusion detection testing and evaluation plays a vital role in enhancing the security posture of IoT networks. Study work like the IoTForge Pro testbed, which generates enormous datasets for simulating an immense array of attack patterns, presents valuable resources for enhancing security protocols (Kumar et al., 2025). Applying advanced machine learning techniques on such data, practitioners can systematically experiment with the performance of different IDS models and tune them to best counter changing threats. This iterative exercise not only helps build more secure systems but also fosters a culture of continuous improvement in security practice in IoT systems. Lastly, the necessity for secure security solutions in IoT is not merely a technological requirement; it is an integral component of the provision of security, privacy, and operational integrity within an increasingly dynamic digital landscape.

8.6.3. Final Thoughts on the Future of Intrusion and Anomaly Detection in IoT

As we glance toward the future of intrusion and anomaly detection for the Internet of Things (IoT), the extremely rapid development in artificial intelligence (AI) is the most significant driver. Integration of AI techniques, namely machine learning (ML) and deep learning (DL), has proven to drive significantly enhanced threat detection across many IoT applications. For instance, these technologies can take live data from a host of devices, inferring patterns over time to identify anomalies that represent security threats. By utilizing AI-based models, organizations can achieve detection rates of over 90% in test beds, as established in existing literature. This is a critical direction, especially with IoT systems becoming more integrated with industrial control systems (ICS), where problems can have far-reaching effects (Bajwa et al., 2025). Also highlighted by the emphasis on real-time analysis of data is a paradigm shift regarding the way we approach cybersecurity in IoT environments. Future systems will be founded on continuous monitoring and predictive analytics to determine anomalies prior to them being major violations. The creation of smart home security systems, for example, illustrates this trend so that AI algorithms interpret data derived from devices that are connected in order to offer smart notification and initiate automated responses against identified threats (Bisht, 2025). This aggressive method not only optimizes security but also keeps the users adequately informed and empowered in defending their internet environment. As the number of IoT devices grows, it will take a coordinated effort to combat the complexity of threat detection in the form of developing robust frameworks that constantly adapt to emerging risks and technological challenges. Lastly, ongoing development of industry-specific cybersecurity systems will play an irreplaceable part in shaping the future topography of intrusion and anomaly detection. With inherent weaknesses in some of the IoT applications—i.e., agriculture, healthcare, or smart cities—solution-specific defense mechanisms will be essential. Countermeasures to adversarial attacks and data integrity issues will also influence the security position of IoT applications. Furthermore, collaboration among industries, academia, and regulatory bodies will result in devising standards enhancing overall resistance to cyber-attacks. Through the integration of these highly dimensional methods and the implementation of developments achieved in AI, the future of intrusion detection for the IoT can potentially not only adapt to but also anticipate countermeasures for new threats, thereby securing critical infrastructure and affording more public trust in these systems.

REFERENCES

1. Abdullah, J., Ahmad, F., Ahmad, Z., Khan, et al. (2020). Network intrusion detection system: A systematic study of machine learning and deep learning approaches. https://core.ac.uk/download/337891688.pdf (accessed on 17th October 2025).
2. Adebisi, B., Baker, T., Belguith, S., et al. (2020). Network traffic analysis for threats detection in the Internet of Things. https://core.ac.uk/download/323058053.pdf (accessed on 17th October 2025).
3. Ahmadinia, A., Javed, A., Larijani, H., et al. (2016). Intelligent intrusion detection in low power IoTs. https://core.ac.uk/download/293881756.pdf (accessed on 17th October 2025).
4. Alatawi, T., & Aljuhani, A. (2022). Anomaly detection framework in fog-to-things communication for industrial Internet of Things. *Computers, Materials & Continua, 73*, 1067–1086. https://doi.org/10.32604/cmc.2022.029283 (accessed on 17th October 2025).
5. Ali, M., Raza, A., Akram, M. A., Arif, H., & Ali, A. (2025). Enhancing IoT security: A review of machine learning-driven approaches to cyber threat detection. *Journal of Informatics and Interactive Technology*. https://www.semanticscholar.org/paper/69efc0b55cdd220e0be38fb38ff743fcff05fdea (accessed on 17th October 2025).
6. Almalawi, A., Baecher, B., Boldea, B., Bouchti, S., Brand, M., Byres, E., et al. (2017). Assessing and augmenting SCADA cyber security: A survey of techniques. https://core.ac.uk/download/293885085.pdf (accessed on 17th October 2025).
7. Al-Naimat, R., Aldreabi, E., Alzaqebah, M., et al. (2024). Ensemble learning with sleep mode management to enhance anomaly detection in IoT environment. https://core.ac.uk/download/621742843.pdf (accessed on 17th October 2025).
8. Alsoufi, M. A., Abd Razak, S., Md Siraj, M., Nafea, I., Ghaleb, F. A., Saeed, F., & Nasser, M. (2021). Anomaly-based intrusion detection systems in IoT using deep learning: A systematic literature review. *Applied Sciences, 11*, 8383–8383. https://doi.org/10.3390/app11188383 (accessed on 17th October 2025).
9. Alzuabi, W., Elmedany, W., et al. (2023). Using machine learning for security issues in cognitive IoT. https://core.ac.uk/download/590956997.pdf (accessed on 17th October 2025).
10. Amrullah, A. (2025). A review and comparative analysis of intrusion detection systems for edge networks in IoT. https://core.ac.uk/download/641047319.pdf (accessed on 17th October 2025).

11. Apthorpe, N., Doshi, R., & Feamster, N. (2018). Machine learning DDoS detection for consumer Internet of Things devices. http://arxiv.org/abs/1804.04159 (accessed on 17th October 2025).
12. Babuta, A., Janjeva, A., & Oswald, M. (2020). Artificial intelligence and UK national security: Policy considerations. https://core.ac.uk/download/305121521.pdf (accessed on 17th October 2025).
13. Bajwa, A., Tonoy, A. A. R., Rana, S., & Ahmed, I. (2025). Cybersecurity in industrial control systems: A systematic literature review on AI-based threat detection for SCADA and IoT networks. *ASRC Procedia: Global Perspectives in Science and Scholarship*. https://www.semanticscholar.org/paper/1e167f2c2e379a0494201f9ec24da609187b9478 (accessed on 17th October 2025).
14. Bisht, K. S. (2025). IoT-based smart home security system with AI-powered intrusion detection. *International Journal for Research in Applied Science and Engineering Technology*. https://www.semanticscholar.org/paper/688872020ddf8c6788ecda4ee143a73a7ef82167 (accessed on 17th October 2025).
15. Butun, I., Sari, A., & Österberg, P. (2018). Security implications of fog computing on the Internet of Things. http://arxiv.org/abs/1809.10492 (accessed on 17th October 2025).
16. Chen, K. C., Hanzo, L., Jiang, C., et al. (2019). Thirty years of machine learning: The road to Pareto-optimal wireless networks. http://arxiv.org/abs/1902.01946 (accessed on 17th October 2025).
17. Chen, Z., Djukic, P., Kantarci, B., et al. (2022). Machine learning-enabled IoT security: Open issues and challenges under advanced persistent threats. http://arxiv.org/abs/2204.03433 (accessed on 17th October 2025).
18. Comuzzi, M., Rhee, K. H., & Tama, B. A. (2019). TSE-IDS: A two-stage classifier ensemble for intelligent anomaly based intrusion detection system. https://core.ac.uk/download/225164258.pdf (accessed on 17th October 2025).
19. Dinkar, A. K., & Choudhary, A. K. (2024). Exploring intrusion detection systems (IDS) in IoT environments. *Seminars in Medical Writing and Education*. https://www.semanticscholar.org/paper/29b0117b1414486a60f2e0199d7103f7632ea84d (accessed on 17th October 2025).
20. Ferrag, M. A., Friha, O., Hamouda, D., & Janicke, H. (2022). Edge-IIoTset: A new comprehensive realistic cyber security dataset of IoT and IIoT applications for centralized and federated learning. *IEEE Access, 10*, 40281–40306. https://doi.org/10.1109/access.2022.3165809 (accessed on 17th October 2025).

21. Haque, A., Chowdhury, M. N. U. R., Soliman, H., Hossen, M. S., Fatima, T., & Ahmed, I. (2023). Wireless sensor networks anomaly detection using machine learning: A survey. *arXiv (Cornell University)*. https://doi.org/10.48550/arxiv.2303.08823 (accessed on 17th October 2025).

22. Jauhar, A., Marojevic, V., Reed, J. H., et al. (2018). Deep predictive coding neural network for RF anomaly detection in wireless networks. http://arxiv.org/abs/1803.06054 (accessed on 17th October 2025).

23. Karim, M. F., Rafi, M. N. A., Rukon, M. I. A., et al. (2024). Enhancing network security: A framework for proactive cyber defense using artificial intelligence and big data. https://core.ac.uk/download/636358637.pdf (accessed on 17th October 2025).

24. Kumar, P., Mullick, S., Das, R., Nandi, A., & Banerjee, I. (2025). IoTForge Pro: A security testbed for generating intrusion dataset for industrial IoT. *IEEE Internet of Things Journal, 12*, 8453–8460. https://www.semanticscholar.org/paper/ec41c1e3e1d275bed4984ea428d61f672630a897 (accessed on 17th October 2025).

25. Latifi, S., Pirouz, M., Raste, N., et al. (2018). A cognitive framework to secure smart cities. https://core.ac.uk/download/215451692.pdf (accessed on 17th October 2025).

26. Mishra, A. (2025). AI-powered cybersecurity framework for secure data transmission in IoT network. *Volume 7*, 05–13. https://doi.org/10.35629/5252-07030513 (accessed on 17th October 2025).

27. Nguyen, D. C., Ding, M., Pathirana, P. N., Seneviratne, A., Li, J., & Poor, H. V. (2021). Federated learning for Internet of Things: A comprehensive survey. *IEEE Communications Surveys & Tutorials, 23*, 1622–1658. https://doi.org/10.1109/comst.2021.3075439 (accessed on 17th October 2025).

28. Paolini, D., Dini, P., Soldaini, E., & Saponara, S. (2025). One-class anomaly detection for industrial applications: A comparative survey and experimental study. *Computers*. https://www.semanticscholar.org/paper/092ae3267fbf3ce72bb8fc011bb6aeea6ba63c66 (accessed on 17th October 2025).

29. Pawlicki, M. (2023). Short paper: Strengths and weaknesses of deep, convolutional and recurrent neural networks in network intrusion detection deployments. https://core.ac.uk/download/587843559.pdf (accessed on 17th October 2025).

30. Sadikin, F., & Wiranda, N. (2023). Anomaly detection in Zigbee-based IoT using secure and efficient data collection. https://core.ac.uk/download/567623347.pdf (accessed on 17th October 2025).

31. Schmitt, M. (2023). Securing the digital world: Protecting smart infrastructures and digital industries with artificial intelligence (AI)-enabled malware and intrusion detection. *Journal of Industrial Information Integration, 36*, 100520–100520. https://doi.org/10.1016/j.jii.2023.100520 (accessed on 17th October 2025).
32. Shaik, K. M. N. (2025). Harnessing artificial intelligence to strengthen intrusion detection in modern network system. *International Journal of Scientific Research and Management (IJSRM)*. https://www.semanticscholar.org/paper/bbed5027862994e90c7d6f51c91df71b4c8efc01 (accessed on 17th October 2025).
33. Sharma, S. B., & Bairwa, A. K. (2025). Leveraging AI for intrusion detection in IoT ecosystems: A comprehensive study. *IEEE Access, 13*, 66290–66317. https://www.semanticscholar.org/paper/b0147387c139d1eacbfa5ff196b9c5c1dddb6f42 (accessed on 17th October 2025).
34. Suarez Gomez, A., Gutierrez Portela, F., & Diaz Triana, O. A. (2024). Intrusion detection system for IoT using anomaly detection techniques. *2024 IEEE VII Congreso Internacional en Inteligencia Ambiental, Ingeniería de Software y Salud Electrónica y Móvil (AmITIC)*. https://www.semanticscholar.org/paper/c326a0731e7796d5e3ac1c3c4e480e9ff53d236d (accessed on 17th October 2025).
35. Udoh, E. (2019). An energy aware and secure MAC protocol for tackling denial of sleep attacks in wireless sensor networks. https://core.ac.uk/download/305119264.pdf (accessed on 17th October 2025).
36. Wang, Y., Su, Z., Zhang, N., Xing, R., Liu, D., Luan, T. H., & Shen, X. (2022). A survey on metaverse: Fundamentals, security, and privacy. *IEEE Communications Surveys & Tutorials, 25*, 319–352. https://doi.org/10.1109/comst.2022.3202047 (accessed on 17th October 2025).
37. Yaseen, A. (2020). Uncovering evidence of attacker behavior on the network. https://core.ac.uk/download/603939725.pdf (accessed on 17th October 2025).
38. Zhukabayeva, T., Ahmad, Z., Adamova, A., Karabayev, N., & Abdildayeva, A. (2025). An edge-computing-based integrated framework for network traffic analysis and intrusion detection to enhance cyber–physical system security in industrial IoT. *Sensors (Basel, Switzerland), 25*. https://www.semanticscholar.org/paper/66554566e9e1b41faa2efd71021d4148f6b38190 (accessed on 17th October 2025).

CHAPTER 9

IOT SECURITY STANDARDS AND FRAMEWORKS

Contents

INTRODUCTION

Internet of Things (IoT) is one of the biggest strides in technological innovation, linking various types of devices to the internet and enabling data acquisition and exchange of data. The connectivity has, however, spawned an array of security loopholes posing big dangers to users, organizations, and infrastructure. As the IoT ecosystem expands, there is a need to implement robust security guidelines and frameworks that govern device inter-compatibility and data privacy.

Without them, cybercriminals will easily exploit the vulnerabilities, leading to unauthorized access, data losses, and compromised functionality. Thus, understanding existing regulatory structures and security practices becomes crucial in reducing such threats and safeguarding the integrity of IoT networks, paving the way for secure usage across sectors, ranging from home systems to industrial operations. A comprehensive analysis of current IoT security practices results in a fragmented regulatory framework, rendering it challenging to devise cohesive compliance practices. Various organizations, from government bodies to global standards organizations, have proposed frameworks such as the NIST Cybersecurity Framework and the EU Cybersecurity Act to combat the problem of IoT security. Yet, as suggested in the literature, such initiatives struggle to offer consistent guidance, and hence, implementation and compliance become patchy among manufacturers and service providers. Lack of standardized practices not only degrades the user data but also prevents mass adoption of IoT technologies, as stakeholders may hesitate to invest in systems with undefined security positions. Therefore, a scrutiny of these regulations is necessary to identify gaps and provide actionable recommendations for enhancement in IoT security practices in different domains. In addition, the relationship between consumer education and regulatory policies plays a pivotal role in establishing the effectiveness of IoT security protocols. What research shows is that consumers themselves are not aware of the privacy and security concerns of IoT devices and are thus vulnerable to potential risks. With the use of IoT devices becoming increasingly active in our daily lives, consumer education is vital in providing safer usage. Combined with successful regulation enforcement, consumer consciousness initiatives are able to strengthen the IoT ecosystem. Such a relationship emphasizes the importance of integrating educational campaigns with tangible policy measures in a bid to empower the users. A shared methodology involving standardization, compliance, and consumer engagement is required in creating a safe IoT ecosystem to sustainably facilitate innovation and protect stakeholders from future threats with an emphasis on the critical imperative for comprehensive knowledge of IoT security frameworks and standards in today's digital environment.

9.1. OVERVIEW OF IOT SECURITY CHALLENGES

With Internet of Things (IoT) pervasively interweaving itself into various industries, the consequent security problems that it brings are becoming more apparent. IoT devices, with their contribution to a more convenient life through increased connectivity and automation, are simultaneously subject to a variety of cyber threats. IoT security is a complex scenario with risks dispersed among the device, network, application, and data layers. Issues such as insecure interfaces, compromised firmware, and weak encryption are prevalent and can lead to grave consequences including unauthorized access and data compromise. It is therefore important to have a general comprehension of the issues as the foundation for developing adequate IoT security standards and frameworks that can address threats and vulnerabilities. The sheer scale and diversity of IoT devices only complicate it further to create uniform security protocols.

Figure 9.1. Robust standards and frameworks should take this heterogeneity into account, promoting the development of adaptable security solutions suited for diverse environments.

Source: https://bpi.com/wp-content/uploads/2022/03/Adaptive-Zero-Trust-Finance-cover.jpg.

As compared to traditional computing systems, IoT devices exhibit a wide range of capabilities, which affect the security they require. Some may have modest processing capabilities and hence require low-level security protocols, while others may have performance-specific capabilities. Such variability has a wealth of different attack targets, which can be exploited by attackers through the specific vulnerabilities of different devices and systems. The importance of respecting these diverse security needs cannot be overstated, for the optimization of heterogeneous security mechanisms optimized for specific IoT applications will be crucial in constructing resilience to cyber attacks. Robust standards and frameworks must take this heterogeneity into account, promoting the development of resilient security solutions relevant to disparate environments. Further, the impact of IoT security attacks is not just that of mere device vulnerabilities; they can bring down essential services and even threaten public safety. For instance, in smart city ecosystems, hacked IoT devices can make mission-critical services such as water supply management, traffic systems, and power grid distribution systems break down. Real-life accidents have already demonstrated the potential disastrous consequences that security failure may have on city operations and individuals' well-being. Such a fact underlines the importance of a multilevel security solution that is not only technical protection but also official policy and public awareness campaigns. By integrating extensive protection solutions in various dimensions, we can design a secure IoT system to promote innovation while ensuring public interests and ultimately constructing resilient and secure smart cities that can withstand future attacks (Figure 9.1).

9.1.1. Vulnerabilities in IoT Devices

The sudden explosion of Internet of Things (IoT) devices also comes with enormous security threats that desecrate user privacy and system integrity. The majority of consumer IoT devices, from domestic appliances to health monitoring equipment, are typically not designed with robust security features due to aggressive development timelines and cost constraints. This is exacerbated by weak regulatory frameworks that fail to deploy important security controls, leaving little motivation for manufacturers to care about security. The more devices that are connected, the greater the number of potential attack surfaces. Insecure communication protocols and weak authentication mechanisms, for instance, are readily breached, opening up attack opportunities for intruders to obtain unauthorized access to data and systems. Therefore, taking advantage of vulnerabilities in IoT devices not only requires technological innovations but also appropriate oversight from regulatory agencies to implement the use of standardized security procedures. Vulnerabilities in IoT devices are beyond software vulnerabilities and involve hardware vulnerabilities as well, especially in medical IoT devices. For example, firmware vulnerabilities in medical devices, such as insulin pumps and pacemakers, have great bearing on patient safety and data integrity. A qualitative IoT medical study sees the connection between vulnerabilities and factors such as device age, manufacturing practices, and compliance with regulation, indicating the need for proactive security on an immediate basis. With medical IoT devices now more deeply integrated into healthcare networks, prioritizing their security is crucial to protect patient data against breach. This scenario is a significant appeal for organizations to institute stronger security practices and also motivate manufacturers to develop advanced secure design concepts. Healthcare device security not only safeguards individuals' privacy but also improves overall resiliency of healthcare systems against cyber-attacks. The IoT security challenge landscape is constantly changing, with new technologies continuously altering the way vulnerabilities are being conceived and dealt with. Existing legislations and frameworks fall short to keep up with the fast-shifting rhythm of IoT technologies, and they generally have loopholes that can be exploited to their benefit by bad actors.

Security audits and manual testing are presently the primary approaches to IoT security; nevertheless, they are tremendously expensive and non-scalable, limiting their use on a larger scale. Current trends suggest that mandatory security certification and standardized testing can be a viable solution towards enhancing consumer IoT security. Proposals pending ensure to foster industry-standardization and support automated testing practices for testing device vulnerabilities in an enhanced manner. Bridging the existing gaps in security measures through collaboration between manufacturers, regulators, and researchers will play a vital role in developing a more secure IoT network (Figure 9.2).

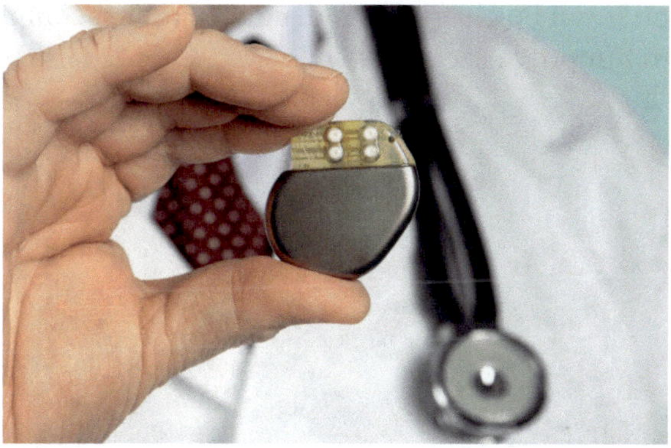

Figure 9.2. As medical IoT devices become increasingly integrated into healthcare systems, ensuring their security becomes paramount to protect sensitive patient information from breaches.

Source: https://relevant.software/wp-content/uploads/2023/11/NVxyeI-yeckypIfHFmW5aCNC59CDbtwfuWr5v5TjvBrYAAoDYR3k3v9BrKK-gzMNBf6qyMeooTqRGMbwB0lYvLd1ZU704mAq8yxfjwIxN1JLcEAC-qgamO-DuCm8G7K-Yp2mkjaiJmDGHrib__wuCvv3vE.png.

9.1.2. Risks Associated with Inadequate Security Measures

The risks of poor security controls in the Internet of Things (IoT) network are expanding into a priority factor with the rising visibility of interconnected devices. Homogeneous IoT applications—from homes to infrastructure—betray vulnerability points to cyberattacks that perpetrators exploit. A lack of standardized security controls is likely to return inadequate defenses that leave devices open to exploitation in the form of unauthorized access and data exfiltration. The high prevalence of occurrences accentuates the need for stringent security measures; failure to adhere to effective models can lead to compromised individual data and even life-threatening situations, especially in sectors like medicine. Managing these weaknesses entails an end-to-end strategy involving security as part of the design methodology of IoT devices with a view to proactive deployment rather than reactive healing of occurrences. In addition, the cost of poor security measures is high, affecting both organizations and consumers. When these breaches happen, impacted companies are not only faced with short-term recovery expenses, but compromised consumer confidence may be lost in the long term. Another dimension is regulatory compliance, as organizations can face substantial fines in case of deficiency in their obligation to provide security under different legal schemes. Through consideration of regulatory environments, like the NIST Cybersecurity Framework and the EU Cybersecurity Act, it can be clearly seen that more robust compliance programs would significantly improve security levels.

Figure 9.3. When breaches occur, affected companies face not only immediate recovery costs but also long-term reputational damage that can erode consumer trust.

Source: https://cdn.prod.website-files.com/634f8a681508d6180f9a2128/68779c6c8b2e0c9762bde47d_medium-shot-man-with-hoodie-holding-laptop.webp.

Those organizations that actively align procedures with industry standards not only reduce the risk of compromise but also put themselves ahead of the competition in a marketplace. This approach, in return, enables customers through standardized security behavior and trust, indicating the symbiotic existence of robust security measures and business resilience. Additionally, IoT device attacks have become more sophisticated, and this creates the need for new solutions with regard to related threats. Current security mechanisms are typically insufficient, particularly when it comes to handling particular low-power device challenges and heterogeneous network configurations. With recent research, the integration of new technologies like lightweight cryptography, machine learning-based anomaly detection, and blockchain can provide an end-to-end security framework with IoTs specific requirements. The hybrid approach not only improves data integrity but also augments anomaly detection, significantly reducing the points of attack. Continuous development in IoT security frameworks emphasizes the imperative for flexibility, as techniques continue to evolve in conjunction with threats that they attempt to counteract. Such creative methods not only increase security but also facilitate increased user trust in IoT devices, which is essential for the mass deployment and feasibility of such devices in this rapidly evolving technological landscape (Figure 9.3).

9.1.3. Impact of Security Breaches on Users and Organizations

With IoT expansion, the impact of security incidents on businesses and customers has increased. Security threats of IoT devices have the potential to create colossal financial losses and user distrust. For instance, a data breach can expose sensitive personal information, which may result in identity theft or impersonation. Customers are likely to experience emotional distress and inconveniences after such incidents. Organizations do bear the financial consequences, including the cost of restoration, fines by legal authorities, and potential fines from regulatory bodies. Furthermore, an offense can disrupt business operations, with the loss of reputation, which, in turn, impacts customer retention and loyalty over time. The so-called dangers coupled with insufficiency in security measures call for excellent IoT security standards that protect both users' information and organizational integrity as IoT technology seeps into daily life (Shao, 2025). The consequences of security breaches go beyond explicit monetary loss, so it is essential to have world-class IoT security frameworks. The majority of the users are not even conscious about threats against their devices, further exacerbating the problem. Studies indicate that poor awareness and non-standard updates might increase the risk of incidents (Shao, 2025). For businesses, it means a two-forked approach: they need to fortify their security system, as well as user education so that they have a greater understanding of potential threats. Awareness programs can train users in safe practices, such as regular firmware updating and utilization of secure authentication methods, hence creating a more secure ecosystem. Utilizing a proactive strategy that brings together technological abilities with user training, organizations can minimize the impact of security incidents and enhance overall system security. In IoT terms, adopting a Zero Trust Architecture (ZTA) would be vital to assisting in de-escalating security matters and limiting breach damage. ZTAs core precept of never trust, always verify forces companies to interrogate every user and device that seeks to access their networks. This rigorous verification mechanism enables enhanced security through minimized risks of unapproved access and enhanced overall networks integrity. Furthermore, ZTA facilitates constant monitoring and analytics to be able to respond in real-time to threats, reducing the vulnerability window. While there are challenges involved in migrating towards a Zero Trust model, such as integration with existing systems and employee training, its implementation can lead to improved compliance with regulatory requirements and a radical reduction in the likelihood of security breaches. Finally, the deployment of ZTA is a vital step towards protecting users and organizations in the new landscape of IoT security (Figure 9.4).

Figure 9.4. Within the realm of IoT, adopting a Zero Trust Architecture (ZTA) could be instrumental in alleviating security concerns and limiting the damage inflicted by breaches.

Source: https://media.licdn.com/dms/image/v2/D4D12AQEvdCN2XyeF1Q/article-cover_image-shrink_600_2000/article-cover_image-shrink_600_2000/0/1691660363589?e=2147483647&v=beta&t=ZBoLE2uL-pYkikagy5LLrXDT7Y4Ufv-rozQtVhzaJ0dA.

9.2. KEY IOT SECURITY STANDARDS

The growing complexity of the Internet of Things (IoT) ecosystem necessitates the implementation of comprehensive security measures that counter a multitude of threats. ISA/IEC 62443 and the NIST Cybersecurity Framework are two critical frameworks on which IoT network security stands based. The ISA/IEC 62443 series is particularly applicable to industrial settings, outlining an end-to-end strategy for security across an asset's lifecycle. It emphasizes prevention and resistance to cyber-attack, which is consistent with the threat posed by the rapidly evolving nature of IoT ecosystems. In contrast with this, the NIST Cybersecurity Framework has a more adaptable model which is able to be tailored in most industries with a focus on an expansive process of risk management. Hence, both standards contribute to an active security position responding to threats in advance while ensuring ongoing operational integrity in IoT environments. Moreover, with the increasing number of devices extending the IoT outward, more stringent data governance becomes an important part of effective security solutions. With the higher levels of interconnectivity of devices and data aggregation from various sources, developing policies and processes for managing data is crucial. Effective data governance models not only concentrate on data quality and confidentiality but also support compliance with different regulatory demands, especially since the data processed by IoT devices is sensitive in nature. Customized approaches, particularly in industries such as healthcare and finance, highlight the need for organizations to implement these governance models within security practices. This holistic approach not only mitigates risks from data breaches and unauthorized access, but also fosters trust in IoT systems, hence propelling larger adoption and innovation across industries (Chukwurah et al., 2024). Last but not least, emerging trends such as machine learning and artificial intelligence are poised to transform IoT security frameworks. The merging of such advanced technologies makes pre-emptive security measures capable of identifying abnormalities in real-time and tracking activities, so that they can make a critical contribution towards preventing cyberattacks. In addition, the integration of physical and cyber systems requires re-defining existing security standards to adapt to new threats. For instance, although standards like ISA/IEC 62443 provide the foundation, they need to catch up with technology advancement so that features such as AI-driven risk evaluation and self-healing can be incorporated. Additionally, with increasing IoT settings, new issues arise, which call for continuous development of security measures. Last but not least, it will be the solution to implementing dynamic and resilient IoT security standards that will render connected devices secure and reliable and will encourage innovation within a secure setting (Olaitan et al., 2025).

9.2.1. ISO/IEC 27001 and Its Relevance to IoT

Implementation of ISO/IEC 27001 within the Internet of Things (IoT) context becomes more vital as organizations employ IoT devices to collect and process vast quantities of data. The standard, which outlines a systematic approach to the management of sensitive information, provides a framework for designing, establishing, implementing, maintaining, and continually improving an information security management system (ISMS). By adhering to the guidelines defined in ISO/IEC 27001, organizations can be certain that the appropriate security controls are in place to mitigate risks associated with IoT networks and devices. With local authorities adopting Smart City initiatives founded on connected IoT systems, ISO/IEC 27001's necessity becomes increasingly important; it assists in safeguarding essential information and promoting public confidence in digital governance (Hossain et al., 2024). Furthermore, the application of ISO/IEC 27001 in an IoT environment also extends to handling specific cybersecurity challenges in Smart Cities. Since cities continue to get increasingly digitized, they are exposed to particular vulnerabilities that can lead to interruptions in essential services. Using ISO/IEC 27001 principles enables stakeholders to establish credible policies for those challenges, thereby making such critical infrastructure such as power systems, transport, and healthcare systems more resilient.

Figure 9.5. The integration of ISO/IEC 27001 within the Internet of Things (IoT) ecosystem is becoming increasingly paramount as organizations leverage IoT devices to collect and process vast amounts of data.

Source: https://coruzant.com/wp-content/uploads/2024/07/Internet-of-things.jpg.

The application of this standard not only enables tactical cyber defense but also establishes a culture of cybersecurity. Moreover, as highlighted during debates in African urban development on the use of Smart Cities, there is now more recognition of the importance of end-to-end cybersecurity models to mitigate risks arising from the interconnectivity of IoT systems (Ahmad et al., 2024). In conclusion, the link of ISO/IEC 27001 to IoT security is critical in ensuring the safety and sustainability of connected spaces. The anticipatory measures that are in the standard enhance ease of detection and handling of security threats, enabling organizations to secure data assets as well as user privacy. As the adoption of IoT increases within various industries, public services, education, and healthcare, the level of standard established by ISO/IEC 27001 becomes a precious resource. By stakeholder collaboration and best practice alignment against international standards, organizations are able to enhance their security position as well as assist in making the IoT ecosystem more robust and comprehensive. Lastly, ISO/IEC 27001 integration is an essential building block towards creating a secure and trusted IoT infrastructure (Figure 9.5).

9.2.2. NIST Cybersecurity Framework for IoT

The National Institute of Standards and Technology (NIST) Cybersecurity Framework for the Internet of Things (IoT) is a valuable handbook for organizations seeking to enhance their security in a hyper-complex digital landscape. With its frameworks that combine best practices, standards, and guidelines, the framework presents a systematic approach that enables IoT stakeholders—namely manufacturers, providers, and users—to assess and improve their cybersecurity position. Specifically, the model emphasizes identification, protection, detection, response, and recovery processes that are essential to managing IoT-related risks. Such a structured process allows organizations to navigate the unique challenges of connected devices, including increased susceptibility to cyberattacks and managing sensitive data. Its use not only aids compliance in organizations but also enhances the overall resilience of IoT ecosystems to potential attacks or breaches. The need for proper application of the NIST Cybersecurity Framework is brought into the limelight by growing reliance on IoT technologies across various sectors, ranging from healthcare to smart cities. The interconnection of IoT devices has a tendency to create the expanded attack surfaces, subjecting organizations to higher risks of cyber incidents, such as data breaches or illicit access to critical systems. Therefore, the emphasis of the framework on continuous monitoring and assessment becomes essential for organizations that want to ensure operational integrity. Finally, the application of a risk-driven methodology implies that organizations optimize their cybersecurity efforts in line with the type of threats they are facing. By being diligent in their risk assessment and alignment of these to appropriate security controls, organizations can balance innovation and security and have an environment in which IoT technologies can be used safely and for their benefit. Facilitating next-generation cybersecurity models, such as the Zero Trust method of the NIST Cybersecurity Framework, also helps to secure IoT deployments. Zero Trust frameworks encourage stringent access controls and verification measures, minimizing the presumption of inherent trust within network perimeters. This paradigm change is very vital, particularly in IoT environments where devices may regularly reside outside standard security perimeters. Through the use of micro-segmentation, encryption, and continuous authentication, as detailed in the framework, considerable progress can be made in mitigating threats from possible vulnerabilities (Syed et al., 2022). By deploying such advanced security techniques along with NIST guidelines, organizations can make their defenses more resistant to future cyber threats, thereby enabling secure deployment and management of IoT systems. Such a comprehensive cybersecurity approach not only promotes resiliency but also allows for long-term digital transformation initiatives within organizations (Saeed et al., 2023) (Figure 9.6).

Figure 9.6. The need for effective implementation of the NIST Cybersecurity Framework is underscored by the growing reliance on IoT technologies across various sectors, ranging from healthcare to smart cities.

Source: https://cdn.prod.website-files.com/651e8862627bb76b91f2a4e6/6752cdae17001e6cd9d43026_Hero%20Cybersecurity%20in%20IoT%20Ecosystems.jpg.

9.2.3. ETSI EN 303 645 and its Guidelines for Consumer IoT Security

The advent of the Internet of Things (IoT) revolutionized consumer technology to make common devices increasingly connected. With this increased connectivity, however, has come increased vulnerabilities that need robust security measures. In recognition of these needs, the European Telecommunications Standards Institute (ETSI) developed the EN 303 645 standard, which serves as the beginning point for improving consumer IoT security. This standard outlines minimum security requirements that must be met by manufacturers, such as using strong authentication mechanisms, secure software update, and data privacy. By introducing a shared baseline of security capabilities, ETSI EN 303 645 aims to promote consumer trust in IoT devices while mitigating threats from potential cyber-attacks. Furthermore, the emphasis placed by the standard on usability guarantees that security solutions at no point interrupt the user experience, integral to the mass deployment of IoT solutions. The ETSI EN 303 645's overall approach aims to accentuate its compatibility with broader cybersecurity frameworks, such as those outlined in the Cyber Resilience Act, a move integral to furthering proactive measures in European cyber defenses. By mandating all digital products to adhere to the standard, the regulation tries to improve the general consumer device security stance. ETSI EN 303 645 is not just a technical standard but also an integral component of a larger cyber resilience strategy. As described in relevant research, this system necessitates the coordination of European Standards Organizations (ESOs) to render standards up-to-date and effective against the evolving character of threats. The policy integration of standards not only increases the standards of industrial practice but also makes manufacturers accountable, representing a paradigm shift towards a security-conscious market. Also, the implementation of ETSI EN 303 645 is bound to influence global cybersecurity practices since European standards also serve as pilot schemes for the globe. By applying its guidelines, non-European producers can gain insight into the value of possessing firm security frameworks, thus facilitating the building of a global consensus of IoT safety. Adherence to global cybersecurity objectives enhances the robustness of safeguard measures aimed at repelling different threats. As practice and research keep advancing the frontiers of new solutions, the processes of partnership development encouraged by the Cyber Resilience Act will enable sharpening and defining standards like ETSI EN 303 645. These collaborative strategies indicate a return to first principles in designing cybersecurity, from reactive defense measures to an all-encompassing strategy with a maximum prevention and resilience against ever-evolving cyber threats, as emphasized in nearby literature (Abdullahi et al., 2025; Kamara, 2024).

9.3. FRAMEWORKS FOR IOT SECURITY IMPLEMENTATION

Successful frameworks for IoT security need to be employed in order to address the unique challenges presented by the growing amount of connected devices. As the devices become more widespread, they create extensive networks that organically increase the potential avenues for vulnerability. A successful security framework should include extensive policies and practices for protecting the data as well as protecting the devices. The emphasis on proactive threat management and risk assessment helps minimize risks of IoT, as there can be a deficiency of standardization that can lead to security measures being unevenly distributed among platforms and devices. It is crucial for organizations to pay attention to establishing a sequential process that promotes integration among cybersecurity professionals and device manufacturers, in the end ensuring security becomes an integral part of the device life cycle from design to deployment. Such efforts not only enhance the trust of the public in IoT technology use but also provide the foundation for long-term innovation within a more digital landscape. One of the main requirements in the deployment of IoT security is the application of well-acknowledged cybersecurity standards such as the ISO/IEC 27000 series. Implementation of such standards, in particular ISO/IEC 27001, provides organizations with a framework for creating an Information Security Management System (ISMS) that is effective in protecting confidential information against cyber-attacks. This formal approach allows organizations to identify and assess risks, design measures against such risks, and continuously observe their position of security.

Figure 9.7. A robust security framework must integrate comprehensive policies and practices designed to protect both the data and the devices.

Source: https://images.prismic.io/secureframe-com/7d4038fb-5bfa-4c7c-b5c1-852166a0e4ef_security-frameworks-illustration.png?auto=compress,format&rect=150,0,1285,608&w=1268&h=600.

Secondly, the incorporation of standards like ISO/IEC 27017 and ISO/IEC 27018, dealing with cloud services and protection of personally identifiable information, respectively, has the potential to secure IoT infrastructures. While organizations avail themselves of the benefits of IoT, syncing their security practices to adhere to these standards will maintain regulatory compliance while creating a security-conscious culture as well as being accountable at all levels of operation (Folorunso et al., 2024). In order to combat the multitude of difficulties in IoT security, frameworks should also encompass sound data governance measures. Data governance plays a significant role in ensuring high data quality, security, and compliance with privacy regulations. It is the responsibility of organizations to establish proper policies, processes, and metrics against data management and security practices. Having stakeholders involved at the implementation stage ensures that various perspectives are considered and thus more effective frameworks. Additionally, companies must be adaptable and adaptable to the rapidly evolving nature of threats. This means realizing new threats and reacting by modifying governance models, as appropriate, through the integration of next-generation technologies such as artificial intelligence and machine learning for enhanced security. Through striking a balance between compliance and new data governance strategies, organizations can utilize IoT to the fullest while safeguarding themselves against significant threats to their information assets (Chukwurah et al., 2024) (Figure 9.7).

9.3.1. The OWASP IoT Top Ten Project

OWASP IoT Top Ten Project is a landmark set of guidelines for the discovery and resolution of the most serious security vulnerabilities in Internet of Things (IoT) products and systems. By sorting out these weaknesses, OWASP is providing a structured approach for developers, engineers, and organizations to efficiently prioritize security initiatives. The project emphasizes the importance of inculcation of security throughout the product's life cycle, from design conception to deployment and upkeep. After understanding the rapid pace of technological advancement in IoT and the consequent security threat, the OWASP IoT Top Ten Project is a valuable resource that assists stakeholders in mitigating risk and improving their security stance. The project also determines a number of shared vulnerabilities, including insecure network services, inadequate authentication, and exposure of sensitive data. These vulnerabilities point to the multi-dimensional interdependencies in IoT systems because they are likely to consist of interlinked devices that communicate over different channels. Detection of such threats is important in developing secure security architectures. For instance, cross-program propagation of infected data can lead to catastrophic security vulnerabilities if proper measures are lacking. It is ranking very high in the OWASP IoT Top Ten, underlining the requirement for deep examination that considers not only the security of an individual device but also the interaction of devices in an IoT setup (Mandal et al., 2020). Thus, vulnerabilities are discovered before their potential for exploitation. In addressing these vulnerabilities, organizations can leverage the OWASP IoT Top Ten as a central part of their overall IoT security initiative. The initiative aims to facilitate an integrated understanding of system architectures, including incorporating security factors at every level of the design and deployment process. Developing an end-to-end architecture that incorporates data standards is essential to achieving this vision. As highlighted in pro-research in intelligent frameworks, effective management practices must be supported with technical architectures to develop an IoT system that is resilient to possible threats (Wang, 2022). Through the embrace of such a comprehensive security approach, organizations are able to secure their IoT deployments against the ever-changing landscape of cyber threats and enjoy the fullest benefits of IoT technologies.

9.3.2. The Industrial Internet Consortium (IIC) Security Framework

The IIC Security Framework is central to the larger IoT security standards debate, providing a structured approach to respond to the unique challenge presented by the convergence of industrial systems with Internet technology. This framework reacts to a level of security challenges tailored to the Industrial Internet of Things (IIoT), calling for rigorous control because of the interdependence and sensitivity of environments built on interdependent devices. By implementing measures in secure communications, access control, and risk management, the IIC Security Framework encourages industries to place cybersecurity as the ultimate priority as an integral part of infrastructure. Furthermore, it emphasizes resilience requirements so that vital systems can continue to operate effectively even in the case of likely security attacks. One of the benefits of the IIC Security Framework is that it emphasizes integrating security into all layers of an IIoT architecture. It encourages a comprehensive approach including device and network security, data integrity, and even managing vulnerabilities in software. This comprehensive strategy is particularly valuable when IIoT environments are increasingly complex with multiple stakeholders and technologies. The framework provides directions for the deployment of security mechanisms that incorporate machine-learning techniques, as evident from recent research applying these methodologies for network traffic analysis and intrusion detection in IIoT contexts. Through its definition of specific methodologies like k-nearest neighbors and random forest algorithms for threat identification, the IIC Security Framework not only educates industries but also enriches the broader conversation around effective cybersecurity action in evolving digital spaces. Perhaps most importantly, the IIC Security Framework not only establishes best practices, but it is a call to action regarding regulatory alignment and compliance within the evolving IoT landscape. With diverse standards across jurisdictions, the framework mandates harmonized policy that holds manufacturers accountable, thus reaffirming the need for a harmonized approach to cybersecurity. Empirical evidence places on the fore that jurisdictions that have stringent regulations have fewer breaches in security, thereby reiterating the framework's mandate for policy establishment. The role of education among consumers in ensuring cybersecurity cannot be exaggerated; educated users serve the vital role of checking vulnerability that is inherent in IIoT deployments. Therefore, IIC Security Framework comes forth as an inclusive tool which not only addresses technological problems of security but also highlights the socio-political factors necessary for long-term stability and trust in IoT (Zhukabayeva et al., 2025; Bonsu et al., 2025) (Figure 9.8).

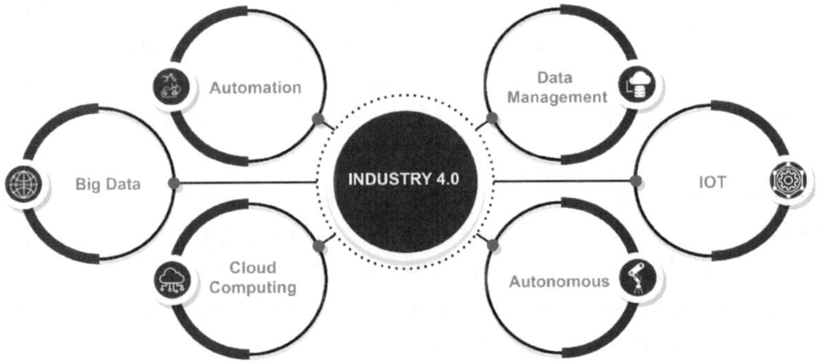

Figure 9.8. The industrial internet consortium (IIC) security framework is a pivotal element within the larger discourse on IoT security standards, providing a structured approach to mitigate the unique challenges posed by the convergence of industrial systems and Internet technology.

Source: https://www.mdpi.com/sensors/sensors-23-07470/article_deploy/html/images/sensors-23-07470-g001.png.

9.3.3 The Cloud Security Alliance (CSA) IoT Security Framework

The Cloud Security Alliance (CSA) IoT Security Framework is a valuable effort to address the unique security requirements of the Internet of Things (IoT) ecosystem. With the increased deployment of IoT devices, so does the complicating element of securing these devices within an environment of diverse threats. The standard serves as a top-down guide for organizations interested in safeguarding their IoT deployments by promoting safe design practices and operation. By providing one language and a defined approach, the CSA framework facilitates collaboration and communication among stakeholders, including developers, makers, and end-users, all of whom have an interest in IoT system reliability and safety. In order to implement the CSA IoT Security Framework, organizations must begin by familiarizing themselves with its central building blocks, namely security controls, best practices, and compliance requirements. All of them are designed to assist in providing a roadmap to identifying vulnerabilities and mitigating the threats of IoT devices.

For instance, the framework emphasizes the importance of security throughout the entire device life cycle, from design to deployment and through continuous management. That is also in alignment with broader regulatory thinking on, say, GDPR compliance, which demands stringent controls on privacy and security, such as the embedding of security within cloud system service-level agreements (SLAs) (Dominiak et al., 2019). The CSA IoT Security Framework similarly recognizes the utility of incessant flexibility to offset the ever-evolving nature of cyber threats. With emerging technologies and new threats being discovered, organizations must be watchful at all times in strengthening their security posture. Adoption of new technologies itself is not sufficient but also ongoing training and awareness programs among the employees tasked with implementing security control measures. Hence, the framework supports a holistic cyber defense strategy that entails technological advancements, employee awareness, and sound risk management practices (Anglano et al., 2018). Through this multi-faceted approach, the CSA aims to establish a more robust IoT ecosystem capable of resisting the sophistication of today's cyber-security threats (Figure 9.9).

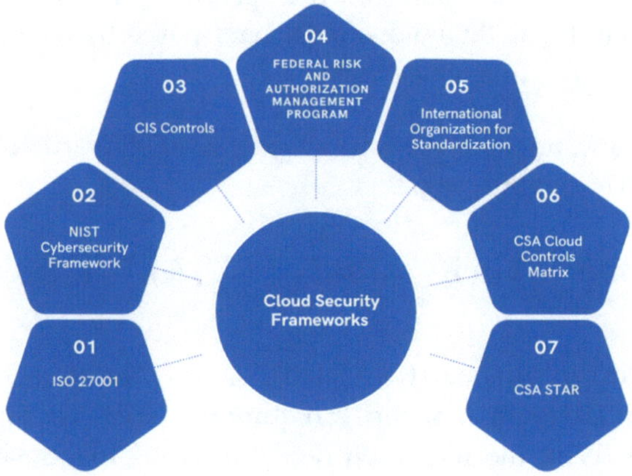

Figure 9.9. Cloud security alliance (CSA) IoT security framework.

Source: https://www.wattlecorp.com/wp-content/uploads/2024/08/Cloud-Security-Frameworks-.webp.

9.4. REGULATORY AND COMPLIANCE CONSIDERATIONS

The conjunction of compliance and regulatory elements with the Internet of Things (IoT) security landscape is crucial to the preservation of the integrity and reliability of connected devices. As IoT technologies spread across the globe, regulatory bodies around the world are actively developing frameworks that govern the use of their applications. The proposed frameworks are designed to minimize threats of data breaches and unauthorized access, addressing the specific vulnerabilities associated with IoT devices. Particularly, legislation such as the EU Cybersecurity Act provides a structurally sound framework that demands compliance from producers and service providers. However, there is the challenge of the regulatory environment being fragmented and immensely varied per region, making compliance a challenge for international actors. Effective harmonization of these regulations is necessary to make compliance processes rational and ensure robust security procedures are enforced across all IoT environments, thus facilitating increased consumer trust in such technologies.

A vital aspect of this compliance is the positive engagement of industry players in the development of legislation and standards governing IoT security. Collaborative efforts between government ministries, private enterprises, and institutions of education contribute to making more effective holistic approaches to confronting emerging threats. Collaborative efforts are categorically imperative in developing relevant guidelines and best practices that remain sensitive to the rapidly evolving technology landscape. Compulsory frameworks can be particularly beneficial as they instill a culture of ongoing development and innovation. For instance, the NIST Cybersecurity Framework encourages firms to assess their posture for security and implement consistent best practices, fueling active compliance. However, in the absence of enforceable requirements, voluntary standards may lead to uneven adoption across the industry, diluting the collective effectiveness of IoT security strategy as reported in studies that analyze the impact of regulatory consistency on breach incidents (Bonsu et al., 2025). Besides, consumer awareness is also an important aspect of the success of compliance initiatives in IoT security. While regulatory frameworks set the foundation for minimum security requirements, informed consumers play a great role in making the attempt successful by enabling a more security-conscious market place. Efforts that create awareness about device security—such as secure setup processes, patching, and knowledge of data privacy importance—play an important role. In service of this objective, education must align with compliance efforts so that consumers understand their place in the IoT ecosystem. Moreover, adding Privacy Enhancing Technologies into compliance efforts can help counter the user privacy and security demands. This integration is important in addressing the legal challenges brought by legislations such as the GDPR, which underscores the importance of an integrated strategy for IoT security standards that deals with regulation elements (Llamas et al., 2025).

9.4.1. GDPR and its Implications for IoT Security

The General Data Protection Regulation (GDPR) is a foundation for the enhancement of data protection and privacy across the European Union, with significant effects on the Internet of Things (IoT) ecosystem. IoT devices often handle immense amounts of personal information in real-time, raising concerns over user privacy and data security. The GDPR demands that strong consent management is put in place and expects organizations to ask for transparency in data practice. This rulebook compels IoT developers and manufacturers to incorporate privacy and security functionality into device design itself, an approach called privacy by design. This type of approach not only safeguards personal data but also reduces risks associated with data breaches, considering that noncompliance with GDPR is punishable with hefty financial sanctions. Therefore, GDPR compliance not only increases consumer confidence but is also essential to form a secure IoT ecosystem, highlighting the need for end-to-end security architectures in this space. In case of IoT, GDPR presents unique challenges, particularly with the amount and diversity of information collected by intelligent products. Most IoT applications execute in real-time and generate a constant stream of personal data, making it challenging to comply with GDPR requirements. The requirement for data minimization and limitation of purpose, for instance, necessitates a lot of consideration through the process of gathering data. The requirement for right to erasure and portability of data by the regulation also creates technical challenges for IoT devices, whose nature makes them lack an option to erase or port data with ease. To fight these difficulties, standards such as ISO/IEC 27001 can contribute considerably to establishing processes and controls that are compliant with GDPR requirements. By applying rigorous security controls and following data governance principles, IoT manufacturers can effectively deal with these regulatory barriers, ultimately fostering stronger security and privacy outcomes for customers. In addition, the relationship between GDPR and IoT security emphasizes the need for ongoing testing and enhancement of security controls. The proliferation of IoT devices at an exponential rate increases the potential attack surface against cyber-attacks, which necessitates proactive security. GDPR not only states regulatory demands but also nudges organizations to undertake extensive security practices, such as encryption, secure coding, and ongoing threat monitoring. The amalgamation of standards' guidelines such as ISO/IEC 27002 and other pertinent ISO standards can enable IoT stakeholders to build strong security stances. With the ever-changing nature of cyber threats, it is possible to respond to these threats with a nimble approach to adjusting security protocols, thereby maintaining GDPR compliance while safeguarding user information from unauthorized use and breaches. Together, a synergistic approach that combines GDPR directives and experienced security paradigms will be paramount to protecting the growing IoT infrastructure, facilitating trust between users as well as stakeholders.

9.4.2. HIPAA Requirements for IoT in Healthcare

The integration of Internet of Things (IoT) technology in the healthcare industry has the promise to revolutionize it but also raises real issues regarding the protection of sensitive patient information. The Health Insurance Portability and Accountability Act (HIPAA) prescribe stringent privacy and security measures that health care organizations must navigate while implementing IoT devices. HIPAA mandates that any electronic transmission of Protected Health Information (PHI) be accomplished with adequate safeguards to ensure confidentiality, integrity, and availability. In the age of pervasive connected medical devices, adherence to these regulations is crucial in order to lower the risk of data breaches and unauthorized access. Non-adherence not only jeopardizes patient confidence, but also places organizations at serious financial risk and liable to legal action. Thus, an understanding of HIPAA requirements is imperative for healthcare professionals to leverage the benefits of IoT without losing sight of robust data protection. In addition, the unique aspects of IoT devices make it more difficult to comply with HIPAA regulations. The majority of IoT devices collect and transmit patient data in real-time, often without healthcare professionals' monitoring. This ease of data collection can also inadvertently lead to HIPAA regulation breaches if proper measures are not adopted. For instance, the healthcare organizations must implement access controls, encryption techniques, and regular security checks to protect the data coming from such devices. In addition, there is a pressing need for organizations to ensure that IoT device manufacturers are themselves HIPAA compliant so that vulnerabilities are not created within the overall healthcare system. Sharing sensitive information through connected devices is one reason all-encompassing security infrastructures that can effectively respond to the evolving healthcare technology environment are critical (Paul et al., 2023). In a bid to introduce IoT securely into health care organizations, new technologies provide innovative approaches to HIPAA compliance. One of these is the application of privacy-enhancing techniques such as Federated Learning that will provide artificial intelligence-based applications without compromising patient data confidentiality. These novel approaches allow data to remain on local devices without compromising participation in larger algorithm training, minimizing the privacy threat of data centralization. As cited in the literature, developing such new forms of data sharing under the era of AI is required both for the protection of patients' privacy and for the promotion of the diffusion of AI-based healthcare applications. The necessity of a balanced approach based on harmony between technological development and compliance requirements is central to the effective integration of IoT into healthcare settings (Khalid et al., 2023). Thus, organizations must remain vigilant about evolving HIPAA regulations yet remain receptive to advancements in technology (Figure 9.10).

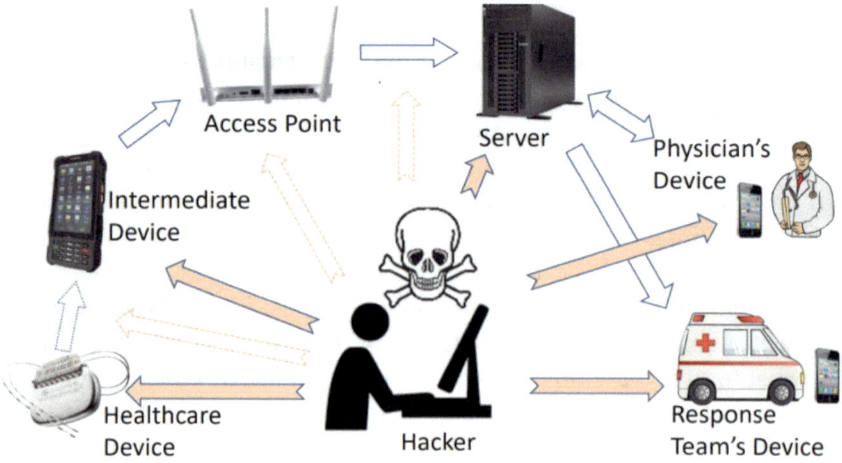

Figure 9.10. The health insurance portability and accountability act (HIPAA) establishes stringent privacy and security requirements that healthcare organizations must navigate as they implement IoT devices.

Source: https://www.mdpi.com/applsci/applsci-12-01927/article_deploy/html/images/applsci-12-01927-g006.png.

9.4.3. Emerging Regulations and their Impact on IoT Security

The arrival of regulatory models within the era of Internet of Things (IoT) security is an evolutionary achievement in the safeguarding of devices and systems that now characterize modern living. As the proliferation of IoT devices goes unchecked, so does the need for efficient security measures to silence the many vulnerabilities attached to interconnected technology. Recent research shows a link between sound regulatory policy and decreased cyber incidents, with integral, enforceable rules having the potential to dramatically decrease the threats of IoT insecure practices. Yet the very disparate nature of current rules habitually results in loopholes that manufacturers and consumers have to navigate, causing uneven security postures throughout the sector. The regulatory framework must change, accordingly, to provide more explicit direction that covers best practices and assigns accountability to stakeholders, ultimately fostering a safer IoT landscape that protects users and their information from increasing threats (Bonsu et al., 2025). Additionally, as regulations must be formulated, ensuring that they are implemented in a realistic fashion that is IoT-friendly is likewise essential. Current compliance measures have a tendency to overlook the inherent heterogeneity of IoT devices, ranging from household appliances to complex industrial automation systems.

Figure 9.11. Emerging regulations must thus be tailored to address specific vulnerabilities tied to different types of devices and their respective environments.

Source: https://orca.security/wp-content/uploads/2024/06/Vulnerability-Management-Blog-Hero-1980x1176-1.png.

It is not possible to implement homogenous security standards because measures that are effective in one domain will not be effective in another. New regulations need to be device-specific to address specific vulnerabilities related to different kinds of devices and their relevant environments. Effective audit processes can play a big role in doing so; still, much of the existing frameworks cannot keep pace with the rapid development and availability of IoT products. The need is thus initiated for adaptive and agile regulatory approaches with the demand for continued monitoring, danger analysis, and a feeling of capability to act quickly on surfacing security risks as they emerge (Dar et al., 2024). In addition to enhancing regulatory transparency and tailored implementation, future regulations must also accord maximum priority to consumer education and awareness. As one of the primary shortcomings of IoT security, most end-users lack the basic information necessary for identifying potential threats or utilizing available security features effectively. With increasing regulations, they have to incorporate mandatory guidelines that promote customer awareness of IoT threats and safety measures so customers can make responsible choices towards device security. Furthermore, implementation of certification schemes with the support of regulatory bodies can incentivize manufacturers to adopt better security practices while designing products, all for the good of the customer. With emphasis put on education alongside regulatory frameworks, an educated public can help the overall security position of IoT ecosystems. This multi-faceted approach will not only address risks associated with IoT technologies but also foster a security-conscious culture that is important in the increasingly expanding, interconnected world (Bonsu et al., 2025) (Figure 9.11).

9.5. BEST PRACTICES FOR IOT SECURITY

In today's globalized era, security best practices for IoT are essential to ensuring device integrity and data confidentiality. A best practice is the implementation of strong authentication methods as a basis of security programs. Requiring strong, multi-factor authentication programs reduces threats due to unauthorized access significantly. Some of the practices involve the use of biometrics, smart cards, and one-of-a-kind device identifiers. Moreover, periodic updates and patching of IoT devices are a requirement, as the vulnerabilities will be used in the long term. Ignoring this can result in security breaches that impact not only individual devices but also the entire network that these devices are part of. Thus, having a regular maintenance plan for updates is elementary to maintaining an effective security posture across IoT environments. Network segmentation is another important component of IoT security best practices. By isolating IoT devices from core business networks, organizations are able to compartmentalize likely breaches, thus minimizing the attack surface. This procedure confines the scope of any security incidents, so that if one device gets breached, it does not provide access to attackers in more sensitive portions of the network. Also, intrusion detection systems and firewalls can assist further, monitoring network traffic in real time and notifying admins of possible issues. As the industry literature has emphasized, the synergistic combination of segmentation and vigilant monitoring can create a strong security framework responsive to the ongoing evolution of cyber threats in the IoT context, as it has been outlined in new standards such as ISA/IEC 62443 (Olaitan et al., 2025) and others. Lastly, encouraging security culture within organizations is the solution for bolstering IoT security practices. Standard training programs that acclimatize workers to potential attacks and optimum methods enable them to act as the initial line of defense when attacked. In addition to enhancing personal vigilance, this practice ensures collective action towards security measures, particularly in an environment where there are numerous stakeholders who operate in conjunction with IoT systems. Secondly, compliance with data governance standards, as described in protocols for addressing the intersection of data security and privacy, maintains data integrity. Considering the compliance issues of the organization while embracing new technologies is critical while developing a robust security strategy that responds to the complexities introduced by IoT environments (Chukwurah et al., 2024). This whole-of-defense approach is critical to protecting critical assets in an increasingly digitalized world.

9.5.1. Device Authentication and Access Control

In the accelerating world of the Internet of Things (IoT), authentication of devices and access control have become the principal aspects of security mechanisms. With a rise in the number of devices connected to the network, there is a need for only authenticated devices to be allowed on the network and exchange data. The problem is compounded by the limited processing capacity and memory of most IoT devices, rendering the use of traditional cryptographic procedures difficult. Therefore, innovative solutions with heightened security without overloading the devices are the pressing need of the hour. Incorporating decentralized technologies like Blockchain can make device authentication more secure. Models like these enhance security by eliminating single points of failure and leveraging complex cryptographical algorithms, which make the overall network more resilient against unauthorized access and data breaches (Khan et al., 2024). Access control systems play an important role in the management of privileges and regulation of interactions between various IoT devices on a network. A proper access control method should ensure that devices only get the resources to which they are intended, thereby ensuring confidentiality and integrity of sensitive data. Zero-knowledge and identity-based schemes combined provide a solution that is both efficient and effective where devices can authenticate themselves without pre-shared keys or instance-specific information. This new method not only simplifies the authentication procedure but also ensures that it is more secure by limiting the possibility of man-in-the-middle attacks. Seamless coordination between access control and authentication procedures within a unified framework is crucial in handling distinct security requirements of IoT applications, eventually resulting in more secure and interoperable IoT landscapes (Simsek, 2024). Incorporating strong authentication and access controls not only guarantees that IoT networks are secured against future attacks but also facilitates it to become easier to develop scalable and efficient systems. These actions are imperative because they reconcile the demands of robust security with the functional constraints of IoT devices. Architectures that incorporate smart contracts and adhere to established cryptographic standards allow users to define strict access controls and provide an open audit history of device communication. Additionally, these architectures significantly enhance supply chain transparency, an issue of increasing concern in industries that deploy IoT technology. By using technologies like Blockchain, IoT systems can make authentication and access controls agile and scalable, effective in safeguarding sensitive information while adaptable to the diversity of functionalities required by various applications (Khan et al., 2024; Simsek, 2024) (Figure 9.12).

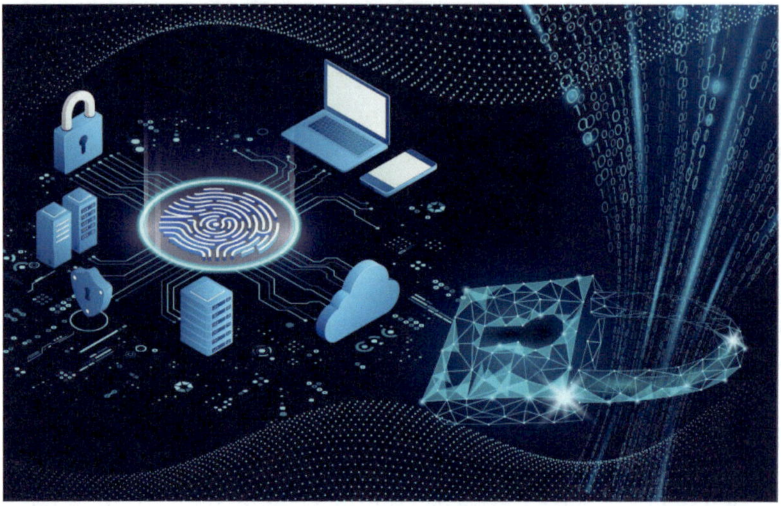

Figure 9.12. As the number of interconnected devices grows, ensuring that only authorized devices can access the network and exchange data is paramount.

Source: https://kotaielectronics.com/wp-content/uploads/2023/11/IoT-Security-Threats-and-Solutions-Blog-Fetaured-Image.jpg.

9.5.2. Regular Software Updates and Patch Management

In light of the dynamic pace of the Internet of Things (IoT) ecosystem, periodic software updates and patching have emerged as essential elements in the maintenance of robust security systems. These are needed to protect IoT devices that are regularly deployed within ecosystems that are not monitored by multiple cyber threats that are able to exploit vulnerabilities present in outdated software. Periodic updating gives such vulnerabilities, making devices secure against imminent threats. Because all the major IoT applications, such as precision agriculture, rely so much on advanced technologies to function optimally, the absence of current maintenance could lead to catastrophic failure not only in production but also in safeguarding sensitive data. Therefore, the inclusion of systematic updating mechanisms within IoT standards is critical in enhancing overall device resilience and operational integrity, thereby promoting customer confidence in such technologies (Karunathilake et al., 2023). Patch management is equally critical in the mitigation of identified vulnerabilities that would otherwise compromise the IoT ecosystem. Through systematically recording discovered security weaknesses and applying patches, organizations are able to thwart the danger posed by cyber adversities that will seek to exploit the weaknesses. As crucial as it is to maintain firmware and software updates, effective patch management also requires solid strategies for testing update releases before deployment. This practice is most vital in advanced IoT frameworks, where functionality and compatibility must be considered to avoid disrupting network functionality. Cybersecurity as a field heavily impacts these patch management policies, with researchers in the field emphasizing that there is an urgent need for complete understanding of risk management directed towards the IoT environment context. As such, imposing rigid patch management protocols becomes the final strategy to make IoT systems resilient against evolving threats (Tariq et al., 2023). Besides, the successful implementation of regular software updates and patch management necessitates a coordinated effort from various stakeholders including manufacturers, developers, and users. Tight collaboration is needed in the execution of overarching security policies that not only decide update frequencies but also define roles in monitoring and managing vulnerabilities. For instance, they must commit to providing ongoing support for the devices throughout their lifecycle, while consumers must take care to install available updates. Ignoring these shared duties can lead to global security flaws that permit unauthorized access and leakage of data. Finally, establishing a culture of proactive management of software maintenance and security patches is a part of establishing effective IoT security standards and frameworks, which operate to secure individual users and the overall ecosystem (Karunathilake et al., 2023).

9.5.3. Data Encryption and Secure Communication Protocols

The demand for robust data encryption and secure communication protocols is never lower than a top priority as the Internet of Things (IoT) extends its claws to various industries. Data encryption is still the first line of defense, mapping readable data into encrypted data which can only be decrypted by the desired receivers. In the IoT system where numerous devices communicate with each other through networks, the application of encryption techniques such as Advanced Encryption Standard (AES) ensures that sensitive information is protected from unauthorized access. Encryption ensures data integrity by making it extremely challenging for malicious parties to alter information being transferred between devices. The use of security protocols such as Transport Layer Security (TLS) also enhances the security system with an extra secure channel over the untrusted networks that are usually present in IoT environments. The union of these technologies thus poses a challenge to existing loopholes and offers a vital defense mechanism within IoT security protocols. In the specific scenario of smart grids, increasingly connected via IoT, secure communication protocols have a central position in assuring operational integrity. Real-time data sharing and monitoring through smart grids allow for efficiencies in energy management; however, such systems are the perfect targets for cyber-attacks due to the high connectivity of the same. Secure communication involves encrypting information that is passed between IoT devices, e.g., smart meters and grid management systems. Several encryption options, including lightweight cryptography that finds a middle ground between security and performance, are on the table.

Figure 9.13. Advanced encryption standard (AES) ensures that sensitive information remains safeguarded against unauthorized access.

Source: https://www.paubox.com/hubfs/What%20is%20the%20Advanced%20Encryption%20Standard%20%28AES%29.jpg.

In addition to encryption, authentication processes ensure that devices passing information in the network are authenticated to protect against unauthorized access. Multidimensionality of issues stems from the requirement to maintain system efficiency while implementing stringent security protocols; however, safe protocols are an integral part of energy infrastructures that must be smartness-resilient for future technology (Enemosah et al., 2024). Secure communication protocol development and implementation must address vulnerabilities in existing IoT ecosystems as well. Protocols used in traditional networks may not be sufficient due to the unique constraints and operational requirements of IoT devices, which are likely to have limited processing power and battery life. This has led to interest in lightweight security protocols with high levels of performance but also high protection against typical attacks such as man-in-the-middle and denial-of-service attacks. By analyzing various protocols available, researchers attempt to deploy maximum security solutions that deflect such threats without disrupting the functionality of IoT devices. Moreover, researching innovative protocols that provide regular updates and self-healing functionality can enhance resilience against evolving cyber fronts. A review of such safe communication protocols brings to the foreground the importance of continuous IoT security protocol updating to counter new threats effectively without reducing operational efficiency (Soni et al., 2024) (Figure 9.13).

9.6. CONCLUSION

In thinking about the multifaceted landscape of IoT security, the necessity for setting sound standards and frameworks cannot be more forcefully underscored. As more IoT devices find their way into networks, so too do the risks involved in deploying them. By adhering to standardized security protocols, stakeholders can rid themselves of threats and strengthen the resilience of these networked systems. Effective frameworks not only underlie technical solutions but also a principle of guidance in accordance with industry best practices. Integrating advanced methodologies such as the Fermatean-FDOSM framework makes it possible for security countermeasures to be ordered against widespread attacks like Denial-of-Service attacks to ensure that there is a systematic approach to securing IoT infrastructures. The results indicate that the criteria weighting is essential explicitly as it informs decision-making procedures that aim to address specific vulnerabilities within various IoT environments, thereby strengthening worldwide security (Al-Hchaimi et al., 2022). In addition, the research on Digital Twin technologies reveals the integration of IoT technological trends and disruption of industrial paradigms. Specifically, the Digital Twin provides a bridge to real-world data synchronization among physical objects and their virtual twins. This integration produces an environment whereby security solutions are experimented and optimized in simulation environments before actual implementation in real-world applications. The comprehensive review of current research on Digital Twins is the epitome of their potential for revolution across industries, including manufacturing and smart cities. These technologies can generate insights that shape the creation of security frameworks tailored to IoT environments from experiences gleaned from successful operation and pitfalls (Fuller et al., 2020). This means there is an inevitable need for ongoing evolution of these frameworks to keep pace with the rapid rate of technological advancement as well as the evolving threat environment. Finally, it is essential to develop effective IoT security standards and frameworks in order to safeguard the integrity of connected systems in today's digital era. As seen, a multi-faceted solution—the convergence of advanced methods like the Fermata-FDOSM for security evaluation and the groundbreaking power of Digital Twin technologies—is an integrative way to address the different challenges facing IoT security. By placing these methods within the context of existing research and best practice, organizations can proactively approach threats and have a secure and resilient IoT environment. The necessity for continuous improvement and development of these frameworks will ultimately dictate the success with which the future of IoT can be navigated, comforting stakeholders in their investment in a securely connected world (Al-Hchaimi et al., 2022; Fuller et al., 2020).

9.6.1. Summary of Important Points Discussed

The issue of IoT security frameworks and standards has evolved quite significantly in recent years, with the increased complexity and vulnerability of connected devices. Key arguments made include the necessity for universal security measures capable of addressing the unique challenges of the Internet of Things. As devices multiply, they generate enormous amounts of sensitive data, and it becomes imperative to comprehend and implement stringent security measures. Standardization of security protocols not only enhances protection against threats at the development stage but also encourages credibility amongst users and stakeholders. Enhanced frameworks assist in unifying fragmented systems and facilitating more effective management of security threats across diverse environments. In the end, robust IoT security standards are essential for safeguarding user data and maintaining the integrity of connected ecosystems. Secondly, the integration of advanced technologies, such as Artificial Intelligence (AI) and Machine Learning (ML), into IoT security solutions has been among the prominent themes in the discussion. Both of these technologies offer new tools for network behavior analysis, anomaly detection, and automatic response to potential threats. Based on data analysis, systems are able to learn and adapt to emerging vulnerabilities, thereby creating a more dynamic security environment. Evaluations of existing protocols reflect a need for continuous updating, namely due to the ever-growing pace of technological advancements. Moreover, the suggested use of integrated sensing and communications (ISAC) in IoT security systems promises potential to enhance data-transmission security and reliability. This intersection has the double benefit of enhancing communications while concurrently enhancing sensing capabilities, projecting a better future of IoT networks (Liu et al., 2022). Finally, the legislative framework of IoT security is equally relevant to current discourse. The policymakers are becoming more aware of regulatory environments imposing compliance with instituted security standards. The standoff is finding a balance between innovation and responsibility so that the implementation of security controls does not undermine technological progress. To this end, various nations are instituting policies whose aim is to provide best practices in IoT security management while also safeguarding user privacy simultaneously. The examination of such regulatory blueprints emphasizes the need for multi-stakeholder engagements where industry, academia, and government have to work together to develop shared standards. Such a collaborative approach is essential in light of the complexity of IoT security and the requirement that defenses need to be effective in evolving environments (Dwivedi et al., 2022).

9.6.2. The Necessity of Adopting Security Standards and Frameworks

In a world of hurricane-speed technological transformation, the call to adopt security standards and frameworks for the Internet of Things (IoT) has never been greater. As products communicate with one another, they create ever more advanced networks exposed to a multitude of security threats. The expansion of IoT across multiple industries from healthcare to transport to smart cities raises the stakes on these risks. With non-standardized security practices, each device is an independent unit and hence more susceptible to cyber-attacks that can compromise confidential data or services. Having detailed security architectures in place is important in the case of avoiding this risk, as it ensures connectivity of devices without sacrificing security. Furthermore, the embracement of security standards facilitates accountability and trust cultures among the stakeholders of the IoT ecosystem. Not only does it allow manufacturers to adhere to best practices of security in the phases of design and development but also provides consumers with confidence in the integrity of the devices employed. By encouraging compliance with established standards, organizations are able to effectively prevent risks of data breaches or exploitation. This is particularly important because the majority of IoT devices operate in an environment that is sensitive by nature, i.e., hospitals or homes, where abuse can lead to extremely severe implications. Adhering to security standards ensures everyone involved—developers, users, and regulators—has a shared understanding and consensus on maintaining robust security controls throughout. In addition, the use of security standards is not only about protecting against threats now, but also about pre-emptive protection of technology against future threats. Technology advances very fast, and the development of matching security solutions is usually slower, so there are usually gaps to be filled by malicious actors, who are keen to use them. Adaptive and constantly evolving frameworks allow organizations to react to new exposures in advance. In today's environment, where privacy, trust, and ethics are at the top of everyone's agenda, the IoT must be designed with security as a foundational concern. As cities and businesses increasingly embark on digital transformation, awareness of and the application of IoT security best practices and standards will be critical in safeguarding society from the adverse consequences of a world linked together, such as those of the impact noted in Dwivedi et al. (2022) and Moreno et al. (2021).

9.6.3. Call to Action for Stakeholders in the IoT Ecosystem

The burgeoning world of the Internet of Things (IoT) necessitates an immediate call to action for its players. With the burgeoning rate of devices and the accelerating increase in interconnectivity, the security and data privacy stakes increase exponentially as well. It is essential for manufacturers, developers, and lawmakers to make it a priority to have improved IoT security standards and frameworks. It is essential that these stakeholders unite to develop integrated standards that not only address current weaknesses but also anticipate potential threats in the future. This cooperative approach will foster trust among consumers, leading to extensive implementation of IoT technologies. This type of forward-looking engagement is essential in developing a secure space that enables innovation while upholding user privacy and data integrity, thereby averting potential cybersecurity meltdowns that might bring down the entire ecosystem. Members of the IoT community are encouraged to share best practices and expertise to create a shared environment that supports security measures between devices and applications. This involves bringing together learnings across various industries, like those derived from the experiences of such industries as manufacturing, where IoT applications have transformed the efficacies of operations, as showcased in the broader environment of Industrie 4.0. By adhering to a shared framework, stakeholders can tackle shared security challenges, make compliance processes easier, and support interoperability between devices. In addition, bringing in broader perspectives from specialists who understand the implications of emerging technologies will make the debate more robust, promoting an integrated approach towards secure IoT models. Finally, having mechanisms for continuous feedback and revision of these standards is needed to ensure that they are up to date considering the rapidly evolving technology landscapes. The evolving speed of the IoT also presents stakeholders with an opportunity to embrace the latest technologies like edge computing and artificial intelligence, which possess the potential to completely secure security implementations. As technologies like these begin to become integrated at large, their ability to foster resilient IoT environments cannot be underestimated. For instance, leveraging advancements in Industrie 4.0, the stakeholders can design versatile frameworks that not only mitigate the threats but also foster flexible infrastructure committed to the special needs of industries like healthcare and intelligent cities. With a single methodology that integrates core security standards and innovative advancements, stakeholders can develop a highly robust IoT ecosystem that is not only secure but also set for sustainable development. This dual-pronged strategy will ultimately result in increased public trust and easy integration of IoT solutions into daily life, paving the way for a more connected and secure future.

REFERENCES

1. Abdullahi, S. M., & Lazarova-Molnar, S. (2025). On the adoption and deployment of secure and privacy-preserving IIoT in smart manufacturing: A comprehensive guide with recent advances. *International Journal of Information Security, 24.* https://doi.org/10.1007/s10207-024-00951-8 (accessed on 17th October 2025).
2. Ahmad, I., Anyanwu, A., Onwusinkwue, S., Dawodu, S. O., Akagha, O. V., & Ejairu, E. (2024). Cybersecurity challenges in smart cities: A case review of African metropolises. *Computer Science & IT Research Journal, 5*, 254–269. https://doi.org/10.51594/csitrj.v5i2.756 (accessed on 17th October 2025).
3. Ahmed, A., Shahzad, A., Naseem, A., Ali, S., & Ahmad, I. (2025). Evaluating the effectiveness of data governance frameworks in ensuring security and privacy of healthcare data: A quantitative analysis of ISO standards, GDPR, and HIPAA in blockchain technology. *PLOS One, 20.* https://www.semanticscholar.org/paper/72bb1133a3a910cb213630f4873ed4cd520f64b3 (accessed on 17th October 2025).
4. Akinsanya, M. O., Ekechi, C. C., & Okeke, C. D. (2024). Security paradigms for IoT in telecom networks: Conceptual challenges and solution pathways. *Engineering Science & Technology Journal, 5*, 1431–1451. https://doi.org/10.51594/estj.v5i4.1075 (accessed on 17th October 2025).
5. Alauthman, M., Aldweesh, A., & Al-qerem, A. (2024). IoT security challenges in modern smart cities. *2024 2nd International Conference on Cyber Resilience (ICCR).* https://www.semanticscholar.org/paper/853161bcf24a3792e9043959f3eadb3f598b1bc5 (accessed on 17th October 2025).
6. Al-Hchaimi, A. A. J., Sulaiman, N., Mustafa, M. A., Mohtar, M. N., Hassan, S. L. M., & Muhsen, Y. R. (2022). Evaluation approach for efficient countermeasure techniques against denial-of-service attack on MPSoC-based IoT using multi-criteria decision-making. *IEEE Access, 11*, 89–106. https://doi.org/10.1109/access.2022.3232395 (accessed on 17th October 2025).
7. Anglano, C., Aniello, L., Antinori, A., Armando, A., et al. (2018). The future of cybersecurity in Italy: Strategic focus area. https://core.ac.uk/download/188830442.pdf (accessed on 17th October 2025).
8. Babu, S., Kumar, A. S., Premalatha, J., Alisha, M., Chekuri, N., & Saravanan, V. (2025). Data-driven security frameworks: AI-infused digital twin software solutions for IoT. *International Journal of Computational*

and Experimental Science and Engineering. https://www.semanticscholar.org/paper/fddf3cd625f551ef72298f4ac23505b3fdb56384 (accessed on 17th October 2025).

9. Boateng, F., Aroba, O., & Patel, S. S. (2025). Sustainable strategies and factors influencing IoT adoption frameworks in library management in educational institutions: A systematic literature review. *Routledge Open Research*. https://www.semanticscholar.org/paper/02a3b12fd21ee825dfed75c5b905ae209ca39873 (accessed on 17th October 2025).
10. Bonsu, M. A., Oware, D. A., & Donkor, A. A. (2025). The role of cybersecurity regulation, policy, and compliance in strengthening IoT security and reducing consumer risks. *World Journal of Advanced Research and Reviews*. https://www.semanticscholar.org/paper/d04e9abef428594990395d516b4f78703de06e7a (accessed on 17th October 2025).
11. Chukwurah, N., Ige, A. B., Adebayo, V. I., & Eyieyien, O. G. (2024). Frameworks for effective data governance: Best practices, challenges, and implementation strategies across industries. *Computer Science & IT Research Journal*. https://www.semanticscholar.org/paper/19f75d8dc8ba5d16368080453604d372767cc675 (accessed on 17th October 2025).
12. Dar, A., Reegu, F., Ahmed, S., & Hussain, G. (2024). Strategic security audit protocol: Safeguarding smart home IoT devices against vulnerabilities. *2024 11th International Conference on Computing for Sustainable Global Development (INDIACom)*. https://www.semanticscholar.org/paper/26732483c198e23bcb3f5f9012f48a17cf3f4e14 (accessed on 17th October 2025).
13. Dominiak, J., Gonzalez Moctezuma, L., Iturbe, E., Larrucea, X., et al. (2019). Service level agreement-based GDPR compliance and security assurance in (multi)cloud-based systems. https://core.ac.uk/download/186637586.pdf (accessed on 17th October 2025).
14. Dwivedi, Y. K., Hughes, L., Baabdullah, A. M., Ribeiro-Navarrete, S., Giannakis, M., Al-Debei, M. M., Dennehy, D., et al. (2022). Metaverse beyond the hype: Multidisciplinary perspectives on emerging challenges, opportunities, and agenda for research, practice and policy. *International Journal of Information Management, 66*, 102542–102542. https://doi.org/10.1016/j.ijinfomgt.2022.102542 (accessed on 17th October 2025).
15. Ejiofor, O. E., Olusoga, O., & Akinsola, A. (2025). Zero trust architecture: A paradigm shifts in network security. *Computer Science & IT Research Journal*. https://www.semanticscholar.org/paper/e80cdf0b81708d61f94578a611f362d534e25312 (accessed on 17th October 2025).

16. Enemosah, A., & Ifeanyi, O. G. (2024). Cloud security frameworks for protecting IoT devices and SCADA systems in automated environments. *World Journal of Advanced Research and Reviews*. https://www.semanticscholar.org/paper/200b4c7f1399b2679904026408687b2aa738081b (accessed on 17th October 2025).

17. Fayayola, O. A., Olorunfemi, O. L., & Shoetan, P. O. (2024). Data privacy and security in IT: A review of techniques and challenges. *Computer Science & IT Research Journal, 5*, 606–615. https://doi.org/10.51594/csitrj.v5i3.909 (accessed on 17th October 2025).

18. Folorunso, A., Mohammed, V., Wada, I., & Samuel, B. (2024). The impact of ISO security standards on enhancing cybersecurity posture in organizations. *World Journal of Advanced Research and Reviews*. https://www.semanticscholar.org/paper/dadf19b9bb86bffa5dc90cb7dd3b8bd3877636bc (accessed on 17th October 2025).

19. Fuller, A., Fan, Z., Day, C., & Barlow, C. (2020). Digital twin: Enabling technologies, challenges and open research. *IEEE Access, 8*, 108952–108971. https://doi.org/10.1109/access.2020.2998358 (accessed on 17th October 2025).

20. Hossain, M. M., Kayas, G., Hasan, R., Skjellum, A., Noor, S., & Islam, S. (2024). A holistic analysis of Internet of Things (IoT) security: Principles, practices, and new perspectives. *Future Internet, 16*, 40. https://www.semanticscholar.org/paper/f1de68c90760ced2e91ce9b27b599682048e8f28 (accessed on 17th October 2025).

21. Hossain, S. T., Yiğitcanlar, T., Nguyen, K., & Xu, Y. (2024). Local government cybersecurity landscape: A systematic review and conceptual framework. *Applied Sciences, 14*, 5501–5501. https://doi.org/10.3390/app14135501 (accessed on 17th October 2025).

22. Hushwah, B., Yadav, U., Bansal, N., & Kumar, J. D. (2024). The connected future: Internet of Things (IoT) overview and real-world applications. *Conference Proceeding*. https://www.semanticscholar.org/paper/24fc3590bccdb2cd651fba28839b396302c2a9f3 (accessed on 17th October 2025).

23. Kagermann, H., & Wahlster, W. (2022). Ten years of Industrie 4.0. *Sci, 4*, 26–26. https://doi.org/10.3390/sci4030026 (accessed on 17th October 2025).

24. Kamara, I. (2024). European cybersecurity standardization: A tale of two solitudes in view of Europe's cyber resilience. *Innovation: The European Journal of Social Science Research*. https://doi.org/10.1080/13511610.2024.2349626 (accessed on 17th October 2025).

25. Karunathilake, E. M. B. M., Le, A. T., Heo, S., Chung, Y. S., & Mansoor, S. (2023). The path to smart farming: Innovations and opportunities in precision agriculture. *Agriculture, 13*, 1593–1593. https://doi.org/10.3390/agriculture13081593 (accessed on 17th October 2025).

26. Katsuya, R., & Liu, X. (2025). Policy and management implications of firmware vulnerabilities in medical IoT devices: A multi-case analysis. *Journal of Science and Technology Policy Management*. https://www.semanticscholar.org/paper/240b27e2e1f9c2eb6958969c35c083bdf5b6fca3 (accessed on 17th October 2025).

27. Khalid, N., Qayyum, A., Bilal, M., Al-Fuqaha, A., & Qadir, J. (2023). Privacy-preserving artificial intelligence in healthcare: Techniques and applications. *Computers in Biology and Medicine, 158*, 106848–106848. https://doi.org/10.1016/j.compbiomed.2023.106848 (accessed on 17th October 2025).

28. Khan, N. S., Mir, R. N., Chishti, M., & Saleem, M. (2024). B-ERAC: Blockchain-enabled role-based access control for secure IoT device communication. *Scalable Computing: Practice and Experience, 25*. https://www.semanticscholar.org/paper/0561f35a5268bd02e09de5a25b54382340025f0f (accessed on 17th October 2025).

29. Kumar, A., Jain, S., Kumar, S., & Sharma, H. K. (2024). Hybrid fusion of lightweight security frameworks using data mining approach in IoT. *Fusion: Practice and Applications*. https://www.semanticscholar.org/paper/50b9e5ab9af8eb922c82791237c6948ba871b52c (accessed on 17th October 2025).

30. Liu, F., Cui, Y., Masouros, C., Xu, J., Han, T. X., Eldar, Y. C., & Buzzi, S. (2022). Integrated sensing and communications: Toward dual-functional wireless networks for 6G and beyond. *IEEE Journal on Selected Areas in Communications, 40*, 1728–1767. https://doi.org/10.1109/jsac.2022.3156632 (accessed on 17th October 2025).

31. Mandal, K., Ferrara, P., Khlyebnikov, Y., Cortesi, A., & Spoto, F. (2020). Cross-program taint analysis for IoT systems. *Proceedings of the 35th Annual ACM Symposium on Applied Computing*. https://www.semanticscholar.org/paper/e5b3051090551113e43f4808b7f3acbdd24a064e (accessed on 17th October 2025).

32. Martínez Llamas, J., Vranckaert, K., Preuveneers, D., & Joosen, W. (2025). Balancing security and privacy: Web bot detection, privacy challenges, and regulatory compliance under the GDPR and AI Act. *Open Research Europe, 5*. https://www.semanticscholar.org/paper/40de1ff1c16de4cd4db131fe03a89f0c1bed5b46 (accessed on 17th October 2025).

33. Mohammed, A. H. (2024). Recent advances in IoT security for real-time data integration. *International Journal of Scientific Research in Computer Science, Engineering and Information Technology*. https://www.semanticscholar.org/paper/74c49b7508ddf143c492d8043785f126ed7c988f (accessed on 17th October 2025).
34. Moreno, C., Allam, Z., Chabaud, D., Gall, C., & Pratlong, F. (2021). Introducing the "15-minute city": Sustainability, resilience and place identity in future post-pandemic cities. *Smart Cities, 4*, 93–111. https://doi.org/10.3390/smartcities4010006 (accessed on 17th October 2025).
35. Nzeako, G., Okeke, C. D., Akinsanya, M. O., Popoola, O. A., & Chukwurah, E. G. (2024). Security paradigms for IoT in telecom networks: Conceptual challenges and solution pathways. *Engineering Science & Technology Journal, 5*, 1606–1626. https://doi.org/10.51594/estj.v5i5.1111 (accessed on 17th October 2025).
36. Olaitan, O. F., Akatakpo, O. N., Victor, C. O., Emejulu, C. J., Ayoola, T. M., Olayiwola, D. E., & Ajibola, A. (2025). Secure and resilient industrial IoT architectures for smart manufacturing: A comprehensive review. *Journal of Engineering Research and Reports*. https://www.semanticscholar.org/paper/5cff4b3452d238332108cfb942fa1352db8df090 (accessed on 17th October 2025).
37. Paul, M., Μαγλαράς, Λ., Ferrag, M. A., & Almomani, I. (2023). Digitization of healthcare sector: A study on privacy and security concerns. *ICT Express, 9*, 571–588. https://doi.org/10.1016/j.icte.2023.02.007 (accessed on 17th October 2025).
38. Saeed, S., Altamimi, S. A., Alkayyal, N. A., Alshehri, E., & Alabbad, D. A. (2023). Digital transformation and cybersecurity challenges for business resilience: Issues and recommendations. *Sensors, 23*, 6666–6666. https://doi.org/10.3390/s23156666 (accessed on 17th October 2025).
39. Samonte, M., Ampiloquio, P. I. R., Bataller, A. C. B., & Medina, I. J. S. (2024). Integrating cloud security in ensuring privacy on medical healthcare records. *2024 4th International Conference on Computer Systems (ICCS)*. https://www.semanticscholar.org/paper/988596ecffb73add6490af5141b0cbf957da59e5 (accessed on 17th October 2025).
40. Schöttle, P., Janetschek, M., Merkle, F., Nocker, M., & Egger, C. (2025). Large-scale (semi-)automated security assessment of consumer IoT devices–A roadmap. *2025 10th International Conference on Smart and Sustainable Technologies (SpliTech)*. https://www.semanticscholar.org/paper/ab76118b0972920bb54d2eafb060fca64e55d5b6 (accessed on 17th October 2025).

41. Shao, T. (2025). Exploring the vulnerabilities of IoT (Internet of Things) devices and proposing solutions to enhance their security. *Science and Technology of Engineering, Chemistry and Environmental Protection.* https://www.semanticscholar.org/paper/9f67878337939ec10e23115f17547c2bf9d82014 (accessed on 17th October 2025).

42. Simsek, I. (2024). Authentication, authorization, access control, and key exchange in Internet of Things. *ACM Transactions on Internet of Things, 5*, 1–30. https://www.semanticscholar.org/paper/34ba9988b7413ff2d5091e4b4b5198ab97d66a60 (accessed on 17th October 2025).

43. Soni, V., Kumar, N., Jain, V., Santhoshkumar, G. P., Y. B., et al. (2024). Secure communication protocols for IoT-enabled smart grids. *2024 International Conference on Innovative Computing, Intelligent Communication and Smart Electrical Systems (ICSES).* https://www.semanticscholar.org/paper/c4ad30c3be967a8c7a2e479715f33ddff6377935 (accessed on 17th October 2025).

44. Syed, N., Shah, S. W. A., Shaghaghi, A., Anwar, A., Baig, Z., & Doss, R. (2022). Zero trust architecture (ZTA): A comprehensive survey. *IEEE Access, 10*, 57143–57179. https://doi.org/10.1109/access.2022.3174679 (accessed on 17th October 2025).

45. Tariq, U., Ahmed, I., Bashir, A. K., & Shaukat, K. (2023). A critical cybersecurity analysis and future research directions for the Internet of Things: A comprehensive review. *Sensors, 23*, 4117–4117. https://doi.org/10.3390/s23084117 (accessed on 17th October 2025).

46. Wang, Y. (2022). Construction of an intelligent platform based on the perspective of IoT data analysis. *2022 Sixth International Conference on I-SMAC (IoT in Social, Mobile, Analytics and Cloud) (I-SMAC).* https://www.semanticscholar.org/paper/6bc2663e0d59dde1e05144a3eedcc5ccec54abc4 (accessed on 17th October 2025).

47. Zhukabayeva, T., Ahmad, Z., Adamova, A., Karabayev, N., & Abdildayeva, A. (2025). An edge-computing-based integrated framework for network traffic analysis and intrusion detection to enhance cyber–physical system security in industrial IoT. *Sensors (Basel, Switzerland), 25.* https://www.semanticscholar.org/paper/66554566e9e1b41faa2efd71021d4148f6b38190 (accessed on 17th October 2025).

CHAPTER 10

EMERGING TECHNOLOGIES IN IOT SECURITY

Contents

INTRODUCTION

The rapid advancement of technology has ushered in a new era characterized by the global spread of the Internet of Things (IoT), a group of connected devices that offers data exchange and automation services across various industries. This development has necessitated revolutionary improvements in security systems, as mounting threats to such vast networks have left them exposed to attacks. New technologies are of utmost significance to enhance IoT security since they bring new solutions that are specifically created to protect sensitive information and maintain user trust. In healthcare, for instance, the value of utilizing advanced security tools is particularly profound since real-time tracking and data integrity are crucial for effective patient care and outcomes. Healthcare use of IoTs is one of the demonstrations of how emerging technologies have the ability to bring security and functionality together in a manner whereby systems become not only effective but also safe and reliable (Abdulmalek et al., 2022). Addition of artificial intelligence (AI) to IoT security systems has come across as a revolutionary approach to manage vulnerabilities in smart devices. AI technology enhances predictive analytics so that systems can identify potential security threats in advance. With the development of AI, its integration with IoT becomes increasingly apparent; jointly, they enable intelligence and active security solutions to become increasingly responsive to emerging threats. This integration is critical as cyber-attacks become increasingly intelligent and pervasive across industries. The capacity of AI to augment IoT security not only mitigates threats but also advances a proactive security strategy, which is important for the maintenance of integrity of sensitive environments. As is indicated in the deliberations of AIs revolutionary role, such an intersectionality of technology and security disposes off the emerging trends that will define the IoT security capabilities (Jiang et al., 2022). IoT security issues surpass the field of technology innovation; they include regulatory, ethical, and infrastructural issues. With the growth of IoT usage in critical sectors such as smart cities and transportation networks, there is a pressing need for robust security systems. The stakeholders must go through a challenging situation filled with privacy concerns, regulatory issues, and ethics of data utilization. Recent studies emphasize the need for all-encompassing methods that address the security of health care, data safeguard, and user anonymity, and they outline some of the significant challenges requiring immediate response. Since this chapter delves deeper into the future technologies that enhance IoT security, evidently an assortment of methods—ranging from technological developments to policy reform and stakeholder collaboration—is required in order to facilitate a secure, robust IoT environment. The future of IoT security is in integrating all these fragmented domains into a cohesive framework that safeguards both technological and human interests.

10.1. BLOCKCHAIN TECHNOLOGY IN IOT SECURITY

Utilization of blockchain technology in Internet of Things (IoT) security is an innovative approach to addressing the intrinsic weaknesses of networked devices. The decentralized nature of blockchains makes it a simpler system that eliminates data integrity and confidentiality concerns, which are critical in IoT applications. Through cryptographic techniques, blockchain renders information transacted between IoT gadgets immutable and traceable, thus establishing trust within the network. The immutable ledger erases unauthorized alterations, severely deterring cyberattacks that typically aim at IoT vulnerability. According to recent research, the inherent vulnerabilities of IoT systems pose major threats that blockchain readily counteracts through its advanced security frameworks (Mendez et al., 2017). Besides, the use of blockchain on IoT enables security systems to be automated, such as smart contracts, that can carry out transactions without a third party. These contracts are able to enforce set conditions automatically and can react in real-time to security incidents. Automation, in this instance, not only streamlines processes but also minimizes latency of traditional security systems to render systems very responsive to potential intrusions.

Figure 10.1. Blockchains decentralized architecture facilitates a secure framework that mitigates issues related to data integrity and confidentiality, which are critical in IoT applications.

Source: https://media.licdn.com/dms/image/v2/D4D12AQGee1m0RK1dMw/article-cover_image-shrink_600_2000/article-cover_image-shrink_600_2000/0/1696676280590?e=2147483647&v=beta&t=7mF09OtB3RCFrqFBGAimCi48k3g8VHgPnkmwtud46R8.

The potential of such technology is high, allowing for enhanced operational effectiveness and resource management across various industries reliant on IoT solutions. Researchers have begun to explore these dynamics, proposing that the confluence of blockchain and IoT could have a profound impact on security architecture needed in coming smart applications (Novakovic et al., 2019). Lastly, while the prospect of blockchain as the enabler of IoT security is intriguing, care must be taken to note the issues associated with its implementation. Scalability of the blockchain network remains a flag of concern, particularly as more and more IoT devices are being installed exponentially. Moreover, the energy required to fuel blockchain transactions has been criticized as unsustainable. Overcoming these challenges will require a multi-dimensional response, integrating technological innovation, regulation, and cooperation among industries. Through its identification by researchers, an in-depth exploration of the security environment in IoT systems confirms the necessity of continuous research into blockchain technologies to ensure that new technologies not only enhance security but also that they are efficient and sustainable (Mendez et al., 2017) (Figure 10.1).

10.1.1. How Blockchain Enhances Data Integrity

In the realm of Internet of Things (IoT) security, data integrity enhancement using blockchain technology offers a revolutionary solution for extensive issues relating to trust and transparency. Traditional centralized databases are vulnerable to various types of cybersecurity threats, where attackers can tamper with data, leading to severe consequences. By using a decentralized system, blockchain ensures that information input into the system is not modifiable and can only be modified based on the agreement of multiple nodes. This feature not only ensures that information is not corrupted but also allows for real-time auditing. Additionally, the open environment of blockchain provides traceability, where there is an auditable history of transactions and actions performed, greatly increasing the user's confidence in the integrity of the system. Deep research shows that blockchain technology can curb the risks of unauthorized access and data breaches in IoT networks, thereby strengthening the overall security architecture of such connected devices (Abdolee et al., 2019). The application of blockchain technology in IoT networks addresses some of the key challenges, particularly data authenticity. With an increasing number of IoT devices, the amount of data being generated is gigantic and creates problems concerning its vulnerability as well as fraud. Since blockchain uses cryptographic algorithms and is decentralized, it makes all the data being generated legitimate as well as safe. For instance, in supply chain management, IoT sensors can be employed to monitor product movement, and then blockchain makes it tamper-proof. This combination not only guards against double-spending but also encourages accountability by participants taking on varying roles across the supply chain. Last but not least, the adoption of blockchain technology allows organizations to embrace an active role in monitoring and validating the integrity of data, resulting in enhanced operational efficiencies and reduced risks of data tampering (Franke et al., 2020). Finally, while blockchain contains an enormous amount of potential for enhancing data integrity, its successful usage in IoT networks must consider challenges such as computational workload and bandwidth constraints inherent to decentralized networks. Usage of blockchain protocols must find a balance between security and efficiency because extremely computationally intensive processing would generate latency and interfere with real-time IoT application operation. Accordingly, top-down solutions are required to overcome these challenges while leveraging the potential of blockchain. For instance, enhanced consensus algorithms can reduce the power consumption and processing time, and thus ensure that the benefits of increased data integrity come without compromising the performance of the system. As researchers continue to explore these dynamics, the collaborative promise of blockchain and IoT technology can lead to a new era of secure, efficient technology solutions that preserve data integrity across many industries (Abdolee et al., 2019) (Figure 10.2).

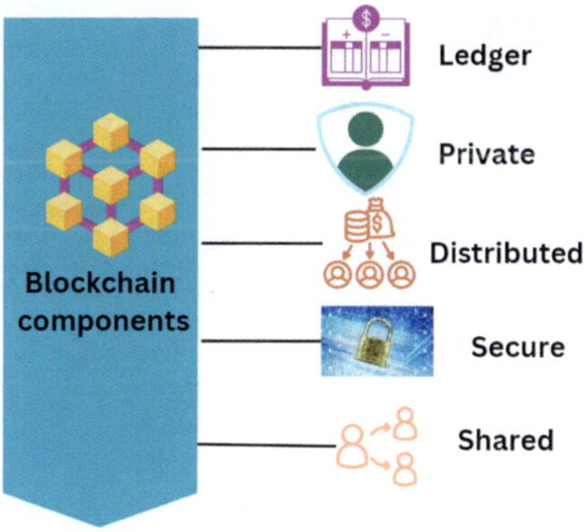

Figure 10.2. The application of blockchain protocols should strike a balance between security and efficiency, as excessive processing requirements can introduce latency and hinder real-time performance of IoT applications.

Source: https://media.springernature.com/lw1200/springer-static/image/art%3A10.1038%2Fs41598-024-68529-x/MediaObjects/41598_2024_68529_Fig9_HTML.png.

10.1.2. Decentralization and Its Benefits for IoT Security

The increase of Internet of Things (IoT) devices has led to increasing security concerns, particularly because such devices are known to operate within centralized systems that can be attacked. Decentralization is a strong answer to such a scenario, fundamentally altering the dynamics of security in IoT. With the distribution of device control and management over a network, decentralized systems make it easier to reduce single points of failure, which in turn makes it much harder for attackers to take control of multiple devices in coordination. The shift in network topology is not only made more resilient but also makes autonomous decision-making more effective at the device level. This transformation has the ability to enable devices to send and receive information and make secure transactions without the need for a centralized party, in essence protecting user data and system integrity in a manner that cannot be achieved by conventional methods. Blockchain technology integrated into IoT networks is a prime example of the security advantages of decentralization. Blockchain provides a secure framework to record transactions in a clear and unalterable manner, which guarantees data integrity and accountability throughout the IoT network.

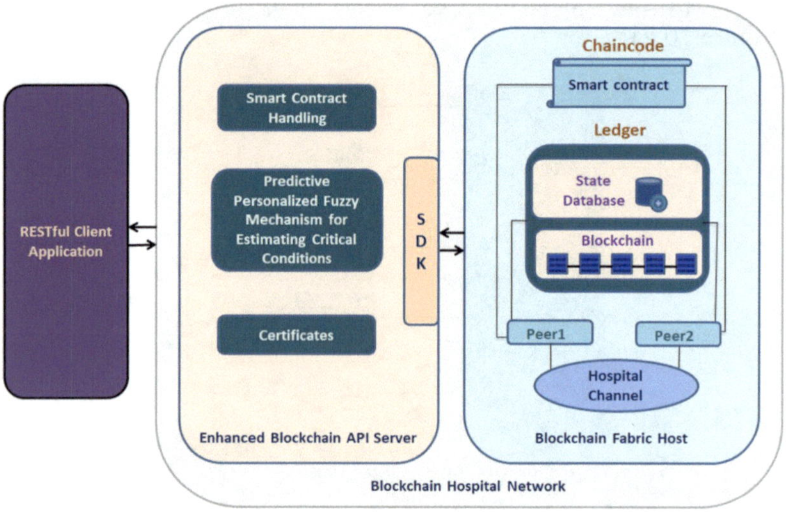

Figure 10.3. By enabling peer-to-peer interactions devoid of middlemen, blockchain can facilitate secure, automated transactions among devices while minimizing the risk of data tampering and unauthorized access.

Source: https://media.springernature.com/lw1200/springer-static/image/art%3A10.1186%2Fs12911-024-02708-8/MediaObjects/12911_2024_2708_Fig4_HTML.png.

This decentralization approach would be particularly beneficial when addressing trust issues in multiple IoT stakeholders. In enabling peer-to-peer interactions devoid of intermediaries, blockchain would enable secure, automatic transactions among devices with minimal opportunity for data tampering and unauthorized access. Besides, the light-weighted nature of blockchain technology through proposals that utilize proof-of-work mining strategies for resource-limited devices demonstrates a path to achieving scalability and security in IoT (Yan et al., 2020). This manner, therefore, decentralized technologies not only assure superior security but also offer room for vast adoption of IoT. Even though significant advantages of decentralization are present, pragmatic limitations can negatively impact its deployment in limited resource IoT systems. Decentralized protocols are complex and thus need computational power beyond that available in most IoT devices, which leads to inefficiency and non-scalability. Recent advances are proving the way decentralized models can be integrated within without surpassing the capabilities of IoT devices. For instance, using reconfigurable hardware for lightweight blockchain applications promises to save energy and computational resources while maintaining a high transaction rate (Yan et al., 2020). With advancements in such technologies, they offer all-around solutions for the security problem of IoT, guaranteeing the possibility of devices operating independently and securely in the future. The promise of decentralization and the scalable nature of technological advancements have enormous potential to reimagine security in the rapidly expanding realm of IoT (Figure 10.3).

10.1.3. Case Studies of Blockchain Implementation in IoT

The use of blockchain technology within the Internet of Things (IoT) setting is picking up momentum, with various case studies that confirm its ability to enhance security as well as efficiency. For instance, in the health sector, an implementation based on Hyperledger Fabric has brought out the advantages of blockchains immutability as well as decentralized features. This case study highlights how patient data, when held on a blockchain, mitigates unauthorized access and increases data integrity between devices. Second, comparative analysis of blockchain platforms confirmed that Hyperledger Fabric outperformed Ethereum for both throughput and latency, making it particularly suitable for private networks integral to IoT healthcare settings. These findings emphasize the importance of selecting appropriate blockchain solutions depending on the relevant use cases in the IoT field, which further enhance performance and security aspects in key fields like healthcare (Ucbas et al., 2023). Another example would be the combination of Software Defined Networking (SDN) and blockchain technology to mitigate the multilateral security challenges of IoT environments. Studies exploring this integration establish how blockchain, when combined with SDN, delivers a secure environment for the management of network resources as well as the privacy of data and users. The architecture of Blockchain-enabled Software-Defined IoT (BC-SDIoT) not only facilitates real-time monitoring of IoT devices but also fosters trust through enhanced access control and authentication mechanisms. Establishment of secure communication pathways between devices, with the power of blockchains' decentralization, avoids threats of data tampering and maintains compliance with data privacy regulations. This new model can be employed by organizations to increase resistance against cyberattacks and further enhance the fundamental components of IoT security (Turner et al., 2023). Furthermore, several case studies have explained the application of blockchain solutions for supply chain management in an IoT environment. Leveraging blockchain's open and immutable ledger, firms are able to trace the origin of goods in real time for better accountability and traceability. These applications have demonstrated not just improved operational effectiveness but also increased security layers against frauds and counterfeits. For instance, a leading logistics project used a blockchain system to give more visibility across the supply chain, lessening conflicts and developing more trust between participants. Blockchain technology's authentication gives IoT ecosystems a more secure space, which, by nature of tradition, are victimized by disconnected processes. These advancements are typical of the ongoing research on blockchain potential to improve IoT security, eventually creating a more secure digital platform (Ucbas et al., 2023).

10.2. ARTIFICIAL INTELLIGENCE AND MACHINE LEARNING

New technologies, particularly machine learning (ML) and artificial intelligence (AI), are transforming the Internet of Things (IoT) security paradigm with more ability to predict, detect, and block cyber-attacks. AI solutions are effective in analyzing extensive amounts of data to detect patterns and deviations and can recognize security hacks with unprecedented speed and accuracy. As the rollout of IoT devices increases, possible attack surfaces increase as well, requiring more robust security controls. With AI and ML, organizations can design anticipatory steps that are always evolving based on developing threats, thereby making security effective against novel vulnerabilities at all times. It is critical in the such as smart cities and industrial IoT, where integration of devices opens up numerous avenues of cyberattack. The interaction between AI, ML, and the resulting data in IoT settings is pivotal in crossing security frameworks. Among the challenges has been, nonetheless, harnessing the abundance of information created in smart cities, which remains under-leveraged. As quoted in recent discourses in the discipline, there is an urgent need for creative ML approaches capable of coping with the fluid nature of such information. Semi-supervised learning methods, in particular, are emerging as effective alternatives to solve the issue of unlabeled data prevalent in such environments. The ability to leverage both labeled and unlabeled data sets allows predictive security models to be fine-tuned, which can respond to threats in real time without causing undue false positives. Thus, successful fusion of AI and ML can ensure these technologies not only deliver security enhancements but also contribute to the overall efficiency of IoT systems. Besides, application of AI and ML for IoT security presents formidable factors related to ethical and privacy considerations. With devices becoming smart and networked, data that they generate is likely to hold sensitive personal information, thus raising concerns related to data protection and consent. The process of balancing the employment of AI for enhanced security and user privacy protection is vital. Developers and policymakers must implement guidelines that control the use of AI in this regard with the goal of transparency and accountability. It is important, as claimed in the discussion of incorporating AI technologies, to establish an environment where users are safe and well-informed on how their data is utilized. For this purpose, their technical and ethical dimensions must be handled carefully to foster trust and adoption of these emerging technologies for IoT security as a whole.

10.2.1. Role of AI in Threat Detection

The advent of the Internet of Things (IoT) has exponentially raised the volume of security threats, for which smart threat identification solutions are necessary. Artificial intelligence (AI) is a game-changer in the management of the threats by analyzing huge amounts of data generated by IoT devices in real time. Using algorithms to identify patterns of user activity, AI is able to distinguish normal usage from potential security breaches that may indicate unauthorized access or malicious activity. This feature is particularly critical in healthcare settings, where IoT devices continuously receive sensitive patient data. AIs ability to detect anomalies in network traffic not only enhances security interventions but also promotes a proactive vulnerability management strategy, thus preventing risks from escalating into full-fledged threats, as quoted in current debates regarding AI-based models for security in the health sector (Bajpayi et al., 2024). Integration of AI into IoT security also enables the creation and deployment of deep learning algorithms, which introduce greatly improved threat detection features. Artificial neural network-based, these algorithms provide effective analysis of complex data sets and can update and improve themselves as they learn from new information. For example, convolutional neural network-based intrusion detection systems can inspect the patterns of network traffic to identify and quarantine malicious botnet traffic. Multilayer perceptron's and recurrent neural networks are adept at recognizing and classifying cyber threats and thus are vital tools for organizations working towards a secure IoT environment. Not only does this enhance organizational resilience but also enhances the comprehension of cyber threats, thus allowing timely action and well-informed decisions (Ghillani, 2022). In addition, the use of AI in threat detection platforms triggers a transition towards a more dynamic approach for handling IoT security. As organizations adopt a zero-trust approach, AIs role becomes more crucial in building sound security infrastructures that constantly assess and evolve with prospective vulnerabilities. With AIs predictive analytics functionalities, businesses can foresee and sidestep threat risk associated with novel threats. This kind of flexibility is essential in the dynamic cyber threat landscape where traditional methods are bound to fail. Consequently, implementing AI-based approaches not only raises the detection of familiar threats but also allows for detection of newly emerging vulnerabilities, thus enhancing the overall security position of IoT systems and enabling higher confidence in their deployment (Bajpayi et al., 2024) (Figure 10.4).

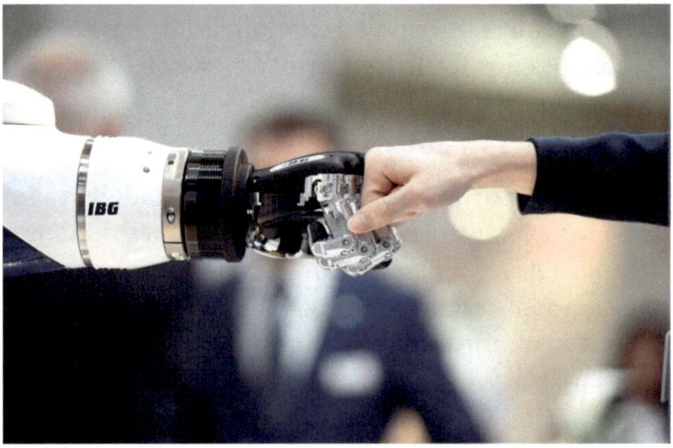

Figure 10.4. Artificial intelligence (AI) plays a transformative role in addressing these challenges by analyzing vast amounts of data generated by IoT devices in real-time.

Source: https://www.brookings.edu/wp-content/uploads/2018/04/robotics.jpg?quality=75&w=1500.

10.2.2. Predictive Analytics for Proactive Security

The application of predictive analytics within IoT security has emerged as a critical component in building pre-emptive security protocols. By employing historical facts and machine learning algorithms, organizations are able to forecast future security intrusions. Not only does it make security procedures more efficient, but it also enables a faster reaction to evolving threats. Predictive analytics allows businesses to monitor device activity and identify abnormal behavior that could indicate a breach or cyber-attack. Therefore, businesses can then mitigate risks successfully, limiting the potential impact to their business and safeguarding sensitive data. The inclusion of predictive analytics within robust security architectures ultimately results in greater organizational resilience and enhanced regulation compliance (Żywiołek, 2025). With respect to Industry 4.0, predictive analytics is increasingly being combined with data security, thus enabling ongoing improvement. Due to its ability to handle enormous data from IoT sensors, there is potential for threat detection and management in real time. Not only can predictive analytics detect vulnerabilities in the infrastructure, but it is also able to quantify the effectiveness of existing security measures, spurring innovations in cybersecurity practices. As security threats evolve in an ever-changing manner, organizations understand that a proactive measure fueled by predictive analytics leads to improved decision-making as well as organizational efficiency.

Figure 10.5. Predictive analytics empowers businesses to monitor device behaviors and identify anomalous activities that may indicate a breach or cyber-attack.

Source: https://exeon.com/wp-content/uploads/2025/06/3-reasons-why-machine-learning-is-critical-against-corporate-cyber-threats-1024x571.png.

These innovations facilitate a culture of continued improvement in which organizations are able to manage changes in regulatory requirements while maintaining high data privacy and security standards (Żywiołek, 2025). Moreover, the relationship between predictive analytics and cyber resilience facilitates a proactive risk management strategy. By incorporating predictive capabilities to traditional defense mechanisms, organizations can move from reactive to proactive by anticipating and reacting to threats before they escalate. This change is particularly critical in a hyper-connected world with IoT and cloud computing, where systems are subject to more vectors of attack. The clear convergence of threat intelligence with predictive analytics enhances not just security infrastructures but also enhances a culture of digital trust for stakeholders. With the management of the complexities of modern-day cybersecurity environments, the emphasis on pre-emptive controls is essential to provide the integrity and availability of information. Such technology is vital in ensuring long-term stability and development in an increasingly insecure digital environment (Figure 10.5).

10.2.3. Challenges in Implementing AI Solutions

The use of Artificial Intelligence (AI) in IoT security systems has numerous challenges that hamper efficient implementation. To begin with, AI algorithms have a tendency to demand high-level technical expertise that may not be readily available in organizations. This lack of skills may lead to the absence of ideal system configurations or data misinterpretation that ultimately discredits the security measures supposed to be established. Moreover, the sheer pace of technological advancement means that security professionals must continuously learn and adapt in order to remain ahead of emerging threats. While organizations are attempting to understand AI, specialized training programs are needed, but they are typically time and resource-intensive. The human element of security cannot be overlooked as the fate of AI deployment relies solely on the know-how and knowledge base of the workforce involved in IoT security initiatives (Ismail et al., 2025). Additionally, ethical concerns and data privacy concerns are significant threats that need to be addressed while deploying AI solutions in IoT environments. The application of AI is usually required in the gathering of enormous quantities of data, both sensitive and personal in nature, to be handled appropriately. Violations of privacy not only catch regulatory eyes but are also likely to lead to irreparable damage to public confidence in the technology and its providers. Apart from this, big data analysis to be used in AI training can lead to biases if not controlled properly, thereby resulting in ineffective or even harmful security systems. This gives rise to the challenge of organizations developing clearly defined ethical standards and compliance processes alongside AI technologies. Balancing the application of data for enhanced security and the protection of individual privacy is a difficult but important exercise that needs collaboration between technologists, ethicists, and policymakers (Khan et al., 2025). Finally, the incorporation of AI in IoT security measures must overcome significant cost implications that pose entry challenges to the majority of organizations. The initial investment in AI technology, hardware, software, and infrastructure that is needed can be prohibitively costly, particularly for small businesses with insufficient funds. Furthermore, frequent updates, maintenance, and potential expansion of AI infrastructure establish a recurring budgetary need that should not be overlooked. These budgetary concerns could discourage organizations from leveraging sophisticated AI features, ultimately causing them to fail to adequately enhance IoT security. With threats across the internet evolving and needing ever more sophisticated defense mechanisms, there is a need for organizations to weigh upfront costs with benefits from AI integration over the long term. Training resources and incentives provided by tech firms can soften some of these costs to make the adoption of AI-powered IoT security platforms simpler (Ismail et al., 2025).

10.3. EDGE COMPUTING AND SECURITY

The advent of edge computing represents a revolution for the Internet of Things (IoT) by bridging the gap between data generation and processing. In the sense that it allows data to be processed at or near where it is generated, edge computing basically reduces latency and bandwidth consumption, which are key challenges in conventional cloud-based models. This paradigm is particularly important for IoT use cases that entail real-time data analysis and decision-making, such as autonomous vehicles and intelligent health sensors. Although increased reliance on computing at the edge enhances responsiveness and diminishes latency, it also comes with the sledgehammer of a myriad of security concerns. Being a new infrastructure, edge environments are susceptible to a variety of attack vectors, such as unauthorized access and data breaches. Deployment of robust security measures therefore becomes imperative to secure the integrity and confidentiality of sensitive information generated in such networks. As much as its advantage is enhanced by edge computing, there also emerge different security challenges brought that need new solutions. The variability and evolvement of IoT environments complicate the application of conventional security approaches, rendering them more unsuitable in reaction to some edge vulnerabilities. Devices may be resource-constrained, rendering the use of conventional security mechanisms impractical. In addition, the lack of centralized authority makes it worse for device-to-device communication exploitation attacks. Future technologies such as blockchain offer a promising solution to enhance edge security in terms of decentralized identity verification and safe storage of data. As addressed by existing frameworks, blockchain can be applied to secure end-to-end communication and fulfill authentication and data integrity issues in IoT networks. Thus, designing a synergistic platform that integrates edge computing with proper security practices will play a crucial role in mitigating vulnerabilities and taking advantage of the strengths of agile and responsive data processing. The future of IoT security is increasingly tied to improved capabilities of edge computing and its ability to facilitate advanced security features. As evidenced by the unprecedented growth in 6G wireless networks and convergence of Generative AI, there is room for an unprecedented leap in vulnerability detection and response features. Traditional security controls fall short in treating dynamic threats appropriately because they are not intended to handle sophisticated attack channels in the present IoT ecosystem. Organizations can bolster their security frameworks with adaptive learning and contextual threat detection by employing Generative AI technologies such as Variational Autoencoders (VAEs) and Large Language Models (LLMs). This end-to-end method not only secures edge devices but also improves overall resilience in the IoT environment. Thus, identifying and embracing these emerging technologies under the umbrella of edge computing will be the foundation for creating a secure and robust framework for the future of IoT security (Erukala et al., 2025; Yang et al., 2025).

10.3.1. Definition and Benefits of Edge Computing

Edge computing is a revolutionary new method of processing, storing, and analyzing data within the Internet of Things (IoT) scenario. In definition, edge computing is the decentralization of computation where computations are performed nearer to the sources of data rather than relying entirely on remote cloud servers. This shift in design goes a long way toward making IoT applications more responsive and effective, particularly those that are security-integrated. The real-time edge processing of data minimizes latency limitations, enabling devices to respond in real-time, which is critical for security solutions that are dependent on timely threat detection and response. Through the implementation of computation power towards the network edge, organizations also reduce bandwidth consumption and improve the system's overall performance, hence overcoming the unique challenge being posed by the exponentially rising volume of IoT-generated data. One of the most significant benefits of edge computing is the fact that it can deliver heightened security for IoT deployments. Traditional cloud-oriented paradigms endanger data by exposing it to threats while being transferred, thereby increasing chances of interception or data leaks. With edge computing, sensitive information is processed locally, minimizing opportunities for data leaks or interception. This local solution not only enhances security but also enables compliance with data privacy regulations, as organizations gain more control over the where and how personal data is processed. Furthermore, edge computing platforms can execute advanced security controls in real-time, facilitating rapid updates and responses to emerging threats, a key differentiator in the ever-evolving landscape of cybersecurity threats IoT devices face. The intersection of edge computing with emerging technologies such as digital twins also improves its benefits in IoT security. Digital twins, being virtual representations of real assets that enhance real-time monitoring and decision-making, can tap into the strength of edge computing to analyze huge volumes of operational data. As stressed in the literature, these virtual replicas can provide insights that enable predictive analysis and enhance the efficacy of security control methods by simulating various scenarios and potential attack routes (Fuller et al., 2020). Additionally, since digital twins rely on actual-time data provided by edge computing infrastructure, they are able to identify inconsistencies and potential security vulnerabilities in advance, enabling organizations to take necessary steps ahead of time. Thus, the partnership of digital twins with edge computing represents a promising advance in IoT system security, encouraging a responsive and resilient operational environment (Rasheed et al., 2020) (Figure 10.6).

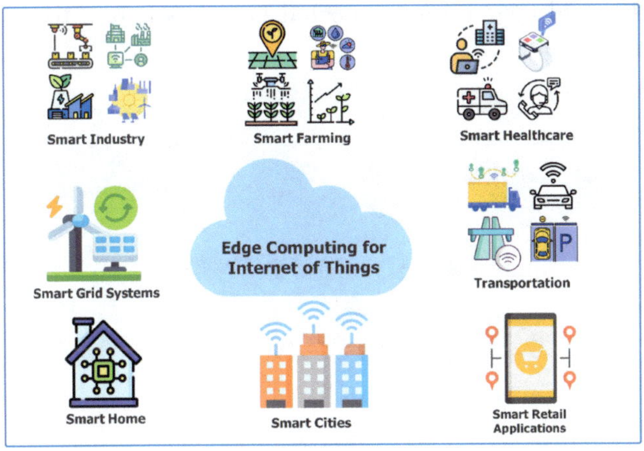

Figure 10.6. Edge computing represents a transformative shift in the way data is processed, stored, and analyzed within the Internet of Things (IoT) ecosystem.

Source: https://media.springernature.com/lw1200/springer-static/image/art%3A10.1007%2Fs11277-023-10669-w/MediaObjects/11277_2023_10669_Fig1_HTML.png.

10.3.2. Reducing Latency and Enhancing Security

In the rapidly evolving landscape of the Internet of Things (IoT), reducing latency and enhancing security are imperative requirements. Emerging technologies, particularly those related to network architecture, are the prime movers in addressing the challenges. Fifth-generation (5G) networks, for example, offer faster data speeds and reduced latency, making real-time communication possible between devices. This low-latency aspect is of supreme importance in applications such as autonomous vehicles and smart cities, where data transfer should be done in real-time for safety and efficiency. The use of edge computing also adds to these technologies by executing data processing close to the source, thus minimizing delay and response times. As the IoT network grows and matures, the need for speed and security increases more and more to support the interconnectedness of devices and buffer against potential vulnerabilities inherent in this complex web (Elechi et al., 2025). More and more, enhancing security within IoT devices while relying on upgrading security is a matter of leveraging developments from emerging technologies like machine learning and artificial intelligence. These technologies enable enhanced monitoring systems that can instantly analyze trends in data in real time and search for anomalies that might indicate security breaches. By employing sophisticated algorithms that learn dynamically from the network's traffic, organizations can proactively flag and respond to suspected breaches before they escalate into full-blown security incidents.

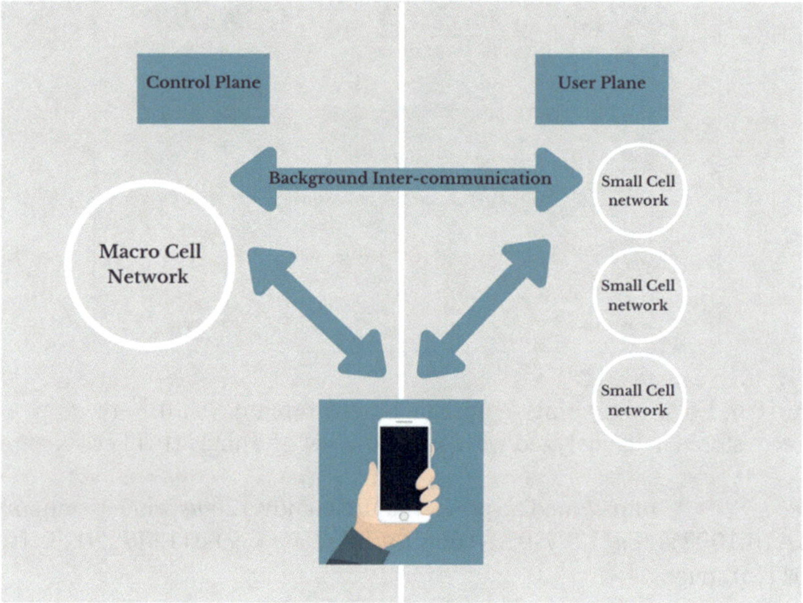

Figure 10.7. Fifth-generation (5G) networks, for example, offer significant improvements in data transmission speeds and reduced latency, facilitating real-time communication between devices.

Source: https://media.springernature.com/full/springer-static/image/art%3A10.1038%2Fs41433-021-01450-z/MediaObjects/41433_2021_1450_Fig1_HTML.png.

In addition, vehicle-to-everything (V2X) communication is essential in offering enhanced security between connected vehicles so that they can share vital information about hazards and traffic conditions. The combined effect of low-latency communication through 5G networks and robust security systems complemented by artificial intelligence powers a safe IoT infrastructure, whereby devices can operate efficiently while guarding sensitive information from impending attacks (International et al., 2025). As demand for real-time processing of data and secure communication increases, the research on quantum technologies presents exciting prospects in reducing latency as well as improving security. Quantum key distribution (QKD) allows the establishment of secure communication channels that are theoretically unbreachable to interception by eavesdropping. The technology allows the exchange of encryption keys between devices in a manner that no unauthorized intrusion into confidential information can be made. Coupled with millimeter wave (mmWave) technologies, which offer high-speed wireless communication, the feasibility of real-time secure data exchange is significantly enhanced. While the promise brought by these emerging technologies is encouraging, issues of implementation costs, standardization, and developing robust infrastructure to counteract persist. Addressing these challenges will be crucial in effective deployment, achieving a safer and more efficient IoT system that prioritizes both data integrity and high-speed response (Elechi et al., 2025) (Figure 10.7).

10.3.3. Edge Device Security Measures

Within the realm of new technologies of IoT security, edge device security has emerged into the spotlight due to the influx of connected devices functioning at the edge of networks. Edge devices regularly handle sensitive data and are often physically exposed, thus they present a clear target for cyber-attacks. Because these devices are intermediaries between cloud services and users, there must be rigorous security implementation in the sense of secure boot protocols, firmware updates, and real-time monitoring. Secure boot ensures that only authentic firmware runs on such machines and that no malicious software is run. Real-time monitoring is at the heart of this matter because it enables anomalies to be detected which can indicate security breaches or compromised devices. By applying end-to-end holistic security practices to the edge, organizations can make their defenses strong against a wide range of cyber threats typical of the IoT ecosystem (Ali et al., 2024). According to conventional security practices, edge device security will also entail encryption techniques designed to protect data both in transit and resting. Since edge devices frequently transfer sensitive information across various networks, employing strong encryption protocols minimizes data in-transit interception possibilities. Moreover, adding hardware-based security modules can enhance the integrity of edge devices by providing a trusted enclave where sensitive information is processed and stored. These measures not only act as a shield against unwanted entry but also facilitate adherence to regulatory frameworks that necessitate the privacy and safety of sensitive and personal data. With IoT ecosystems in motion, encryption will become increasingly essential, and money must be pumped continuously into state-of-the-art cryptographic technologies to fill future exposures pertaining to edge computing environments (Nalini, 2024). Finally, identity and access control management in edge devices is the difference maker in improving security for IoT systems. Identity management infrastructures like network access controls and role-based access controls ensure only authorized parties have access to edge devices and data generated by them. Effective access management incorporates multi-factor authentication measures that further slow down unauthorized access. In addition to periodic audits and assessments, these security controls offer a robust framework for edge device monitoring and user access and interaction authentication. With threats evolving as well, organizations must also remain ahead of the curve, continuously refining their security practices and policies in an attempt to neutralize potential edge vulnerabilities. This holistic approach to security of edge devices ends up being the foundation of the integrity of IoT networks, which creates trust and reliability across stakeholders and users (Ali et al., 2024) (Figure 10.8).

Figure 10.8. Real-time monitoring plays a pivotal role as it enables the detection of anomalies that may indicate security breaches or compromised devices.

Source: https://lirp.cdn-website.com/38309653/dms3rep/multi/opt/openart-image_FueYOWIp_1719453409197_raw-640w.jpg.

10.4. ENCRYPTION TECHNIQUES FOR IOT

The integration of IoT devices with smart infrastructures such as Smart Grids requires robust encryption processes to safeguard sensitive data and allow secure communication. As power systems shift from traditional systems to Smart Grids, they must possess a two-way stream of data rendering them extremely vulnerable to cyber threats. Encryption is therefore an essential security system that ensures protection for data transferred between sensors, smart meters, and centralized control networks. Encryption techniques like Advanced Encryption Standard (AES) and Elliptic Curve Cryptography (ECC) are used extensively to assist in keeping the information confidential, thus shielding it from any form of unauthorized access and tampering. Additionally, these techniques are used significantly in environments that have many IoT devices networked since the high volume of data creates more avenues for potential intrusion and thus requires an aggressive security model in IoT deployments (Copeland et al., 2019). For security in IoT, lightweight encryption algorithms are gaining popularity since most IoT devices have limited capabilities. In contrast to mainstream systems, which have enough capability to handle the processing required for complex encryption methodologies, IoT devices require cost-effective methods that do not drain battery life and functioning efficiency. Methods like RC4 and Chacha have been modified for application in these spaces in a way that keeps data secure without overloading device function. Lightweight alternatives are more critical by the day as IoT landscapes continue to grow, with devices implemented in smart traffic systems, health care, and home automation. Thus, the scientists are always seeking novel lightweight algorithms that can offer sufficient security without compromising on the limited resources typical in IoT devices, marking a basic step toward secure IoT deployments (Anglano et al., 2018). The security arena for IoT continuously changes, where utmost emphasis is given to advanced encryption techniques as basic weapons in the battle against cyber-attacks. With more devices and complex applications, data in motion is an even tougher challenge to secure. This is made even more challenging by the varying capabilities of devices within the network, resulting in a need for scalable encryption mechanisms that can adapt and cope with diverse operating environments. Future cryptography techniques for IoT must strike a very thin line between robust security and economical utilization of resources, resulting in new solutions combining machine learning and adaptive security measures. A multi-layered encryption strategy coupled with continuous monitoring and anomaly detection could be an effective step to enhance the integrity and confidentiality of IoT networks against evolving threats (Copeland et al., 2019).

10.4.1. Importance of Encryption in Data Transmission

The landscape of information transmission has changed quite significantly with the advent of the Internet of Things (IoT) where a multitude of devices are continuously communicating, generating information, and making autonomous decisions. With these technologies being everywhere, encryption has become the critical aspect in ensuring data confidentiality and integrity. With connected devices transmitting sensitive information ranging from personal health records to financial transactions, interception and unauthorized access are becoming very dangerous. Implementation of robust encryption algorithms not only protects information while being transmitted but also instills trust in users. With increasing and growing IoT applications in the pipeline, such as smart health networks and smart cars, secure transmission processes are more than ever required to facilitate protection of user information against malicious attacks, thereby shaping a secure digital world that is part of the technological evolution in the field. Secondly, encryption is also crucial in maintaining adherence to mounting data protection legislation and regulation.

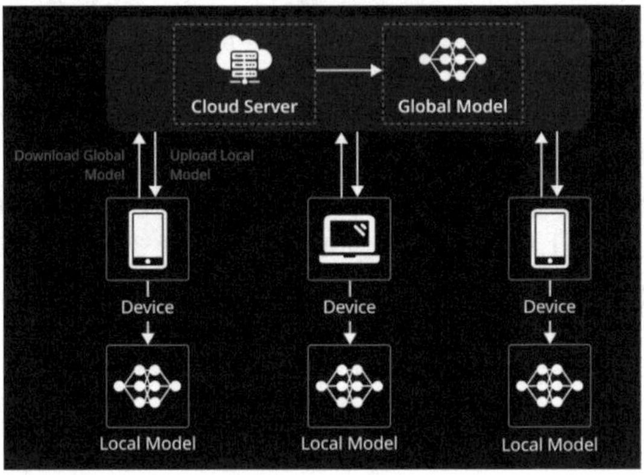

Figure 10.9. The integration of Federated Learning (FL) offers an innovative solution by allowing distributed data processing without compromising privacy, as it enables the collaborative training of machine learning models while keeping raw data local.

Source: https://d3lkc3n5th01x7.cloudfront.net/wp-content/uploads/2024/01/17044114/Federated-learning-1.png.

Given mounting awareness of global concerns of data privacy, rules such as the General Data Protection Regulation (GDPR) emphasize ensuring personally identifiable data is safeguarded in transit. Failure to comply with these regulations results in heavy fines and organizational loss in terms of reputation for businesses that use IoT technology. By incorporating advanced encryption techniques in their data transmission processes, companies can minimize compliance risk and demonstrate that they take protection of users' data seriously. Integration of Federated Learning (FL) is an innovative approach since it facilitates distributed data processing while being private since it supports collaborative training of machine learning models while raw data is kept local. This indicates the shifting situation under which both encryption and novel solutions like FL become relevant in offering data security in IoT applications, particularly where traditional solutions may be insufficient

(Nguyen et al., 2021). While encryption offers strong protection for data during transmission, due consideration must be given to the balance between security, performance, and user experience. Cost of computation of encryption can conflict with latency, which may be detrimental to real-time applications such as intelligent transportation systems where timely data delivery is crucial. Emerging technologies such as Mobile Edge Computing (MEC) and intelligent machine learning algorithms attempt to overcome these issues by optimizing data processing at or close to the data source. Here, Federated Learning provides a solution where the models are trained locally, thus reducing the transmission of sensitive data without compromising privacy and confidentiality (Lim et al., 2020). Thus, firms must strategically employ encryption when using these new technologies so that transmission of data does not happen without impacting usability and efficiency. The convergence of encryption with new methods of managing data reflects a proactive vision for securing IoT networks in today's digital world (Figure 10.9).

10.4.2. Types of Encryption Used in IoT

The surge in Internet of Things (IoT) devices poses serious issues with regard to data security, and hence proper encryption methods are essential to secure information. Among the many forms of encryption employed in IoT, symmetric encryption stands out because of its speed and efficiency. It uses the same key for decryption as well as encryption and is computationally less expensive, an aspect that is very important when dealing with resource-limited IoT devices. Though it has its advantages, symmetric encryption also possesses problems, primarily regarding key distribution and management, which introduce potential vulnerabilities. To offset this, some newer models of encryption combine symmetric and asymmetric processes, which further protect the process while attempting to maintain low processing requirements. The hybrid approach reflects a common trend in IoT for optimizing encryption methods to enable different devices to communicate securely while maintaining equilibrium for performance and computational strain (Gu et al., 2021). As the IoT environment evolves, more robust encryption techniques like the Elliptic Curve Cryptography (ECC) are more in demand due to their high security with low computational expense. ECC utilizes elliptic curves' algebraic structure over finite fields, offering more robust encryption via shorter keys than traditional ones like RSA. This is particularly suitable for IoT devices as they typically have limited processing capacity as well as power resources. Besides, ECC's effectiveness renders it suitable for deployment in applications such as secure key exchange and digital signatures, which are increasingly crucial as IoT applications increase. Possessing the capability to provide high levels of security while maintaining resource consumption at minimal levels renders ECC a potential area of focus at the boundary between IoT and encryption technology, enabling secure communication in the modern digital world (Lim et al., 2020). To address the unusual problems caused by the IoT ecosystem, novel encryption algorithms are being developed for low-power, low-computation gadgets. One such development is the development of image encryption algorithms for green IoT applications requiring efficient data handling while ensuring security. These algorithms typically employ methods such as chaotic encryption, which employs chaotic systems to create secure pseudo-random numbers for encryption keys. This approach is beneficial in scenarios when devices are slowed down by low computational power, as they can still provide a robust level of security while enhancing performance. Focusing on affordable and efficient encryption mechanisms, researchers are pioneering the path towards the future of IoT security to deliver these devices with safe operation without jeopardizing system integrity or user privacy (Gu et al., 2021).

10.4.3. Challenges in Implementing Encryption

The integration of encryption technologies within the Internet of Things (IoT) security paradigm presents several key challenges that organizations must overcome. One of the biggest challenges is the inherent difficulty of implementing robust encryption protocols across a wide range of IoT devices, which run under a diverse set of operating environments and technological standards. These ranging from simple sensors to complex automation systems have varied capabilities that complicate the use of uniform encryption mechanisms. For example, many low-power devices may lack the processing power for sustaining complex encryption algorithms and therefore demand a careful selection of encryption techniques offering security needs versus device limitations. While organizations attempt to use comprehensive security devices, they encounter the daunting task of making these devices interoperable without compromising the integrity of the encryption process, as seen in the dynamic threat landscape (Agunuru, 2025). On top of this, organizations typically have to deal with regulatory and compliance matters while using encryption on their IoT infrastructure. The compliance regime surrounding data protection is complex, with varying degrees of compliance that are not merely geographic but also industry-specific. This complicates the ability of organizations to fully know local and international regulations, a chore that is perhaps best left undone by many organizations looking to warp their encryption strategies to suit. With growing regulatory oversight to safeguard personal and financial sensitive information, especially in sectors like finance and property, organizations must have clearly articulated procedures for deploying encryption that capture such diversities. The challenge is that tight security measures, here encryption, to secure data while maintaining operational efficiency enhances the challenge of applying it to an already complicated regulatory framework (Avvari, 2025). Finally, staff acceptance and training mandated for employees are significant drivers of the successful implementation of encryption products to IoT security. Organizations need to develop a security culture among employees since the success of encryption depends heavily on users understanding its importance and applying it appropriately. This includes educating employees to recognize possible security threats and be assisted by best practices when handling data through encryption tools. Resistance to change or inadequacy of security training may lead to inadvertent compromise or exploitation of encryption mechanisms. Moreover, the cost of commencing such training programs may be considered a barrier, especially to small organizations with limited budgets. Thus, resolution of these human elements is crucial to ensure that encryption serves its intended function, providing effective security against new cyber threats in IoT environments (Agunuru, 2025) (Figure 10.10).

Figure 10.10. Resistance to change or a lack of security training can lead to unintentional breaches or misuse of encryption protocols.

Source: https://i0.wp.com/faisalyahya.com/wp-content/uploads/2024/06/ae0bf451-9aa6-4d30-b40a-da304848e4d6.jpg?fit=1200%2C669&quality=89&ssl=1.

10.5. SECURE DEVICE AUTHENTICATION

The IoT ecosystem has expanded exponentially, introducing an enormous number of networked devices that enhance comfort and efficiency across industries. But along with this pervasiveness comes severe security concerns, particularly in the realm of device authentication security. Robust authentication protocols are needed to assist in establishing device-to-device trust without permitting unauthorized devices to gain access and data breaches. Current practices are often derived from traditional security paradigms that may be inadequate when applied to dealing with the unique vulnerabilities of IoT systems. The new technologies must then be used to develop sophisticated authentication paradigms that are flexible, adaptable, and resilient against dynamic cyber threats. The complexity of the verification of a network that continues to expand for devices necessitates a transition to more sophisticated mechanisms capable of supporting the needs of various applications while maintaining the integrity of sensitive information (Rathod et al., 2025). One of the most promising methods of improving secure device authentication is the application of Zero Trust models, which posit that no device, from whatever source, should be trusted by default. This paradigm of authentication is focused on continuous verification and sensitivity to context within the authentication process. By including Attribute-Based Access Control (ABAC) and risk-adaptive policies, organizations have the ability to dynamically adjust access authorization according to real-time contextual factors like user activity and device health. This enables an experience-specific model of authentication, where devices receive access based on a comprehensive assessment of risk rather than static conditions.

Through the implementation of advanced AI algorithms that monitor user activity and the external environment, companies can minimize potential threats and amplify the overall security posture of IoT devices such that authentication for these networks is not only more efficient but also much safer (Kumar, 2025). With increasingly advanced IoT ecosystems on the horizon, the need for innovative means of authentication becomes increasingly imperative. New device authentication methods must incorporate advanced protection like privacy-preserving identity authentication and decentralized identity solutions. The new methods aim to empower consumers by giving them greater control over their online identities with the added advantage of reducing the threat of centralized data breaches. Along with it, the incorporation of AI-enabled risk monitoring heightens the efficacy of such security steps by enabling organizations to constantly watch and modify authentication processes in accordance with the changing threat landscape. These advancements do not simply increase security but also adhere to industry-specific standards, which make it possible for a more holistic approach to IoT security. By adopting these new models of authentication, stakeholders can better protect sensitive data, build user trust, and ultimately facilitate sustainable IoT technology development (Rathod et al., 2025).

10.5.1. Methods of Device Authentication

The growing deployment of Internet of Things (IoT) devices has necessitated the establishment of robust device authentication processes that ensure security and privacy. Traditional modes of authentication such as passwords and personal identification numbers (PINs) have not been able to satisfy the needs of IoT devices due to the unique limitations of these devices, for example, limited processing power and battery life. In response, improved measures such as biometric authentication, multi-factor authentication (MFA), and certificate-based authentication are gaining traction. Biometric identification is based on unique physical characteristics, which provide high confidence in the user's identity. On the contrary, MFA involves multiple different verification processes, which provide an additional security layer by requiring more than a single form of identification. These advances are called for in addressing the built-in weaknesses of the IoT environment, as indicated in the comprehensive survey of privacy and security concerns related to IoT technology (Mendez et al., 2017). In addition to biometric and MFA protocols, emerging technologies such as blockchain offer new answers for device authentication in IoT environments. The decentralized structure of blockchains provides an immutable ledger of device identities that provides data integrity and safeguards against unauthorized access.

Through a trustless framework, devices can securely authenticate themselves with minimal intervention by centralized authorities. Secondly, the employment of smart contracts within blockchain technology provides for the automatic enforcement of authentication protocols, which reduces response times to security threats immensely. This real-time responsiveness to needs addresses the ever-evolving nature of cyber threats, which can potentially compromise traditional authentication measures. As the IoT landscape becomes increasingly sophisticated, the arrival of blockchain authentication is an important milestone toward a secure infrastructure, supporting the urgent need for increased security measures highlighted under IoT issues (Ali et al., 2019). Lastly, the role of machine learning (ML) in enhancing device authentication is becoming revolutionary. ML algorithms are able to browse large volumes of data to look for patterns, distinguishing between legitimate and illegitimate device activity. By learning from new data in real time, such programs can adapt to new threats in real time, effectively enhancing the security of authentication processes. Anomaly detection technology with ML offers a dynamic solution that can recognize unusual deviations from normal behavior and enable proactively taking measures to combat possible security breaches. Moreover, the integration of AI and device authentication can automate the authentication process itself, rendering it not only more secure but even more convenient. As

IoT continues its progress, both ML and traditional methods of authentication will converge to offer a safe platform, ultimately forming the larger discourse on IoT security challenges, as expounded in existing academic literature (Ali et al., 2019) (Figure 10.11).

Figure 10.11. By establishing a trustless system, devices can securely authenticate themselves and transact with minimal intervention from centralized authorities.

Source: https://www.apriorit.com/wp-content/uploads/2019/09/smart-contracts.jpg.

10.5.2. Role of Biometrics in IoT Security

The advent of the Internet of Things (IoT) has introduced unparalleled convenience but also profound security challenges. In emerging technology for enhancing IoT security, biometrics has become widely noted in its promise to utilize unique physiological characteristics for user identification. The process includes the comparison of biological characteristics such as fingerprints, facial recognition, or iris patterns to stored templates, which offers a robust identity verification solution for IoT. As IoT sensors become more ubiquitous—from smart home appliances to wearables—the installation of biometric systems can discourage identity theft and unauthorized entry, hence reinforcing the overall security architecture. Biometrics integration into the IoT is not just about improving security but also about easing user interaction by substituting cumbersome password systems with seamless, convenient access controls. The security context surrounding IoT also has the issues of scalability and interoperability, which are very important because the number of devices connected increases exponentially. Biometric solutions can be particularly useful in addressing these issues by enabling scalable security features that can adapt to various device environments. For instance, multi-factor biometric authentication can improve the security measures of IoT ecosystems to permit access by only authenticated individuals. As biometric systems are also advanced further, they can be designed to operate on heterogeneous platforms and devices beyond the fragmentation that is typical of IoT systems. This ability arises as a response to the demands for effective and responsive coordinated security, hence aligning with the conditions set in the overall context of the new technologies in IoT security. Nevertheless, the use of biometrics in IoT security does not exist without its complicities. Data privacy, data storage, and biometric information management are issues of challenge that have to be addressed to ensure user trust. With increasing instances of data breaches and cyberattacks, there is a high risk of mismanaging biometric data with grave consequences. New technology in the form of encryption and decentralized storage, such as put forth in the scenario involving blockchain use, could offer solutions to safeguard biometric data. The evolving paradigm of digital identity and security necessitates the need for effective measures to be employed to secure biometric data while, concurrently, availing of enhanced security aspects offered by biometrics. With the continued growth of the metaverse and future IoT applications, ensuring the robustness of biometric security systems will be paramount to their capacity to protect users in such networked spaces (T-The et al., 2023; Wang et al., 2022).

10.5.3. Challenges in Maintaining Authentication Protocols

The rapid proliferation of Internet of Things (IoT) devices has introduced a crucial challenge of maintaining secure authentication schemes in the system. As the devices proliferate, heterogeneity in their capabilities, processing capacities, and communication protocols ensures it is challenging to implement standardized security. The traditional schemes of authentication are likely to struggle to scale to the resource constraints of most IoT applications, particularly when fog computing is involved and devices can possess even limited processing capabilities and memory. This limitation requires the development of innovative solutions that will be strong enough to enforce hard security and yet agile enough to operate effectively in constrained environments. Surprisingly, when the number of connected devices rises, the possibility of unauthorized access also rises, emphasizing the need for strong authentication methods able to effectively secure sensitive data and accommodate the dynamic nature of IoT networks (Sahoo et al., 2025). Compounding the complexity of the IoT security landscape is the requirement that authentication procedures must accommodate a wide spectrum of levels of trust between devices being connected. The range's variability precludes one-size-fits-all, single-method approach to authentication from being truly effective. More sophisticated processing devices, for instance, can employ more sophisticated encryption and multi-factor authentication, with lower devices employing token-based or lightweight methods. The issue is that of scaling an approach that will be able to concurrently provide strong authentication for high-risk devices while ensuring usability and efficacy for low-risk devices. Furthermore, new technologies such as LPWAN introduce further aspects of complexity, such as in the example of LoRaWAN, where secure authentication is absolutely essential to network integrity (Kassimov et al., 2025).

Figure 10.12. As cyber threats evolve, the vulnerabilities exposed through poorly maintained or outdated authentication mechanisms can lead to severe breaches and data compromises.

Source: https://www.okoone.com/wp-content/uploads/2024/06/Product-Design-173.jpg.

This diverse environment necessitates continuous adjustment of authentication practices to respond to evolving threats and diverse device capabilities. Furthermore, the dynamic nature of threats further complicates it to maintain strong authentication measures in IoT environments. As cyberattacks evolve further, the attacks that could be launched on vulnerable devices leveraging compromised or outdated authentication frameworks result in deep breaches and loss of data. For instance, fog computing, which optimizes data processing at the edge, also comes with unique security challenges, including potential latency and resource limitation that can hinder proper authentication (Sahoo et al., 2025). Real-time adaptation to new attack vectors is a must; hence, leveraging machine learning and artificial intelligence solutions can provide the needed agility to improve authentication resilience. All these technologies can enhance mechanisms by detecting anomalies and dynamically adjusting security controls. Finally, the intersection of disparate device capabilities, disparate levels of trust, and ongoing change in cyber threats requires an integrated, dynamic approach in providing security by strong authentication protocols in IoT environments (Kassimov et al., 2025) (Figure 10.12).

10.6. FUTURE TRENDS IN IOT SECURITY

The extremely fast evolution of the Internet of Things (IoT) offers immense possibilities for enhancing security mechanisms. As IoT devices mushroom across most sectors, the necessity for creating enhanced security protocols increases day by day. The future direction is towards a combined paradigm that integrates traditional security techniques with emerging technologies. For instance, advances in machine learning and AI are likely to revolutionize threat detection mechanisms so that systems can identify anomalies in real-time. In-depth analysis of data patterns will help organizations anticipate probable intrusions by deploying predictive models, hence reducing the attack surface significantly. As a result, the organizations that embrace these advancements will not only strengthen their security defenses but also facilitate greater consumer trust in IoT solutions because the ramifications of security breaches can be disastrous. The growing complexity of security requirements in IoT platforms has also led to the development of new frameworks like Zero Trust, which encourages embracing the shift away from traditional perimeter-based security models. As companies adopt cloud computing and an increasing number of devices become networked, the traditional safety nets do not work and hence the need for this paradigm shift. The Zero Trust model operates on the premise that no element either within or external to the network can be trusted implicitly. This minimizes vulnerability by requiring strict identity confirmation for all devices and users attempting access to resources. In addition, future IoT security advancements will be influenced by regulatory and ethical concerns that emphasize the necessity of multidimensional frameworks that engage different stakeholders. These factors will necessitate ongoing dialogue among governments, organizations, and academics so that emerging technologies are assured to comply with safety standards that protect data and privacy. With the changing digital landscape, the inclusion of quantum computing in the security of IoT is a trend breaker. As current cryptographic mechanisms are outmatched by preventing increasingly advanced attacks, quantum computing can offer answers that have the potential to reshape security protocols. The ability of this technology to perform calculations at speeds previously unimaginable can assist in the development of new cryptographic protocols, also known as post-quantum cryptography, which are immune to imminent quantum-fueled attacks. Also, the integration of behavioral biometrics into IoT devices is likely to enhance security through constant authentication of the user's identity via unique behavioral patterns, and hence an added level of protection. New trends, therefore, not only take into account the requirement for adaptive solutions in IoT security but also emphasize the necessity for continuous learning and investment in new technologies to secure networks against future threats (Rao, 2025; PellReddy, 2025).

10.6.1. Anticipated Technological Advancements

The security of IoT is on the verge of a revolutionary makeover with expected technological advancements. One of the foremost advances is the deployment of 5G wireless technology, which offers high-throughput and low-latency connectivity for secure IoT communication. The integration of 5G with other emerging technologies such as artificial intelligence (AI), big data, and machine learning offers fertile ground for enhancing security features. These technologies synergistically empower IoT devices to make decisions in real-time against enormous datasets, finally leading to more intelligent and adaptive security. With such converging advancements, the immunity of IoT systems against cyberattacks will not only be enhanced but a new era of health-based applications will also be inaugurated, finally bolstering global health systems as envisioned within the framework of the UN Sustainable Development Goals (Farooq et al., 2017). Another major field of innovation is in the development of Federated Embedded Systems (FES) mechanics that relook the manner connected devices interact within the IoT environment. The FES concept involves embedded, networked, and heterogeneous control systems that provide inter-device collaboration while ensuring secure and efficient functions. As the technology advances, the interdependence of technologies such as cyber-physical systems and multi-agent systems increasingly becomes apparent, laying a fertile ground for innovation in security solutions. This interdependence offers a higher capacity to monitor and respond, which is greatly needed in the detection and prevention of threats. By the exploitation of synergies between disparate technology domains, IoT security will benefit from an integrated solution that guarantees vulnerability but improves more interoperability reliability within devices (Axelsson et al., 2012). Breakthrough in future quantum computing also has very deep implications for IoT security. Quantum technologies may revolutionize encryption mechanisms to provide more secure data transmission across networks against evolving cyber-attacks. As traditional forms of encryption fall prey to sophisticated hacking techniques, quantum cryptography offers a new option that leverages the principles of the quantum mechanics in creating virtually unbreakable security codes. Such developments not only enhance the security of one IoT device but also the overall integrity of a network. With society becoming more reliant on IoT networks, the transition to quantum-based security solutions will prove vital. Through the fight against both current and potential threats, these technological improvements will be crucial for developing a safer, more secure Internet of Things, backing the necessity for continued investment and research in this critical area of security (Figure 10.13).

Figure 10.13. Quantum technologies have the potential to revolutionize encryption methods, making data transmission across networks more secure against evolving cyber threats.

Source: https://outshift-headless-cms-s3.s3.us-east-2.amazonaws.com/Post-Quantum%20Cryptography%20%281%29.webp.

10.6.2. Evolving Threat Landscape

As the Internet of Things continues to grow, the new threat landscape presents a significant challenge to the practice of cybersecurity. The connectivity of devices creates an ecosystem that, while it enhances data exchange and automation, also widens vulnerabilities. Devices that were once in isolation have become the conduit for data intrusion and cyberattacks, with attackers targeting weaknesses in weak areas to exploit. Several reports show that as such devices grow in numbers, the complexity of the network progresses, making it difficult to protect from new kinds of threats. This reality requires more knowledge about cybersecurity hygiene, with more emphasis on the importance of adherence to best practices for the protection of IoT system integrity and maintaining user trust in the technologies that increasingly govern functionality in everyday life, as seen in Mughal et al. (2019). Moreover, the cyber threat environment keeps evolving with new technologies and improvements in the attack mechanisms. The new malware and ransomware designed to exploit IoT infrastructure brought an added level of complexity to already prevalent threats. The DDoS attack has now become another tool in the arsenal of an attacker to break into entire networks, thereby exposing serious shortcomings in traditional security systems as well. Recent publications suggest that IoT devices are predisposed to have poor security features right from the initial stage of their design phase, and thus they are prone to exploitation. Knowledge about such vulnerabilities marks the beginning of gaining insights into the synergy between technological advancements and the added threats it poses. Addressing these vulnerabilities begins with a proper examination of the IoT architectures and imposing stringent frameworks for the sake of enhancing security. The solution to this dynamic threat landscape must involve not only technical solutions, but also collaborative strategies bridging the gap between various parties. Governments, manufacturers, and security professionals need to work together to develop resilient IoT ecosystems. As impending threats become increasingly interconnected with complex global perils, multilateral cooperation will be central in developing effective countermeasures. IOT security discussions must be extended beyond technical barriers to include societal attitudes and legislative factors in security. It is important to facilitate debates between business, government, and civil society to develop creative solutions that address the multifaceted challenges presented by new technologies in a connected world. Collaboration will be necessary to minimize risks and foster an environment that is secure for technological innovation.

10.6.3. Predictions for IoT Security Solutions

As the Internet of Things (IoT) continues to reach a wide range of industries, security solutions are increasingly given more importance. Future prospects of IoT security solutions indicate that integrating Artificial Intelligence of Things (AIoT) will be critical in maintaining robust security measures. With AI, IoT systems can scan huge datasets in real-time and detect anomalies so that they can take proactive actions against threats. This shift to data-oriented security is imperative, with more and more IoT devices being used and traditional security methods not being sufficient. But its use has problems; problems of privacy of sensitive user data remain all-pervasive, particularly in respect to vulnerability to possible threats of data extraction through model weaknesses. Mitigating these problems with innovative methods such as federated learning could provide an avenue to deliver security with maintaining user anonymity, hence being the focus of future IoT security advancements (Yang et al., 2024). In addition to AI advancements, machine learning-based algorithms are bound to become the foundation of IoT security solutions, particularly in developing countries where infrastructures may be insufficient.

Figure 10.14. Enhanced public-private partnerships can facilitate the sharing of best practices and resources necessary for building secure IoT environments.

Source: https://emudhra.com/hs-fs/hubfs/digital-composite-image-person-touching-invisible-illuminated-screen-c.webp?width=1200&height=600&name=digital-composite-image-person-touching-invisible-illuminated-screen-c.webp.

The particular challenges of these regions call for light and cost-effective security measures that can be enabled by machine learning. Pattern recognition on security breaches enables machine learning programs to learn and refine themselves over a timeframe, and as a consequence, even as threats evolve, the protective system of the security system keeps up in a like manner. Furthermore, utilization of blockchain technology extends an extra layer of security through immutable storage and identity verification. These technologies combined provide a thrilling prospect for IoT security improvement, particularly where financial and technological ability is constrained. Strategic investment in digital infrastructure as well as the development of capacity will be vital to the efficient deployment of these technologies among vulnerable groups (Tewera et al., 2024). Future outlooks on IoT security solutions emphasize the importance of collaborative public-private sector effort to develop scalable as well as integrated security frameworks. Given the integrated character of IoT systems, regulatory efforts will need to be correspondingly coordinated for acting on the diverse set of devices and usage. Enhanced public-private collaborations can result in knowledge sharing and resources needed to develop secure IoT ecosystems. Further, digital literacy development can enable users to engage with IoT technologies securely, reducing the risks associated with user complacency. The confluence of emerging technologies calls for an encompassing approach that manages not only technological developments but also social implications and the digital divide. Ultimately, an overarching strategy will be called for to create secure, sustainable, and just IoT ecosystems in the future (Tewera et al., 2024) (Figure 10.14).

10.7. CONCLUSION

As the discussion around next-gen technologies in IoT security reaches its conclusion, it is essential to recognize the vast opportunities and difficulties created by the innovations. Continual innovation in technologies such as artificial intelligence, machine learning, and blockchain offers unprecedented opportunities to enhance security mechanisms within IoT environments. These technologies, along with supporting real-time threat detection and response, create a culture of proactive security management. But the effects of these technologies extend beyond technical considerations; they bring new ethical considerations and social challenges that must be addressed. Researchers and practitioners must meet these technologies head-on critically in order to realize their potential while limiting privacy, trust, and general user-experience risks, marking a watershed in advocating for IoT security advancements. Furthermore, the integration of technology and human nature becomes increasingly relevant as companies adopt such new technologies. The integration of IoT devices into everyday life entirely transforms customers' relationships with technology and, consequently, how organizations develop their marketing ideas. As the research attests, electronic word-of-mouth negatively can stem from security breaches, incurring potential reputation damage and mistrust from customers. This emphasizes the need for a multifaceted awareness of the socio-economic effects of IoT security solutions. The conversation needs to widen to encompass numerous viewpoints from marketing, consumer behavior research, and ethics in order to have a multifaceted view of the security landscape so as to promote a climate that not only spurs innovation but also puts consumer well-being and societal trust at the forefront. In the end, IoT security in the future will depend on the marriage of technological development and ethical thinking. According to the literature, the breakdown of boundaries between digital and physical worlds in emerging technologies demands a multi-disciplinary effort to be able to effectively deal with the challenges in this sector. Maintaining solutions to the challenges introduced by potential misinformation, privacy concerns, and changes in consumer behavior will require continued communication between stakeholders like researchers, policymakers, and industry experts. By means of an ethical dialogue, we are able to create bedrock values that shall guide the responsible development of IoT technologies. Deliberation over these important issues not only will guide strong security architecture but also build a general knowledge base within society regarding the implications of our increasing connectivity, linking technological progress with moral accountability.

10.7.1. Summary of Key Points

As the Internet of Things (IoT) continues to advance further, it has become clear that the integration of new technologies is essential to enhance security controls. One of the key components of securing IoT devices is the usage of Cyber-Physical Systems (CPS), which is directly linked to the Industry 4.0 paradigm. This new industrial revolution combines physical and virtual worlds, improving manufacturing processes and enabling new business models that strongly shape the marketplace. As demonstrated through recent studies, the integration of CPS and IoT provides for real-time information exchange and analytics, with a safer environment being created. These advances, nonetheless, also require increased vigilance in cybersecurity defense, as the presence of more interlinked devices increases the attack surface for potential assaults (Acemoglu et al., 2017). Hence, IoT security has to keep pace with such quicker-paced technologies in an effort to uphold data integrity and secrecy. Another key field in IoT security is the newly emerging solutions based on cutting-edge communication technologies, such as Optical Wireless Communication (OWC). With the increased demand for high-data-rate applications, traditional radio frequency (RF) spectrums proved to be inadequate, leading to innovative alternatives such as OWC. This technology not only offers vast unregulated spectrum coverage but also enhances IoT networks' security by limiting risks of interception typically associated with RF communication. By employing mechanisms like visible light communication and free-space optical communication, organizations are able to provide secure data transmission over various distances. Hence, OWC has emerged as a viable solution to the increasing complication of IoT applications and their security requirements (Chowdhury et al., 2018). The integration of such technologies in the IoT environment gives a fillip to the necessity of adopting robust security systems. Lastly, the convergence of emerging technologies and IoT security underlines the necessity of taking a holistic approach towards transcending potential vulnerabilities. As more and more devices get connected, there is greater exposure to cyber-attacks, and therefore, it is crucial to have architectures that involve higher encryption methods and machine learning patterns. These types of strategies can enhance threat detection and response mechanism, thereby making the IoT environment more resilient to cyberattacks. Ongoing research and development in securing IoT devices cannot be overemphasized since development not only increases security but also encourages consumer acceptance and trust. Ultimately, technological and security synergy takes center stage, ensuring that the evolving IoT environment of today can withstand an ever-evolving tide of cyber threats and vulnerabilities. By comprehending these then, stakeholders are adequately prepared to work through the intricacies of protecting IoT systems in a challenging digital world.

10.7.2. Importance of Continuous Innovation in Security

In the constantly evolving IoT ecosystem, the call for relentless security innovation cannot be overemphasized. As more and more devices get networked, corresponding attack surfaces for cyber-attacks also expand in similar proportion, necessitating an evolutionary cybersecurity stance. Emerging technologies, driven by Industry 4.0 concepts, need to be leveraged to develop fault-tolerant security infrastructures that can effectively counter complex and dynamic threats. The integration of advanced security measures into IoT devices not only makes them stronger against external threats but also creates consumer trust in such systems. Such continuous development keeps manufacturers competitive while maintaining regulatory compliance and standards by bodies, ultimately supporting mass industry evolution in safe technology rollouts. Security innovation is also the solution to overcoming the numerous challenges presented by IoT ecosystems. As observed in the case of the food industry under the Industry 4.0 philosophy, the interconnection of manufacturing processes in the modern era has particular vulnerabilities in spite of offering opportunities for improved operation. The food industry, particularly in food and beverage sectors, has greatly to gain from adopting security technology protecting sensitive data and processes. This flexibility not only guards' assets but is also promoting a safety culture that is resonating across other sectors. By admitting that flexible security solutions are necessary, companies can manage complex regulatory environments while leveraging the top technologies at their disposal to safeguard their information systems against the next big threats. Continuing innovation in security also plays a critical role in influencing the wider research and development framework pertaining to IoT cybersecurity. It is imperative that organizations act in unison and focus on the identification of those technologies that must be protected and effective risk management practices to be implemented. The importance of formulating competent individuals through training and awareness exercises cannot be overemphasized, as an aware workforce forms the frontline of protection against cyber-attacks. With the clearly defined areas of interest proposed by the Italian Nation research community, technological progress and proactive cyber defense mechanisms are important to achieve synergy. It conveys the mutually dependent behavior involved in building a safe IoT ecosystem and thus marks the pivotal role that innovation will take in building a robust digital ecosystem needed in the future for all industries operating under the IoT paradigm (Anglano et al., 2018; Córdoba-Roldán et al., 2017).

10.7.3. Call to Action for Stakeholders

With the acceleration of Internet of Things (IoT) technology adoption, the stakeholders must aim for a harmonized strategy towards improving security systems. The increasing complexity of IoT networks introduces unforeseen threats that will threaten organizational data and user privacy. With the volume of data generated by IoT devices, effective financial management and operational performance rely on secure systems that can adapt as new threats emerge. The cooperation of stakeholders, including industry players, policymakers, and researchers, is important to design effective security protocols that will safeguard sensitive information. Through unification of resources and intelligence, these stakeholders can engage in a proactive effort in responding to expected security attacks, thereby imparting confidence and trustworthiness on IoT solutions in various industries. Being part of constant discussion and exchange of information will provide a rich ground for innovative solutions, reflecting the need for better security in our increasingly interconnected world. Furthermore, embracing new technologies such as blockchain within IoT security measures presents a vast opportunity for stakeholders to reengineer data protection systems. As the research underscores, blockchain possesses unique traits like decentralization, immutability, and transparency, which make it a preferred solution for protecting digital content in complex IoT environments (T-The et al., 2023). Stakeholders should highlight embracing blockchain solutions that address urgent issues related to data interoperability, privacy, and secure data sharing. With the use of blockchain, organizations are not only in a position to enhance data security measures but also establish user trust in their IoT devices. This synergy between blockchain and IoT security can provide a more resilient foundation for data management, ultimately contributing to higher operational efficiency and driving innovation in the industry. Finally, a call to action by stakeholders calls for collaboration towards establishing industry standards and best practices in IoT security. The rapid evolving context of IoT demands a commitment towards ethical values that can guide the wise deployment of such technology. Stakeholders must engage in detailed deliberations to define the impact of IoT and related technologies on data security with due consideration of the options of possible threats (Allioui et al., 2023). A blend must exist to form a governance model that advocates for transparency, accountability, and protection of consumers. By creating a culture of shared responsibility, stakeholders are well equipped to take on the sophisticated security challenges of IoT technologies. In cooperation, this combined effort is central to creating a secure IoT infrastructure that covers existing needs as well as emerging trends in technology and security needs.

10.7.4. Future Outlook on IoT Security Developments

As the Internet of Things (IoT) goes on an increasingly expansive mode, the future of IoT security innovations will be radically altered. The most critical sector that requires attention is the application of decision support systems (DSS) capable of visualizing and reducing cyber threats pertaining to IoT technology. Businesses are increasingly turning towards embracing such methods, especially in supply chains where cyber vulnerabilities usually remain invisible. A recent study presents a step-by-step process for designing DSS systems with the ability to effectively map and neutralize cyber attacks fostered by IoT deployments. The anticipatory method enables organizations to create risk management strategies best tailored to their requirements, thereby enhancing their immunity against future cyber-attacks. Since these systems are being embraced by businesses, there is a possibility for a paradigm shift in how firms approach cyber risk, pointing to a bright future for IoT security enhancements (Burnap et al., 2019). Furthermore, with the advent of technologies such as 5G, the future of IoT security is poised to make enormous leaps. The combination of high-speed connectivity with IoT offers unparalleled sharing of data, expanding potential attack surfaces in the process while simultaneously enabling more sophisticated security protocols. With current technologies such as artificial intelligence and machine learning, the security of IoT can see the implementation of predictive and adaptive models that are always ahead of cyber threats. The convergence of these technologies not only promises to upgrade security systems but also complements the global health agendas that are incorporated into the UN Sustainable Development Goals. With the application of 5G and other next-generation technologies, healthcare systems and other essential sectors can optimize their efficiencies of operations while addressing existing security challenges (Farooq et al., 2017). In the years to come, the dynamic innovation of IoT devices will necessitate that security measures improve and keep pace with constant research and development. As more interdependent systems are deployed in industries, from domestic homes to industrial automation, the shifting landscape of cyber threats necessitates reactive and informed action on the part of stakeholders. This concerns not just technology developers but regulatory bodies tasked with compliance and safety. The IoT future security will predominantly depend on cooperative efforts between public and private sectors, learning from each other through experiences, best practices, and research to effectively combat new threats arising in the future. As organizations establish the foundation for long-term solutions to secure their IoT infrastructure, it becomes evident that being adaptable and innovative will play a crucial role in designing a secure digital future for everyone who's affected by IoT technology.

REFERENCES

1. Abdolee, R., Maroufi, M., & Tazekand, B. M. (2019). On the convergence of blockchain and Internet of Things (IoT) technologies. http://arxiv.org/abs/1904.01936 (accessed on 17th October 2025).
2. Abdulmalek, S., Nasir, A., Jabbar, W. A., Almuhaya, M. A. M., Bairagi, A. K., Khan, M. A. M., & Kee, S. H. (2022). IoT-based healthcare-monitoring system towards improving quality of life: A review. *Healthcare, 10*, 1993–1993. https://doi.org/10.3390/healthcare10101993 (accessed on 17th October 2025).
3. Acemoglu, D., Almada-Lobo, F., Atzori, L., Borgia, E., Cardoso, D., Chui, M., Dombrowski, U., et al. (2017). A review of the meanings and the implications of the industry 4.0 concept. https://core.ac.uk/download/154275592.pdf (accessed on 17th October 2025).
4. Agunuru, A. K. R. (2025). Data security in real estate: A technical perspective. *World Journal of Advanced Research and Reviews*. https://www.semanticscholar.org/paper/20bdbf2e0f67781e749fc1b3e08ef320d166c0c0 (accessed on 17th October 2025).
5. Akindote, O. J., Adegbite, A. O., Dawodu, S. O., Omotosho, A., & Anyanwu, A. (2023). Innovation in data storage technologies: From cloud computing to edge computing. *Computer Science & IT Research Journal, 4*, 273–299. https://doi.org/10.51594/csitrj.v4i3.661 (accessed on 17th October 2025).
6. Al Ali, A., Al-Blooshi, O., Al Ali, R., & Hamadi, H. A. (2024). Securing the Internet of Things (IoT) application: Best practices and challenges in IoT software. *2024 Advances in Science and Engineering Technology International Conferences (ASET)*. https://www.semanticscholar.org/paper/90aaf729edcff2e07a245187445798bf4d3c7545 (accessed on 17th October 2025).
7. Al-Fuqaha, A., & Mohammadi, M. (2018). Enabling cognitive smart cities using big data and machine learning: Approaches and challenges. http://arxiv.org/abs/1810.04107 (accessed on 17th October 2025).
8. Ali, I., Sabir, S., & Ullah, Z. (2019). Internet of Things security, device authentication and access control: A review. http://arxiv.org/abs/1901.07309 (accessed on 17th October 2025).
9. Allioui, H., & Mourdi, Y. (2023). Exploring the full potentials of IoT for better financial growth and stability: A comprehensive survey. *Sensors, 23*, 8015–8015. https://doi.org/10.3390/s23198015 (accessed on 17th October 2025).

10. Alwahedi, F., Aldhaheri, A., Ferrag, M. A., Battah, A., & Tihanyi, N. (2024). Machine learning techniques for IoT security: Current research and future vision with generative AI and large language models. *Internet of Things and Cyber-Physical Systems, 4*, 167–185. https://doi.org/10.1016/j.iotcps.2023.12.003 (accessed on 17th October 2025).

11. Amanlou, S., Hasan, M., Mokhtar, U. A., Malik, K., Islam, S., Khan, S., Khan, M. A., et al. (2025). Cybersecurity challenges in smart grid systems: Current and emerging attacks, opportunities, and recommendations. *IEEE Open Journal of the Communications Society, 6*, 1965–1997. https://www.semanticscholar.org/paper/ec606566bb9dbbdbdc877a71e438bb51f08f0042 (accessed on 17th October 2025).

12. Anglano, C., Aniello, L., Antinori, A., Armando, A., et al. (2018). The future of cybersecurity in Italy: Strategic focus area. https://core.ac.uk/download/188830442.pdf (accessed on 17th October 2025).

13. Asokan, N., Frassetto, T., Hafeez, I., Marchal, S., et al. (2016). IoT Sentinel: Automated device-type identification for security enforcement in IoT. http://arxiv.org/abs/1611.04880 (accessed on 17th October 2025).

14. Avvari, S. S. N. (2025). The technological pillars of FinTech: Data integration and security. *Technix International Journal for Engineering Research*. https://www.semanticscholar.org/paper/67ae06a9eecdf83b178d57ed9a7d41bfdcc4a7d2 (accessed on 17th October 2025).

15. Axelsson, J., & Kobetski, A. (2012). Federated embedded systems – A review of the literature in related fields. https://core.ac.uk/download/11434985.pdf (accessed on 17th October 2025).

16. Bajpayi, P., Sharma, S., & Gaur, M. S. (2024). AI driven IoT healthcare devices security vulnerability management. https://doi.org/10.1109/icdt61202.2024.10488939 (accessed on 17th October 2025).

17. Burnap, P., De Roure, D. C., Montalvo, R. M., Nurse, J. R. C., et al. (2019). Methodology for designing decision support systems for visualizing and mitigating supply chain cyber risk from IoT technologies. http://arxiv.org/abs/1903.12582 (accessed on 17th October 2025).

18. Chowdhury, M. Z., Hossan, M. T., Islam, A., Jang, Y., et al. (2018). A comparative survey of optical wireless technologies: Architectures and applications. http://arxiv.org/abs/1810.02594 (accessed on 17th October 2025).

19. Copeland, R., Crespi, N., Rehmani, M. H., Saleem, Y., et al. (2019). Internet of Things-aided smart grid: Technologies, architectures, applications, prototypes, and future research directions. http://arxiv.org/

abs/1704.08977 (accessed on 17th October 2025).

20. Córdoba-Roldán, A., de las Heras García de Vinuesa, A., Luque Sendra, A., Peralta-Álvarez, M., et al. (2017). State of the Industry 4.0 in the Andalusian food sector. https://core.ac.uk/download/185608711.pdf (accessed on 17th October 2025).
21. Dwivedi, Y. K., Hughes, L., Baabdullah, A. M., Ribeiro-Navarrete, S., Giannakis, M., Al-Debei, M. M., Dennehy, D., et al. (2022). Metaverse beyond the hype: Multidisciplinary perspectives on emerging challenges, opportunities, and agenda for research, practice and policy. *International Journal of Information Management, 66*, 102542–102542. https://doi.org/10.1016/j.ijinfomgt.2022.102542 (accessed on 17th October 2025).
22. Dwivedi, Y. K., Ismagilova, E., Hughes, D. L., Carlson, J., Filieri, R., Jacobson, J., Jain, V., et al. (2020). Setting the future of digital and social media marketing research: Perspectives and research propositions. *International Journal of Information Management, 59*, 102168–102168. https://doi.org/10.1016/j.ijinfomgt.2020.102168 (accessed on 17th October 2025).
23. Elechi, P., Ekolama, S. M., Okowa, E., & Kukuchuku, S. (2025). A review of emerging technologies in wireless communication systems. *Innovation and Emerging Technologies*. https://www.semanticscholar.org/paper/30e2328192db5e0bf0d8209957f77b34ecb760a1 (accessed on 17th October 2025).
24. Erukala, S., Tokmakov, D., Perumalla, A., Kaluri, R., Bekyarova-Tokmakova, A., Mileva, N., & Lubomirov, S. (2025). A secure end-to-end communication framework for cooperative IoT networks using hybrid blockchain system. *Scientific Reports, 15*. https://www.semanticscholar.org/paper/ec8b785b1a43b27a415c881f54b68ce8db0515d6 (accessed on 17th October 2025).
25. Farooq, S., Imran, M. A., Latif, S., Qadir, J., et al. (2017). How 5G wireless (and concomitant technologies) will revolutionize healthcare? https://core.ac.uk/download/143476480.pdf (accessed on 17th October 2025).
26. Franke, L., Salomo, S., & Schletz, M. (2020). Designing a blockchain model for the Paris Agreement's carbon market mechanism. https://core.ac.uk/download/287885254.pdf (accessed on 17th October 2025).
27. Fuller, A., Fan, Z., Day, C., & Barlow, C. (2020). Digital twin: Enabling technologies, challenges and open research. *IEEE Access, 8*, 108952–108971. https://doi.org/10.1109/access.2020.2998358 (accessed on 17th October 2025).
28. Ghillani, D. (2022). Deep learning and artificial intelligence framework to

improve the cyber security. *Authorea (Authorea)*. https://doi.org/10.22541/au.166379475.54266021/v1 (accessed on 17th October 2025).

29. Gu, Z., Li, H., Khan, S., Deng, L., Du, X., Guizani, M., & Tian, Z. (2021). IEPSBP: A cost-efficient image encryption algorithm based on parallel chaotic system for green IoT. *IEEE Transactions on Green Communications and Networking, 6*, 89–106. https://doi.org/10.1109/tgcn.2021.3095707 (accessed on 17th October 2025).
30. Huynh-The, T., Gadekallu, T. R., Wang, W., Yenduri, G., Ranaweera, P., Pham, Q.-V., da Costa, D. B., et al. (2023). Blockchain for the metaverse: A review. *Future Generation Computer Systems, 143*, 401–419. https://doi.org/10.1016/j.future.2023.02.008 (accessed on 17th October 2025).
31. Ismail, A. I. I., Ismail, M. A. H., & Johari, S. (2025). Smart cities implementing IoT applications for security technologies and future recommendations. *International Journal of Innovative Research and Scientific Studies*. https://www.semanticscholar.org/paper/fec2b3754c977ddd2fbdbb1aa8395fcb3f99d11d (accessed on 17th October 2025).
32. Jiang, Y., Li, X., Luo, H., Yin, S., & Kaynak, O. (2022). Quo vadis artificial intelligence? *Discover Artificial Intelligence, 2*. https://doi.org/10.1007/s44163-022-00022-8 (accessed on 17th October 2025).
33. Kassimov, A., Khizirova, M., Yermekbaev, M., Abdikhan, D., & Marxuly, S. (2025). Mobile application for remote monitoring and control of LoRaWAN networks. *International Journal of Innovative Research and Scientific Studies*. https://www.semanticscholar.org/paper/8eb937769a9ade5ef2869372ed8913b91f47466c (accessed on 17th October 2025).
34. Khan, R., & Ved, A. (2025). Innovative technologies for climate-smart food supply chains: Solutions for climate change challenges. *International Journal for Multidisciplinary Research*. https://www.semanticscholar.org/paper/898c6440b04bb7c4bbcd2973ecf6681fb2e00075 (accessed on 17th October 2025).
35. Kumar, P. (2025). Next-generation secure authentication and access control architectures: Advanced techniques for securing distributed systems in modern enterprises. *International Journal of Computational and Experimental Science and Engineering*. https://www.semanticscholar.org/paper/3b204c315ae4492d8173bf25985138335ab20c43 (accessed on 17th October 2025).
36. Lim, W. Y. B., Luong, N. C., Hoang, D. T., Jiao, Y., Liang, Y. C., Yang, Q., Niyato, D., et al. (2020). Federated learning in mobile edge networks: A comprehensive survey. *IEEE Communications Surveys & Tutorials, 22*,

2031–2063. https://doi.org/10.1109/comst.2020.2986024 (accessed on 17th October 2025).

37. Mendez, D. M., Papapanagiotou, I., & Yang, B. (2017). Internet of Things: Survey on security and privacy. http://arxiv.org/abs/1707.01879 (accessed on 17th October 2025).
38. Mughal, A. A. (2019). Cybersecurity hygiene in the era of Internet of Things (IoT): Best practices and challenges. https://core.ac.uk/download/568392999.pdf (accessed on 17th October 2025).
39. Nalini, D. (2024). Securing smart cities: A cybersecurity perspective on integrating IoT, AI, and machine learning for digital twin creation. *Journal of Electrical Systems*. https://www.semanticscholar.org/paper/8eec19498e098cf774fffa8780a6c895509d89c1 (accessed on 17th October 2025).
40. Nguyen, D. C., Ding, M., Pathirana, P. N., Seneviratne, A., Li, J., & Poor, H. V. (2021). Federated learning for Internet of Things: A comprehensive survey. *IEEE Communications Surveys & Tutorials, 23*, 1622–1658. https://doi.org/10.1109/comst.2021.3075439 (accessed on 17th October 2025).
41. Novakovic, T., Rammel, C., Voshmgir, S., Wildenberg, M., et al. (2019). Sustainable development report: Blockchain, the Web3 & the SDGs. https://core.ac.uk/download/286370731.pdf (accessed on 17th October 2025).
42. PellReddy, R. (2025). The future of cybersecurity: Predicting trends and preparing for emerging threats. *Asian Journal of Research in Computer Science*. https://www.semanticscholar.org/paper/443582b89e4ead6bf4c455d96e6fdcb2917ed58c (accessed on 17th October 2025).
43. Rao, P. V. (2025). IoT-enabled environmental monitoring systems: Trends, challenges, and future directions. *International Journal of Environmental Sciences*. https://www.semanticscholar.org/paper/df924a3de1974ac1dfcb2ec5b79521444032a196 (accessed on 17th October 2025).
44. Rasheed, A., San, O., & Kvamsdal, T. (2020). Digital twin: Values, challenges and enablers from a modeling perspective. *IEEE Access, 8*, 21980–22012. https://doi.org/10.1109/access.2020.2970143 (accessed on 17th October 2025).
45. Rathod, P., Bhatt, N. V., Nema, R., & Jyotheeswari, P. (2025). A comprehensive review on IoT security challenges and solutions. *2025 Seventh International Conference on Computational Intelligence and Communication Technologies (CCICT)*. https://www.semanticscholar.

org/paper/930e6fcff2fd6e5b4f8b6cf33231b64387046a32 (accessed on 17th October 2025).

46. Sahoo, S. S., & Das, D. (2025). Design of key agreement authentication scheme with IDS using OS-RVFL neural network for secure fog computing. *IEEE Internet of Things Journal, 12*, 28521–28530. https://www.semanticscholar.org/paper/f14a242bbecd1280e6c4d92e9420038e670702da (accessed on 17th October 2025).
47. Sarker, I. H. (2022). AI-based modeling: Techniques, applications and research issues towards automation, intelligent and smart systems. *SN Computer Science, 3*. https://doi.org/10.1007/s42979-022-01043-x (accessed on 17th October 2025).
48. Tatiya, M., Verma, A., Talekar, S., Kumar, S., Kiran, V., Bhosale, S., & Kumar, S. (2024). Cybersecurity in IoT-based smart grids: A comprehensive survey. *Computer Fraud and Security*. https://www.semanticscholar.org/paper/ff649180f5b7aee7d169df66dc584fc40de08439 (accessed on 17th October 2025).
49. Technology March Harvard International, Bolaji-Adetoro, D. F., Adedotun, K. J., Shola, I., & Raji, A. K. (2025). Real-time object detection and collision avoidance in IoT-enabled autonomous vehicles. *Harvard International Journal of Engineering Research and Technology*. https://www.semanticscholar.org/paper/0387a3b34ab1ac17313a6057c4fbacbf031dfc81 (accessed on 17th October 2025).
50. Tewera, D., Zhou, M., & Gavai, P. (2024). Enhancing IoT security for socio-economic development in the mirror of challenges, emerging technologies, and holistic solutions. *2024 3rd Zimbabwe Conference of Information and Communication Technologies (ZCICT)*. https://www.semanticscholar.org/paper/2a11d9a702e9e29a4340518d776b4fc0e81344c4 (accessed on 17th October 2025).
51. Tiwari, A., Chauhan, S. S., Singh, S., & Singh, V. (2024). Evolution of cybersecurity in the age of IoT and cloud computing. *2024 International Conference on Augmented Reality, Intelligent Systems, and Industrial Automation (ARIIA)*. https://www.semanticscholar.org/paper/4b35ec76a2f58b134475e66eebf1fc1bd8151a07 (accessed on 17th October 2025).
52. Turner, S. W., Karakuş, M., Güler, E., & Uludag, S. (2023). A promising integration of SDN and blockchain for IoT networks: A survey. *IEEE Access, 11*, 29800–29822. https://doi.org/10.1109/access.2023.3260777 (accessed on 17th October 2025).
53. Ucbas, Y., Eleyan, A., Hammoudeh, M., & Alohaly, M. (2023). Performance and scalability analysis of Ethereum and Hyperledger Fabric. *IEEE*

Access, 11, 67156–67167. https://doi.org/10.1109/access.2023.3291618 (accessed on 17th October 2025).

54. Wang, Y., Su, Z., Zhang, N., Xing, R., Liu, D., Luan, T. H., & Shen, X. (2022). A survey on metaverse: Fundamentals, security, and privacy. *IEEE Communications Surveys & Tutorials, 25*, 319–352. https://doi.org/10.1109/comst.2022.3202047 (accessed on 17th October 2025).
55. Yan, W., Zhang, N., Njilla, L., & Zhang, X. (2020). PCBChain: Lightweight reconfigurable blockchain primitives for secure IoT applications. *IEEE Transactions on Very Large-Scale Integration (VLSI) Systems, 28*, 2196–2209. https://doi.org/10.1109/tvlsi.2020.3014155 (accessed on 17th October 2025).
56. Yang, S., Zheng, X., Xu, J., Li, J., Song, D., Chen, Z., & Ngai, E. C. H. (2025). Generative AI for vulnerability detection in 6G wireless networks: Advances, case study, and future directions. https://www.semanticscholar.org/paper/d09127ffa4c8076c3ab5b1ef501ebf22ec4f14c8 (accessed on 17th October 2025).
57. Yang, Z., Xiong, B., Chen, K., Yang, L. T., Deng, X., Zhu, C., & He, Y. (2024). Differentially private federated tensor completion for cloud–edge collaborative AIoT data prediction. *IEEE Internet of Things Journal, 11*, 256–267. https://www.semanticscholar.org/paper/8f5940446bd8f08120d6ec28ba90649e6f40eb1a (accessed on 17th October 2025).
58. Żywiołek, J. (2025). Continuous improvement: Leveraging data security in Industry 4.0 settings. *Scientific Papers of Silesian University of Technology Organization and Management Series*. https://www.semanticscholar.org/paper/685bc0a21c3bf3e0f78321be0a9733156ad0e905 (accessed on 17th October 2025).

INDEX

N

O

P

Q

R

S

T

U

V

W